THE
CORPORATE ROLE
AND
ETHICAL BEHAVIOR

THE
CORPORATE ROLE
AND
ETHICAL BEHAVIOR

Robert J. Litschert, *Virginia Polytechnic Institute and State University*
Edward A. Nicholson, *Wright State University*

CONCEPTS
AND
CASES

PETROCELLI / CHARTER   NEW YORK 1977

036752

Printed in the United States of America

1 2 3 4 5 6 7 8 9 10

Acknowledgement is made for material reprinted from *The
New York Times*, © 1966, 1967, 1969, 1970, 1971, 1972,
1973, 1975 by The New York Times Company. Reprinted
by permission.

Library of Congress Cataloging in Publication Data

Litschert, Robert J.
 The corporate role and ethical behavior.

 Includes index.
 1. Industry—Social aspects—United States—Case
studies. I. Nicholson, Edward A., joint author.
II. Title.
HD60.5.U5L58   301.18'32   76-30799
ISBN 0-88405-402-0

CONTENTS

Contents

PREFACE

The theme of this book is socially responsible behavior. There are numerous views of what constitutes socially responsible behavior and, in a sense, the concept is sufficiently abstract and elusive of definition that it seems unreasonable to ask students to be concerned about it. Yet the concern for responsible behavior is so pervasive and cogent for businessmen in this age that one cannot avoid discussing the ethics and social impact of the businessman's behavior in nearly all college courses in business. Courses in marketing, finance, organizational behavior, accounting, computer sciences, and so on, must concern not only the principles and techniques of decision making in the respective disciplines but need to address the larger issue of how certain decisions affect the social and natural environment.

This book primarily presents a method of answering the question: In this situation what would be the socially responsible decision? The text is not prescriptive. It attempts to avoid making value judgments. It considers behavior from the individual's viewpoint, the organization's viewpoint, and from the point of view of the environment. The method is subtle and complex and requires of students disciplined analysis and additional research to present a good case analysis. The cases are not short incidents; rather, they are "broad brush" vignettes of complex business problems. To analyze the cases properly, students should undertake further research into the problem area represented by each case.

We wish to express our gratitude to the many graduate students who helped research the cases over the last three years; special thanks needs to be expressed to Professor Sang Lee whose editorial assistance was much appreciated.

SECTION ONE

A
CONCEPT
OF THE
SOCIAL ROLE
OF
BUSINESS

CHAPTER 1

SOCIAL ROLES
AND
BEHAVIOR
IN
ORGANIZATIONS

Social Roles

This chapter is concerned with behavior—the behavior required of men and women in managerial roles in business organizations. As in most textbooks, we are concerned with present behaviors, what causes these, what supports their continuation, what are the more desirable types of behavior, and how can we change to the more desirable behaviors.

To answer these questions, we borrow a concept from the behavioral sciences—social roles. A social role is defined as a set of behaviors expected of someone occupying some position or participating in an organization, in the community, or in any social institution such as the family, religion, or democracy. For example, we expect the pastor of a local church to act out his role by engaging in certain behaviors: preaching, visiting the sick and shut-in, counseling parishioners, and performing religious rites. We also expect him *not* to engage in other behavior such as: intemperate drinking of alcohol, extramarital sexual relations, conspicuous displays of wealth, or even bad temper. However, for those who are lay parishioners in the same church, we typically do not expect constant evidence of "religious" behavior. Preaching by a layman in some churches may be considered condescending or presumptuous. A display of pious behavior considered excessive could even be threatening to other parishioners who believe that the person is trying to assume a higher status than theirs in the organization. On the other hand, we may be willing to tolerate some intemperance in parishioners, we may be more understanding of extramarital affairs, and we may even encourage conspicuous displays of financial well-being (note how well-dressed churchgoers are on Easter Sunday).

The term *role behavior* refers to how people actually behave in some position. *Role expectations* is a term used to indicate how people should act in their positions. Lawless points out that "role expectations are anticipatory (there is a regularity to the expected behavior of both role partners), and obligatory (we feel a person is obligated to fulfill our expectations)." [1] In other words, as two or more people encounter each other they anticipate certain behavior from the other(s) based upon the roles that they perceive are being played. If one fails to exhibit the expected behavior or if one engages in unexpected behavior, this upsets the others in the encounter. Think for a minute about the role expectations you maintain for a used-car salesman. Picture yourself going to a car lot because you are attracted by a shiny, red, three-year-old sports car. You glance quickly at the exterior of the car; it appears to be in excellent condition. The sticker price is $3500. You open the door and observe the odometer. Great! The car only has about 26,000 miles on it. A salesman approaches and tells you that this is probably the best buy on the lot. You counter that it is a clean-looking car but $3500 is much too high; you will consider buying for $2800. He exclaims that he paid more than that for the car but feels that his manager might let it go for $3100. That seems reasonable to you, so you get in the car and go for a test ride as the salesman goes to discuss his offer with the manager. As you drive back onto the lot, thoroughly convinced that this is a sound used car, you are excited and hopeful that the manager agrees to the price. Both the salesman and the manager are waiting for you. The manager speaks first: "We have decided to price the car at $2500 because I was informed this morning that the car's actual mileage is closer to 60,000 rather than the 26,000 recorded on the odometer. We did not turn the mileage back and actually paid $2650 for the car at wholesale. However, it is our company's policy to charge fair prices regardless of profits; we, therefore, have determined that $2500 is a fair price for a car like this one with 60,000 miles."

Would you buy the car? Perhaps not. Would you be puzzled by the manager's behavior? Probably. Most likely you would be very suspicious of his motives because his actions would not meet your expectations. He could have sold you that car for $2800 or even $3100; instead he asks less! Why? What is he trying to do? His behavior, because it is unlike what you expect from someone in the role of a sales manager, might cause you not to buy the car.

Not only might the would-be buyer be perplexed, but the salesman also might feel confusion, perhaps even anger. He expects the sales manager to help him sell cars, not hinder him. He had a sale; he went to the manager not only to get approval of a price but to get the manager's support for a price higher than the customer offered. A typical sales ploy would be to come back to a customer and inform him that the price offered was so low that the manager wouldn't approve it. If the customer is willing to pay $200 more, the salesman would argue, the sales manager might be convinced to let it go.

There is a third dimension to this problem of role behavior. The sales manager is concerned about his own behavior. He knows that he did not act as he was expected to by either the salesman or the customer. He knows that he is expected by salesmen and by his boss, the agency owner, to sell cars profitably. But, only yesterday the new owner of the agency changed the name of the establishment. It is now called "The Consumer's Automobile Mart," and the new owner insists that complete honesty is the best policy and emphasized for hours at yesterday's meeting that both the new-car sales manager and the used-car sales manager must become the customers' advocate and protect them from deceptive or dishonest sales practices. The owner ended the meeting by saying that he was convinced that if both managers try, they could increase gross profit on sales by 10 percent in the coming year.

The used-car sales manager in our example has just experienced considerable role conflict. He is attempting to meet conflicting expectations: his boss expects him to protect the interest of the customer and increase profits; the salesman expects the sales manager to help him sell cars and does not anticipate that the manager must be candid with the customer about a situation that will likely frighten him away. Moreover, the sales manager may personally disagree with the role of consumer advocate forced on him by the new owner. His values may lead him to believe that the buyer should be intelligent enough to make his own deal so long as salesmen do not engage in illegal practices.

Socially Responsible Role Behavior

Keeping our example in mind, let's turn to the relationship between role behavior and social responsibilities. What is meant when someone makes the statement about another: "I believe he acts responsibly"? We believe that the person making that judgment is saying that, in his opinion, this other person is engaging in appropriate role behavior. Most judgments about the responsibleness of another's actions are actually assessments of the extent to which the other person has met legitimate role expectations. Note, however, that it is the person making the judgment who defines the legitimate expectations, not the person being judged.

This concept of responsible behavior is based upon the commonly accepted notion that organizations are role systems. Professors Katz and Kahn explain that ". . . the organization consists of the patterned and motivated acts of human beings, [and] . . . will continue to exist only so long as the attitudes, beliefs, perceptions, habits, and expectations of human beings evoke the required motivation and behavior. In short, each behavioral element is to a large extent caused and secured by the others." [2] The relationships that people have with each other in formal organizations, and therefore their effect on each other's behavior, is influenced greatly by the office they hold. "Office is essentially a relational concept, defining each position in terms of its relationship to others and to the system as a whole." [3]

The expected behavior is the role that individuals must play in a particular office if they wish to be considered "responsible officeholders." The officeholder's superior, his subordinates, and his peers holding other offices in the organization communicate in both subtle and overt ways how they expect someone in his position to behave. They depend upon his behavior, and often the proper performance of their responsibilities requires that he act appropriately.

This *role sending* on the part of others is intended to influence behavior in predictable ways. However, it is not what is sent that directly affects behavior. Rather, it is what is received that immediately influences the officeholder's actions. His own expectations of how someone in his position should act tend to distort the signals of others. Katz and Kahn argue that the individual, ". . . comes to the job in a state of . . . role-readiness, a state which includes the acceptance of legitimate authority and compliance with its requests, a compliance which for many people extends to acts which they do not understand and which may violate many of their own values." [4]

In perspective, then, the pressure from peers, subordinates, superiors, and one's own idea about how the role should be played influences actual behavior. As we observed previously, these "pressures" often call for conflicting behavior. To understand the relationship between "socially responsible" behavior, we must extend our view of role expectations to the larger society and ask how contemporary society views the role of the officeholder in business because, in part, the contemporary view determines the role-readiness of individuals in organizations.

Popular literature frequently discusses the changing role of the manager, the professional, and the worker in business. Note that "worker" tends to conjure up a picture of someone working on an assembly line, or in the mines, or otherwise laboring. It typically doesn't extend to even a plumber or an electrician. When we think of a professional, we first consider an attorney, a physician, perhaps a nurse, and increasingly we include teachers, psychologists, and others in this category. Turning to our idea of a manager, we may see a picture in our mind's eye of a president of a firm, a vice president, a staff manager, a middle manager, a first-line supervisor, and so on. Each of these sub-classifications reflect our view of different offices in a business organization. We have somewhat different sets of role expectations for each of these positions and, we argue, different views of what constitutes socially responsible behavior for each. For example, do we expect first-line supervisors to attempt to implement "equal employment opportunity" practices in their departments independent of, and perhaps contradictory to, the policies and practices of the firm as a whole? Not normally. However, we do expect the president, with the aid of his personnel staff, to develop and implement policies and practices that bring the firm in line with laws governing equal employment opportunity.

In other words, we (society) view each role and its relationship to a social problem somewhat differently. Not only can these different expectations be found among roles within a particular firm, but the concept also can be extended to include different expectations of what constitutes socially responsible behavior among business organizations. Do we expect the president of General Motors to act differently than the president of Echo Tool and Die? General Motors, a large, financially sound, mature firm is more charged with the public interest than a small, financially weak firm that, since its inception two years ago, has not been able to operate at a profit, as is the case with Echo. It may not be sufficient for General Motors to abide by the laws of business in order to be judged socially responsible by the public. Programs that go beyond compliance to the extent of making a positive effort to help solve society's problems may be necessary to fulfill the public's role expectations. On the other hand, few would argue that Echo should make an effort to employ low-skilled, disadvantaged minority workers if they are less skilled and efficient than white workers seeking employment.

We can extend our concept of social role expectations in another direction. During the 18th century, many employers had rules and policies that attempted to regulate the deportment of employees when they were not at work. For example, a large department store in Chicago had a policy requiring employees not to be seen in public "dressed beyond their station" or partaking of expensive cigars. In addition, written policy in this store urged church attendance, abstinence from alcoholic beverages, and avoidance of frivolous activities. As late as 1930, unmarried women teachers were required to sign employment contracts that forbade pregnancy, marriage, and frequent unchaperoned public appearances accompanied by men. In the past, these were serious public issues and employers were expected to become involved with and concerned about this type of behavior. These practices of the past are humorous, but any attempt by employers at regulating non-job related behavior today risks a court suit or at least strong pressures from employee groups.

More directly, social role expectations change over time and differ from one type of employer to another, from one position to another, and even among industries. To define socially responsible behavior, one must analyze the public's expectations of how someone in a particular position, in a certain firm within a specified industry is expected to act under the historical and social conditions he faces. These expectations define what is or is not responsible behavior.

The idea of role behavior applied to an occupational class is analogous to the sociological concept of ideology. The following discussions present, as an analytical framework, three business ideologies in the form of the role of the entrepreneur, the role of the bureaucrat, and the role of the professional manager. Although the discussions present the historical progression of each role, the reader should keep in mind that they also represent current expectations of role behavior and, therefore, are influential in explaining the actions of businessmen and women.

Role Behavior and Entrepreneurship

The importance of the sociological concept of role behavior for understanding the nature of entrepreneurship has long been recognized. Arthur Cole in his study of entrepreneurship states:

> It is enlightening to think of the relationships existing between the entrepreneur and the various elements of his organization in the terms provided by sociology. The bearers of the entrepreneurial function are viewed as playing a role in the Lintonian sense; and the execution of the several aspects of the role is stimulated by positive and negative sanctions exercised by the various individuals and groups with which these role bearers have relationships. [5]

The concept of entrepreneurship has played an important part in the history of economic development in the Western world. There is no agreed upon definition of entrepreneurship, and many writers include in the concept both the small businessman and the corporate executive employed by a large firm. In this section, we will explore the historical development of the role and the behavior expected of an entrepreneur.

In everyday usage, the term *businessman* is generic and refers to nearly all who are employed in private business except the rank-and-file worker. A *manager* is used to denote anyone who supervises others; a *bureaucrat* has the connotation of someone who works in a large organization and has little authority because it has been diffused throughout many offices similar to his—a bureaucrat also is thought to adhere to or administer the rules of the organization; an *executive* refers to anyone who has considerable influence and power in the organization. Researchers may prefer more precise definitions of these terms, but our concern is with how these roles are differentiated in the mind of the public.

Each of these terms conjures up an image of how someone in the role behaves. This image constitutes the basis of the role expectations in the community. To some people, even the generic term businessman has a negative connotation, but for most people these roles have both positive and negative connotations.

THE HISTORICAL ROLE OF THE ENTREPRENEUR. Reinhard Bendix traces the history of entrepreneurship to the late eighteenth and early nineteenth centuries in England. He finds that early entrepreneurs ". . . were struggling for recognition in a relatively hostile environment . . . . In common with other rising social groups, they were engaged in a fight for public recognition of their economic activities and for acceptance of their own position in society." [6] Their ideology was founded on middle-class values that were intended to ensure their social recognition, promote disdain for the ruling aristocracy, and gain influence over a rapidly growing industrial labor force. In a sense, then, the notion of the entrepreneur resulted from the early industrialists' attempts to justify their economic position and to establish a social class.

Bendix points out that the concept of social class defines a group of people with common interests who ". . . give rise to unifying ideas and united actions but whose cohesion is more or less unstable." [7] This instability exists because the ideology of the group (that is, their unifying ideas) adapts to the changing conditions in society in order to serve the practical interests of the members. It is important to note that ideology serves the purpose of justifying the position of influence and power of the social class and, at the same time, tends to structure the role behavior of group members. In other words, the ideology of these early industrialists reflects what is socially acceptable and expected from them as a group and as individuals.

Many writers have addressed the question of what justifiable function the entrepreneur performs in society. Most agreed that he is more than simply a provider of goods and services, a merchant, or an investor. Joseph Schumpeter argued ". . . that the function of entrepreneur is to reform or revolutionize the pattern of production by exploiting an invention or, more generally, an untried technological possibility for producing a new commodity or producing an old one in a new way, by opening up a new source of supply of materials or a new outlet for products, by reorganizing an industry and so on." [8] Schumpeter's emphasis on entrepreneurial innovation, which he called "creative destruction," did not require the entrepreneur to invent things; the function of the entrepreneur, in his words, consisted of "getting things done."

J. W. Gough presents another well-accepted view of the entrepreneur's function: ". . . personal enterprise and personal involvement are of the essence of entrepreneurship, this in part at any rate is because it is his own fortune, his own capital that the entrepreneur places at risk. . . . the archetypal entrepreneur is not only a man of initiative, but the man who 'runs his own show.' " [9] In this view, the entrepreneur is one who personally bears the risk of enterprise not solely as an investor, but as one who owns and operates the business and who expects no interest on his invested capital nor wages for his time, but expects and works toward profits as a return for his services. In the Western world, the notion of the entrepreneur as an owner of property that he risks for profit is an important dimension of his social role.

Another facet of the entrepreneurial function relates to the authority that accompanies this role. In the United States, the authority of the entrepreneur emanates from two sources: the institution of private property and the ideas of personal freedom that argue that ". . . authority in industry is justified explicitly on the ground that the man who already enjoys the good things in life has earned them and is entitled to the privileges (power) which they confer." [10]

Adolph Berle and Gardner Means, in their famous study of *The Modern Corporation and Private Property,* put forth the basic idea of private property:

> Since the use of industrial property consists primarily of an effort to increase its value—to make a profit—the owner of such property, in being entitled to its full use, has been entitled to all accretions to its value—to all the profits which it could be made to earn. In so far as he had to pay for the services of other men or other property in order to accomplish this increase in value, these payments operated as deductions; the profit remaining to him was the difference between the added value and the cost of securing these services. To this difference, however, the owner has traditionally been entitled. The state and the law have sought to protect him in this right. [11]

The legal basis of ownership of the means of production protected the early entrepreneur in his pursuit of profits, and the social ethic often associated with Protestantism encouraged individuals in the eighteenth and nineteenth centuries to pursue economic activities as a means to salvation. A doctrine of self-dependence and individual responsibility for one's own position in life was formulated during the industrial revolution which supplanted the old master-servant ethic that held the employer morally responsible for his employees. The new ethic, often referred to as "social Darwinism" urged the poor and unpropertied to imitate the entrepreneur by being frugal, industrious, and "morally abstinent" in sexual activities so as to become successful. Success as an entrepreneur was evidence of one's moral superiority and conferred the qualities of leadership that enabled the employer to direct the efforts of others in the interest of society.

Finally, Adam Smith's argument in the eighteenth century that self-seeking economic behavior was the "invisible hand" that led the way to increased national wealth created the social sanctioning of the pursuit of profits by entrepreneurs. He argued that the pursuit of self-interest frequently promotes the interests of society more effectively than when one really intends to do so.[12] Smith's philosophy is at the heart of the exhortation that entrepreneurs should act to maximize profit, for only through this type of behavior would the "natural laws" of economics work to the benefit of society. Under Smith's *laissez faire* economics, labor was a factor of production to be used as efficiently as other factors—to be purchased at the lowest possible cost—and to do otherwise would only detract from the welfare of society. Profit became the standard by which this new social class was judged, and profit maximization was the basis of the entrepreneur's moral claim to leadership over workers in the interest of the nation.

In summary, during the eighteenth and nineteenth centuries an ideology was created to further the aims of a new class of industrialists and to justify their economic power. This ideology justified their social position and established the role of the entrepreneur. The social function of the entrepreneur created by the ideology was to innovate in the economic sphere, assume financial risk, and pursue the goal of economic efficiency. There were positive moral, social, and economic sanctions established that encouraged this behavior. It was argued by many that successful economic endeavor was evidence of moral superiority and the means for success and salvation were held to be available to all who had the discipline to be frugal, industrious, and morally abstinent. The economic philosophy of *laissez faire* justified and encouraged the goal of profit maximization; and the institutional principle of private property permitted this new class to increase its power as it increased its profits to the practical benefit of the individual entrepreneur and the theoretical benefit of society.

HISTORICAL PERSPECTIVE. Although this brief sketch may seem naive and anachronistic to the modern student of business, we argue that these antecedent beliefs continue to influence the role of today's businessman because they remain, within some segments of society, the prevailing role expectations. This is not to deny that changes have taken place, for they have. Nor are we suggesting that the entrepreneurial role is not a legitimate one in today's industrial society. Our major purpose is to establish in the reader's mind a view of how the archetypal entrepreneur is expected to behave.

The Growth of the Corporation and the Role of Bureaucrat

The success of the industrial revolution resulted largely from the efforts of early entrepreneurs who, in their pursuit of personal gain, created and dominated for a short period of time the mass production industries. Railroads, steel making, oil production, auto making, to name but a few, were dynasties created by a handful of successful men in the United States during the eighteenth century. The success of what often began as a modest entrepreneurial undertaking resulted in a large-scale effort serving mass markets both domestically and abroad. As these organizations grew, such as Ford Motor Company or Carnegie Steel Company, two major changes tended to take place. First, the form of ownership changed from a closely held, family-owned organization to a publicly owned corporation. Secondly, the organization was restructured as a bureaucracy. As a result of both of these occurrences, the role of the businessman changed.

Regarding the growth of the public corporation, it was becoming evident during the early part of the twentieth century that the use of the corporation as a legal device to protect and promote the propertied interests of entrepreneurs was changing. Berle and Means pointed out in 1932:

> In its new aspect the corporation is a means whereby the wealth of innumerable individuals has been concentrated into huge aggregates and whereby control over this wealth has been surrendered to a unified direction. The power attendant upon such concentration has brought forth princes of industry, whose position in the community is yet to be defined. The surrender of control over their wealth by investors has effectively broken the old property relationships and has raised the problem of defining these relationships anew. The direction of industry by persons other than those who have ventured their wealth has raised the question of the motive force back of such direction and the effective distribution of the returns from business enterprise. [13]

The significance of this historical change is that the concept of private property was modified as the business corporation became a quasi-public institution ". . . in which a large measure of separation of ownership and control has taken place through the multiplication of owners." [14] The ideology of the entrepreneur that exhorted him to engage in a quest for personal gain (profits) was a practical incentive that was to ensure the success of the social order. However, with the growth of the large corporations and the diffusion of ownership to the public in the form of stock rights, control over the physical assets fell to managers who seldom owned much of the stock but were expected to act in the interest of the stockholders. The growth of absentee ownership brought into question the efficacy of the old ideology. According to Berle and Means:

> . . . . it is no longer the individual himself who uses his wealth. Those in control of that wealth, and therefore in a position to secure industrial efficiency and produce profits, are no longer, as owners, entitled to the bulk of such profits. Those who control the destinies of the typical modern corporation own so insignificant a fraction of the company's stock that the returns from running the corporation profitably accrue to them in only a very minor degree. The stockholders, on the other hand, to whom the profits of the corporation go, cannot be motivated by those profits to a more efficient use of the property, since they have surrendered all disposition of it to those in control of the enterprise. The explosion of the atom of property destroys the basis of the old assumption that the quest for profits will spur the owner of industrial property to its effective use. It consequently challenges the fundamental

economic principle of individual initiative in industrial enterprise. It raises for reexamination the question of the motive force back of industry, and the ends for which the modern corporation can be or will be run.[15]

The second major force that brought about a change in ideology was the growth of bureaucratic structures in large business enterprises. Bureaucracy is used today often as a pejorative term to assail the real and imagined social dysfunctions that come from working in or dealing with large organizations. However, the "principles" of bureaucracy amount to an ideology that, as Bendix argues, explains and justifies the authority of managers.

The nature of bureaucracy was set forth by Max Weber in the form of the following principles:

Modern officialdom functions in the following specific manner:

  I. There is the principle of fixed and official jurisdictional areas, which are generally ordered by rules, that is, by laws or administrative regulations.

    1. The regular activities required for the purposes of the bureaucratically governed structure are distributed in a fixed way as official duties.

    2. The authority to give the commands required for the discharge of these duties is distributed in a stable way and is strictly delimited by rules concerning the coercive means, physical, sacerdotal, or otherwise, which may be placed at the disposal of officials.

    3. Methodical provision is made for the regular and continuous fulfillment of these duties and for the execution of the corresponding rights; only persons who have the generally regulated qualifications to serve are employed.

In public and lawful government, these three elements constitute "bureaucratic authority." In private economic domination, they constitute bureaucratic "management." Bureaucracy, thus understood, is fully developed in political and ecclesiastical communities only in the modern state, and, in the private economy, only in the most advanced institutions of capitalism. . . .

  II. The principles of office hierarchy and of levels of graded authority mean a firmly ordered system of super- and subordination in which there is a supervision of the lower offices by the higher ones. Such a system offers the governed the possibility of appealing the decision of a lower office to its higher authority, in a definitely regulated manner. With the full development of the bureaucratic type, the office hierarchy is monocratically organized. The principle of hierarchical office authority is found in all bureaucratic structures; in state and ecclesiastical structures as well as in large party organizations and private enterprises. It does not matter for the character of bureaucracy whether its authority is called "private" or "public". . . .

  III. The management of the modern office is based on written documents ("the files"), which are preserved in their original or draught form. There is, therefore, a staff of subaltern officials and scribes of all sorts. The body of officials actively engaged in a "public" office, along with the respective apparatus of material implements and the files, make up a "bureau." In private enterprise, "the bureau" is often called "the office". . . .

In principle, the executive office is separated from the household, business from private correspondence, and business assets from private fortunes. The more consistently the modern type of business management has been carried through the more are these separations the case. . . .

IV. Office management, at least all specialized office management—and such management is distinctly modern—usually presupposes thorough and expert training. This increasingly holds for the modern executive and employee of private enterprises, in the same manner as it holds for the state official.

V. When the office is fully developed, official activity demands the full working capacity of the official, irrespective of the fact that his obligatory time in the bureau may be firmly limited. . . .

VI. The management of the office follows general rules, which are more or less stable, more or less exhaustive, and which can be learned. Knowledge of these rules represents a special technical learning which the officials possess. It involves jurisprudence, or administrative or business management. . . .[16]

The structure of bureaucracy is one which, in the interest of efficiency, attempts to eliminate personalized relationships and "nonrational" considerations. It is an attempt to standardize the behavior of individuals in clearly defined roles (offices) by establishing a framework for pre-existing rules that govern the behavior of one appointed to an office. In a sense, it is also an ideology that serves the same purpose as any ideology—to explain and justify the ideas, behavior, and authority of group members and to promote and protect the interests of the class in the larger society. Moreover, it defines expected and accepted behaviors of those occupying bureaucratic offices in the same manner that the entrepreneurial ideology governs the behavior of its members.

Weber's conceptualization was the ideal type, and large organizations are bureaucratized to varying degrees. We wish to avoid the impression that we are opposed to bureaucracies. On the contrary, as Weber argues, they are often the most efficient means to socially desirable ends, economic or otherwise. The concern here is with the behavior of those in bureaucratic roles. If the entrepreneur was expected to pursue personal financial gain in the interest of the larger society, what ends should the bureaucrat seek and how do they relate to social well-being?

The bureaucrat is expected to pursue the goal of technical competence. It is argued that, since the bureaucracy is a rational creation of an organization to serve social needs, the bureaucrat need only concern himself with becoming as technically competent as possible. As he better performs the duties of his office, he furthers the goals of the organization and thus the needs of society. In Bendix's words, whereas "entrepreneurial ideologies reflected the interaction among social classes brought about by industrialization . . . managerial ideologies are a response to the problems of coordination and direction in large-scale enterprises." [17]

The force of coordination and control in bureaucratic organizations is the social system. Precision, reliability, and efficiency are attained through conformity of behavior to prescribed rules. The discipline required of officeholders, Merton points out, ". . . can be effective only if the ideal patterns [of behavior] are buttressed by strong sentiments which entail devotion to one's duties, a keen sense of the limitation of one's authority and competence, and methodical performance of routine activities. The efficacy of social structure depends ultimately upon infusing group participants with appropriate attitudes and sentiments." [18]

What are these attitudes, sentiments, and beliefs that form the bureaucratic personality? First, there is a belief in strict devotion to rules to the extent that these rules, originally intended as means to socially desirable ends, may become ends in themselves. Second, the belief that nonconforming behavior is *per se* inefficient and therefore should not be tolerated. Third, the conviction that individuals higher in the hierarchy are better qualified to make decisions than those lower in the organization. Finally, an insistence on loyalty to the organization, its rules, and one's superiors is standard. These beliefs, to a greater or lesser extent, seem to pervade the large modern business organization.

This ideology has had both functional and dysfunctional consequences for society and for employees in the organization. Without question, the industrial strength and the unrivaled material standard of living in the United States is directly related to the creation of large, efficient manufacturing and marketing organizations. However, industrialization has brought urban decay, environmental pollution, and, many argue, a blight on the humanism of modern man. More importantly for our purposes, it is argued that the bureaucratic ethic has produced a "trained incapacity" in industrial leaders to respond in unique ways or to adapt readily to special conditions or a changing environment. Behavior often serves to perpetuate the vested interests of bureaucrats even to the detriment of the client groups the organization is designed to serve. Most importantly, bureaucracies, as rational designs, are not imbued with moral or ethical purposes as were early entrepreneurs and masters in traditional (nonindustrial) societies. Entrepreneurs of an earlier age, while not as efficient as their bureaucratic successors, were considered defenders of the capitalistic faith and the best examples of the American values of personal freedom, hard work, and individualism.

The most cogent criticism of the bureaucrat and his rise to power in the twentieth century is expressed by Clarence Walton:

> There was fear that the businessman of the new breed was rising to power because of his organizational [sic manipulative] skills and not because of his entrepreneurial qualities; there was concern that the conscientious small entrepreneur was in danger of being ground down by the conscienceless corporation. Thus, the system came under attack not because it was inefficient, but because it allegedly debased the moral quality of the country. [19]

Walton's view is that, while the bureaucrat performs his technical/business role efficiently, he has not sustained the moral/social relationship very well. The modern bureaucrat, guided by the "rational" policies of the bureaucracy appears unguided by ethical considerations outside of the organization unless they become codified in the rules governing the behavior of offices.

While this is a telling denunciation of bureaucratic behavior that not every researcher accepts, it has had sufficient public support to help foster a movement toward the development of a new business ethic with concomitant attempts to define the social responsibilities of managers in modern organizations.

The Developing Role of the Professional Manager

Benjamin Selekman, in the late 1950s, wrote that business was in search of a moral philosophy that ". . . might be explained in terms of 'industry in search of an ideology.' " [20] This search, in his view, resulted both from the upheaval of the Great Depression, which challenged the social viability of capitalism, and the growth of a new managerial class that wished to distinguish itself from the entrepreneur of former days. This new class was attempting to "professionalize" itself by establishing the traditional criteria of a profession: a body of knowledge, a repertoire of accepted techniques, an educational process that provides recognized credentials (Masters in Business Administration or other similar designations), and a code of professional ethics.

As in former times, the ideology was needed both to explain and to protect the power and authority of the people who controlled industry. If managers did not risk their own capital, what special economic purpose did they serve? If they were salaried and did not fully benefit from maximum profitability, what assurances were there that they would always seek economic efficiency? If they succeeded in bureaucratic organizations through conformity to rules and loyalty to superiors, what social justification was there for their considerable power over and leadership of the economic institutions of society? As with the ideology of the entrepreneur, the ideology of the professional manager must serve as both a social justification of the class and a guide to decision making for those who are in the role. The technocratic ideal of Weberian technocracy ignored these questions and the criticism that arose in the 1950s from writers such as Chris Argyris, who published *Personality and Organization* in 1957, arguing that modern bureaucracies inhibited personal fulfillment, was only the beginning of a growing criticism that business, and especially managers, were not fulfilling their social responsibilities.

The criticism of writers such as Argyris, McGregor, and Likert [21] became *de rigueur* in graduate education in business and found popular appeal among a small group of businessmen in the 1950s who were leaders of some of the largest and most powerful corporations in America. [22] The fifties was a period of intellectualizing about a new social responsibility and the need for a new business ideology. In many ways, the following decade of the 1960s was the coming together of these intellectual forces and activist groups of women, young people, racial minorities, and consumers, who made their causes felt at the highest levels of nearly all major corporations in the United States. The radical sixties brought a realization on the part of the public in general and among most managers that business was being challenged seriously, even in the midst of unparalleled prosperity, to justify its control over jobs and product markets and its ill-effect on the quality of the environment.

The challenges, intellectual and activist, resulted in strains on the role of manager in society. As Sutton, et. al., conceive it, these strains form the bases for a managerial ideology. In the *American Business Creed*, Sutton, et al., outline a theory of how business creeds develop and change. Their thesis is essentially the one put forth by this chapter. More specifically, they recognize the following major sources of role conflict that result in the development of ". . . a patterned reaction to the patterned strains of social role"—namely, an ideology: [23]

1. *The need for personal achievement.* In America, the emphasis on career achievement, especially relative to others in the same occupation, is an important source of role strain. While the pressure to achieve is great, even the casual observer is aware that success befalls many for unknown reasons. Tangible accomplishment alone does not assure success; the standards for success have been generalized and products and methods of business have lost their intrinsic significance. The generalized standards are size, rate of growth, profitability and market share.

> By these criteria, pills are as good as poetry, and what factory may be more successful than a bookstore. A firm making sewer pipes, cheap dresses, or artificial flowers may be more successful than one producing elegant china. [24]

The emphasis is upon achieving results in terms of the generalized standards ". . . however unorthodox or inelegant the means." [25] The strain of generalized standards results from the demand and interest in product quality, the delights of esoteric technical processes, and the esthetic qualities of merchandise, all of which must be subjected to the economic standards to determine if they "pay." Only if they meet the general standards are they legitimate to pursue. [26]

2. *Uncertainty, limited control, and responsibility.* The manager's role is one which gives him complete responsibility for achievement in an uncertain world where he tends to have little direct control over the forces which affect achievement. To cope with these strains, the managers attempt to reduce uncertainty by sponsoring protectionist legislation, trying to control suppliers, eliminate competitors and monopolize markets, all of which tend to incur the displeasure of various segments of the public at large. [27]

3. *Business hierarchies.* Although the responsibility for the success or failure of a venture is pushed to the top management of the organization, those lower in the hierarchy do not escape role strain. "The demands made upon junior executives for initiative, flexibility, and cooperation are a major source of strain." [28] As with top executives, the junior executive in the organization has no clear standards to guide behavior.

> His prospects depend to an unusual degree upon the opinions of a very few superiors, or perhaps one man. He is judged by practical results but, like his superiors, he may be judged by results over which he has very little control. [29]

4. *Social relations.* An important source of role strain is the requirement by organizations that the manager act impartially toward others. He is exhorted to restrain his personal likes and dislikes to promote efficient relationships within the firm. In addition, ". . . the enterprise may be legitimately self-oriented, and the

interests of others or the community at large rarely have to be considered." [30] These two strains come together and often cause problems for the manager who wishes to act out of his feelings of personal attachment or responsibilities for others, but the proscriptions of the firm will not allow the manager to protect the incompetent executive, over forty years old, even if he has a family of seven children. The manager ". . . feels it is his duty to judge people fairly according to their competence." [31]

5. *The bounds of legitimacy.* "The self-orientation of business means that the businessman as such feels only limited moral responsibilities toward other persons and groups." [32] Yet, there are limitations on the means he can use in the pursuit of achievement. These limitations are not well-defined, but the sanctions for going beyond the boundaries of accepted business practices are real and encountered often by those who pursue an aggressive policy. "[The manager] has difficulty in keeping a balanced moral judgment of his practices." [33]

6. *The social structure.* The businessman is often called on to play many other roles in society. The roles of statesman, benefactor of the arts, and leader in religious and civic associations are often an important part of the successful executive's life. Reconciling the demands of these roles with the role of manager is often a source of strain. [34]

The role of the professional manager is an emergent one and represents an evolution of the entrepreneurial and bureaucratic ideologies in response to the role strains implicit in modern society. The six sources of role strain above represent a taxonomy of the major forces that come together and influence the role perceptions of the modern professional manager. The modern manager is professional in the sense that his orientation leans toward "the profession" rather than toward the bureaucracy that employs him. Entry into the occupation often requires specific formal education or training. Educational credentials are becoming much more important for entry level positions, and a body of techniques and knowledge is building in business schools throughout the nation. What is lacking, many argue, is an explicit "code of ethics" to guide the professional manager in making socially responsible decisions. This has been a criticism and lament of many who wish management to achieve the professional status of law, medicine, or the clergy. In a sense, this is tilting at windmills. Thomas Petit makes this point by arguing that ". . . business ethics is never in a state of being; it is always in a process of becoming. A manager should never reach the point where he is certain for all time to come to his ethical position. . . . To be effective, a socially responsible manager must be tuned in to broad social trends and comprehend their significance for the corporation." [35] Even more specifically, "when we talk about *socially responsible managers*, what we are really doing is calling attention to a particular type of emphasis in the expectations of the manager's role." [36] In agreement with Petit, we believe that, for analytical purposes, the manager must continually engage in an explicit process of role definition to ensure that he is meeting the test of social responsibility. His code of ethics, his ideology, result from this examination and evolve as a result of the changing expectations of society.

A Contingency View of Socially Responsible Behavior

The previous section examined three archetypical social roles found in varying degrees in modern business enterprises. Pure types are seldom found in large firms. Rather, some firms tend to encourage one type of behavior more than another or, under certain conditions, a manager may be expected to act like an entrepreneur, while under other circumstances, he must play the role of professional manager. The role of professional manager appears to be in the ascendency; there are cultural and environmental reasons that make this type of behavior more appropriate today than in the past, although it should be emphasized that there are conditions that require managers to play other roles. Recognizing the contingency nature of role behavior, a good case can be made for defining socially responsible behavior within the firm as playing a role that is consistent with the organizational model adhered to by the firm. But the firm is charged with a social responsibility that, although not independent of the behavior of its managers, is clearly separable from individual roles. In a sense, the firm plays a social role that must be judged. The socially responsible firm may be viewed as one that adheres to an organizational model and employs coping strategies that are consistent with the environment.

In Figure 1.1, we depict a relationship among the four variables: the organizational model of the firm, managerial roles, coping strategies, and environmental conditions. The social model that a firm may choose, which influences considerably the dominant role behavior expected of managers and the coping strategies employed, must be consistent with the nature of the firm's environment. We know that role expectations are important determinants of organizational behavior. Individuals tend to conform to roles to avoid sanctions and to meet the expectations of others that are considered legitimate. The model that the firm adheres to is reflected

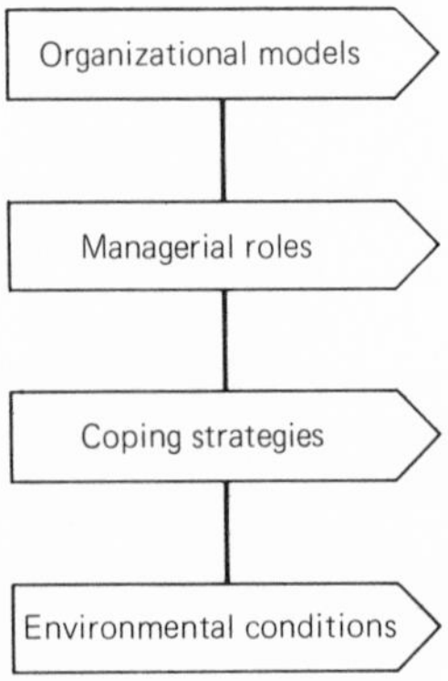

FIGURE 1.1 Variables determining socially responsible behavior

mainly in its goals, and these goals, plus social ideologies, greatly influence what expectations managers consider legitimate. Addressing a concern for socially responsible behavior, Thompson and McEwen point out that "the goal-setting problem (of organizations) is essentially determining a relationship of the organization to the larger society which in turn becomes a question of what the society . . . wants done or can be persuaded to support . . . the setting of goals is essentially a problem of defining desired relationships between an organization and its environment. . . ." [37] Clarence Walton appears to be in agreement with this view in setting forth his *models* of socially responsible enterprises. Figure 1.2 lists these models, their primary goals, and their primary beneficiaries. [38]

1. *The austere model.* Walton's austere model is based upon the proposition that the firm is made up of basically two elements: ownership rights and resources. However, the ownership rights extend to the resources that are employed by the owners, for their benefit. The owners are not the same as the *employees* of the firm. They are the risk-takers who risk their capital and therefore "rightly deserve all profits."

> The austere model is predicated on the following factors: (a) large numbers of owners who are willing to commit their resources in risk-taking ventures for profit; (b) competitive markets for all products; (c) ability to substitute one resource for another when the competitively set cost-price equation makes another form of resource combination more profitable; (d) acceptance by all of the owners of the principle of self-interest as the motivating force in all economic activity. . . .
>
> An austere philosophy aims to save corporate executives from all philanthropy by reminding them that the stockholders are the self-reliant elements of our society; their concern in business affairs is self-interest, which is served by profit-maximizing corporations whose doors must be locked against all deviations represented by so-called social responsibilities.
>
> Vigorous pursuit of the stockholder's interests becomes the socially responsible function of corporate management. [39]

This model is the classical view of the firm in a capitalist economy.

2. *The household model.* This model asserts the rights of employees. Walton explains that:

FIGURE 1.2 Organizational models of socially responsible firms

Model	Primary Goal	Primary Beneficiary
1. Austere	Profit Realization	Stockholders
2. Household	Resource Utilization	Employees
3. Vendor	Sales Volume	Customers
4. Investment	Survival	Firm as Entity
5. Civic	Health and Welfare	Public at Large
6. Artistic	Education and the Arts	Cultural Community

The household model accepts, as its first proposition, the fact that human resources are a firm's most precious asset; consequently, anything that depersonalizes the employee or assigns him a low rating in the corporation's list of priorities is to be rejected as unsound. Employees (managers and blue-collar workers) have, therefore, a claim that is equal, if not superior, to that exercised by stockholders.[40]

This model is a departure from the classical view and places social values above purely economic ones. Providing employees good wages, good working conditions, and economic security becomes the socially responsible function of management along with the pursuit of the stockholders' interest.

3. *The vendor model.* This view of social responsibilities goes one step beyond the household model and brings the consumer's interests into consideration.

If the household model of social responsibility accords priority to industrial policy (employment opportunities, incomes, and rights) over financial policy (profit maximization), the vendor model thrusts the consumer into the picture as the 'forgotten' man of modern economics—forgotten because big business and big unions have produced a species of accommodations where the rewards of increased productivity are shared with these groups rather than with the consumer. Both financial and industrial policy look inward to the stockholder and to the worker, respectively. Market policy looks outward to the rights, interests, and tastes of the consumer.

In every state jurisdiction, there are laws governing the sale of certain products to certain potential consumers and the sale of liquor to minors is one example. The Pure Food and Drug Act seeks to protect the health of the consumer by restricting certain products from general sale. Hence, there exists a fair amount of compulsion in the vendor model. There are, however, other areas where options do exist to promote consumer interests. Defaults in these responsibilities include acts such as deliberately engineered product obsolescence, shoddy service on consumer durables, excessive and hidden charges for credit, and the withholding of new products from the market.[41]

4. *The investment model.* In this model, there is a shift of focus from internal to external claimants. In the vendor model there is a recognition that the success of the firm is dependent upon maintaining a good relationship with customers, while the investment begins to go beyond the customer to a consideration of other external interests such as education, medical research, or charitable organizations. The connection between the success of the firm and the interests of these groups is vague and tenuous. Nevertheless, the connection is rationalized by an appeal to a view of "enlightened self-interest" that asserts that the firm must serve these groups to ensure the long-term success of the firm. Management's responsibilities are to employ resources to support social institutions that are important for the future success of the firm.[42]

5. *The civic model.* This model differs from the others on the assumption that the business corporation has a responsibility to the major institutions in society: the industrial system and the political system. Managers are given a franchise from society to engage in certain activity in the interests of the people of that society. To re-

tain the franchise they must act ". . . with due concern for the public interests, and they must behave as responsible citizens."

> Thus, citizenship, as defined in the civic model, is not limited simply to a discharge of formally imposed obligations any more than citizenship for the individual is fully met by paying taxes or by voting. The civic model envisages a positive business commitment to the political system of democracy. It means willingness to help alleviate unemployment and to preclude chronic business cycles; it asks business to participate in public dialogues on important issues. Like every other citizen, the corporation is free to determine where and how it can best meet such commitments. [43]

6. *The artistic model.* This model is an emergent one that at present, Walton argues, is indistinct but developing in some corporate circles. In this model, management is called on not only to serve the social claimants, but to go beyond reacting to needs to one of helping create a new social order beyond the constraints imposed by a doctrine of enlightened self-interest. Managers are to use their talents and the firm's resources ". . . as servants in the cause of a higher civilization and culture" regardless of the long-term consequences to the firm. [44]

The role of modern manager is a *melange* of ideology that incorporates many elements of the entrepreneur, the bureaucrat, and increasingly the professional manager. In focusing on the role of the manager we argue that individual managers have a social responsibility within the organization. Perhaps the most important determinant of how the manager should act is the role his organization is expected to play in the economic scheme of things. For example, the farm owner/manager who operates in a highly competitive market is expected to act differently than the chief executive of a large agri-business corporation. Additionally, more might be expected in the way of concern for employees of a local firm than one that is international in its operations. Walton's models describe, in a sense, six strategies that corporations might follow in fulfilling their perceptions of their social responsibilities. The reader should keep in mind, however, that some firms may adhere to one of these models and be judged responsible, while firms in different circumstances may find adherence to the same model inappropriate.

The connection between individual roles and organizational models has been made. To complete our analysis of the socially responsible firm, the model must be connected to the environment. Before we describe the nature of the connection it is important to understand differences among environments. One can define the environment faced by organizations from many abstract views. One that we believe is especially useful for our purposes here is a taxonomy developed by F. E. Emery and E. L. Trist. [45] Strategies are ways in which organizations attempt to attain goals in an uncertain future. The strategic problem is how to reallocate resources to meet the challenge of a changing environment. Uncertainty is a function of change or the instability of the environment; therefore, Emery and Trist classify environments according to their expected stability. They analyze environments along the four point continuum in Figure 1.3.

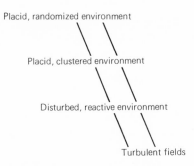

FIGURE 1.3 Types of organizational environments

1. *Placid, randomized environment.* This type of environment is one in which there are no connections among environmental parts. The environmental forces are constantly and randomly changing, and the firm can do little to affect the nature of the environment. This environment is similar to the classical economy of pure competition in which every organization is faced with the same set of competitive forces and responds by ". . . attempting to do one's best on a purely local basis" [46] whatever the circumstances. The pursuit of self-interest is expected, even necessary, for organizational survival and does not affect the tactics of other firms in the market.

2. *Placid, clustered environment.* This is the case of imperfect competition in which success, perhaps even the survival of the firm, depends upon knowledge of the changing environment. Success depends upon how the environment changes and how other firms react to the changes. In a situation where there are many sellers of a product competing for what might be considered the changing tastes of the consumer, success or failure of one firm will be dependent upon the extent of knowledge about how tastes are changing, what competitors are likely to do to meet changing consumer demand, and the firm's ability to meet the instability created by the anticipated changes in consumer tastes.

Unlike the previous example, firms in a placid, clustered environment believe they can and need to exercise some control over the environment. Faced with this type of environment, strategy is distinct from tactics. Some divisions of the organization are required to subordinate their resources to the main plan. A product division may be required to forego growth in market share so that resources might be diverted to other product divisions in the interest of strategic goals. Or, firms may refrain from short-run profit maximizing behavior in the interest of increasing profits in the distant future. Also, some firms may develop "distinctive competencies" that serve a segment of the market while allowing or encouraging others to serve the remaining segments. "Organizations under these conditions, therefore, tend to grow in size and also to become hierarchical with a tendency toward central control and coordination." [47]

3. *Disturbed, reactive environment.* The dominant characteristic of this type of environment is that all organizations must be aware that they may compete for the same future position. "Knowing this, each will wish to improve its own changes by hindering the others. . . ." [48] Now one must not only choose a strategic objective and engage in tactics that draw the organization to the objective, but one may need to mount operations that take into consideration "a planned series of tactical initiatives" that consider the actions and reactions of other organizations in the environment. Stability can come about only by ". . . 'coming-to-terms' between competitors, whether *enterprises, interest groups,* or *governments.*" [49] Thus, in this environment various forms of accommodation between like but competitive organizations whose fates are to a degree negatively correlated are established.

4. *Turbulent fields.* In this environment there is a marked increase in uncertainty because one must deal not only with competitors but also with a fast-changing environment made up of nearly the entire cultural-economic fabric of society. The outcome of actions becomes increasingly more unpredictable; to cope with the relative uncertainty, firms must become concerned with changing community values, ethical codes, and cultural priorities. Even then, the accelerating rate and complexity of change may very well exceed the organization's capacity for prediction and control of the compounding consequences of its actions. Under such conditions instability pervades both organization structure and social roles.

The important managerial question is: if we are faced with one of these environments, how shall we act? This is a normative concern, and our answer is tentative; however, Thompson and McEwen's view is that firms choose one of three strategies to deal with uncertainty and relate the organization's goals to the environment. Figure 1.4 illustrates their continuum. In a relatively stable environment, perhaps one similar to the *placid, randomized environment,* the appropriate strategy of the firm should be competition—competition not only with one's competitors in the product market but competition in the sense that "it includes scrambling for resources as well as for customers or clients, and in a complex society it includes rivalry for potential members and their loyalties." [50] As instability increases, the appropriate organizational response moves more and more in the direction of *co-optation.* This is a process of introducing more and more elements, or points of view, into the firm's decision-making processes to avert a threat to the firm's survival. While in a disturbed reactive environment cooperation is required between like, but competitive firms, turbulent environments also require cooperation among dissimilar organizations whose fates are positively correlated. In Thompson and McEwen's view ". . . co-optation is an important social device for increasing the likelihood that organizations related to one another in complicated

FIGURE 1.4 Organizational coping strategies

Competition ⟶ Co-optation ⟶ Coalition

ways will in fact find compatible goals." [51] At the extremes of instability, if an organization finds itself in a *turbulent field*, perhaps the proper response is to form *coalitions*. The firm may combine with other organizations in the environment to pursue a common purpose. "Coalition requires a commitment for joint decision of future activities and thus places limits on unilateral or arbitrary decisions." [52]

Emery and Trist also suggest possible means of contending with particularly turbulent field environments. [53] They point out that, in such an environment, the ability of an organization to maintain stability declines drastically. One possible solution is the use of social values as coping mechanisms. For instance, as an organization's actions are amplified through the environment, values may provide conditions similar to rules or at least guides. However, the authors also state that even if successful, the use of social values as guides only helps transform turbulent environments into disturbed or clustered environments. Once values are inculcated into the organization, the firm may be described as institutionalized in the sense that goals congruent with the organization's own character must now offer maximum convergence with goals in the interest of other parties. One danger the authors also see is a failure to recognize turbulent environments. In these instances, solutions are always inappropriate because they are based on the assumption that organizations operate in either disturbed or clustered environments.

We now have a tentative model of how a firm and its managers should act in particular environments to be considered responsible. Figure 1.5 indicates that as a firm moves into unstable environments, the appropriate coping response is in the direction of co-optation and coalition; however, to accomplish this the role behavior of the manager must move away from the entrepreneur's role in the direction of the professional manager. To reinforce the role behavior of decision makers, the firm must adopt a consistent model away from the austere toward the artistic. We wish to emphasize that the reader must deal with these abstractions as forces that propel one toward a need for change, not as mechanical prescriptions for choosing one or the other model to suit a static analysis of the nature of the environment. Rather, the reader should ask in what direction has the environment moved? Is there a need for a different strategy? What changes are needed in role behavior?

FIGURE 1.5 Responsible behavior

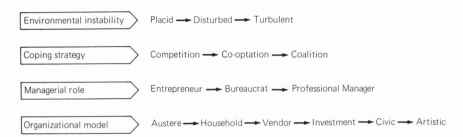

Prescriptions in this complex area are like cliches; everyone is aware of them but few find them useful to guide behavior.

FOOTNOTES

[1] David T. Lawless, *Effective Management: Social Psychological Approach* (Englewood Cliffs, New Jersey: Prentice-Hall, Inc., 1972), p. 283.

[2] Daniel Katz and Robert L. Kahn, *The Social Psychology of Organizations* (New York: John Wiley and Sons, Inc., 1966), p. 172.

[3] *Ibid.*, p. 173.

[4] *Ibid.*, p. 179.

[5] Arthur H. Cole, *Business Enterprise in Its Social Setting* (Cambridge, Mass.: Harvard University Press, 1959), p. 53.

[6] Reinhard Bendix, *Work and Authority in Industry* (New York: Harper and Row, Publishers, 1963), p. 23.

[7] *Ibid.*, p. 7.

[8] Joseph A. Schumpeter, *Capitalism, Socialism, and Democracy* (New York: Harper and Bros., Publishers, 1942), p. 132.

[9] J. W. Gough, *The Rise of the Entrepreneur* (New York: Schocken Books, Inc., 1969), p. 17.

[10] Bendix, *Work and Authority in Industry*, p. 11.

[11] Adolph Berle and Gardner Means, *The Modern Corporation and Private Property* (Harcourt, Brace, and World, Inc., 1932), p. 294.

[12] George Soule, *The New Science of Economics: An Introduction* (Greenwich, Connecticut: Fawcett Publications, Inc., 1948), pp. 20–22.

[13] Berle and Means, *The Modern Corporation and Private Property*, p. 4.

[14] *Ibid.*, p. 5.

[15] *Ibid.*, p. 9.

[16] Excerpted from *From Max Weber: Essays in Sociology*, edited and translated by H. H. Gerth and C. Wright Mills. Copyright 1946 by Oxford University Press, Inc. Renewed 1973 by Dr. Hans H. Gerth. Reprinted by permission.

[17] Bendix, *Work and Authority in Industry*, p. 9.

[18] Robert K. Merton, "Bureaucratic Structure and Personality," *Social Forces*, Vol. 18, 1940, as reprinted in Joseph A. Litterer, ed., *Organizations: Structure and Behavior* (New York: John Wiley and Sons, Inc., 1963), p. 375.

[19] Clarence C. Walton, ed., *Business and Social Progress* (New York: Praeger Publishers, 1970), p. 126.

[20] Benjamin M. Selekman, *A Moral Philosophy for Management* (New York: McGraw-Hill Book Co., Inc., 1959), p. 3.

[21] See Chris Argyris, *Personality and Organization* (New York: Harper and Bros., Publishers, 1957), Douglas M. McGregor, *The Human Side of Enterprise* (New York: McGraw-Hill Book Co., 1960), and Rensis Likert, *New Patterns of Management* (New York: McGraw-Hill Book Co., 1961).

[22] Thomas A. Petit, *The Moral Crisis in Management* (New York: McGraw-Hill Book Co., 1967), pp. 51–53.

[23] Francis X. Sutton, Seymour E. Harris, Carl Kaysen, James Tobin, *The American Business Creed* (Cambridge, Mass.: Harvard University Press, 1956), p. 307.

[24] *Ibid.*, p. 328.

[25] *Ibid.*, p. 328.
[26] *Ibid.*, p. 330.
[27] *Ibid.*, pp. 332–333.
[28] *Ibid.*, p. 337.
[29] *Ibid.*, p. 337.
[30] *Ibid.*, p. 339.
[31] *Ibid.*, p. 340.
[32] *Ibid.*, p. 343.
[33] *Ibid.*, p. 344.
[34] *Ibid.*, pp. 345–346.
[35] Petit, *The Moral Crisis in Management*, p. 169.
[36] *Ibid.*, p. 73.
[37] James D. Thompson and William J. McEwen, "Organizational Goals and Environment: Goal-Setting As An Interaction Process," *American Sociological Review*, no. 23 (Feb. 1958), p. 23.
[38] Clarence C. Walton, *Corporate Social Responsibilities* (Belmont, California: Wadsworth Publishing Co., Inc., 1967), p. 126.
[39] *Ibid.*, pp. 127–129.
[40] *Ibid.*, p. 130.
[41] *Ibid.*, pp. 132–133.
[42] *Ibid.*, pp. 134–136.
[43] *Ibid.*, pp. 136–139.
[44] *Ibid.*, pp. 139–141.
[45] F. E. Emery and E. L. Trist, "The Causal Texture of Organizational Environment," *Human Relations*, Vol. 18, No. 1 (1965), pp. 21–32.
[46] *Ibid.*, p. 24.
[47] *Ibid.*, p. 25.
[48] *Ibid.*, p. 25.
[49] *Ibid.*, p. 26.
[50] Thompson and McEwen, "Organizational Goals and Environment," p. 26.
[51] *Ibid.*, p. 28.
[52] *Ibid.*
[53] Emery and Trist, "The Causal Texture of Organizational Environment," pp. 28–30.

CHAPTER 2

ANALYZING THE CORPORATE DILEMMA

It is fashionable to point to the changing economic, technological, and cultural scenes and conclude that our environment is changing at a more rapid pace than in the past. This rapid rate of change is said to be causing many of the frustrations and concerns that are involved in defining socially responsible business behavior. Of course we are involved in a changing social milieu. Perhaps it is changing at a more rapid rate than in the past; perhaps it is not. The concern over the rate of change has become almost a lament for "the good old days" when people knew right from wrong, knew their place, respected authority, and fulfilled the role expectations of others.

Alvin Toffler in his popular book *Future Shock* argues that many of the social problems that confront America are the result of accelerated change that, independent of the substance of the change, causes modern people to become maladaptively oriented. The pace of change has become so rapid that before we adapt to a perceived change in the environment we are well into further change that makes our previous response inadequate. ". . . the increased rate at which situations flow past us vastly complicates the entire structure of life, multiplying the number of roles we must play and the number of choices we are forced to make. This in turn, accounts for the changing sense of complexity about contemporary life." [1]

"Decision stress" is one result of the rapidly changing environment and in Toffler's view many of us are forced ". . . to quicken the tempo of private and public decision-making. New needs, novel emergencies, and crises demand response. Yet the very newness of the circumstances brings about a revolutionary change in the nature of the decisions [we] are called upon to make." [2]

No longer are we able to cope with the diversity of interests affected by our decisions. We are faced with a large number of response patterns to problems and opportunities in the environment, we are provided with voluminous information about the potential effects of our choices, and we are expected to choose responses that are suitable not only to our interest but are compatible with many other interests that claim to be affected by our decisions. Each complex decision may require trade-offs of the interest of the many or few affected by our choices because their interests are in conflict. For example, the rising young executive frequently faces the choice of having to move from place to place every few years, disrupting family life, interfering with or breaking strong social ties if he wishes to be successful as a manager. Other family members may be better served *if* social ties would remain unbroken, *if* a sense of community attachment were retained, but only *if* he could become "successful" without having to move from place to place. The choices are often painful to make because every alternative falls short of meeting the legitimate demands of the parties affected by the decision.

Whether it is the pace of change, as Toffler argues, that causes the decision stress, is a debatable but ultimately irrelevant question in considering the notion of socially responsible business behavior. The businessman has always been faced with making painful decisions for an uncertain future. He has always preferred more certainty to uncertainty and therefore always laments the rapidly changing environment. How he adapts to the changes in his environment is the product of his decisions and it is this product that is judged according to its social responsibility—its deference to the public interest. However, the result is seldom judged independently of the decision maker's role behavior. For example, faced with growing financial losses Detroit automobile manufacturers begin massive employee layoffs. These decisions result in a 30 percent rate of unemployment in Detroit, increases in violent crime and the number of suicides, and a cutback on services as tax revenue diminishes and the costs of welfare programs increase. The results of the decision to lay off employees is certainly costly to many public interests—the poor, the young, the unskilled, the nonwhites, and the emotionally unstable. But, was the decision to lay off workers socially irresponsible? The answer to that question depends upon what auto companies are expected to do. At what cost to the interest of the stockholders and the financial viability of the business should management retain unneeded workers?

These questions, of course, cannot be answered in precise terms but, traditionally, the prevailing ideology and the roles that are created to bring about behavior consistent with that ideology provide the answer.

The dilemma of socially responsible behavior relates not so much to the pace of change as it does to the changing social ideology. Votaw and Sethi point out: "Traditional corporate values and ideologies often appear to aggravate rather than alleviate contemporary social conflicts and problems. Time-tested responses to social challenge appear to make conditions worse rather than better—or not to have measurable effect at all." [3] Furthermore, they conclude:

> . . . the rationality of decision-making is based on a selected ideological assumption that leads to specific types of behavior. For example, with respect to product line mix, a rationalized self-interest orientation will probably lead to a profit-maximizing product mix decision, even if the products have to be forced through the marketing channel. A predisposition to maximize consumer preferences, on the other hand (given a fixed volume assumption), would lead to a differ-

ent, probably less profitable, set of product offerings. In each case, the underlying ideology is quite different. Given the basic ideological commitment, the selection of appropriate behavior can be made rationally—self-interest, consumer interest, or whatever.

Difficulties are encountered when the corporate ideology is obscure, not thought out, or unconscious, at a time when the objectives of the corporation come into conflict with other social needs and norms. Decisions come into conflict with other social needs and norms. Decisions that have to be made on nonconventional business problems, e.g., disclosure of minority employee lists, are likely to fall into one of the categories mentioned above. Where there is an apparent lack of rationality in the behavior of the corporation, it suggests the total absence of an ideology or an ideology that is unstated, unadmitted, or unrecognized. The absence of an ideology means an absence of normative orientation—the lack of a set of "oughts" which the corporation should follow. Faced with a new problem for which it has no ideological referent, the corporation may become paralyzed or make a decision on the basis of a nonapplicable norm. In either event, the consequences are likely to be disastrous, which underlines the value of anticipating problems before they arise so that a conscious behavior decision can be made, based on the selected ideology. While this would solve the problem of being taken by surprise without a developed ideology, the problem of dealing with unstated, unadmitted, or unrecognized ideologies remain.[4]

The Analytic Process

If this is the case, then it is fitting that the student pursue an analysis of each of the corporate dilemmas in this volume by examining the "apparent" ideological perspective of the firm in each of the cases. The ideological perspective determines the rationality of policy decisions. The cases should be analyzed as policy issues that can be "solved" by the establishment of the proper criteria for success (goals), the communicating of these policies throughout the organization, the development of specific plans for attaining these goals, the institution of policy control procedures to monitor progress toward goals, and a proper reward system to motivate goal accomplishment.

The cases found in Section II are representative of some of the major social problems facing business in the 1970s. As we noted earlier ideology is a changing pattern of responses to a changing pattern of strains that impinge upon the organizations and individuals who make the decisions about how to respond. There are no answers that the reader can hope to arrive at and feel confident that his prescription for socially responsible behavior is the only correct one for that case for all times. Formulas for solving the major policy decisions of organizations do not exist nor will they be developed. The best we can hope for is to improve the quality of our decisions by improving the process by which these decisions are made. The process suggested by this chapter is one that should lead the reader to an understanding of the social forces that compelled the responses of the actors and organizations in each case. Furthermore it is a process that recognizes the dynamic nature of organizational environments and is useful in analyzing whether more appropriate responses should be made, what those responses could be, and how one might change an organization's response to social problems.

In analyzing these cases the reader should not rely on the facts of the case but should attempt to analyze the complex environment in which each case is set, discover the rationale of the organization's response, understand the role behavior of individual decision makers, and develop and defend any changes in either organizational or individual responses that are appropriate. To do this, the reader is urged to answer the following questions for each case.

1. What is the nature of the organization's environment? Has it changed recently? What is the anticipated direction of change?

2. What type of coping strategy seems to dominate the organization? Is this appropriate? What, if any, change in coping strategy would appear to be desirable? In the future, what would be the most appropriate coping strategy? How does one bring about a change in strategy?

3. What type of managerial role behavior is dominant? Is it appropriate for the environment? What, if any, change in role behavior would be desirable? How might the change be affected?

4. What is the dominant role model of the organization? Is it an appropriate model? What changes should be brought about? How is an organization's model behavior changed?

Of course, answering these questions will not solve the case. Solutions require that explicit goals, policies, procedures, and criteria for success be established. These questions represent a model for analysis that will avoid or overcome the problems encountered when the ideology is "obscure, not thought out, or unconscious." The student should analyze each case by answering the questions enumerated above recognizing that "solutions" to the case require policy formulation. As with most models of complex phenomena, the usefulness of the model is dependent upon the perspective that can be gained through its use in explaining the phenomena and the insight one might gain into the relationships among the forces in the environment.

The remainder of this chapter illustrates the use of the method of analysis suggested by this book by examining a case similar to those in Section II of the book: "Disney vs. the Sierra Club: A Question of Land Use." The case analysis presented here is abbreviated and does not constitute a complete analysis. Rather, the intention is to illustrate concisely how the method outlined might serve to guide the analysis of a case. The authors are not suggesting that their analysis is the only acceptable one. It is not the "school solution" by any means, nor does it solve the problems. However, the reader should readily see that the analysis is suggestive of policy changes that could be elaborated. Moreover, we recommend that this case be used as the first case for analysis. Students may consider our analysis first and then discuss the policy implications of this analysis for Walt Disney Enterprises.

FOOTNOTES

[1] Alvin Toffler, *Future Shock* (New York: Bantam Books, Inc., 1970), pp. 33–34.
[2] *Ibid.*, p. 355.
[3] Dow Votaw and S. Prakash Sethi, *The Corporate Dilemma* (Englewood Cliffs, New Jersey: Prentice-Hall, Inc., 1973), p. 5.
[4] *Ibid.*, p. 52.

Case Example
Disney vs. Sierra Club:
A Question of Land Use

Mineral King Valley

Mineral King Valley is 228 miles from Los Angeles, 271 miles from San Francisco, and 55 miles from Visalia, the nearest large city in the Central Valley. The valley is composed of approximately 15,000 acres nestled in the Sierra Nevada Mountains in Tulare County, California, adjacent to Sequoia National Park. The valley has been described as a spectacular wild mountain valley, an alpine paradise of peaks, ridges, and high passes. Within its circumference are 22 mountain lakes, open to the hardy by horseback and foot in the summer and by skis and snowshoes in winter.

During 1967 this little-known valley became the center of a classic conservation fight, demonstrating the pressures on recreation space for a growing population.

Mineral King was first visited by white men in the late 1850s. The valley was mistakenly thought to have rich mineral deposits, and during the seventies and eighties there was a modest, short-lived silver rush. When Sequoia National Park was created in 1890, the valley was not included because a few remaining mining interests lingered, a condition considered incompatible with national park standards. Even though all mining ceased long ago, and the few buildings associated with mining have disappeared, the attitude still prevails. In 1926 the area was designated as the Sequoia National Game Refuge.

The United States Forest Service, which is entrusted with the maintenance and administration of national forests, began in the late 1940s to give consideration to Mineral King as a potential site for recreational development. The decision to develop Mineral King was made unilaterally by the Forest Service with no public hearings or other opportunity for public comment.[1] In 1949 the Forest Service issued a prospectus inviting bids from private concerns to develop Mineral King as a winter sports resort. There was considerable interest, but no bids were made. There were no state or federal funds available for a new road, and none of the interested private developers was willing to spend the millions of dollars needed to build a twenty-five mile, all-weather road in mountainous terrain.[2]

Prodded by a rapidly increasing demand for skiing facilities, in 1965 the Forest Service again published a prospectus, inviting bids from private developers for the construction and operation of a ski resort that would also serve as a summer recreation area. The proposal of Walt Disney Enterprises Inc. was chosen from those of six bidders, and Disney received a three-year permit to conduct surveys and explorations in the valley in connection with its preparations of a complete master plan for the resort.

Walt Disney Productions

In the year 1966 Walt Disney Productions estimated that, around the world, 240,000,000 people saw a Disney movie; 100,000,000 watched a Disney television show every week; 800,000,000 read a Disney book or magazine; 50,000,000 listened or danced to Disney music or records; 80,000,000 bought Disney-licensed merchandise; 150,000,000 read a Disney comic strip; 80,000,000 saw Disney educational films at school, in church, on the job; and 6.7 million made the journey to that peculiar mecca in Anaheim, California insistently known as "Walt Disney's Magic Kingdom" in the company's press releases, and more commonly referred to as Disneyland. From a state of profitability near zero in 1954, the company progressed over the years to the point where its net income was $12,392,000 on a gross of $116,543,000, which meant that the magic kingdom was very close to joining the magic circle—the five hundred largest corporations in the nation.[3]

In order to understand something about Disney Productions, one must look closely at Walt Disney, the man who literally put the organization together and ran it as an extension of his personality during his life. The man pursued an old private dream dating back to the 1930s—the creation of an amusement park suitable for his own children—and he managed to lay the groundwork for the kind of diversification that all the other film companies lust after but rarely achieve.

Disneyland offers an ancient entertainment form that had fallen on dreary days and was ripe for fresh innovations. More important, it is felt that this project claimed the largest share of Disney's psychic energy during his later years and indicates his real "genius." Richard Schickel, author of *The Disney Version*, believed Disney's talent was not that of artistic expression as many argue, but rather a genius for the exploitation of technological innovations.[4] James Rouse, a leading figure in the "New Town" movement, states, "The greatest piece of urban design in the U.S. today is Disneyland. Think of its performance in relation to its purpose."[5]

The Disneyland Project led to larger related efforts which, though retaining elements of the Disney dream, were more accurately seen as attempts to reexamine the customs of urban design (such as Disney World in Florida) and of recreational design (such as the Mineral King project). In part, awareness of urban recreational design was accidentally imposed upon the Disney organization as it sought to learn how to handle large crowds efficiently, keeping them in a happy frame of mind.[6]

Forest Service

The Forest Service guiding principle of land management is "multiple use." On the 187 million acres of public land administered by the Forest Service, a wide variety of activities are permitted including lumbering, hunting, livestock grazing, mining, and even some private cabin building.

Within the last decade the focus of national attention upon the country's recreational potential, combined with the spiraling magnitude of the billion dollar recreational business, has alerted the federal government's largest landholding bureaus to the task of accommodating a prodigious number of special recreation interests, ranging from motorboating to motorcycling, and from skiing to skimobiling. In the case of skiing, the Forest Service has leased public lands to commercial developers who operate such well-known ski meccas as Aspen, Vail, Sun Valley, Mt. Snow, and Sugarbush.

Thirty-seven of the over 190 ski areas on Forest Service land are located in California. Nevertheless, that state's current population of about 19 million is growing rapidly; it is expected to reach about 25 million in 1976, and perhaps 40 million by the year 2000. The Forest Service predicts that the use of California's national forests for winter sports will climb from a level of about 2 million annual visits in 1968 to 6 million in 1976 and 12.4 million in year 2000.[7]

The Disney Enterprises Plan

It was decided that Mineral King Valley would be developed by Disney Enterprises, Inc., of Glendale, California. The Mineral King Valley is approximately two miles long. The valley floor has an altitude of 7800 feet and is surrounded by peaks that reach as high as 12,405 feet. It is one of the few areas in the United States that offers uninterrupted ski runs as long as four miles with a vertical drop of over 3700 feet. Eight major basins in these mountains offer snow conditions among the most dependable in North America and provide ski terrain equivalent to six Squaw Valleys. The downhill runs are also judged to equal Europe's best.[8]

The Disney organization plans a $35-million complex in the valley consisting of an alpine village, 14 ski lifts, a heliport, a golf course, a reservoir skating pond, swimming pools, and an auto service station. Tourists will be lodged in two hotels, a 500-room dormitory, and 1200 cabins; there will be an underground facility large enough to hold the expected 2500 automobiles daily. Nearby, food storage and preparation areas and accommodations for nearly 1000 employees are also planned.[9]

Horse-drawn sleighs are to be the principal mode of transportation, while cars remain hidden in the underground garage 1¼ miles from the village. An electric cog railway will carry the visitors from their vehicles to living facilities.[10]

In the first year of operation nine food-service facilities seating 1300 people are planned. They are designed to cater to all tastes and degrees of affluence: snack bars and coffee shops, "buffeterias," a "teen center," and a "gourmet restaurant" atop a village hotel. By the fifth year, there are supposed to be 13 facilities seating 2350 people. Among these will be a 150-seat sandwich shop at the Midway Gondola Terminal on Miner's Ridge at an altitude of 9200 feet—1400 feet above the valley floor. At the end of the gondola line, a place called Eagle's Crest, is planned a 150-seat coffee shop located in the "enclosed lift terminal." [11]

Approximately two million customers are expected to visit the complex annually for both summer and winter sport. Disney expects an annual income of about $23 million from the resort during the first few years of operation, with this sum increasing according to the area's popularity. [12]

Disney Enterprises defends its project on the assumption that people will continue to go to the mountains regardless of facilities. Isn't it then far better for their government to help set aside specific and suitable areas for their enjoyment and recreation? If we fail to develop selected areas, such as Mineral King, the 50 million people who will be living in California before the end of this century will spill over the sides of the coastal cities and ravage the Sierra with unplanned and undirected enthusiasm for the vanishing outdoors. [13]

Sierra Club: Its Position on the Project

The Sierra Club is an 80-year-old non-profit club mainly known for "saving the redwoods." It was founded in 1892 to "explore, enjoy, and preserve the Sierra Nevada and other scenic resources of the United States." The club still devotes a large portion of its $3-million budget and 60-man staff to hiking and camping activities. It has offices in New York, Washington, Seattle, Tucson, and Alaska. With new applications averaging 3000 per month, membership has soared to nearly 100,000. The club obtains one-third of its revenue from dues, one-third from publications, and one-third from outings. [14]

The Sierra Club went to war with the Forest Service over the Mineral King development because of the Forest Service's deviation from its original guidelines for the area, the magnitude of the project, the estimated damage to the area, and the Forest Service's apparent lack of concern about the effect of such a project on the environment.

The Forest Service is permitted by statute to lease no more than 80 acres to a concessionaire for the purpose of recreational development. The Mineral King complex would involve thousands of acres. But the Forest Service maintains that the letter of the law has not been violated. The 80-acre law limitation dates from a 1915 law passed by the U.S. Congress and amended in 1956, which states that the Forest Service may lease up to 80 acres to a concessionaire, for a duration of thirty years. However, as demand for bigger and more complex recreation developments grew, the agency responded by combining various types of permits so as to enable the concessionaire to construct the necessary facilities: lodges, ski runs, hiking trails, parking facilities, and so on. Thus, such "terminable permits" may involve hundreds or even thousands of additional acres. [15] For instance, with regard to Mineral King, the approximately 13,000 acres not leased to Disney would still be affected by construction of gondolas, chair lifts and ski runs.

However, precedents for this action do exist. The Mineral King plans, and the manner in which they have been administered, are not unique. Scores of ski areas, including some of the most popular in the United States, happen to be located on national forest land and also happen to cover a great deal more than eighty acres. The Forest Service is, of course, alarmed that a decision against this practice of combining permits would make all these areas illegal.

Also, the Forest Service has never before attempted to manage such a complex concessionaire. It has never been involved in the hotel business to the extent required by the Disney plan. The 1700-room hotels recommended by the plan are among the largest in the general area. For example, the largest hotel in Los Angeles is the 1500-room Biltmore, and the eleven-story Disneyland Hotel has only 608 rooms.

One of the major concerns of the Sierra Club is the congestion likely to occur and its impact on the area's ecological balance which is particularly delicate during the summer months. A comparison was made with the Yosemite Valley to emphasize this contention. Yosemite Valley is seven miles long and one mile wide while Mineral King is only 1½ miles long and only approximately ¼ mile wide. Furthermore, Yosemite is heavily forested and Mineral King is only lightly wooded. Even before it reached the level of two million annual visitors, Yosemite was infamous for its crowded conditions. Yet, Disney expects to attract about the same number of people in the much smaller valley. [16]

The Sierra Club sees damage to this alpine environment taking many forms. They conjure up pictures of tourists picking the ground clear of unusual rock fragments, wild flowers, evergreen cones, and other elements of the alpine landscape; of skiers watching candy bar wrappers being tossed from gondolas attached to the aerial tramways; of erosion caused by construction activity; of sewage pollution in the Kaweah River; and of the intrusion of automobiles, buildings, and large numbers of visitors upon the mountain landscapes. [17]

The congestion is not expected to be limited to Mineral King but to extend to the back country beyond the valley because of its increased convenience created by the project. Facilities at Mineral King will give many more people the ability to travel the back country. If the number of people reaching Mineral King increases fortyfold, the number getting into the back country might increase by an even greater factor. At Mineral King, the situation will be aggravated by the existence of chair lifts, some of which will go all the way to the ridge at the boundary of the national park. There are literally thousands of people who would not think of hiking five or six strenuous miles entailing an altitude gain of 3,000 feet, but would gladly pay several dollars to ride a chair lift. [18]

The Forest Service claims that both it and Disney are aware that Mineral King can stand development to only a certain level. Disney contends that it does not plan, and the Forest Service would not permit, a development beyond that "capacity threshold." But "capacity threshold" appears to lend itself to subjective interpretation, and what the term means to the Forest Service is apparently quite different from the connotation given by most of those opposed to the project. The Forest Service interprets this level as maintaining a minimum amount of ecological damage, whatever the level of construction and human visitation. On the other hand, the Sierra Club defines the concept in terms of wilderness, in which case the threshold would likely be exceeded on the resort's first day of operation.[19]

Finally, the Forest Service is being accused of not making any studies of the impact of increases in population upon the natural flora and fauna. The Sierra Club believes that studies should include such items as deer forage after the valley floor is covered with the village and the impact on plant life of the heavy foot and horse traffic.

However, the lack of studies may not be because the Forest Service is a blundering, inefficient bureaucracy, or because decisions have been made by inept or venal people. If the assumption is made that the development is in the public interest, and that the bigger the better, then the only studies one needs to make will focus on how to develop. The question of whether to develop was apparently never raised by the Forest Service.

The Sierra Club's basic position is that the Mineral King site should be incorporated into Sequoia National Park. The site, controlled by the National Forest Service, is bordered by the park on three sides.

The Road

The present road into the mountains was built in 1880 when a silver boom brought the first influx of miners. It is a tortuous, windy path climbing to the canyon wall of the east fork of the Kaweah River from near the small town of Three Rivers. It runs through Sequoia National Forest land, then for six miles across an area of Sequoia National Park, and out again into the National Forest. The first heavy rains and snows of the late autumn close the partly paved, partly dirt road to all but four-wheel-drive automobiles and snow vehicles until spring. During the winter the 26-mile journey normally takes a minimum of 2½ hours when the road is not completely closed.

A new all-weather road has become the key to opening Mineral King and is also one of the major areas of dispute between the warring factions. The road, to be built at the expense of the state of California, would be a wide two lanes with scenic turnouts and would provide access to the valley in both summer and winter in a half-hour. The cost of maintaining the road through the winter, if the expected heavy ski traffic materializes, would likely be the highest of any in the state. Early in 1967 the California Highway Commission had to make a decision whether or not to commit $20 million or more for the road in order to make the valley accessible to perhaps 2.5 million visitors per year by 1976.

Secretary of the Interior Stewart Udall disapproved of the new road. He felt that it would prove a "blighting influence" upon Sequoia National Park. He felt the blasting of rock and removal of eight million cubic yards of soil would scar park terrain, cause erosion and consequent siltation of the Kaweah River, pollute the air with auto exhaust fumes, pose a threat to giant sequoias and other large evergreens, and would, in general, compromise "park values." [20]

It was also felt the road would enhance the likelihood of congestion and its accompanying problems. A high-grade highway would bring millions of visitors into the mountain neighborhood and encourage less rigid protection of adjoining land. It was also feared that the presence of a high-grade road reaching halfway across the Sierra Nevada range may be used as a rationalization for extending the pavement another thirty miles to create a new Trans-Sierra highway through one of the country's last enclaves of primitive landscape. [21]

It is pointed out that the country's recreation facilities are mainly for the middle- and upper-income groups and Mineral King will not be an exception. In that case the congestion predicted by the Sierra Club will be made up primarily of people who produce the greatest amount of pollution on a per capita basis. Gaining access to a national park or forest, for example, is frequently contingent upon automobile ownership. And such pursuits as skiing, motorboating, and the more elaborate forms of camping require a considerable investment to purchase and operate the necessary equipment. The typical ski-family in the western states has an annual income of $9,500 ($2,000 above the average income for the area); an adult member of such a family owns about $300 worth of ski equipment, and spends over $20 per day on ski trips. The Sierra Club argues that federal money may be better spent on a recreation area nearer the heavily populated areas in California. This would allow the lower-income group to enjoy some of its own taxes. [22]

Those opposing the road have provided studies showing that most Americans would never visit such a place as Mineral King if there were no highway. Ninety-five percent of the human traffic in our national park system occurs in only five percent of the total parkland within or immediately adjacent to the formal campsites, visitor centers, and other developed portions of the parks. [23]

In 1967 Three Rivers was a small unincorporated town of approximately 300 population located on state route 198, the origin of the road to Mineral King. The prospective Mineral King development has led to a sharp division among townspeople. Bitter words have contributed to what one resident described as "extremism" on both sides. Oldtimers want to keep things as they are while a younger, more liberal group has sought to gain adequate zoning and replace the present clutter along the Kaweah River with a greenbelt or scenic park. The small river front view now is blocked by stores, restaurants, hotels, a garage and post office. [24]

Speculation on land to be used for motels and restaurants has caused some residents to speak of the "greed" of outside people who want to make a fast buck without regard to the problems the Mineral King project might bring to the town. One six-acre parcel of prime commercial land along the river recently sold for $135,000. This was said to be more than half again its worth prior to announcement of the Disney plan. [25]

The Disney Image and Further Controversy

One of the assets that Disney Corporation has is its "Disney Image." After being honored by a number of nature-oriented organizations—ranging from the National Audubon Society to the National Wildlife Federation—and after thirty years of producing such films as *Bambi, Beaver Valley,* and *Nature's Half Acre,* it hardly seems possible that the Disney firm would consent to undertake a project that would in any way prove detrimental to the great out-of-doors. The integrity and quality image of Walt Disney Enterprises has already been presold in the public minds. [26]

Some of Disney's opposition tries to look behind this image. They claim that, because of Disney's farm background and bad rural experiences, he shared many of the feelings of the poor, rural Midwesterners. Schickel believes Disney possessed the operative instinct attributed to the farmer, which is to cut away the underbrush, clear the forest, and thus drive out the untamed, nonutilitarian creatures. This tradition of the American farmer is to take up more land than can be worked and, rather than let it stand untouched, clear it and let it stand fallow until it can be used. This instinct may be seen throughout our urban society, which abhors empty land as nature does a vacuum and rushes to fill it with something, even if it is only a parking lot or a hopeful sign promising future development. [27] Schickel further argues that Disney's drive to develop Mineral King was a result of such a tradition. He comments the development will be "accessible to every moron who could lay hands on an automobile and a picnic lunch (the debris of which he could scatter out the window)." In its undeveloped state it is "useless," closed to all but the hardiest most of the year behind a barrier of snow. [28]

Karl Menninger, a Kansas psychiatrist, stated, "They [rural Midwesterners] are much conditioned by the hatred of dirt and of the land that needs cleansing, training, and even paving before it can be said to be in genuine working order." [29] This is compared with a part of the plan concerning Mineral King. The plan states: "Grooming and manicuring of most slopes without destroying the naturalness of the area, particularly for intermediates, will require extensive bulldozing and blasting in most lower areas and extensive rock removal at higher elevations." [30]

Time magazine compared the confrontation between the Sierra Club and Disney Enterprises as motherhood coming smack up against apple pie. When this happens, it is plainly anybody's ball game.

During 1966 and 1967, Disney Enterprises gained many political allies at both the local and federal levels. In September 1966, Walt Disney and California's governor, Edmund Brown, flew into Mineral King by helicopter to survey the area. Shortly thereafter, the Brown administration applied for and received a $3-million federal grant to partially finance the twenty-six mile access road's construction. The California Highway Commission then voted to provide the remaining $20 million needed for construction from the state's highway tax fund.

Governor Reagan frequently endorsed the project during his election campaign but said little after his election. Both governors based their support on its projected economic impact on the state. Tax revenues are expected to increase from several sources. Added income should be generated from visitors arriving during both summer and winter months, and approximately 2400 new jobs should be created in the Tulare County area, an area of chronic unemployment and low income.[31] Gordon Luce, Director of the State Transportation Agency and a member of the State Highway Commission stated, "We cannot turn our backs on a project which will have a great impact on the economy of our state." [32]

On the other hand, several state assemblymen attacked the road project as atrocious. They accused the Reagan administration of being outrageous for cutting the state's Parks and Recreation budget from $33 million to $1 million in one case, and then giving $20 million away to facilitate a private venture.[33]

In the wake of the controversy, several alternatives to the road have been put forth. There has been talk but no serious consideration given to tramways and helicopters. Secretary of the Interior Udall, who opposed the road, proposed an overhead monorail or tramway system of transporting sightseers and skiers to Mineral Valley, but the plans were objected to by both Disney and the Forest Service as being too expensive. The cost of installing such a system—unlike the tax-financed roadway—would be borne by Disney Enterprises. Supporters of the project do point out that the Disney plan limits vehicles to the entrance of the valley and transports visitors into the valley on "people movers," a constantly moving belt of small cars.

By mid-1967, California's two senators, several representatives, lieutenant governor, many state legislators, and Los Angeles' Mayor Yorty stood solidly behind the Disney plan. This support was echoed by Tulare County politicians and newspaper columnists. All viewed Udall's reluctance to approve the access road as an obstructionist tactic.[34]

The federal government entered the picture in the summer of 1967. It happened that just as the fight for the permission to build the road reached a peak, bills seeking the establishment of a new national park were introduced in Congress. One of the proposed national parks would encompass two existing state parks and these, of course, would have to be ceded to the federal government by California. President Johnson felt that Governor Reagan would be more amenable to the installation of Redwood Park in his state if he were offered certain concessions in return. One of the several concessions offered the state was the administration's active support of the Mineral King development and its access road.

Because the road must cross the six miles of national park land, the National Park Service must give its approval to any plans. The park surrounds the national forest on three sides. During this same period the park service was in the process of submitting its final plans for adding parts of the park to the National Wilderness System, a plan set up by Congress, to preserve wild areas in their natural state. Disney plan supporters wanted a wide corridor through the park to provide for the road. But conservationists urged that the wilderness boundaries be set right down to the existing right-of-way, thus squeezing out the hopes for a wide all-weather road. This "squeeze" plan was backed not only by the Sierra Club but also such major conservation organizations as the National Park Association and the Wilderness Society.[35]

In December 1967, a high-level Mineral King meeting was called. Attendants in favor of the project included: Secretary of Agriculture Freeman, California Senators Kuchel and Murphy, Congressman Mathias, and, for the administration, Phillip Hughes. Attendants opposed: Stewart Udall. Shortly after the conference, Freeman issued a press release announcing that the right-of-way for the road through Sequoia Park was being prepared by the Department of the Interior and that the Disney development would proceed as planned.[36]

As Secretary of the Interior, responsibility for final approval of the road across national park land fell to Stewart Udall. For nine months he had sought to reverse the plan of the Department of Agriculture's Forest Service for the road and the Disney development. He contended it would "violate" the valley and create water and air pollution problems. However, after the confrontation, Udall reluctantly bowed to the request of the Secretary of Agriculture and Budget Bureau. The agreement would enable the California Division of Highways to proceed with an all-weather, two-lane road into the valley.

The Budget Bureau was involved because it acts for the President to supervise such programs and is interested in revenue producing projects. The Disney people were to pay rental to the government at an amount not determined. The Agriculture Department, which runs the Forest Service, is also interested in the revenue possibilities.

In an attempt to quell the fears of Udall and conservation organizations opposing the project, Secretary Freeman emphasized that each phase of the development would be carefully scrutinized to make sure that the highest standards were met, and the aesthetic and ecological values of the area were protected. "This will be a model project that will be copied, not criticized," he said.[37]

Three agencies of the federal government are to be involved in order to provide triple protection against erosion and pollution during and after construction of the road and the Disney recreation facilities. In agreement with the Forest Service, the National Park Service will control the routing of the new road and oversee construction. It also will govern erosion and pollution control. The Federal Water Pollution Control Administration, another agency of the Interior Department, will govern measures to prevent the pollution of the Kaweah River, which runs out of Mineral King through the park and down the mountains to towns below. In addition, the Forest Service, which supervises more than 250 ski and recreation areas in national forests, will provide an overall check on the Disney work.[38]

The Disney Position

In stating Disney's position, Robert Hicks, the Mineral King Project Manager, echoed the stand taken by United States Senator Thomas H. Kuchel. As a senior member of the Senate's Committee on Interior and Insular Affairs, Kuchel was an author of the bills creating the Redwood National Park and the Point Reyes National Seashore. Hicks stated:

The demand for suitable winter sports sites has increased dramatically during the last few years and will continue to grow. But areas suitable for winter sports development are extremely limited. Most have already been developed. This need is particularly critical in California where, according to a recent study, 35 percent of all skiers in the nine western states now live. [39]

We must make balanced judgements on whether any given resource should be developed commercially, developed for recreation, or maintained in its natural state. These are difficult judgements for which there are all too few guideposts. But if we fail to allocate a balanced portion of our total resources to each of these needs, sheer economic and demographic pressures will lay waste to the remaining wilderness we possess. [40]

Elaborating on this position, Disney Productions argued emphatically that the value of much public land is lost because the land is inaccessible. A professor of economics backed the Disney position with the following statement:

Mineral King is like all other economic resources: it is desired by different people for different purposes and there is not enough for everyone to have all he wants. This problem is dealt with every day by having different groups bid against each other . . . . It is obvious that these bids are based on—and thereby represent—the individual demands of thousands of potential customers for each of the alternative services that can be provided by the area. [41]

The Sierra Club countered this type of argument with one of its own. If Disney were to build a thirty-lane bowling alley in the center of Mineral King Valley, the lanes would soon be in constant use. Disney would then counter all objections by pointing out that, obviously, bowling was what people wanted and their needs had been met. American mores demand that land be used, that undeveloped land is wasted; that, all men being equal, all are entitled to use the public lands; and that all types of use are equally valid. [42]

The Sierra Club Suit

On January 21, 1969, with neither public notice nor opportunity for review, the Forest Service accepted Disney's master plan for the development of Mineral King. Before the development permit could be issued, the Sierra Club, on June 5, 1969, filed suit in the District Court in San Francisco, seeking preliminary and permanent injunctions against the project.

In the suit, the Sierra Club contended that the Forest Service and Department of Agriculture exceeded the limits of their authority in granting such a permit to Disney. While legal technicalities were involved, the argument actually centered on the right of the Forest Service to lease more than the 80 acres stipulated by law to Disney, the concessionaire, for the purpose of recreational development. The Forest Service, after granting Disney a thirty-year lease on 80 acres, also granted year-to-year leases on 300 additional acres. This was land that would be permanently altered by the construction of the village and its associated facilities. Most of the remainder of the Sequoia National Game Refuge—some 13,000 acres—

although not under lease to Disney, would be affected, as mentioned earlier, by construction of gondolas, chair lifts, and ski runs. The lawsuit charged that the lease arrangement is a clear and patent effort to circumvent the 80-acre limitation. The suit also charged that the proposed use of the valley by Disney is a violation of its status as a national game refuge and that the Forest Service violated its own rules by failing to hold public hearings on whether Mineral King should be developed. [43]

While the size of the proposed project was the Sierra Club's principal objection, there were others. They also included the National Park Service and the Department of Interior in their lawsuit for allowing the construction of the access road across national park land. The Club argued that both agencies violated their own statute, which holds that no right-of-way shall be approved through a national park that will be used for "non-park purposes." The question revolved around the issue of the primary purpose of the road: Will it be used as a scenic roadway through Sequoia National Park or to provide access to the Disney development? [44]

On July 23, 1969, United States District Judge William Sweigart granted to the Sierra Club a preliminary, temporary injunction against the Department of Agriculture and the Department of the Interior to block the development of Mineral King until the Supreme Court decided whether or not to hear the case.

Judge Sweigart commented:

> We find that the plaintiff has raised questions concerning possible excess of statutory authority, sufficiently substantial and serious to justify a preliminary injunction against both Agriculture and Interior pending trial of these issues. The court is not concerned with the controversy between so called progressives and so called conservationists. Our only function is to make sure that administrative action, even when taken in the name of progress, conforms to the letter and intent of the law as laid down by Congress. [45]

The Forest Service and Disney Productions were disappointed in the decision, but they continued to believe that the project would be approved soon. The Sierra Club was overjoyed and issued the following statement:

> Judge Sweigart's decision to grant a preliminary injunction breaks new ground for conservationists. For the first time, the judiciary has caused the Secretaries of Interior and Agriculture to stop their machinery while conservationists get a chance to plead their case. The judiciary is providing a forum that neither department would furnish. At last, there will be an opportunity for a hearing before an impartial tribunal on some of the essential elements of the proposal. [46]

The government appealed. On September 17, 1970, the United States Court of Appeals for the Ninth Circuit by a 2-to-1 vote overturned the injunction, ruling that the Sierra Club had no legal standing by which to contest actions of the federal officials who approved the Mineral King development. The appeals judges also ruled unanimously that the Sierra Club's argument against the project was so weak that Judge Sweigart had erred in issuing the injunction.

Sierra Club president Phillip S. Berry stated, "it's an extremely unfortunate decision. We think the judges are dead wrong on the law." [47] The three-judge panel noted that the Mineral King project was supported by the U.S. Ski Association and pointed out to the Sierra Club that the nation's natural resources are not the property of any particular group. [48]

After five years of dispute, the Supreme Court agreed to hear, in November 1971, the Sierra Club's challenge to the federal government's action granting the Disney organization permission to go ahead with the proposed recreation area.

Formally entitled *Sierra Club* v. *Morton, et al.*, it was the membership of the Sierra Club that claimed in the courts to be the aggrieved party. A complicated case, the outcome was expected to be considered a landmark decision in the history of environmental law. Five months after hearing the case, on April 19, 1972, the Court, in a 4-3 opinion, decided that the Sierra Club did not have sufficient standing to sue. It was a significant setback for the conservation organization, which had purposefully set out to enlarge the public's right to sue the federal government. It was obvious during oral presentation during November that the case would probably be decided on the issue of standing. Questions by the justices dealt not so much with the merits of the case as with the justification the Club could give concerning right to sue.

The Club desired a test on the standing issue, and so argued that the organization's concern about the environment gives it the right to sue on its own behalf. They failed to convince a majority of the Court that their status as a membership organization with a special interest in the conservation and sound maintenance of the national parks, game refuges, and forests of the country gave them sufficient standing to sue on behalf of the general public. Justice Potter Stewart, voting with the majority, declared:

> The Sierra Club failed to allege that it or its members would be affected in any of their activities or pastimes by the Disney development. Nowhere in the pleadings or affidavits did the Club state that its members use Mineral King for any purpose, much less that they use it in any way that would be significantly affected by the proposed actions of the respondents. [49]

Justice Harry Blackmun dissented from this opinion on the grounds that the Mineral King case was not an ordinary suit, but posed serious and fundamental environmental questions. He argued that the Sierra Club should have been given standing, in order that the case could be heard on its merits.

Justice Douglas, also dissenting, offered a rather creative solution for the standing issue: the fashioning of a federal rule that allows environmental issues to be litigated before federal agencies or courts in the name of the inanimate object about to be "despoiled, defaced, or invaded by roads and bulldozers and where injury is the subject of public outrage." Environmental objects such as rivers, lakes, groves of trees, air, and so on would have the same legal status as do corporations and ships. [50]

The effect of this decision on the Sierra Club and the environmental movement is difficult to assess at this time. It is certain, however, that the conservationists did not win additional legal rights. The Supreme Court chose to adhere to the traditional notion of standing, which does not allow a group or individual the right to sue solely to protect "the public interest." Thus the center of conflict appears to involve what constitutes the public interest in the area of land-use policy; it is clear there is yet no agreed-upon definition of the public good pertaining to land-use decisions.[51]

FOOTNOTES

[1] John W. Rettenmayer, "Letters to the Editors," *Natural History*, January 1969, p. 68.

[2] Peter Browning, "Mickey Mouse in the Mountains," *Harper's*, March 1972, p. 66.

[3] Richard Schickel, *The Disney Version* (New York: Simon and Schuster, 1968), p. 19.

[4] *Ibid.*

[5] *Ibid.*, pp. 22–23.

[6] *Ibid.*, p. 24.

[7] Jack Hope, "The King Besieged," *Natural History*, November 1968, p. 56.

[8] W. E. Towell, "Mineral King a Golden Opportunity," *American Forests*, April 1969, p. 36.

[9] Hope, "The King Besieged," pp. 72–73.

[10] "Mom vs. Apple Pie," *Newsweek*, February 10, 1969, p. 25.

[11] Browning, "Mickey Mouse in the Mountains," p. 68.

[12] Hope, "The King Besieged," p. 73.

[13] Robert B. Hicks, "Letters to the Editors," *Natural History*, January 1969, p. 70.

[14] "Sierra Club Mounts a New Crusade," *Business Week*, May 23, 1970, p. 65.

[15] P. L. Nelson, and R. C. Eckhardt, "Sequoia, Looking Toward the King," *National Parks*, December 1969, p. 30.

[16] Rettenmayer, "Letters to the Editors," p. 68.

[17] Hope, "The King Besieged," p. 73.

[18] Browning, "Mickey Mouse in the Mountains," p. 70.

[19] Hope, "The King Besieged," p. 74.

[20] *Ibid.*, p. 78.

[21] *Ibid.*, p. 74.

[22] Browning, "Mickey Mouse in the Mountains," p. 56.

[23] Hope, "Letters to the Editors," *Natural History*, January 1969, p. 70.

[24] William M. Blair, "Conservationists Fight Disney Resort Plan," *The New York Times*, March 13, 1967, p. 44.

[25] *Ibid.*

[26] Hope, "The King Besieged," pp. 80–81.

[27] Schickel, *The Disney Version*, p. 52.

[28] *Ibid.*

[29] *Ibid.*, p. 53.

[30] Browning, "Mickey Mouse in the Mountains," p. 68.

[31] Blair, "Conservationists Fight Disney Resort Plan," p. 44.

[32] *Ibid.*

[33] *Ibid.*

[34] Hope, "The King Besieged," p. 80.

[35] Blair, "Conservationists Fight Disney Resort Plan," p. 44.

[36] Hope, "The King Besieged," p. 82.

[37] William M. Blair, "Udall Yields and Opens the Way for a Resort in Sequoia Forest," *The New York Times,* December 28, 1967, p. 27.

[38] *Ibid.*

[39] Hicks, "Letters to the Editors," p. 68.

[40] *Ibid.,* pp. 68, 70.

[41] Peter Browning, "Commentary," *Harper's,* August 1972, p. 103.

[42] Browning, "Mickey Mouse in the Mountains," p. 70.

[43] Jeanne Nienaber, "Supreme Court and Mickey Mouse," *American Forests,* July 1972, p. 30.

[44] Browning, "Mickey Mouse in the Mountains," p. 67.

[45] R. Leadabrand, "Mineral King, Go or Not Go," *American Forests,* October 1969, p. 34.

[46] *Ibid.,* p. 45.

[47] "Sierra Club Will Appeal Ruling on Disney Project," *The New York Times,* September 20, 1970, p. 61.

[48] *Ibid.*

[49] Nienaber, "Supreme Court and Mickey Mouse," p. 29.

[50] *Ibid.*

[51] *Ibid.,* p. 30.

Abbreviated Case Analysis
Disney vs. Sierra Club:
A Question of Land Use

What Is the Nature of the Environment?

The environment in this situation certainly borders on the disturbed reactive type or perhaps even the turbulent field type. The conservationist forces, under the direction of the Sierra Club, are major "competitors" for the use of Mineral King Valley. The major participants in this case have attempted to hinder one another in their planned use of land. While conservationist forces have been active in the United States for a long period of time, their concerns have not always had a major impact on public policy. Today however, there appears to be a growing concern in the public sector over the impact of economic development on our natural resources. During the 1940s and 1950s economic growth prevailed over the interests of those who wished to preserve our unspoiled remaining wilderness. Today, public policy has certainly moved in the direction of more concern for the environment and the creation of the federal Environmental Protection Agency heralded a new approach to monitoring and regulating the effect of private enterprise on our natural environment.

For Walt Disney Productions the perception of the environment may be close to one of turbulent fields. There is a considerable element of uncertainty in the environment and the outcome is made even more unpredictable because social values and cultural priorities are changing in the direction of supporting the position of the

Sierra Club. The dissenting opinions by Justice Blackmun and Douglas may be the vanguard of legal change in support of the Sierra Club's position on this matter and others.

What Coping Strategy is Dominant?

It appears that Walt Disney Productions has adopted a strategy of coalition with some but not all of the major "competitors" in the environment. The state of California, Mayor Yorty of Los Angeles, the National Park Service, and the U.S. Department of Agriculture formed a coalition to pursue the development of the valley. The Sierra Club and some dissident federal officials and townsfolk continued to pursue a competitive strategy and remain outside of the coalition. The coalition, to the extent that the governmental members represent a large portion of the public interest, constitute a formidable force for the commercial development of the valley. Given the priorities, and community values, coalition is certainly the appropriate strategy for Walt Disney Productions to pursue. However, one would hope that there would be some basis for wider public participation in the coalition. Public interest groups, not associated with government, might make a valuable contribution to such a coalition.

What Type of Managerial Role Dominates the Firm?

While there is scant evidence in the case to determine with certainty what type of role behavior is most dominant, it might be inferred that the entrepreneurial role is important in the character of Walt Disney, the founder, chief executive officer, and creative force behind the success of the firm. If this role is important, a note of caution is certainly sounded because the project is so charged with the public interest. Unrestrained pursuit of profits is certainly unwarranted. The assumption of risk is undertaken not only by the firm, but by the other members of the coalition and the public at large. The professional managerial role seems more appropriate. The manager of the development must have a major interest in the "success" of the venture including not only the financial success of Walt Disney Productions, but also success in the sense that the primary social purpose is accomplished. A high degree of ethical commitment to both social goals and the enterprise's objectives is required of management on this because the opportunities for becoming a social malefactor are so great. A manager could be tempted to forsake the accomplishment of social goals by allowing the project to destroy wild-life habitats in order to accomplish the financial objectives of the firm.

Although there is some evidence that Walt Disney frequently acted out of a sense of public good his role as one of the great entrepreneurs of our times is undisputed. Perhaps an alternative to Walt Disney Productions as the sole developer and operator of the recreational sites would be the creation of a public corporation to develop the site and operating agreements with Walt Disney Productions to manage the recreational facilities at the site. This plan would have the advantage of facilitating the hiring of individuals who would be better able to play the role of the professional manager during the all-important physical site development phase and would still retain the expertise and entrepreneurial abilities of Walt Disney Productions.

What Is the Dominant Organizational Model?

There seems little question that the firm has adopted rightly many aspects of the civic model. The franchise to operate comes from society's public institutions. The amount of land planning undertaken demonstrates considerable concern for the public interest and the need to safeguard the environment. Moreover, it is difficult to argue that the development of the valley should be pursued out of an artistic model although the Sierra Club certainly fits that model. The concern for an unspoiled wilderness has not been articulated sufficiently in the case to warrant turning the valley over to the protection of the conservationist forces. There remains a demonstrable public demand for recreational facilities. Furthermore, rational development of the valley may protect it from the ravishments of rapid population growth and the unorganized pursuit of recreational activities by the citizens of California and nearby states, as argued by Walt Disney Enterprises.

What Major Concerns Need Clarification?

As a part of any cost/benefit analysis, one must discuss the economic benefits set forth by members of both the state and federal governments. These include revenues in the form of both state and federal taxes and increased jobs in the state of California. The town of Three Rivers saw both costs and benefits in the new Disney project. Given the mixture and location of the proposed Mineral King facilities and the increased level of the principal clientele, are there alternative recreational projects for which public funds might provide greater social benefits? Furthermore, there is the problem of the public good. One group is attempting to provide needed recreational facilities in the face of growing demand. This group expects an economic return to Disney, California, and the federal government for the use of such facilities. Benefits would include the added recreational facilities and revenue from their use. A major potential cost would occur if the ecology were radically changed due to a miscalculation concerning the impact of the development of the valley. The question arises: does the company become responsible for this error? Who is liable for a remedy? On the other hand, the conservationists are attempting to preserve a natural wilderness on the basis that such states of nature are disappearing. Preservation would allow future generations to observe and know a natural wilderness. This alternative would not provide much income for the community, for nowhere near the same number of people would have access to Mineral King if it remained undeveloped. Thus, if this alternative is selected, noneconomic factors must play a role in the decision. Companies such as Disney typically have much greater experience dealing with issues in which economic factors are basic and thus may tend to apply economic criteria to situations or issues in which they become involved. The different expectations must be reconciled in the public arena before development begins.

Concluding Notes

In the next section, the student should read each case carefully and address those issues that are important. A summary of suggested issues precedes each case but does not list the only issues that might be of concern. Following each case the authors have outlined a series of policy questions that should be answered if the student is required to propose a solution to the case.

CHAPTER 3

CORPORATE
SOCIAL
POLICY
MAKING

Introduction

This chapter presents a paper entitled "Social Responsiveness in the Large Corporation" by Robert Ackerman.* Professor Ackerman's paper describes the process by which two large firms make policy decisions in the realm of social needs. The importance of this paper for this text is that it describes *how* corporate social policy decisions could be made and focuses the reader's attention on the requirements for social responsiveness. Ultimately, large firms that are highly charged with the public interest must develop explicit social objectives, strategies, plans, and tactics. Becoming socially responsive is a managerial issue that does not differ fundamentally from *other* policy decisions such as those regarding the entry of new markets. Therefore, the student must incorporate into his analysis a discussion of the explicit goals, plans, operating policies, and procedures that are required if the firm is to be judged socially responsible.

Social Responsiveness in the Large Corporation †

ROBERT W. ACKERMAN

Considerable discussion in recent years has been devoted to the social responsibilities of business and more generally to the role of the large corporation in society. Purists undoubtedly remain who adhere to the Friedman (1) view that activities for

* Reproduced with permission of the author Robert Ackerman, "Social Responsiveness in the Large Corporation," Academy of Management, Division of Business Policy and Planning, Professional Papers, 1973 National Meeting, Boston, Massachusetts.

† This research was made possible through the generous support of The Russell Sage Foundation, to whom the author is much indebted.

purposes other than the maximization of profit are "fundamentally subversive." However, business leaders in the past decade have increasingly acknowledged the close relationship between the corporation and society and have espoused a commitment to social responsibility as a means of improving it. This position received substantial, though not unanimous, support in a recent report by the Committee for Economic Development (2). Andrews (3) has gone a step further by stating that social responsibilities should be given explicit attention, analysis and weight in the formulation of corporate strategy.

The inquiry described in this paper relates to the process through which two large corporations manage the response to societal needs and demands. My survey of the literature (4) reveals that little attention has been devoted to the implementation of policy in areas of social concern, particularly policy that implies change in the operations of the corporation. This issue has significance for two reasons. First, the structure and processes typical in the large, diversified firm may, in fact, impede its willingness and ability to implement such policies. Yet, unresponsiveness may have a fundamental long-term impact on the flexibility permitted the corporation to define the strategy governing its affairs. Second, by insisting on the execution of corporate policy in this area, the chief executive may risk a reduction in the effectiveness of his organization in dealing with more traditional, economic, technological, and competitive forces. This latter may stem not so much from the reallocation of economic resources, as Friedman (1) might suggest, but from organizational dislocations.

Research Questions

The large corporation in the U.S. has undergone a massive organizational transformation since World War II through the adoption of the divisionalized structure. Chandler (5) documented the development of this structure by Du Pont and General Motors in the 1920s and its subsequent proliferation as a result, he argued, of increasing product-market diversity in American industry. Wrigley (6) and Remult (7) in studies of companies in the *Fortune* 500 found that by 1969 this form had replaced the functional organization as the dominant formal structure.

Organization *	*Estimated Percentage of Firms*		
Structure	1949	·1959	1969
Functional	76.1%	48.9%	20.6%
Divisionalized	23.9	51.1	79.4

* Condensed from Remult (7). His research included a further breakdown of the functional organization into functional (11.2%) and functional with subsidiaries (9.4%) and the divisionalized organization into product (75.5%), geographic (1.5%) and holding company (2.4%). Percentages refer to 1969.

This structural transformation, as Scott (8) has noted, is accompanied by (a) a separation in function and orientation between corporate and division levels with the latter given substantial responsibility for the formulation and implementation of product-market strategy, (b) a reliance for planning and control on result-oriented performance measures, often obtained through the creation of profit centers, and (c) an effort to relate executive evaluation, promotion, and compensation to performance against targets as reflected in the control system.

I have found (9) that the investment process in vertically integrated and diversified corporations differs in the location of responsibility for judging resource commitments and the use of financial measures for business and executive appraisal in the directions suggested by Scott. However, the integrated firms had recently adopted formal structures and reporting systems patterned after those in the diversified enterprise, which suggests that the appeal of the divisionalized firm may extend beyond the diversified firm. Bower (10) has described the critical role played by middle-level general managers in the allocation of resources in the large corporation. Berg (11) found that, relative to old line diversified corporations, the newer conglomerates have accentuated the characteristics of the divisionalized structure.

In the past decade, public interest in corporate behavior has increased significantly. The impact of social needs and demands is felt in most facets of business operations; product line (design, safety, and disposal), production processes (environmental protection, occupational health and safety), work force (equal opportunity, employment practices), marketing (consumerism, promotional practices), etc. Issues vary in degree of public acceptance, codification into law, and social or legal enforcement. Over a period of time, expectations in some areas have become reasonably well defined, while in others, evolution has not progressed as far and in some instances, never may. The businessman has the choice of leading or lagging behind social expectations. He cannot, however, avoid responding to them, even though the response is to resist them by affirming traditional accommodations.

To manage the divisionalized corporation in a fashion that permits flexible and creative responses to changing social demands poses three major dilemmas. First, the separation of corporate and division responsibilities is challenged. The outside world assumes the president is responsible for the conduct of the corporation in these areas. Yet, how is he to secure compliance for corporate-wide policies affecting delegated functions without denigrating the responsibility and accountability of operating units? Second, the traditional financial control system is not relevant to tracking social responsiveness. The measurement problem is twofold; first, what sort of system is appropriate for planning and assessing performance in, for example, pollution control or equal opportunity, and second, how, if at all, can or should that system be integrated into the financial control system? Bauer and Fenn (12) have found that techniques for systematically measuring social costs and benefits are rudimentary at best. Third, executive evaluation and reward processes in divisionalized corporations normally rest on two conditions—reasonably clear responsibilities, and a control system designed to facilitate objectivity, neither of which is present in this instance. How are incentives to be conceived and used to elicit organizational commitment to policy implementation?

The policy questions guiding this research are twofold: (a) How does the large corporation respond to issues of social concern? and (b) What impact does responsiveness have on the corporation's organization structure and processes?

Research Design

In view of the complexity of the issues and the near absence of systematic prior research, in-depth studies of two large corporations was felt to be appropriate as a means of securing an understanding of unfamiliar terrain. The companies selected had sales of roughly $2 billion; both were diversified and divisionalized, though in each case the component businesses bore some product-market relationship to one another. The companies were recognized as leaders in the response to certain issues of social concern. Leaders were chosen because (a) the purpose of the research was to observe and learn from corporate experience in implementation without having to debate the question of intent and (b) openness in discussing sensitive issues was felt to be more likely.

Particular attention was devoted to two areas of social concern: ecology and equality. In both instances these areas (a) are of both lasting significance and immediate concern, (b) are relatively well defined in near term public policy on environmental protection and equal employment, and (c) cannot be entirely avoided, thus insuring an observable response. Consequently, in the selection of both companies and issues, efforts have been made to simplify the research task and increase the probability of securing nontrivial results. Whatever biases or limitations to generalization that may accrue from these choices are acknowledged and represent areas for future research.

Research has been conducted through (a) interviews with top line staff executives to establish the history and current profile of policy and organizational commitment to social responsiveness, particularly in the areas noted above, and (b) tracking a series of specific decision situations from inception to resolution by interviewing participants, attending meetings and analyzing documentation. In one company (designated COA), both areas of social concern were of significance; attention in the other company (designated COB) was focused on equality in employment. As presently defined, ecological issues were not particularly relevant to COB.

Corporate Responsiveness as an Evolutionary Process

The results obtained thus far suggest that corporate responsiveness to a changing social context is an evolutionary process in which the challenges and responses are progressively managerial in character. Three phases have been identified in this evolution, and I suspect there must be a fourth. Each encompasses a period of relative stability in the definition of the problem and the organizational accommodations observed for coping with it. However, there are also destabilizing episodes which burden these accommodations with stress sufficient to force change and transition to a subsequent phase. The transitory situations are difficult, often traumatic experiences for the organization; understanding them provides important clues to the mechanisms through which organizations learn to incorporate social concerns in their operations.

In the following pages, the phases are described first, followed by a summary of the episodes observed to propel the response process forward.

Phases in the Response Process

The phases may best be designated in terms of outcomes or roughly the accomplishment noted below, though it should be recognized that the escarpment between one phase and the next is not always precise and the critical dimensions of earlier phases continue to evolve. Each appears to serve an essential role in a drama that unfolds over a period measured in years. During this time, the degree of definition and enforcement given to the issue in the environment increases as well.

I. Enrichment of Purpose
II. Substantive Development
III. Engagement and Implementation

ENRICHMENT OF PURPOSE. The definition of corporate purpose has long been held to be the province of the chief executive and those senior managers around him, and to be influenced by his values [Andrews (13), Selznick (14)]. The weight of delegated responsibility for establishing product-market strategy in the diversified and divisionalized corporation may have eroded the chief executive's influence. However, his leadership was clearly instrumental in both COA and COB in securing an awareness for social issues and imparting a sense of commitment for corporate response. The patterns were similar. The chief executive in the period 1962–1964 recognized ecology and equal employment (specifically minorities) as legitimate concerns of the corporation. In some cases his rationale was moralistic, in others more narrowly pragmatic. These concerns were manifested by (a) public affirmations of the corporation's obligations, (b) a revised statement of policy to govern the firm's activities, and (c) visible corporate involvement such as participation in the National Alliance of Businessmen (providing jobs and training for the hard core unemployed), membership on commissions, and support for community development projects.

Aside from ad hoc staff assistance, implementation did not call for organizational commitments. In each case the policy stated or implied that equal opportunity and, in the case of COA, pollution control, was a line management responsibility at operating levels. However, there was no effort to secure systematic evidence of adherence to the policy nor were attempts made to translate purpose into a strategy for attaining future results. Operating decisions continued to address the issues in a decentralized mode, often with widely variable postures. For instance, the manufacturing function in one COA division had, since the late 1950s, systematically provided for pollution control in facility planning while other divisions just as systematically ignored it.

The first phase was superseded three to four years * after it began, having two important achievements to its credit: (a) the chief executive had enriched the purpose of the corporation, and (b) he had raised the expectations for future achievement through initiating activities directly under his control.

SUBSTANTIVE DEVELOPMENT. The first phase was followed by a second during which efforts were directed at developing positions on substantive issues and attempts were made to incorporate these positions in operating decisions.

Rather than matters of awareness, obligation, and legitimacy, the concern became one of comprehension. Three massive uncertainties accompanied each issue. The first related to social and political expectations. Since legal requirements and activists' demands for both civil rights and ecology were changing and frequently varied from place to place, the social terrain appeared chaotic and as yet had not been reduced to a plausible map. Second, the nature and feasibility of alternative responses were unclear; the technology for controlling emissions in several of COA's businesses had not been developed, mechanisms for locating qualified minority applicants and successfully integrating them were not known, and so forth. Third, little information existed on the corporation's performance. Consequently, in addition to changing public expectations and unknown remedies, the overall magnitude of the task and the location in the corporation of specific problems was uncertain.

The harbinger of phase two was the appointment by the chief executives of staff specialists from 1966 to 1968 with titles such as minority relations manager or environmental control director to coordinate the corporation's response. In each case, the specialist sought to rationalize this response by accumulating substantive understanding sufficient to answer three questions: (a) What are likely social expectations?; (b) What responses are feasible?; (c) Where in the corporation are problem areas? In doing so, he fashioned a means for scanning both the environment and the activities of operating divisions, the former remaining ad hoc but the latter becoming increasingly systematized.

The specialists provided skills and designed systems that were found to be essential to rationalizing the response process. However, neither the existence of corporate policy nor the availability of specialized knowledge was sufficient to secure implementation. The specialists' impact was constrained by task and role. In the first instance they surveyed a portion of the environment that was both unfamiliar and perceived as a threat by operating managers to performance as traditionally measured and evaluated. Moreover, in addressing ecological or equality issues, the specialists were not primarily concerned with the overall conduct of the business. Hence, the costs, broadly defined, of pollution control or minority hiring were given less weight than engineering performance and head counts. As for role, the

---

* For issues more recently identified, this time span appears to be shorter.

specialists served in staff capacities and could not force responsiveness or sanction the lack of it. Nevertheless, because they were in close proximity to the chief executive, they were perceived by operating managers as a threat to their autonomy. Operating managers' anxieties were attenuated by occasional harsh judgments absorbed by their peers for situations which "got out of control."

ENGAGEMENT AND IMPLEMENTATION. The ambiguities in responsibility and performance evaluation evident during phase two created an unstable situation; either the policy would be tempered or the organizational responsibilities and processes had to be modified to force its incorporation in operating decisions. As Bauer (15) has noted, the adoption of policy requires attention to organizational as well as intellectual processes.

A pattern was observed during 1972–1973 at COA with regard to pollution control and at COB with regard to equal employment that appeared to result in the engagement of the operating divisions in the implementation of the policy. Phase three in these instances exhibited three characteristics that distinguished it from previous phases. First, management at division levels accepted or insisted on responsibility for implementation of the policy; the corporate specialist's involvement in operational decisions was curtailed. Second, targets related to implementation were added to the reporting system and commitments were negotiated in the context of the financial planning cycle or a parallel target-setting exercise. Third, and perhaps most significantly, performance against plan became part of the executive appraisal process.

In neither company was the responsibility for or burden of economic performance eased; implementation represented increased job complexity at middle levels. While COA made funds available for pollution control equipment and COB encouraged expenditures for equal employment programs, both companies sought to recoup the profit decrement from the divisions in the planning cycle by refusing to acknowledge the existence of the decrement in negotiating profit performance expectations. The intent was to reduce whatever cushion might have existed in division forecasts rather than sacrifice earnings or compromise the division manager's responsibility for the affairs of his unit.

Despite the existence of hiring and advancement targets for minorities and females, equal employment at COA remained in phase two. Progress continued to be made through individual efforts and the continued prodding and support of the staff specialist. However, the specialist was promoted and absorbed into the personnel function; division management in most instances remained unwilling to disturb hiring and promotion practices at lower levels; and the distribution of rewards and punishments did not systematically relate to results in implementing equal employment.

The Dynamics of Transition

Lacking from our discussion thus far is a description of the forces which caused transition from one phase to the next and in particular from phase two to phase three. In part, of course, an increasingly demanding environment provided the impetus for transition; the threat of enforcement became credible. However, that did not appear to be the determining element. Instead, transition came as a result of one or more specific episodes in which division autonomy was challenged, thus producing a brief suspension of the rules normally governing corporate-division relationships. The situations were not necessarily significant in themselves but served to demonstrate the willingness of corporate executives to intervene in matters related to the policy. More importantly, they provoked a reaction from operating management which confirmed the adoption of revised organizational accommodations that fostered responsiveness. Two illustrations of transition are described below:

ILLUSTRATION I. In 1967, a plant manager in Division 1 of COA became aware of increasing interest in air pollution in his state. He reported this to the Environmental Control Department (ECD) which was then engaged in research on various control technologies. Over the next year, ECD, working with corporate and division engineering, negotiated a timetable with the state which committed the company to certain dates and performance standards far exceeding current operating experience in the division's industry. This was viewed with some concern by the larger but less profitable Division 2, which had numerous plants in the state employing similar processes and little inclination to invest funds in emission controls unless required by a regulatory agency to do so.

Over the next two years, the technology failed to develop as forecast and the company fell behind its schedule. When the broader implications of this situation for other divisions became clear, the group vice-president responsible for Division 1 (but not Division 2) asked his senior technical manager to review the project. The technical manager immediately raised engineering questions about the capital request then being finalized to cover the control equipment finally selected by ECD and division engineering. He felt the matter should be given further study and with the group vice-president's concurrence, had the request removed from the finance committee docket. The division manager, taking the advice of his engineering and manufacturing departments, contested this action and the request was reinstated. Subsequent efforts during the next month to delay construction were also turned aside by the division manager, making it clear that he was prepared to shoulder the technological and financial risks involved.

Some months later, a second environmental issue arose in another state. Division 1 had anticipated the expenditure in its financial plan, an engineer had been added whose primary function was to adapt environmental programs to operating requirements, and the division manager remained involved. ECD and the corporate level staff provided technical assistance as needed. On this second occasion,

Division 2 was directly confronted with similar environmental demands but had made no provision for the expenditure in its plans; and, for a time, direction of the study remained with the manager of ECD. Progress in resolving technical and scheduling issues was noticeably slower than in Division 1, although both were operating at the state of the art. However, during this period, a new Division 2 manager was appointed who had earlier worked closely with the chief executive in formulating the corporate position on social responsibility. He instigated a division-wide study of future pollution control expenditures and made it clear to his engineering and manufacturing managers that he expected them to incorporate the results of the study in their activities. Division involvement increased, and the pace of implementation quickened.

ILLUSTRATION II. In June 1971, the president of COB received a letter from a group of minority employees accusing a branch manager of certain discriminatory practices. A corporate review of the incident underlying the allegation revealed the need for various corrective actions which were held to be the responsibility of the branch manager and his immediate superior, the regional manager. Six months later, the minority group contacted the president again, saying that no change had occurred and raising the further issue of discrimination in the assignment of sales territories. A more thorough investigation cosponsored by division and corporate resulted in the termination of one manager and the implementation of a number of administrative changes. The president was intimately involved himself and accompanied the division manager to the region when the latter announced the changes.

In July 1972, the chairman issued a letter to all company managers, emphasizing the importance of the equal employment policy. It also indicated that henceforth management appraisals would include explicit reference to performance of agreed-upon targets in this area.

Within weeks, another episode presented itself, this time involving a first-line supervisor at a small service unit in the same division who was accused of discrimination by four black clericals. For the next three weeks, seven levels of management with associated staff specialists attempted to resolve a problem that became ever more explosive. In the end, the president himself made the final decision and in the process countermanded the recommendation approved up the line below him. After these experiences, the division took charge of minority affairs. A number of programs were initiated which, taken together, represented a strategy for managing equal employment, securing organizational commitment, and disengaging the corporate level. Included were management practices audits, awareness seminars, the formal inclusion of minority affairs in the management appraisals process, and systematic reviews of performance against targets for organizational components within the division.

The Process Reviewed

The central argument in this paper is that corporate responsiveness is an evolutionary process in which attention is directed sequentially to the enrichment of purpose, the acquisition of substantive skills and understanding, and the incorporation of responsiveness in the operation of the corporation. The process is summarized in Exhibit 1 and the roles and tasks associated with it in Exhibit 2. Two further comments are warranted.

First, a fourth phase is anticipated. As public expectations in specific areas of social concern become more clearly defined and the corporation's behavior adapts to them, the response to each will pass through the stages which have been described and will eventually become a matter of standard operating procedure. The need for explicit planning, performance evaluation, and corporate staff involvement may fade away.

Second, while some issues may in time become akin to standard operating procedures, others will take their place as new policy issues. Consequently, at any point, a number of issues will be "in process" as the assessment for COA depicts in Exhibit 3. It should be noted that COA has not accorded all issues equal emphasis and may, therefore, occupy varying postures relative to other corporations and to public expectations.

Impact on the Corporation

The responsiveness process has three discernible effects on the divisionalized firms observed in this research—a broader definition of corporate purpose, the addition of new and changing staff relationships, and an increased complexity in executive performance appraisal. On the other hand, the impact of the process on structure and location of responsibility for decisions affecting operations appeared to be

EXHIBIT 1 The response process

	Phase I	Phase II		Phase III
Policy issue	What is legitimate corporate responsibility?	What response is appropriate?		How is the response to be managed?
Requirement	Corporate policy	Information and analysis		Organizational commitment
Organizational involvement	Chief executive	Chief executive Staff specialists	TRANSITIONAL EPISODES	Chief executive Staff specialists Operating managers
Control system	Situational reporting	From situational to systematic reporting		Systematic planning and reporting
Performance evaluation	None	Criticism for specific instances of malfunction		Reward/punishments based on systematic review against plan

Executive Classification	Phase I	Phase II	Phase III
Chief executive	Issue: Policy problem Action: Write and communicate policy	Obtain knowledge	Obtain organizational commitment
	Outcome: Enriched purpose Increased awareness	Add staff specialists	Change performance expectations
Staff specialists		Issue: Technical problem Action: Design information system and rationalize environment	Obtain operating division response Apply information system to planning and performance measurement
		Outcome: Specialized knowledge	
Operating executives			Issue: Management problem Action: Commit resources and modify procedures
			Outcome: Increased responsiveness

EXHIBIT 2 Organizational involvement

EXHIBIT 3 Issues of social concern and the responsiveness process

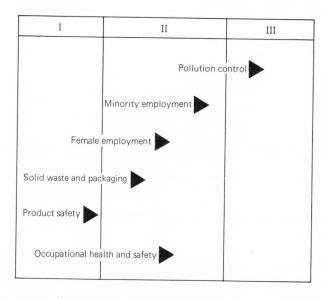

minimal; the companies were reluctant to disturb a structure that had been success-ful in managing product-market diversity. This latter assessment may turn out to be inaccurate, however, if the number of issues demanding response overburdens the capacity of the performance appraisal process to reflect the increased complexity of the middle management job.

Managing the response process was observed to place four demands on the or-ganization, and, in particular, on its chief executive:

The identification of social issues having relevance to the corporation and posi-tioning of the firm relative to them. Bauer (16) has surmised that the chief executive, who must shoulder this burden, is limited by time and credibility in the number of issues he can champion. But his flexibility to accept commitment may be greater than that of his organization which, as we have described, is governed by processes that may obstruct responsiveness unless modified. To raise expectations without recognizing the magnitude of the transition to the third phase of the process may have long-term negative impacts. Consequently, gauging the importance of social issues to the firm is an early and critical assessment which has managerial implica-tions. It is reasonable for firms to seek positions of leadership in some areas but not in others. Such was the case in the corporations studied here.

The incorporation of specialized knowledge and specialist roles in the corporate structure. As response to a particular issue matures, the task performed by the spe-cialist changes from that of information gathering and systems design to facilitating implementation. Two phenomena were observed. The first involved the transfer of knowledge to operating managers. Rather than influencing line managers directly, the specialist frequently worked through staff departments at division levels, possibly augmented by specialists, who had long-standing relationships with line managers. The second related to the specialist's role. As the competence and commitment of the operating divisions increased during phase three, his assistance became viewed as interference. However, new tasks appeared to emerge as the chief executive turned to the same specialist for the rationalization of a new issue. Thus, the minor-ity affairs specialist shifted his attention to female equality with the larger question of worker satisfaction in the background, and the pollution control expert became involved in product safety and noise abatement. Over time, a permanent corporate staff function having to do with managing the effects of social change may be devel-oping.

The modification of the executive evaluation process to reflect increased responsi-bilities for social responsiveness. The first hurdle encountered is gaining credibility for the performance measure as one that is reflective of achievement, equitable in matching responsibility with results, and systematic. The specialist played a major part in designing the system upon which measurement was based. The second hurdle is gaining credibility for top management's intention to use the system in evaluation. There was value seen by operating managers in having a few simple, result-oriented yardsticks such as those in a profit plan. Attempts to introduce complexity were unwelcome. Chief executive commitment was essential in modify-ing performance expectations.

The recognition of transitory episodes. Commitment was enacted through the management of the decision process in time of stress. Precipitating or permitting an organizational crisis to occur and using it as a basis for judgment before the substantive work was well developed produced resentment among middle-level managers. However, once the second phase had been digested, changed expectations appeared to be most easily communicated through example. Responsiveness hinged on corporate executives' ability to sense when precedents were at stake and willingness to permit the organization to learn from them.

The achievement of leadership in social responsiveness was not without organizational cost. Expectations were raised which intensified the pressure on the corporation for performance while paradoxically also increasing its vulnerability to and fear of attack. Middle managers experienced increased ambiguity in determining what was expected of them, which fostered anxiety, resentment, and a diversion of effort from other tasks. Yet, the benefits were acknowledged to be substantial. Most importantly, through its ability to implement policy related to social concerns, the corporation gained greater flexibility in defining and executing product-market strategy for its businesses.

FOOTNOTES

[1] Friedman, Milton, *Capitalism and Freedom* (Chicago: University of Chicago Press, 1962).

[2] *Social Responsibilities of Business Corporations* (New York: Committee for Economic Development, June 1971).

[3] Andrews, Kenneth R., *The Concept of Corporate Strategy* (Homewood, Ill.: Irwin Publishers, 1971).

[4] Ackerman, Robert W., *Public Responsibility and the Businessman* (Cambridge, Mass.: Harvard Business School, 4-371-520, April 1971).

[5] Chandler, Alfred D., *Strategy and Structure* (Cambridge, Mass.: M.I.T. Press, 1962).

[6] Wrigley, Leonard, *Divisional Autonomy and Diversification,* unpublished doctoral dissertation (Cambridge, Mass.: Harvard Business School, 1970).

[7] Remult, Richard, *Strategy Structure and Financial Performance of the Fortune 500,* unpublished doctoral dissertation (Cambridge, Mass.: Harvard Business School, 1972).

[8] Scott, Bruce R., "The Industrial State: Old Myths and New Realities," *Harvard Business Review,* March–April 1973.

[9] Ackerman, Robert W., "The Influence of Integration and Diversity on the Investment Process," *Administrative Science Quarterly,* September 1970.

[10] Bower, Joseph R., *Managing the Resource Allocation Process* (Cambridge, Mass.: Division of Research, Harvard Business School, 1971).

[11] Berg, Norman A., "What's Different About Conglomerate Management," *Harvard Business Review,* November–December 1969.

[12] Bauer, Raymond and Fenn, Daniel, *The Corporate Social Audit* (New York: Russell Sage Foundation, 1972).

[13] Andrews, Kenneth R., *op cit.*

[14] Selznick, Philip, *Leadership in Administration* (New York: Harper & Row Publishers, 1957).

[15] Bauer, Raymond A., "The Study of Policy Formation: An Introduction," in Bauer and Berger, *The Study of Policy Formation* (New York: Free Press, 1968).

[16] Bauer and Fenn, *The Corporate Social Audit.*

SECTION TWO

SOCIAL
ISSUE
CASES

CHAPTER 4

POLLUTION
AND
ECOLOGY

CASE 1
THERMAL POLLUTION

Modern man is man apart from nature; nature is his dominion, to be controlled and used for his benefit. To this end, our technology has been created. However, man may be an endangered species not because he has failed to control the forces of nature but because he has not recognized his interdependence with nature. [1]

However, while there have been a number of undesirable side effects, there are few who would argue that the benefits of modern science and technology do not currently outweigh environmental costs. The pressures of rapidly expanding population, increased (per capita) consumption, and the dwindling sources of fossil fuels have dictated that utility companies use advanced technology to continue to supply power needs, in particular, to metropolitan areas. Florida Power and Light Company found itself in just this kind of situation during the early 1960s and attempted to increase capacity in accordance with forecasted increased demand for power in the Miami-Dade County metropolitan area.

After considering alternatives, the company elected to increase capacity via nuclear energy. Debate over the use of atomic power has continued from the time such power plants were first suggested. However, a potential side effect not frequently publicized and a central issue in the construction of nuclear plants by Florida Power and Light is thermal pollution. Essentially, thermal pollution involves heating water to a point that disrupts the mutual relations between organisms and their environment. Little seems to be known as yet about the nature and impact of such pollution, and this becomes quite evident when various organizations attempt to come to grips with the issue in this case.

The government has clarified considerably its policy on the pollution issue during the last few years. The federal government, and to a lesser extent state and local governments, apparently intend to exercise increasing control over industry and the general public in pollution matters. Since private industry is the chief producer of new technology, the responsibility for eliminating pollution is being placed on the businessman.

It is generally accepted that environmental pollution is a problem and must be dealt with immediately. Yet, there is opposition from business concerning standards of quality, the method of deciding what should be done, and problems associated with the application of rules.

FOOTNOTES

[1] Edward Nicholson, Robert Litschert, and William Anthony, *Business Responsibility and Social Issues* (Columbus, Ohio: Merrill Publishing Co., 1974), p. 76.

[2] Council on Environmental Quality, *Environmental Quality: The Second Annual Report of the Council on Environmental Quality, August 1971* (Washington, D.C.: United States Government Printing Office, 1971).

Thermal Pollution vs. Electricity Brownout: Dilemma of the Florida Power and Light Company

Introduction

On February 26, 1970, federal and state officials ordered the Florida Power and Light Company to curb the discharge of hot water from the Turkey Point Plant into Biscayne Bay. They ruled that the $8 million six-mile canal the company was building to carry the hot water to adjacent Card Sound was not acceptable as a solution because the discharged water could not be sufficiently cooled. Florida Power and Light was given sixty days to come up with proposals for an alternative to the existing system. The Florida Air and Water Pollution Control Commission concurred in the ruling.[1]

This was the situation that Florida Power and Light found itself in after approximately seven years of attempts to both preserve the ecology of the Biscayne Bay region and provide needed power to the greater Miami area.

Biscayne Bay

Biscayne Bay extends from the eastern edge of the city of Miami southward for twenty-five miles almost to Key Largo. It is a semi-enclosed bay, bound on the west by the Florida peninsula and on the east by a string of islands and shallow tidal banks.

The bay contributes to a wide variety of activities. It is considered to be an exceptional ecological area with 58 species of fish, more than 100 species of shellfish, and a dozen species of birds, including pelicans, cormorants, herons, egrets and the rare roseate spoonbill. The bottom of the bay is richly vegetated and serves as a nursery ground for many juvenile sport fish and bait fish. Thus, the bay has become an extremely popular boating and sport fishing area. Evidence of this is the development of commercial boat shrimping in the bay, now a $500,000 per year industry. Also, many people consider the bay to be the major water recreation area of south Florida.

Brooks Atkinson, writing for *Audubon*, gives this account of Biscayne Bay:

> The water is marvelously clear. Since the bay is shallow, the bottom is visible everywhere—a fabulous spread of sponges, turtle grass, clumps of algae, and beds or mounds of shining, intricate coral . . . . the bay is a tropical lagoon.[2]

Biscayne Bay is relatively shallow, with the deepest areas averaging only eight or nine feet. Summertime bay temperatures normally get quite high. Strong solar heating, coupled with shallow water and vast areas of bay bottom that are sometimes exposed during "spring tide," often result in water temperatures as high as 90–92 degrees during the middle of the day in July and August. The average summer water temperature in Biscayne Bay is 86–88 degrees.[3]

Congress has also recognized the unique properties of the area and in 1968 established Biscayne Bay National Monument, a group of islands located in the bay. The monument was established "in order to preserve and protect for the education, inspiration, recreation, and enjoyment of present and future generations of Americans a rare combination of terrestrial, marine and amphibious life in a tropical setting of great natural beauty."[4]

Turkey Point

Turkey Point is an unusually shaped bulge on the Florida coastline that juts out into Biscayne Bay. It is a peninsula inhabited only by birds, fish, and reptiles and a mangrove swamp with no roads or homes. Like the bay itself, it provides a habitat for both plant and animal. More than 100 kinds of birds have been sighted along with rare crocodiles, alligators, raccoons, foxes, otters, manatees, bobcats, and panthers. Orchids and native ferns grow on the mangrove and cottonwood trees.

Florida Power and Light Company

Florida Power and Light Company (FPL) is the largest power company in the state of Florida. It employs approximately 7680 persons and maintains total assets in excess of $1,760,000,000. In the early part of 1963, FPL recognized the growing power needs of southern Florida and made plans to meet these needs by expanding its existing Cutler Plant, which is located in Dade County. On August 7, 1963, FPL applied to the Metropolitan Dade County Commission for the necessary zoning variances for the addition to the Cutler Plant of two oil-fired units of 432,000 kilowatts each.

Almost one year later, March 31, 1964, with expansion plans well under way, the Metropolitan Dade County Commission ruled that expansion would be permit-

67

ted only on the condition that FPL use 100 percent gas in these units. Since gas was not available in the quantity necessary for production of the needed power, FPL planners found themselves searching for a new plant site.[5]

The planners at FPL, based on years of experience, believed that the site had to be remote from population, accessible to cooling water and to transportation necessary to barge fuel oil. Turkey Point was about the last remaining section of waterfront available in Dade County for this expansion. Located 25 miles south of Miami and five miles from the nearest dwelling place, Turkey Point seemed an ideal spot for expansion of the necessary generating facilities.

FPL initially purchased 1800 acres of land at Turkey Point; since then, the site has grown to about 12,700 acres. The Metropolitan Commission granted its permission to operate two conventional oil-burning power plants on June 19, 1964. With the use of some contracts and equipment originally planned for the Cutler expansion, construction began on the two fossil units immediately with an expected completion date of 1968. Community leaders hailed the move as an unusual example of cooperation between industry and the community in the selection of a site that would not interfere with human habitation.[6]

At about the time construction was beginning on the conventional units, company officers forecasted that the 432,000 kilowatt output of these facilities even if upgraded to a generating capacity of 1,286,000 kilowatts would not satisfy the Dade County demand for electric power in the late 1960s. FPL further predicted that the power needs in Dade County by 1975 would increase to approximately 3,940,000 kilowatts and this figure was continually revalued upward.[7] It was obvious that still more generating facilities were needed if FPL was to meet the power needs of the expanding population in the area.

Accordingly, in January 1965, FPL announced to the Florida Public Service Commission that negotiations were underway for a nuclear plant at Turkey Point. On November 15, 1965, FPL announced the planned construction of two nuclear units capable of 760,000 kilowatts. Total cost of the two conventional units and the two nuclear units was expected to be more than $175 million.[8]

On March 26, 1966, FPL applied to the Atomic Energy Commission for a permit to construct the two nuclear units at Turkey Point. Construction was tentatively scheduled to begin in April 1966 and 1970 was set as the date for operation of the first nuclear unit at Turkey Point. FPL officials felt that there was no reason to believe that a 1970 date could not be met.

Turkey Point Facilities

In addition to building generating facilities to meet the power needs of southern Florida, McGregor Smith, chairman of the board at FPL, took a personal interest in developing a miniature conservation project on 1700 acres at the site. The completed project was designated the "McGregor Smith Turkey Point Wildlife Conservation Area," in honor of its creator who died during construction of the project. Civic and government organizations are invited to make use of the land. Buildings, pools, playgrounds and canoes are provided for both Girl Scout and Boy Scout camps. Beaches are available to the public; there are two nature trails for hiking and bird watching; and four miles of channels are open for fishing and swimming.

Not for public use, but also illustrative of the varied uses to which FPL put the area, is an Air Force sea survival school and several large ponds in which shrimp breeding is being studied by the University of Miami.

The project has been described in company literature as "a monument to the men and women of FPL who dreamed this impossible dream . . . It is the bustle of industry, yet it blends into the serenity of the surrounding land." [9] The provision of these facilities by FPL prompted Jay Clarke, writing for *The New York Times*, to say: "This story is a prime example of the marriage that is possible between industry and conservation, and how natural beauty can be created and preserved while meeting the needs of industry." [10]

However, not all persons saw the Turkey Point Plant as preserving natural beauty:

> From every point of view, the most conspicuous feature in the landscape is the generating plant (Turkey Point) of the Florida Power and Light Company. It consists of two tall stacks, from which smoke and combustion effluents drift across the land, and massive buildings that contain the equipment. It is the most conspicuous feature because it is totally alien to the nature of the landscape. Industrial construction on that scale cannot be reconciled with any natural environment. It is an intrusion that cannot be ignored; the eye focuses on it at once because it is out of context. [11]

Thermal Pollution and the Nuclear Units

As is customary with applications to the Atomic Energy Commission for a permit, the FPL application was examined by the U.S. Fish and Wildlife Service of the Department of the Interior. On January 27, 1967, FPL received a letter from the Fish and Wildlife Service expressing concern over possible deleterious effects of the warm water discharges on the marine life of the bay.[12] This was the first communication received by FPL from a public agency suggesting possible harm. FPL began a wide search for information on the subject—thermal pollution—since this had been the first time in forty years of operation that any of its plants had been questioned on this basis.

The company discovered thermal pollution was apparently the result of what happens when a massive environment is suddenly exposed to an unremitting source of heated water that is 7–12 degrees Fahrenheit warmer than normal for that area. Massive use of cooling water to condense steam is an integral part of the generating process carried on by power utilities. In fact the nation's power plants are running neck and neck with irrigation as the chief users of water in this country. Power plants currently use more than 100 billion gallons a day, one quarter of the total "withdrawals" of water for all purposes, and this is expected to quadruple by the year 2020.[13]

Authorities also argue that if the marine environment that is subjected to substantial temperature increases is located in or near the tropics as is Biscayne Bay, the problem might become even more acute. Marine biologists feel that plants and animals living in tropical waters are often close to their natural thermal deathpoint during periods of summer maximum water temperatures, and that only a small temperature elevation might prove fatal.[14] The heat may adversely affect fish by reducing the amount of oxygen in the water, speeding up their metabolism so they have to breathe faster, slowing them down in their pursuit of food, and inhibiting reproduction. It may also kill normal vegetation and stimulate the growth of algae, which, in turn, disrupts the plant-fish-insect-bird "food chain" underlying the ecology of the area.

It is also argued that a marine environment is extremely complex, much more so than a freshwater environment. Many of the biological and physical processes that occur, and their relative importance in the survival of marine organisms, are not completely understood.

Atomic power plants that are superseding fossil fueled ones require even more cooling water than their predecessors. Florida Light and Power's two conventional generators will use 530,000 gallons of Biscayne Bay water per minute to cool the generator condensers. The two nuclear units, when placed in operation, will require an additional 1,340,000 gallons per minute for cooling.[15]

A second and more obvious difference between nuclear and fossil fuel units is the nature of the fuel. Basically, in a nuclear unit, atoms split inside the "core" which is contained in a nuclear reactor. This provides the heat that in a fossil unit comes from the burning of gas or oil in the boiler. Unlike fossil fuels, there is no combustion with nuclear fuel, therefore, no by-products of combustion. In the core, pressurized water is heated to 600 degrees. It then travels through a heat exchange where it turns a second circuit of water to steam. The steam then works, as in a fossil unit, by spinning a turbine that is coupled to a generator.

For both fossil fuel and nuclear units, a separate stream of water, usually drawn from a nearby source, cools and condenses the steam, which returns to water and to the heat exchange, to be converted back to steam again. The cooling water, which itself is now warmer, is cooled and sent back to its source. Thermal pollution occurs when this hot water discharge results in the rise of the normal average water temperature of the source.

Officers at FPL gave two major reasons for shifting to nuclear power at Turkey Point. "First, a nuclear plant shows potential for better overall economics for the generation of power as compared to fossil fuel plants, especially in fuel cycle costs. Second, the company was looking for a proper balance between nuclear and fossil fuel. The use of nuclear helps prolong the use of fossil fuels. Gas and low sulfur oil are getting scarce. In fact a very high percent of low sulfur oil is imported from foreign countries even now." [16]

Senator Muskie and the Committee on Public Works

In January 1967, at the same time the Fish and Wildlife Service of the Department of the Interior was expressing concern about the damage the discharge of warm water from the cooling systems might do the marine life of Biscayne Bay, the subject of thermal pollution and the probable need for quick legislative action caught the eye of Senator Edmund S. Muskie. In the fall of 1967, Muskie asked the AEC authorities for their position on regulating hot water discharges from nuclear power plants. The AEC officials informed Muskie that they claim no authority on the matter—either under its licensing regulations or under an executive order that calls on all government agencies to provide leadership in cutting water pollution.[17]

The AEC had taken the same stand earlier in 1966 in a case involving thermal pollution in New Hampshire. The Licensing Board of the AEC had maintained that it lacked subject matter jurisdiction and refused to consider the question of thermal effects when considering issuing a construction permit. The U.S. Court of Appeals later affirmed the Board's decision in the case of *New Hampshire* vs. AEC. The court agreed that the responsibility of the AEC is "confined to scrutiny of and protection against hazards from radiation." [18]

Hearings before the Subcommittee on Air and Water Pollution of the Committee on Public Works headed by Senator Muskie were held in February and April of 1968 to gather information about the known and unknown effects of thermal pollution. The Sport Fishing Institute reported during these hearings that the greatest source of thermal pollution is the steam-electric station. The Sport Fishing Institute report also stated that thermal pollution has gross adverse biological effects on fish and other aquatic life of major concern. Many long-term effects are much less apparent but may be even more severe.[19]

During the April hearings in Miami, FPL's Chairman of the Board, McGregor Smith, derided the claims of conservationists who had argued that the heated water discharged into Biscayne Bay would cause severe damage to marine and aquatic life. Smith claimed that with all four units in operation, 1.8 million gallons of water per minute would be drawn from Biscayne Bay for use as cooling water. Thus, in any twelve hour cycle, this amounts to 3600 acre/feet of water or the equivalent of 900 acres four feet deep.[20]

The average depth of Biscayne Bay is only about eight feet, and the bay takes in an area of some 220 square miles or 140,800 acres. This means that the bay presumably contains about 1 million acre/feet of water at low tide, claimed Smith. Also, some 280,000 acre/feet of water would flow in and out of the bay during each tidal cycle with the average tide being two feet.[21]

After presenting these figures to the hearing, Smith made the following statement:

> It can be readily seen that the amount of water discharged is quite low compared with the entire body of water in the bay, or even that coming in with the tide. Therefore there is no chance of increasing the temperature of any appreciable part of the bay, as some people suppose.

Our Cutler plant, located a few miles north of Turkey Point, has been borrowing cooling water from Biscayne Bay for some twenty years without harmful results. The only effect we know of is that it seems to have improved the fishing in the area. The truth of the matter is that practically nothing is known about temperature tolerance of species that inhabit south Florida. [22]

Actions Taken By FPL

Shortly after receiving the complaint from the Fish and Wildlife Service in early 1967, FPL took action to deal with the controversy. Richard O. Eaton and Drs. Pritchard and Carpenter of The Johns Hopkins University were retained to study the mixing and flushing characteristics of Biscayne Bay. In April 1967, unit number one at Turkey Point went into operation for the first time.

In January of 1968, Bechtel Corporation, the engineer/constructor of the Turkey Point Plant, was directed to conduct an engineering study of all available cooling water methods and to recommend an augmented cooling water system. This system was to meet the Dade County criterion that the hot water discharge could not raise the average water temperature of Biscayne Bay above 95 degrees Fahrenheit.

At the same time, FPL began biological studies since an intensive search had disclosed relatively little knowledge of Biscayne Bay ecology. Field studies on mixing were conducted in the spring of 1968.

In the summer of 1968, FPL received the report of Bechtel and the report of Pritchard and Carpenter. The latter report disclosed the existence of 20 percent recirculation and predicted 70 percent recirculation with the operation of all four units. The Bechtel report examined several cooling methods, including cooling towers, a pipeline out to the continental shelf, and cooling ponds, and specifically spelled out their disadvantages. The towers were ruled out because of a cost of approximately $30 million and the possible effects that their salt water spray might have on nearby trees, plants, and animal life. The cost also would include the possible added costs of designing towers to withstand hurricane force winds of 140 m.p.h. or better. In response to notification of the cost of towers, McGregor Smith replied, "We will do everything within reason. I'm a conservationist but not a fanatic." [23]

The cooling ponds were rejected because the ponds or lakes simply would take up more space than FPL owns or could acquire in the area.

Construction of a 13-mile pipeline to carry out the hot water to the continental shelf would cost over $110 million which FPL officials indicated was clearly prohibitive. "Besides," a FPL official said, "even then we don't even know if it would work." [24]

McGregor Smith commented, "We are certainly willing to compromise on this issue, because a solution must be found that will be beneficial to all parties." [25]

Smith also knew that, because of the bay's shallowness and lack of circulation, his plant could run into a recirculation problem because of its own effluent. In other words, some of the heated water might be recirculated back into the condensers, possibly causing a shutdown. He stated, "We know this is a possibility. That is one reason why we're so anxious to work out some kind of solution. But we've got to decide before long." [26]

The AEC was also interested in the ecology of Biscayne Bay and granted the University of Miami's Institute of Marine Science $60,000 to support a one-year study. Dr. Durbin C. Tubb, an associate professor at the Miami Institute, believed it possible to make accurate estimates of the maximum temperatures that bay flora and fauna can tolerate. He was also convinced there would be a change in the ecology of the bay once the nuclear units went into operation. For one thing, he said, much elevation of the water temperature above 93 degrees Fahrenheit would bring it close to lethal temperatures. Also, when the nuclear units are running, the temperature of some water could approach 110 degrees Fahrenheit. "They don't have to go much higher than 93 degrees Fahrenheit to affect the nature of protein," he stated. Furthermore, while he didn't believe the entire bay would be affected, he thought there would be "radical change" in perhaps 40% of the area. [27]

However, prior to the completion of this study the Dade County Pollution Control officer, Paul Leach, in the summer of 1968, cited FPL for violating the ordinance which limits the average bay temperature to 95 degrees Fahrenheit. On October 11, 1968, FPL officials asked Leach for a variance until July 1969 at which time they would come up with a feasible method to cool the water. During this same month, Congress established Biscayne Bay National Monument.

One alternative to the cooling methods described above is the use of cooling canals. This would involve digging 5.5 to 6 miles of cooling canals from the plant site due south to Card Sound. The project, which would cost approximately $8 million, would take hot water from generating plants, cool and divert it from Biscayne Bay. This method would eliminate the problem of recirculation which, in turn, would make feasible the utilization of dilution as a means of cooling the water. The company could then conform to the one existing temperature limit.

FPL officials stated that their prime motivation was to avoid recirculation so that the water could be cooled to acceptable limits. Consequently, FPL did two things. First, they retained the University of Florida to study the Card Sound canal and dilution plan in order to determine the temperature fields and possible recirculation. Second, company officials met in Atlanta on October 14, 1968 with members of the Federal Water Pollution Control Administration and the Florida Air and Water Pollution Control Commission to inform these organizations of the canal-dilution system and to ask their opinions. Members of the two groups expressed the opinion that the canal system appeared to be a satisfactory solution to the problem.

On December 6, 1968, the President's Water Pollution Control Advisory Board visited Turkey Point. A presentation was made by FPL officials in which the extended canal and dilution system was explained. At this time, the board stated that an extended canal system to Card Sound was probably the best solution.

In May 1969, the work of the University of Florida was completed and the results were favorable. On June 23, 1969, FPL officials called a meeting to discuss the canal-dilution plan with every interested public agency. Full disclosure of the plan was made to the Federal Water Pollution Control Administration, National Park Service, Fish and Wildlife Service, Florida Board of Conservation, and the Florida Game and Fish Commission. On June 30, 1969, FPL sent a letter to each one of the participants, enclosing copies of all the materials presented at the earlier meeting. There were no responses from these letters, even though they were requested by FPL.

On July 29, 1969, the Dade County Pollution Control Board, composed of three Ph.D.'s in the biological sciences and two professional engineers, heard FPL's presentation of its plan. The plan was approved by the board on December 5, 1969 with stringent conditions for protection of the environment. The board also granted a time extension of the earlier variance request to July 1, 1971.

One of the conditions for approval of the canal required that FPL must fund an ecological and meteorological study acceptable to Dade County, the state of Florida, and the federal government. This study must be in operation for one year prior to the canal's operation and should create a real natural laboratory to obtain facts. Should the results demonstrate that further temperature reduction were necessary, FPL must immediately proceed with steps to accomplish the necessary reduction.

A. M. Davis, vice president of FPL, summarized the situation as follows:

> We have cooperated with every interested public agency. All our research has been made available for scrutiny.
>
> We have participated in conferences, seminars, courses and hearings all over the country in our search for insight into the problem.
>
> We have spent over a million dollars in research and study on this vital problem. We have utilized dozens of experts, hundreds of pages of reports, and thousands of pages of transcript.
>
> The canal system to Card Sound eliminates the need of the people of Florida who we serve with electricity to choose between the environment and an adequate supply of electricity. They'll have both.[28]

Federal/State Conference in Miami

It appeared that FPL had finally solved the problem of thermal pollution by building the canal to Card Sound. However, on December 7, 1969, Governor Kirk of Florida requested U. S. Secretary of the Interior Hickel to hold a federal/state conference concerning the Turkey Point Plant, the canal to Card Sound, and thermal pollution. Governor Kirk claimed that he and certain conservationists were not yet convinced that the Card Sound Canal would eliminate the thermal pollution of Biscayne Bay.

On December 10, 1969, the Department of the Interior announced that a federal/state conference on thermal pollution of Biscayne Bay would be held in Miami on February 24 and 25, 1970. This hearing marked the first time in the thirteen years of federal water pollution abatement actions that a move had been based entirely on thermal pollution. The announced purpose of the conference was threefold. First, it was to bring together representatives of the state of Florida, the U.S. Department of the Interior, and other interested parties to review the existing situation at Biscayne Bay and the progress that had been made. Second, the conference was to lay a basis for future action by all parties concerned. Finally, it was to provide an opportunity for the state and FPL to take any indicated remedial action under state and local law.

On February 24, 1970, the hearings opened with Murray Stein, an official of the Department of the Interior, reading a statement for Walter Hickel, who was absent. Secretary Hickel took a hard line:

> Since the hearings were set in December of last year, we had expected FPL to refrain from taking any action which would change the position of the parties affected by this conference.
>
> However, we have learned that on February 7, 1970, FPL gave its go ahead to have excavating machinery begin the actual digging of the canal. This indicates the company intends to proceed with its projected plan regardless of the deliberations of this federal-state conference.
>
> As evidence of good faith, I want the FPL spokesman at this conference to declare that his company will not proceed with the canal excavation until the federal and state requirements have been established.
>
> If they refuse, I will request the Justice Department to seek appropriate remedies to protect the Biscayne Bay National Monument, including court action if necessary. [29]

During the hearings, the Federal Water Pollution Control Administration reported three major conclusions based on several studies it had performed. First, present heating effluent from the Turkey Point Plant was causing severe damage to the aquatic plant and animal population in lower Biscayne Bay. Second, operation of the two nuclear power generating units at the Turkey Point site would increase the waste heat load by four times over that presently discharged. This increased heat load would intensify the damage in extent, severity, and frequency. Third, if waste heat from the Turkey Point facility were discharged into Card Sound, as proposed by FPL, temperatures in excess of 95 degrees were to be expected in at least 35 percent of Card Sound, five percent of the time. [30]

The Federal Water Pollution Control Administration also recommended that FPL abate the excessive waste heat load being discharged from its Turkey Point Plant to the levels recommended for estuarine waters by the National Technical Advisory Committee and the Secretary of the Interior. The committee recommended that the monthly mean of the maximum daily temperature should not be raised more than 4 degrees during the fall, winter, and spring or more than 1.5 degrees during the summer. These same limits were incorporated in federal/state water-quality standards for all fifty states, now in the final stages of adoption, which will open the way for general enforcement.

The utility denied conference allegations that water, which is heated while cooling generating units, had damaged plant and animal life in the bay. Also FPL officials were still not convinced that the canal to Card Sound would cause damage to marine and aquatic life. One of the spokesmen for FPL at the hearings was Dr. James B. Lackey, a consultant for the company and a doctor of zoology from Columbia University with some thirty-five years experience in water pollution problems, much of it marine. Dr. Lackey stated, "I have studied Biscayne Bay for two years and, despite temperatures in some parts of it of substantially in excess of 95 degrees, it is my considered opinion that the discharge of the Turkey Point cooling water into Card Sound at a temperature not to exceed 95 degrees will not cause damage to the aquatic life. I am totally unwilling to accept the factually unsubstantiated Federal Water Pollution Control Administration report to the contrary." [31]

As the hearing drew to a close, FPL officials had still not given their word that the canal excavation would be stopped. "We have never been requested by the federal government before not to refrain from implementing our plan," said A. M. Davis, FPL vice president for public affairs.

"I guess I'm not going to get that statement not to proceed with the canal excavation," Stein interjected.

"No, sir," replied Davis. [32]

Another FPL official attending the hearings, Vice President F. E. Autrey, said the company would study the Federal Water Pollution Control Administration's requests but added that the canal project was already behind schedule.

"Anything that slows down this project now threatens a power shortage in June of next year," said Autrey. "We will carefully consider their requests and I want to emphasize that, as good citizens, we want to cooperate with all government agencies, but time is critical on the project of such vital importance to this community." [33]

On February 26, 1970, the day after the hearings, federal and state officials ordered the FPL to curb the discharge of hot water from the Turkey Point Plant into Biscayne Bay. As stated above, they ruled that the $8 million six-mile canal the company began building to carry the hot water to adjacent Card Sound was not acceptable as a solution because the discharged water could not be cooled enough. FPL was given sixty days to come up with proposals for an alternative to the present system. The Florida Air and Water Pollution Control Commission concurred in the ruling.

FPL argued it had nowhere to turn. They saw no immediate way to meet the requirements and still supply sufficient electricity to the Miami area by the summer of the next year. The first nuclear unit was scheduled to start up in the spring of 1971. Without it, the company's generating capacity would trail expected demand. The peak load was expected to be 5.6 million kilowatts while the supply, without the nuclear unit, would amount to only 5,565,000 kilowatts. The company might be able to buy some power from neighboring utilities for a time, but it could not rely on it permanently.

Justice Department's Suit

While FPL continued with the canal excavation, the Justice Department filed suit on March 13, 1970 to halt the company from present and future thermal pollution of Biscayne Bay. The suit was filed at the request of Walter Hickel who said that the Interior Department has an obligation to protect the interest of the United States in the fragile ecology of Biscayne Bay National Monument. The complaint stated that microorganisms and other small organisms were killed as the sea water passed through the heat exchanges and, when discharged into the bay, these dead organisms had a visible destructive effect on marine ecology. The suit sought an injunction to stop FPL from discharging heated water from the two existing power generating plants and from the two nuclear facilities under construction.

In 1968, a year after the two plants went into full operation, the complaint stated, the thermal pollution had created a "barren area" of 300 acres. This had more than doubled by 1969 according to the complaint. Also the situation was expected to become much worse when the two nuclear reactors were in operation. To cool these units, the total water withdrawn from the bay would amount to 4.5 million gallons a minute. "At this rate," the Justice Department stated, "water equivalent to all of Biscayne Bay would pass through the plant and its works in less than a month. The high water velocities will scour and disturb an extensive area of bay bottom. The removal of microlife will destroy the existing ecological cycle." [34]

The suit did not ask the court to stop construction of the nuclear plants or operation of the existing ones. It asked the court to order FPL to submit within forty-five days a plan to eliminate the thermal pollution allegedly resulting from the existing plants. In addition, it sought an injunction to stop construction of the canal to Card Sound designed to carry and cool the heated water discharged from the nuclear plants.

While the suit did not ask that the plant be shut down, failure to comply could theoretically result in court action forcing FPL to close its existing oil-fired units. But this would be a difficult decision for the government to pursue since the two units supply 75 percent of the generating capacity in Dade County.

In response to the suit, FPL issued the following statement:

> We regret that the Justice Department has brought this thermal pollution action against our company. The direction we have been taking for handling the cooling water at Turkey Point has the approval of the Dade County pollution control officer and was approved in the best interest of the public in both protecting the environment and assuring necessary electric power. [35]

FPL continued the excavation of the canal and on April 16, 1970, the United States District Court, Miami Division, denied the Justice Department's motion for preliminary injunction to stop the discharge of heated water into Biscayne Bay for failure to show irreparable damage. However, the motion for an injunction to restrain the digging of the Card Sound Canal was granted. The Justice Department's entire suit was based on Section 13 of the Rivers and Harbors Act of 1899 which prohibits the deposit of refuse into navigable waters.

In the ruling, Judge Atkins said:

> At this time, after careful consideration of the evidence presented and a view of the Turkey Point area I have decided that the application for a preliminary injunction should be denied. It is my conclusion that the government has not carried the burden of showing that the present operation of the Turkey Point plant is causing irreparable damage to lower Biscayne Bay. It is a basic principle that preliminary injunctive relief should not be granted in the absence of proof of irreparable harm and a substantial likelihood of success when the case is fully tried on the merits.
>
> I do find that the present warm water discharge causes some damage but it is minimal and retrievable. In this regard plans are in process to reduce the temperature of the discharge water to a benign level by July of 1971. As I do not find irreparable damage, the government's request that FPL be required to submit a plan to cool the discharge water is denied.
>
> While I denied relief sought at this stage pertaining to two nuclear power units being installed at Turkey Point, I am concerned about the large amount of heated water the units will discharge when they begin operation in 1971 and 1972. Therefore, I do plan to receive further evidence on this point at hearings to be scheduled at a later date. [36]

However, FPL knew that Judge Atkins' ruling was only a temporary solution to their problems. Once the two nuclear units went on line, the suit would definitely be reopened. Thus, a means still had to be developed to cool the discharge water to acceptable limits. FPL took steps to comply with the recommendations of the federal/state conference held in February. However, they still strongly rejected the conference assertions that the water cooling system under construction at Turkey Point was inadequate and certainly did not agree that the heated effluent was damaging plant and animal life in the bay. [37]

On April 30, 1970, FPL told federal and state pollution control officials that water temperatures within Biscayne Bay National Monument would not be raised by more than four degrees in the fall, winter, and spring and by 1.5 degrees in the summer as a result of the plant's operation. Also, a monitoring system would be installed to ensure compliance.

In addition, FPL announced that the engineering alternatives for handling the cooling waters would again be reevaluated by an independent engineering firm. An experimental cooling pool would also be built as a possible means of cooling the water.

As time drew near for FPL's nuclear units to go on line at Turkey Point, the Department of the Interior and the Justice Department were still not satisfied that FPL's present cooling system would prevent damage to plant and animal life at Biscayne Bay and Card Sound. The original suit against FPL was reopened by the Justice Department which again wanted to halt the discharging of heated water into Biscayne Bay.

Finally, on September 2, 1971, the Justice Department announced settlement of the suit aimed at halting the discharge of heated water into Biscayne Bay. The agreement was formalized in a consent decree filed in the U. S. District Court in Miami. If accepted by the court, it would terminate the suit that began in March 1970.

On September 9, 1971, the U. S. District Court in Miami accepted the consent decree and thus terminated the suit. It was decreed that, after a stated period, FPL would not discharge into the bay or sound any water used for cooling its condensers at fossil fueled electric generating units and nuclear powered electric generating units, except to prevent excessive concentration of salt in the water of the cooling system, or during national, regional, or reactor emergency, or when health, safety, or welfare of the public might be endangered by an inability of the company to supply electricity from other sources available to it.

The company was allowed to operate all Turkey Point units under strict limitations that were developed in consultation with state and federal agencies, the Department of the Interior, the Corps of Engineers, the Department of Justice, the Environmental Protection Agency, and the Atomic Energy Commission. FPL agreed to construct a closed cooling canal system to be completed within five years at a cost of $35 million. The system requires dredging some 125 miles of canals over 4000 acres of land where the waters will flow to be cooled, monitored, and controlled before returning to Card Sound. A canal to Card Sound to allow discharge of water to prevent excessive concentration of salt in the cooling system must be completed within four years. Also the canals will be open to inspection by government agencies.

FOOTNOTES

[1] Gladwin Hill, "Florida Power Plant Told to Cool Water," *The New York Times*, February 27, 1970, p. 10.

[2] Brooks Atkinson, "Biscayne Bay: The Endless Fight to Save It," *Audubon*, September 1970, p. 45.

[3] Robert Stearns, "Heat Waste," *Sea Frontiers*, May–June 1970, pp. 154–163.

[4] E. W. Kenworthy, "U. S. Suit Fights Heat Pollution," *The New York Times*, March 14, 1970, p. 31.

[5] "Turkey Point: Close-up," *Sunshine Service News* (Florida Power and Light publication), September–October 1970, p. 7.

[6] U.S. Department of the Interior, "Conference: in the matter of pollution of the navigable waters of Biscayne Bay and its tributaries in the state of Florida," February 24 and 25, 1970, p. 395.

[7] *Ibid.*

[8] Jay Clarke, "Biscayne Bay Gets a Wildlife Sanctuary With Its New Power Plant," *The New York Times*, April 2, 1967, p. 3.

[9] "Turkey Point: Close-up," p. 7–8.

[10] Clarke, "Biscayne Bay Gets a Wildlife Sanctuary," p. 3.

[11] Atkinson, "Biscayne Bay: The Endless Fight," p. 46.

[12] *Ibid.*

[13] Gladwin Hill, "Thermal Pollution Issue," *The New York Times*, March 10, 1969, p. 31.

[14] Stearns, "Heat Waste," p. 154.

[15] *Ibid.*, p. 156.

[16] "Turkey Point: Close-up," p. 12.

[17] "Atom Power Plant in Hot Water," *Business Week*, June 29, 1968, p. 69.

[18] Federal Reporter, 2nd Series, Vol. 406, p. 175 (1st Cir. 1969).

[19] Committee on Public Works, "Thermal Pollution—Part 1," February 6 and 13, 1968, February 14, 1968, pp. 5–12.

[20] *Ibid.*

[21] *Ibid.*

[22] *Ibid.*

[23] "Atom Power Plant in Hot Water," p. 72.

[24] "A Power Play Over Pollution," *Business Week*, March 21, 1970, p. 29.

[25] "Atom Power Plant in Hot Water," p. 72.

[26] *Ibid.*

[27] *Ibid.*, p. 70–

[28] U. S. Department of the Interior, "Conference," p. 395.

[29] Gladwin Hill, "Hickel Warns Power Company on Canal," *The New York Times*, February 24, 1970, p. 94.

[30] U. S. Department of the Interior, "Conference," p. 395.

[31] U. S. Department of the Interior, "Conference," p. 395.

[32] Hill, "Hickel Warns Power Company on Canal," p. 94.

[33] "U. S. Threatens Suit to Stop Construction of Canal in Florida," *The Wall Street Journal*, February 25, 1970, p. 34.

[34] Kenworthy, "U.S. Suit Fights Heat Pollution," p. 31.

[35] *Ibid.*

[36] 311 F. Supp. 139 (1970).

[37] "Florida P & L's Profit Fell in First Quarter," *The Wall Street Journal*, April 30, 1970, p. 16.

QUESTIONS

1. What is the nature of role expectations placed on FPL by various segments of its environment?
2. What were the major changes in FPL's environment forcing a search for a different coping strategy?
3. What were environmental constraints impinging on actions taken by FPL to react to the changing environment?
4. What appears to be the role of the Atomic Energy Commission?
5. What appears to be the major reasons for FPL's inability to respond effectively to environmental expectations?
6. On what basis might FPL establish priorities for relating to the different segments of its environment?
7. In what way does the state of the art concerning thermal pollution influence FPL's environment?

8. In what manner did FPL have to redefine its social role? Is this appropriate?
9. Can a cost-benefit analysis solve problems of an ethical nature or problems where economic factors are only secondary?
10. Are there any organizational changes needed in the firm?

CASE 2
WATER DECAY

Environmental pollution has long been recognized as a problem. However, not until recently have industrial expansion, technology, population growth, and other characteristics of a modern society combined to accelerate pollution to the point of critically threatening the natural environment. The destruction of streams, rivers, and lakes is having a far-reaching impact on our civilization.

The issue in this case is very complex for the substance creating pollution here—phosphate—also contributes significantly to the betterment of human existence. Detergents first became commercially available in the early 1930s, but it was not until 1947 when Procter & Gamble's Tide first combined surfactant (surface-active-agent) and phosphates that consumers recognized a noticeable improvement over soaps. With phosphates added, detergents cleaned much better than soap and were cheaper to produce. Other companies quickly followed Procter & Gamble's lead and, shortly thereafter, phosphates were used in nearly all detergents.

A decade or so passed before the first cries of concern over the impact of phosphates on the environment were heard. Phosphorus is a nutrient, as are carbon and nitrogen; apparently when excess amounts are drained into rivers and lakes, it provokes accelerated growth, especially in algae. When the algae dies, as a result of accelerated growth, it robs oxygen from the water in addition to blocking the sunlight, making the water unfit for plants and fish. This process of water decay is known as eutrophication and can be curbed by reducing the amount of phosphates in the water. One study disclosed that at least 32 states have eutrophication difficulties.[1]

As a result of several often conflicting studies, a controversy has erupted in the detergent industry. The issues appear to focus on the amount of danger to the environment and the most effective means of removing excess deposits of the phosphates. Crusaders against pollution have persistently campaigned for removal of phosphates from detergents. Their position is that this is the most effectively controlled source of phosphates. Industry is opposed to this alternative for the following reasons. First, complete removal of phosphates from detergents would require new inventions and the discovery of new cleansing materials, requirements which may take several years. Second, there is no guarantee that nonphosphate detergents will satisfy consumers' expectations or eliminate environmental problems.[2]

The detergent industry argues that phosphates should be strained out of sewage. Industry officials state that the cost of removing phosphates from sewage is relatively low, requiring little new equipment. They point out that modernization of sewage plants, now demanded of many cities by the federal government, might easily include installation of sewage straining equipment.[3] However, opponents disagree and point out that while waste treatment could potentially eliminate 80–98 percent of all phosphates, the cost is likely to be prohibitive.[4]

The detergent industry is dominated by the "Big Three"—Procter & Gamble Company, Lever Brothers Company, and Colgate-Palmolive Company—commanding approximately 90 percent of 1972's $1.4 billion total sales. Among the three, Procter & Gamble is by far the largest with close to 50 percent of industry sales. This company has a very clear-cut management philosophy that includes a very conservative financial structure, a policy of promotion from within, a strong marketing image, and a high sensitivity to the public image of their products. It is also quite clear that Procter & Gamble sees its role regarding phosphates differently from others in the industry.

FOOTNOTES

[1] "Phosphates: Out by 1975," *Chemical Engineering*, Vol. 79, September 18, 1972, p. 84.

[2] "Detergents Battle: No Permanent Damage," *Financial World*, Vol. 136, August 4, 1971, p. 5.

[3] "Why Detergent Makers Are Turning Drag," *Business Week*, February 20, 1971, p. 64.

[4] "Phosphates: Out by 1975," p. 84.

Water Decay vs. Clean Clothes: Dilemma of the Procter & Gamble Corporation

During the late 1960s the soap and detergent industry faced the prospect of having to reduce or completely remove the phosphate content from its detergent products. The movement toward a ban on detergent phosphate was due to the findings of several studies showing that phosphates cause eutrophication, a process of water decay. Phosphates are a nutrient and when excessive amounts of nutrients are discharged into waste streams, then into lakes and rivers, they cause excessive growth of algae. When this algae dies it takes oxygen from the water, making the water unfit for other plants and fish. The other major sources of eutrophication are human and agricultural wastes. A number of studies have revealed that only one-third to one-half of the phosphates in waterways come from detergents. The rest come from human and industrial wastes and fertilizer runoff. Other authorities, however, claim that the entire problem of excess algae growth is caused by phosphates in detergents.

In late 1967 the Soap and Detergent Association (SDA) met with the Secretary of the Interior, Stewart L. Udall, the person responsible for curbing water pollution and improving the condition of the nation's water resources. It was pointed out that scientists in the detergent industry had been working hard to find a satisfactory substitute for phosphates that also would achieve the cleaning and sanitizing demanded by housewives and industry users. At this time it was also emphasized that detergent phosphates are not the only contributors to accelerated eutrophication of the nation's water. For this reason it was agreed that a joint industry/government effort would attempt to solve the problem. Consequently, the Federal Water Pollution Control Administration and the Department of the Interior began a search for a means of controlling phosphates and other plant nutrients in municipal sewage and industrial wastes. After this meeting the SDA stated:

> Research on possible substitutes for phosphates in detergents is being vigorously pursued by detergent manufacturers and their suppliers. Concurrent with its work on possible replacements for phosphates, the industry is supporting, jointly with the government, programs dealing with the removal or control of nutrients through sewage treatment and other means. Since this will remove most nutrients, including phosphates, these programs will be a major contribution to combatting eutrophication. The search for a phosphate substitute is being undertaken in the context of this broader effort . . . an extensive amount of work to date has not uncovered a phosphate substitute. Therefore, the industry believes that removal or control of nutrients through sewage treatment and other means is of primary importance in the overall effort to control eutrophication.[1]

Congressional pressure to change detergent formulation was first initiated in 1963 by Representative Henry S. Reuss (D-Wis.), then chairman of the Conservation Energy and Natural Resources Subcommittee. He had earlier played a key role in forcing the detergent industry to make the conversion from alhylbeuzene sulfonate surfactants (ABS) to linear alhyl sulfonates (LAS). This change reduced both the sudsing and foaming of detergents. Approximately two years after the initial meeting with Secretary Udall the SDA appeared before Representative Reuss' subcommittee and argued that there was still no conclusive proof that detergent phosphates were the key element in accelerated eutrophication. The organization further stated that there was no suitable phosphate replacement available, creating a situation quite different from that which led to the conversion from ABS to LAS.[2]

Thus, as 1970 approached, after a decade of research the detergent industry had not yet discovered a suitable substitute for phosphate. No product had been found that would clean as well or that could be certified safe for man and environment. The industry still contended that it had not been proven that phosphates cause accelerated eutrophication and reiterated that phosphates are not the only source of the problem. Further, they argued that there was no assurance that a phosphate replacement, even if discovered, would be useful in solving the eutrophication problem.

Despite the industry position, in 1970 the Federal Water Pollution Control Administration called for an immediate reduction in the amount of phosphates in detergents and eventual total replacement by substitutes considered less harmful to the environment. The recommendation was based on information gathered by a team of scientists sent to Sweden to study its progress in dealing with lake eutrophication.

Findings gave added credence to the accusation that phosphates are a major component of water pollution.[3]

Procter & Gamble Profile

The soap industry is composed of three major producers—Colgate-Palmolive, Lever Brothers, and Procter & Gamble. These companies control approximately 90 percent of the heavy-duty detergent market and Procter & Gamble possesses more than 50 percent of that market.

William Procter and James Gamble founded Procter & Gamble Co. (P & G) in Cincinnati in 1837 with a capital investment of $7,192.24. The company was originally established to manufacture soap and candles. "By 1847 the firm was earning $27,000 a year. Procter ran the office downtown, while Gamble managed the expanding factories along the riverfront. Every Saturday night they met in Procter's home to discuss the business and make decisions. By 1859 P & G was the largest business in Cincinnati with annual sales of more than $1 million." [4]

As the company grew, the partnership was expanded to include children and other relatives who eventually took over management of the company. However, as long as he lived, Procter held a monthly meeting at his home to discuss the business. The family management was continued until 1930 when Richard R. Deupree became the first non-family chief executive.

Procter & Gamble Co. is "a marketing company." It is the nation's number one advertiser, providing over one-tenth of the television networks' total revenues in 1973. It ranks ". . . number one in the U. S. in laundry detergent (Tide), shampoo (Head and Shoulders), toothpaste (Crest), shortening (Crisco), disposable diapers (Pampers), and toilet paper (Charmin)." [5]

"The secret, in a word, is thoroughness. Procter & Gamble manages every element of its business with a painstaking precision that most organizations fail to approach. Thoroughness extends to the careful and tenacious recruitment of employees, the development of a much admired executive corps, the design of manufacturing facilities, the creation and testing of products." [6] For example, the development of Pringle's potato chips took over fifteen years.

However, critics argue that too much discipline shackles company executives and hampers company growth. One former P & G executive says, "Procter has reached middle age and is full of guys aged 35 making $35,000 who have to ask permission to go to the washrooms." Layer after layer of executives producing memos has resulted in a highly proceduralized company, according to another former executive. [7]

P & G argues that this thoroughness is directed specifically at fulfilling the consumers' wants and needs. Company officials stress that this is most apparent in the development of new products, the lifeblood of any consumer-goods company. The company spends well over $100 million annually on research and development and this function employs one out of every thirteen P & G employees.[8] No product is introduced without thorough testing. In fact, P & G introduced only two new products between 1970 and 1974. Before Chairman Edward Harness will allow a new product to be put on the market, he insists that its superiority (meaning consumer preference for it) be demonstrated by actual tests. According to Harness:

> Some people suggest that product differences in our field are minimal or infinitesimal. I can't agree. When you find a significant body of women who believe the characteristics of what they want are in a product—this is the essence of consumerism, giving them what they want.[9]

P & G does not market a product that has not exhibited some margin of superiority over its competition through employee and consumer panel testing.

The company believes this kind of thoroughness has contributed to both the relatively small number of product failures experienced and the longevity of its products. To support the latter claim it is argued that when left unchanged, a packaged product will tend to increase its market share for a few years after it is introduced, hit a peak, and then sink into decline. A study by the A. C. Nielsen Co. concludes that 85 percent of all new brands can expect less than three years of success before their market share starts declining rapidly. Procter & Gamble, however, has virtually overridden the life cycles: Ivory soap was first sold in 1879, Crisco in 1912, and no Procter & Gamble product has died in the last ten years.[10]

The Problem with Phosphates

The detergent industry generally dates the emergence of phosphates as a public issue to July 31, 1967 when Stewart Udall, then Secretary of the Interior, addressed the industry's leaders in Washington. At that time he asked the soap and detergent industry to work with the government to research and develop substitutes for phosphates.

The basic ingredient of all detergents, phosphate or nonphosphate, is a surface active agent or "surfactant"—a quasi-synthetic soap, derived from petroleum that makes up 15 to 20 percent of a typical heavy-duty formula. Surfactant is the ingredient chiefly responsible for actual soil removal. But it cleans cotton and some other fabrics poorly unless combined with chemicals known as "builders" that create conditions in the wash water that enable the surfactant to work efficiently. For a quarter of a century the most widely used builder has been some form of phosphate, which in recent years has accounted for 35 to 55 percent of most detergents, by weight. Phosphates assist by softening water and by keeping dirt and particles that cause hardness in suspension so that they are not redeposited on clothes or on the machine. Other chemicals possess the power to soften water or to limit redeposition of dirt, but phosphates perform their various functions especially well. Moreover, they are exceptionally free of undesirable side effects inside the washing machine.[11]

In the early 1930s detergents consisted almost entirely of surfactant. It was not until 1947, when P & G's Tide first combined surfactant and phosphates in the same box that detergents aroused any enthusiasm among consumers. With phosphates added, detergents cleaned better than soap and were cheaper. Because they left so little residue, they made possible the design of modern automatic washing machines. During the next few years, soap was relegated to a minority share of the laundry products market.

Phosphates have proven to be unusually safe as well as effective compounds. Their presence enables detergents to clean with less alkalinity even than soap. While the federal government annually receives reports of around 4000 ingestions of cleaning products, mostly by young children, no deaths or even serious injuries are known to have been caused by phosphate laundry detergents in a generation of use. Phosphates, in fact, are a constituent of many foods. Several million pounds are consumed by Americans each year in beer and soft drinks, of which the old-fashioned lemon phosphate was a famous example. In fact, the role of phosphate as a food has created much of the controversy. Included in the organisms that share the universal need for a little phosphorus in the daily diet are aquatic weeds and algae—microscopic plants that live in water. In limited quantity, algae are beneficial, creating oxygen through photosynthesis and forming a link in the aquatic food chain. An excess of algae, though not a cause of death, creates conditions that make the environment unfit for plants and fish.[12]

Many bodies of water cannot support excessive algae because they are too deep, fast moving, muddy, or cold. However, in lakes, ponds, and other slow-moving waters the availability of nutrients is often the factor critical to whether or not algae get out of hand. As stated above the process by which lakes become clogged with algae is eutrophication, usually defined as overfertilization with nutrients. Eutrophication is common in nature, for nutrients enter water from sources as varied as rainfall and the decomposition of dead fish. However, human activities can greatly accelerate the process.

Algae requires fifteen to twenty different nutrients of which phosphorus is quantitatively the third most important, after carbon and nitrogen. There is little hard evidence that phosphorus is chiefly responsible for eutrophication. But of the nutrients that might be responsible, phosphorus is considered the most controllable. Unlike nitrogen, phosphorus is effectively trapped by most farmland and by properly functioning septic systems. In many lakes as much as 70 percent of the phosphorus is believed to flow from municipal sewage plants. Of the phosphorus contained in sewage, 40 to 70 percent often comes from phosphate detergents, and all of these are manufactured by essentially three companies. Thus the simple expedient of forcing three companies to change their product formulas might possibly eliminate approximately 50 percent of all the phosphorus going into some lakes.[13]

NTA, a Potential Substitute

Despite research efforts by the major soap companies aimed at finding a substitute for the phosphate content of laundry detergents, only a substance called sodium nitrilotriacetic acid, or NTA, first produced in Germany during the 1930s was discovered. NTA had for years been considered too expensive for general use. But improved methods of synthesis patented in 1962 by a division of W. R. Grace & Co.

reduced costs, and tests indicated that in some respects NTA was even more effective than phosphates. P & G first used small amounts of NTA in a detergent called Gain during the mid-1960s. Then in 1970 after several years of testing, doubts, and hesitation the company believed it was ready to use NTA on a much larger scale. P & G ran a full-page ad stating, "By May of this year, we will be using NTA to replace 25 percent of the phosphates in approximately one third of the company's laundry detergent volume." [14] The ad run by P & G was titled, "Questions and answers about phosphates in detergent and their possible effect on our lakes and streams." The ad stated P & G's concern for the environment and its desire to find a safe, effective phosphate substitute. The company stated that it:

> . . . is engaged in an all-out effort to reduce and eventually eliminate the phosphate content of its detergents. We have not waited for 'proof' that the elimination of phosphates from our products will have any significant effect one way or the other on lakes and streams . . . . Neither are we waiting for proper sewage treatment facilities which could answer this and other problems. [15]

Dr. David Stephan, associate commissioner for research and development at the Federal Water Pollution Control Administration, called P & G's action a "step in the right direction" and considered NTA to be "the leading candidate" to replace phosphates. [16]

In June 1970, P & G told a Senate subcommittee on air and water pollution that "in the hassle of solving problems in our polluted environment," it had already replaced 25 percent of the phosphates in one-third of its packaged detergent line with NTA and that it was experimenting with a 50 percent replacement. P & G felt that any further lowering of the phosphate level would adversely affect the cleaning results of the detergent and that housewives might compensate for this by using larger amounts of detergent and thus nullify the aim of lowering the phosphate content. [17] Based on its commitment to NTA the company sank more than $150 million into orders for NTA as well as into plant equipment and commitments to help its NTA suppliers build new factories.

At this same June hearing consumer groups called for a public hearing and disclosure of information collected by the FTC during an investigation concerned with enzymes in detergents. Since 1961, when discovered by a Swiss company, enzymes had been added to detergents to attack certain stains more effectively. P & G took the position that there was no possible basis for the implication that a health hazard was involved in the use of detergents containing enzymes. [18] However, it was also concluded that enzymes were added to detergents for competitive reasons and although their removal without replacement would affect detergent performance somewhat, it would not have the devastating affect that removal of phosphates would have.

Phosphate Producers

Despite the upheaval in the detergent industry, producers of phosphate in the United States did not appear to be concerned about the possible annihilation of their detergent market. Spokesmen for the industry continued to remain relatively calm in the face of an antiphosphate campaign carrying the full emotional and political force of an environmental crisis. According to the Soap and Detergent Association the United States produces over 2,500,000 tons of phosphorus compounds a year. Approximately half of this is used in detergents.[19]

1970 P & G Annual Meeting

Despite the confusion taking place in the detergent industry, in 1970 sales of synthetic detergents were still up 18.3 percent in volume and 16.6 percent in value from the previous year.[20]

At their annual meeting in 1970, P & G stockholders were given a special report from President Howard Morgens stating that, by March 1972, P & G would eliminate 500 million pounds of phosphates annually from its production. This is an overall reduction of 38 percent. The report also stated that further steps would be taken to reduce phosphate usage by 100 percent but that this would take new inventions and the discovery of new materials. Morgens went on to say that the phosphates then used in detergents were "absolutely safe for people" and therefore:

. . . any new material must pass rigid long-term tests to prove that it is safe for humans as well as our environment.[21]

He further said that P & G had been running such tests over many years to establish the human and environmental safety of the materials the company was then using as a partial replacement for phosphates. He continued: ". . . if anyone— in government or out—can suggest a more intelligent or responsible course of action from the standpoint of the public interest, we will gladly adjust what we are doing." [22] Morgens also pointed out that a specific schedule for the complete removal of phosphates was difficult because:

. . . no government agency has yet endorsed any effective substitute material. Without waiting for government assurances, Procter and Gamble, based on its own extensive studies over many years, has already ordered well over $150 million worth of one alternate material. New factories are being built to supply it. This should, we feel, provide some evidence of the confidence we have in this material and of our determination to solve the problem as rapidly as possible.[23]

Action by Governments

By late 1970, Governor Rockefeller of New York had decided to ask the 1971 state legislature to ban the sale of phosphate-containing detergents and cleaners. The ban was to become effective in 1972. Rockefeller stated that one-half of the phosphates in most municipal sewage systems was from detergents. He also felt that by delaying the ban until 1972 detergent manufacturers would have time to find a substitute. [24]

Governor Rockefeller's announcement came right after Lever Brothers introduced a liquid laundry detergent, All, containing no phosphates. Lever Brothers indicated that NTA could be used as a 100 percent replacement for phosphates in detergents that were liquids rather than powders. However, the company did not wish to commit itself to NTA completely until federal research on the safety of NTA was completed. [25]

The SDA also expressed wariness over some of the new substitutes that were being used to replace phosphates, including NTA, sodium citrate (STC), and a silicate carbonate base. The SDA felt that the ecological impact as well as the practical effectiveness of these substances had not been tested fully enough. In its view the real solution should feature sewage treatment plants and government aid in research. [26]

Also in October 1970, Chicago enacted an ordinance requiring the removal of phosphates from detergents. This ordinance, passed unanimously, ruled that the phosphorus content of detergents must be cut to 8.7 percent by February 11, 1971, and to zero by June 30, 1972. This drew strong attacks from the SDA. The organization claimed that this action would have no effect on the quality of the water in Lake Michigan, that phosphate substitutes still had unknown factors concerning human and environmental safety, and that this action would in no way speed up research for a phosphate-free detergent because work was being carried out in this area as thoroughly and as quickly as was possible.

The "Ban" On NTA

On December 16, 1970, officials of the detergent industry were called to a meeting in Washington set for the following day. At that meeting another serious blow was dealt industry attempts to reduce the phosphate content in detergents. During the meeting the Health, Education and Welfare Department revealed a study showing that NTA could cause birth defects in animals when combined with metallic wastes (mercury and cadmium) to form a third substance. Fearful that the substance might get into the nation's drinking water and prove harmful to pregnant women, HEW threatened to ban NTA. However, to prevent additional negative publicity and further pressure from the government, the industry agreed to stop using NTA. P & G was hit hardest by this decision since it had committed substantial sums to the use of NTA and had urged several chemical companies, including Monsanto Co., to build or expand NTA production facilities. By some estimates the detergent and chemical companies had committed $100 million to the development of NTA. The industry was particularly disturbed by the threatened action because the results of their own research on NTA were not solicited by HEW. Industry sources argued that their research on NTA was more comprehensive than the HEW studies. In fact one executive present recalled, "We weren't allowed to examine the data. The people we had down there had no technical resources." [27]

It was further believed by some manufacturers that the ban was the result of a power struggle either between HEW and Senator Edmund S. Muskie (D-Me), head of the Subcommittee on Air and Water Pollution or between HEW and the new Environmental Protection Agency. If true, the detergent industry had merely become a pawn in the battle.[28] One reason for this assumption was the manner in which the meeting had been called. The detergent industry was notified on December 16 of the meeting to be held on the 17th, and a decision was demanded of them by the 18th, all just prior to the December 19 opening of Senator Muskie's hearings into detergent problems.[29]

Response of P & G to Ban on NTA

P & G was one of the first to react publicly to the ban on NTA:

> In the quantities which we have used NTA in certain of our products, we are absolutely confident of their safety. Our research on NTA started in 1961. We believe that there has been more research supporting the safety of NTA than there has been supporting the safety of most, if not all, of the materials going into the nation's food products.
>
> The Surgeon General [Jesse L. Steinfeld] does not suggest there is cause for concern about the limited quantities of NTA now in use. However, once the Surgeon General has made the statement he has, public confidence in products containing NTA is bound to be adversely affected. Regardless of the facts, the future usefulness of this material has been largely destroyed. Therefore, we have already moved to phase out use of NTA as rapidly as possible.[30]

A study done for the Senate Public Works Committee by a staff of independent consultants, mostly from universities, reached conclusions similar to the HEW study on NTA. Among these conclusions were (1) available toxicological data on NTA indicate potential human hazards, (2) no toxicological data are available on a wide range of questions critical to the assessment of consumer and environmental safety, and (3) it is improbable that NTA detergents will achieve the stated objective of reducing eutrophication.[31] This study added support to the ban on NTA and increased the likelihood that the ban would not be removed in the future.

However, an A. D. Little study for P & G indicated a low probability of human or environmental hazards at use levels contemplated for the chemical. NTA developer John W. Singer, vice president for W. R. Grace's chemical group, stated that a two-year rat feeding study, on which the ban was based, showed:

1. Except for mammary tumors (to which the rat strain is susceptible) low incidence of other tumors in both control and test animals.
2. No significant increase in specific tumors nor in total tumors.

Criticizing the Surgeon General's statement that the study was inadequate to provide evidence that NTA is not carcinogenic, Dr. Singer pointed out that no compound has ever been proven not carcinogenic.[32]

Response of Small Detergent Companies to Ban on NTA

As soon as the government's results on its NTA studies were released the small detergent companies, which had earlier come out with non-phosphate detergents using NTA as a substitute, claimed to have a suitable alternate ready. These companies stated that they had used NTA only as a stopgap measure while working on a more satisfactory substitute. They apparently were reasonably sure that the government examination of NTA would demonstrate the undesirability of the product. When asked why they had used NTA knowing that it would be found unsuitable, several companies indicated a variety of reasons. Some of the companies didn't have the other substitutes ready at the time they put their products on the market. But a prime reason, according to one executive, was that:

> When P & G says NTA is safe and it commits itself heavily, you have to listen to what a company that size says. Since converting to a new formula is a costly operation for a large company, it doesn't make such a decision unless it is based on extensive research and that's why smaller companies followed P & G's lead. [33]

Another often-asked question was how the smaller companies could find a solution when the big companies could not. The "big three" manufacturers argue that they must do extensive research while small companies do not have to worry about a small amount of a new substance being introduced into the environment. The big companies also accused some of the smaller companies of producing inferior products.

An executive from one of the small companies, however, said that one reason the big companies were having trouble coming up with a substitute was that they were starting at step two instead of step one so that they could use existing equipment and avoid changing the entire manufacturing process. [34]

Continued Disagreement but no Alternatives

With no alternative solution available after the NTA ban, P & G again began producing detergents containing larger amounts of phosphates. The detergent industry continued to campaign for phosphate removal through sewage treatment. The industry reasoned this approach would incur relatively low costs and little new equipment, especially since the federal government was pushing for cities to modernize their sewage plants to control many more problem substances than phosphates. However, the new Environmental Protection Agency was still insisting that the phosphate content in detergents be reduced to achieve a "balance" of control of the problem, both at the source and through sewage treatment. [35]

Besides the attack on phosphates the fight against enzymes in detergents continued. Consumer groups reported scattered complaints of itching and rashes attributed to enzymes. The American Academy of Allergy announced that enzymes "are a potential hazard to public health." Ralph Nader petitioned the FTC to prohibit their sale because they are a "serious health danger." The industry could only dispute the claims and cut back. P & G's President Morgens announced that "we have reduced the number of our brands that contain enzymes." The reason for the change was not safety but a "vague confusion" in consumers' minds. "Regardless of the validity of the questions (concerning enzymes) when consumer preferences change, we adjust." [36]

Amid all the confusion over phosphates, enzymes, and NTA, P & G's share of the market began to decline, falling to 44 percent by mid-1971. Colgate-Palmolive managed to maintain its 17 percent share, but Lever Brothers fell to 15 percent. The largest beneficiaries in this market shift seemed to be the non-phosphate detergent manufacturers, having gained 7 to 13 percent of the market despite warnings against non-phosphate products which the three major producers had issued. These warnings had apparently not been heeded by consumers. [37]

Major new entrants to the detergent industry had been rare, partly because huge advertising budgets are considered necessary. However, confusion following the suspension of NTA created unique opportunities for producers of washing-soda detergents. The common theme heralding the arrival of washing-soda brands was unselfish concern for the environment coupled with intimation of scientific breakthroughs. A classic example was Sears Roebuck's phosphate-free formula, which quickly doubled its share of the market. However, shortly after this accomplishment the Surgeon General warned that certain non-phosphate products could be harmful to health. In fact it was later found that certain brands were sufficiently caustic to damage eyes and mucous membranes irreversibly if splashed or eaten. Also, some non-phosphate detergents do a satisfactory job of removing dirt, but they tend to stiffen fabrics and leave white deposits on dark clothes. [38]

An About Face by the Government

The lack of an acceptable substitute coupled with the subsequent return to original compounds such as phosphate in detergents spurred several consumer groups to demand that at least labels indicating content and potential dangers be required on detergents.

During 1971, in addition to other actions being taken, the Federal Trade Commission did hold hearings on a proposal by Concern, Inc. This citizens' group asked that pollution warnings be required on detergent products and advertisements and that all ingredients be listed on the packages, with percentages of the total content, as in drug items. [39]

However, the passage of any such proposal was severely jeopardized later in the year when the government appeared to change its philosophy on phosphates. Because NTA and the alkali substances that were being used to date were both found to be unsuitable as substitutes for phosphates, the government began recommending increased use of phosphate detergents. The alkali detergents were found to be highly caustic and therefore presented more of a health hazard than did phosphates. Dr. Jesse Steinfeld, the Surgeon General, advised consumers to buy phosphates and recommended that states and local communities reconsider laws and regulations "which unduly restrict the use of phosphates in detergents." [40] It was now felt by the government that the health danger from phosphate alternatives greatly outweighed the water pollution caused by phosphates. In fact, detergent officials at the FTC hearing argued that phosphates were only a pollution problem where sewage flowed into the lakes or other deposits where there was little current. Even in these cases phosphates were only one of many sources of problems. William Ruckelshaus, Administrator of the Environmental Protection Agency, seemed to agree, and stated that he was convinced that phosphates were no problem in at least 80 percent of the country's waters. In the areas where there was a problem Ruckelshaus suggested the government aid in the building of sewage treatment plants. [41] In fact, the federal government was earmarking $500 million to support such construction over the next year.

The new position taken by the Surgeon General was widely condemned as a sellout to the "big three" and in particular to P & G, whose chief lobbyist, Bryce Harlow, was a former Nixon aide. Marketers of the non-phosphate detergents were particularly up in arms over the latest shift in government opinion on their ecology-slanted products; they temporarily halted ads. Ironically, from P & G's point of view the Surgeon General's testimonial hardly offset the immediate financial and marketing impact of the company's defeat on NTA; in fiscal 1971, P & G wrote off $7,100,000 of binding contracts to purchase NTA. [42]

However, continued antiphosphate actions by state and local authorities pointed to a continued lack of common perception of dangers by governmental bodies. For instance, in December 1971, P & G withdrew its products from the Miami, Florida area due to a new regulation in Dade County making it illegal to sell phosphate detergents after the end of the year. P & G explained that it could not use any of the three alternatives to phosphates now available. It said it would not use NTA because of the Surgeon General's request that its use be stopped pending further testing. The company would not use sodium carbonate because it was highly alkaline and corrosive causing a possible danger to humans, washing machines, and the environment. Finally, the company argued it could not remove phosphates completely with no replacement because the resulting detergent would not clean. P & G, therefore, withdrew from the market having no suitable alternative to its phosphate detergents. [43]

By January 1972, however, state and county officials, concerned with the caustic properties of phosphate-free detergents and confused by Dr. Steinfeld's September statements, began to repeal or lighten bans on phosphates in several areas of the country. Michigan passed a state law limiting phosphorus content to 8.7 percent which preempted city laws in Detroit and Grand Rapids calling for zero phosphate levels. Lake County, Florida repealed its ban. Similar proposals were being made elsewhere. [44]

The confusion continued in Washington also. Federal officials backed off somewhat from the earlier statements made by Dr. Steinfeld, saying that phosphate detergents were reasonably safe but could lead to eutrophication. On the other hand, low or non-phosphate detergents were unsafe for use where there were children, and soap was an effective cleaner only in soft-water areas.

Colgate-Palmolive and Lever Brothers, but not P & G, asked for a federal law to limit phosphate content to 8.7 percent. All three supported preemption of state and local antiphosphate laws, now numbering seventy-one. Variations in limits among states forced producers to adhere to the lowest of these requirements.

The debate also continued over NTA. A scientific advisory committee was set up by HEW to review the technical questions surrounding NTA. Dr. Steinfeld was not informed of this action. This new committee was created and started work with great speed. Jack Anderson charged that White House aides, one of which is chief lobbyist for P & G, had exerted undue influence to have NTA put back on the market. Bryce Harlow, now a P & G lobbyist and a former advisor to President Nixon, denied these charges saying that there was no influence-peddling to put NTA back on the market.

Dr. Merlin K. DuVal, the Assistant Secretary of HEW, said he had asked the National Academy of Science to set up a panel to review possible health hazards of NTA. However, because of the time this report would require (6–7 months), Dr. DuVal instead decided to appoint a panel of nine scientists headed by Dr. Lauren Woods, vice president for health sciences at the Medical College of Virginia. Their charge was to examine all relevant health and safety information on NTA. The panel held meetings in a motel in suburban Arlington described by one federal scientist in attendance as rather "puzzling." "There was a smoke-filled room—people sprawled on beds—it just didn't look like an assembly of scientists wrestling with a complicated problem." [45]

Also, Dr. Samuel S. Epstein, a professor at Case Western Reserve University and the first to make public the possible health problems of NTA, stated, "I don't understand the sudden rush to look into NTA again. There may be nothing sinister in this, but it would be madness to put NTA back on the market without a lot of thoughtful study." [46]

Dr. Woods and Dr. DuVal emphatically denied that any political pressure had been exerted to hurry the review along although the latter added, "There have been an enormous number of people who have reminded me of the residual impact of last September's statement." [47]

Dr. Ian A. Mitchell, a special assistant to Dr. DuVal who was also involved in the NTA controversy, said, "I have never felt political pressure, although I have been aware that there are interested parties." [48]

Dr. DuVal also conceded that Dr. Steinfeld had indeed not been fully consulted on all the detergent issues, including the transmission of technical data.

Chicago Bans Phosphate-Based Detergents

Meanwhile, during these panel discussions, Chicago authorities decided to place a total ban on phosphates in virtually all detergents to take effect July 1. However, two Chicago suburbs which passed similar ordinances calling for an outright

ban on detergent phosphates on July 1 extended the deadline, evidently in anticipation of a similar move by Chicago. The Skokie, Illinois, board of trustees repealed
the phosphate ban, but voted to reconsider the matter in six months. Other communities in the Chicago area were considering similar action.[49]

In June 1972, the SDA, on behalf of Procter and Gamble, Colgate-Palmolive,
and Lever Brothers, prepared to go to court to challenge the legality of Chicago's
total ban on phosphates. Some observers felt that the unfavorable results of the
HEW study on NTA had prompted the SDA to press the Chicago suit. The results
of the HEW study released in May concluded that serious toxicity problems had not
been resolved with regard to NTA.

Whatever the reason for the action, the SDA was determined to force a showdown airing all aspects of the detergent controversy and its legal implications. If the
SDA could win the Chicago suit it would have a powerful precedent for blunting
the effect of phosphate-limiting ordinances elsewhere.

SDA's case was expected to stress the legal aspects of phosphate bans. It was expected to try to show that the Chicago ordinance impeded interstate commerce, that
production could not be geared to regional legal requirements, that the ban was not
reasonably related to public safety, that the equal protection clause of the 14th
Amendment was violated because other phosphate products had not been banned,
and that the statute would harm the industry and the public. It was also likely that
the SDA would try to show that present phosphate substitutes were corrosive and
potentially hazardous.[50]

On June 30, 1972, the phosphate ban went into effect in Chicago and once
again P & G withdrew its products from the market, making essentially the same
statement that it had made in Florida. This was P & G's third major withdrawal
from the market, the other one being Erie County, New York (Buffalo). An official
of P & G indicated that P & G had not found a satisfactory non-phosphate detergent
substitute yet and would therefore continue to pull its products out of antiphosphate
markets. The ban was only effective in the city proper, so P & G products were still
available in the suburbs.[51]

Despite the ban, Chicago consumers seemed determined to continue to buy
phosphate detergents. Many suburban stores reported record sales of phosphate detergents subsequent to the ban. One store that normally sold 18–20 cases of Tide per
week sold 800 cases in one week after the ban.[52]

In the meantime, SDA's suit against the ban had been delayed, but some
sources felt that P & G's pullout from the Chicago market would help the company when the suit did go to court. They argued that the company's integrity would
be enhanced by the position that present phosphate substitutes were poor perform-
ers and potentially harmful to people. In addition, the company could presumably
show financial injury.[53] P & G commented that there should be no concern over a
detergent shortage, "because competitive companies have already indicated that
they will supply the kinds of products that we feel we should not supply."[54]

P & G Introduces New Products

With their withdrawal from three large markets, P & G continued to work toward finding a phosphate substitute that they considered effective and safe. In October 1972, Howard Morgens announced that P & G had developed a new cleaning system that would permit about a 50 percent reduction in phosphate content of its laundry detergents. The company had developed a surfactant (surface-active agent) system that was more "calcium insensitive" than those in use. The new formula enabled the reduction of phosphates in their detergents to about a 6 percent level.[55]

Morgens also announced that P & G intended to begin selling non-phosphate detergents in localities where phosphate detergents had been banned. Until now the company refused to sell a low- or non-phosphate product, asserting that the safety and efficacy of phosphate replacements hadn't been proven.[56] The company spent $85 million to find a suitable phosphate substitute and was the last of the "big three" to market a non-phosphate detergent. Two of the P & G non-phosphate entries into the market were a liquid detergent called Era and a reformulated Tide. In both cases, P & G played down the non-phosphate element of the new detergents in their advertising since they still maintained that a small amount of phosphate was necessary for effective cleaning.[57]

P & G continued to employ a strategy characterized by an initial strong advertising thrust. The company achieved substantial success in test markets with Era by using substantial sampling, couponing, and saturation TV advertising. The product became the No. 1 selling liquid detergent two months after its introduction and three months after advertising broke, it was "outselling all competitive powders and liquids." [58]

P & G also introduced a non-phosphate pre-soak, Biz, in Dade County, Florida, with the ad, "Come Clean Dade County, Look at the difference a Biz soak can make in a no-phosphate detergent wash." [59]

The Phosphates Win One

Finally, after eight months, the Chicago ban on phosphates was lifted when Federal Judge Thomas R. McMillen ruled that the June 30 ordinance:

. . . constitutes an unjustified interference with interstate commerce and therefore violates the U. S. Constitution. The evidence is clear that a detergent made with phosphate is a more effective cleaning agent than non-phosphate detergents when used with Chicago's water and is not at all harmful to the persons using it. This [decision] doesn't necessarily mean that similar ordinances in other jurisdictions cannot be sustained where the effects of discharging phosphates into the public water supply may outweigh the interference with interstate commerce.[60]

The city of Chicago appealed the decision to the U. S. Circuit Court of Appeals.

P & G, although it continued to reduce the phosphate content of its detergents, stated that they would: ". . . continue our efforts to present the facts on this complex problem to legislators, the public and to the courts in an effort to bring about a change in laws which force housewives to use inferior products." [61]

Also, despite all the controversy, by mid-1974 phosphate detergents again began to pop up on supermarket shelves. Since the height of the phosphate debate about 1970, at least two dozen states and localities have rescinded or postponed bans on the use of phosphates. In areas that permit phosphate products, the sale of phosphate-free cleaners has fallen from a high of about 14 percent of the detergent market to between three percent and four percent according to the industry estimates. Also it was argued by the Environmental Protection Agency that most areas have found that a phosphate ban isn't the solution once thought. [62]

Back to the Drawing Board

On January 15, 1975, the three judges of the appeals court unanimously accepted the theory that phosphates contribute to the aging process of lakes and rivers by accelerating the growth of algae and plants. They, therefore, upheld the Chicago ban on phosphates reversing the decision of the lower court. The decision stated that, although Chicago's contribution to the phosphates in Lake Michigan might be minimal, the level of phosphates in the lake was so high that any additional amount, no matter how small, could be greatly detrimental. The decision also stated that Chicago's actions should provide an example for other cities around Lake Michigan that were dumping phosphates into the lake. [63] Finally, the appeals court stated the burden of interstate commerce caused by the ban was slight and that companies had failed to prove this was an unreasonable approach to a legitimate objective—controlling water pollution. [64]

The companies then urged that their case be heard in the Supreme Court claiming that the appeals court ruling would "encourage the adoption of disparate and conflicting local restrictions upon the movement of interstate commerce of safe and beneficial goods." [65]

P & G had claimed throughout the court cases that they had lost $4.7 million in sales due to the Chicago ban and that their shipping costs had increased $2.5 million due to changed production arrangements required to comply with the law. [66]

In May 1975, the Supreme Court turned down the appeal of the companies without comment. [67]

FOOTNOTES

[1] "Phosphates-in-Detergents Nut: Efforts to Crack It Please Udall," *Oil, Paint and Drug Reporter*, Vol. 193, January 22, 1968, pp. 4, 42.

[2] "Another Switch for Detergents," *Chemical and Engineering News*, Vol. 47, December 22, 1969, p. 7.

[3] *Wall Street Journal*, February 5, 1970, p. 2.

[4] Peter Vanderwicken, "P & G's Secret Ingredient," *Fortune*, Vol. 90, July 1974, p. 75.

[5] *Ibid.*

[6] *Ibid.*

[7] "Is the Soap Leader Getting Soft?" *Business Week*, July 19, 1969, p. 52.

[8] James W. Nethercott, "The Procter and Gamble Company," *Wall Street Transcript*, Vol. 36, June 19, 1972, pp. 28, 870.

[9] Vanderwicken, "P & G's Secret Ingredient," p. 75.

[10] *Ibid.*

[11] William Simon Rukeyser, "Fact and Foam in the Row Over Phosphates," *Fortune*, Vol. 85, January 1972, p. 71.

[12] *Ibid.*, p. 72.

[13] *Ibid.*, p. 73.

[14] "NTA Gets Big Push in Detergent Powders," *Chemical and Engineering News*, Vol. 48, April 6, 1970, p. 11.

[15] *Ibid.*

[16] *Ibid.*

[17] "Up-to-the-Minute Marketing Reports on the 125 Largest National Advertisers," *Advertising Age*, Vol. 41, August 24, 1970, p. 150.

[18] *Ibid.*

[19] "Phosphate Makers Calm About Pending Detergent Problems," *Industrial Marketing*, Vol. 55, September 1970, p. 12.

[20] *Ibid.*, p. 13.

[21] "Phosphates: Big Wash-Out," *Oil, Paint and Drug Reporter*, Vol. 198, October 19, 1970, p. 18.

[22] *Ibid.*

[23] *Ibid.*

[24] "Rockefeller to Ask State Ban of Phosphates," *Advertising Age*, Vol. 41, September 28, 1970, p. 3.

[25] *Ibid.*

[26] "Phosphate Makers Calm," p. 12.

[27] Rukeyser, "Fact and Foam," p. 166.

[28] "A Phosphate Stand-in Goes Down the Drain," *Business Week*, December 26, 1970, p. 17.

[29] "Why Detergent Makers Are Turning Gray," *Business Week*, February 20, 1971, p. 66.

[30] "NTA Projects 'Deferred' or 'Halted' But Trade Isn't Washing Them Out," *Oil, Paint and Drug Reporter*, Vol. 198, December 28, 1970, p. 14.

[31] *Ibid.*

[32] "Phosphate Debate: Confused As Ever," *Convenience Food Reporter*, Vol. 4, March 15, 1972, p. 95.

[33] Nancy Giges, "Detergent Makers Scramble for No-Phosphate, No-NTA Formulas," *Advertising Age*, Vol. 42, January 11, 1971, p. 52.

[34] *Ibid.*, p. 53.

[35] "Turning Gray," p. 64.

[36] *Ibid.*, p. 66.

[37] "P & G's Detergent Share Tumbles as Non-Phosphates Make Big Gains," *Advertising Age*, Vol. 42, July 12, 1971, p. 8.

[38] Rukeyser, "Fact and Foam," p. 168.

[39] "Detergents Battle: No Permanent Damage," *Financial World*, Vol. 136, August 4, 1971, p. 5.

[40] "Phosphate Turnabout Stuns Alkalis; Advertising Picture Is Uncertain," *Advertising Age*, Vol. 42, September 20, 1971, p. 1.

[41] *Ibid.*, p. 74.

[42] Rukeyser, "Fact and Foam," p. 170.

[43] "P & G Plans to Withdraw Its Detergents From Miami Area," *Advertising Age*, Vol. 42, December 6, 1971, p. 3.

[44] "Retreat on Phosphates," *Chemical Week*, Vol. 110, January 26, 1972, p. 14.

[45] Richard D. Lyons, "Health Aide Fears Easing of NTA Ban in Detergent Study," *New York Times*, April 9, 1972, p. 48.

[46] *Ibid.*

[47] *Ibid.*

[48] *Ibid.*

[49] "Big Three Choose Chicago for Phosphate Showdown," *Chemical Week*, Vol. 110, June 7, 1972, p. 16.

[50] *Ibid.*, p. 17.

[51] Kathryn Sederberg, "P & G Detergents Exit Chicago as Phosphate Ban Takes Effect," *Advertising Age*, Vol. 43, July 10, 1972, p. 1.

[52] Mark Gerchick, "Chicago Housewives Scurry to Suburbs to Buy Detergents Now Banned in City," *Wall Street Journal*, August 10, 1972, p. 6.

[53] "New Detergent Builders in the Wind," *Chemical Week*, Vol. 111, July 19, 1972, p. 45.

[54] Sederberg, "Exit Chicago," p. 8.

[55] "Procter and Gamble Says It Can Cut Phosphates in Detergents by 50%," *Wall Street Journal*, October 11, 1972, p. 24.

[56] "P & G Brands Are Due as Low, No-Phos Detergents," *Advertising Age*, Vol. 43, October 16, 1972, p. 2.

[57] "P & G Testing Heavy-Duty Era Liquid in Two Markets," *Advertising Age*, Vol. 43, November 20, 1972, p. 1.

[58] Larry Edwards, "P & G's Era Liquid Expands, Sets Off Promotion Battles," *Advertising Age*, January 14, 1974, p. 1.

[59] *Advertising Age*, Vol. 43, December 25, 1972, p. 1.

[60] "Ban on Detergents with Phosphates in Chicago Upset," *Wall Street Journal*, March 7, 1973, p. 12.

[61] "Market Newsletter," *Chemical Week*, Vol. 113, September 12, 1973, p. 32.

[62] Michael Oreskes, "Phosphate Is Making Big Comeback In Detergents as States Ease Ban," *Wall Street Journal*, July 29, 1974, p. 12.

[63] "Ban on Phosphates in Chicago Upheld by the Appeals Court," *Wall Street Journal*, January 17, 1975, p. 3.

[64] "Supreme Court Won't Review Phosphate Ban," *Wall Street Journal*, May 20, 1975, p. 5.

[65] *Ibid.*

[66] "Ban on Detergents with Phosphate," p. 12.

[67] "Supreme Court Won't Review Phosphate Ban," p. 5.

QUESTIONS

1. Discuss the manner in which the phosphate controversy affected the environment in the detergent industry. What factors emerged as dominant forces?
2. Identify and discuss variations in roles played by members of the detergent industry. What appeared to be reasons for the variations?
3. What referent group should Procter & Gamble look to for guidance in the process of defining its social role?
4. What were the key issues generated by the controversy?
5. Do you see evidence of potential role conflict inherent in the controversy?
6. If a cost/benefit study were to be carried out to determine, at least in part, the proper social role of firms in the detergent industry, what factors must be taken into consideration?
7. How would you characterize the management philosophy at Procter & Gamble and the company's perception of a proper social role?
8. If social expectations are used as a basis for a company evaluating its socially responsible behavior, do you see clear-cut social expectations in this case?
9. Discuss the contingency nature of role behavior in this case.
10. It is argued that when sanctions appear, a company will meet those believed to be legitimate. What sanctions, if any, did Procter & Gamble view as legitimate?

CHAPTER 5

PLANT
SHUTDOWN

CASE 3
A PLANT SHUTDOWN

The Olin Corporation is a large multinational company operating in several industries. Until the early 1970s the company operated facilities in Saltville, a small community located in a rural area of Virginia along the North Fork of the Holston River.

Saltville bears close resemblance to the archetypical company town. The company's influence reached far beyond being the town's major employer. The community was highly dependent not only economically on Olin but also politically, educationally, socially, as well as psychologically. The company, at least in the minds of the citizens of Saltville, had become a permanent fixture in the community.

Then quite abruptly the company announced it was going to shut down all its Saltville operations over a period of several months. The impact on the community was traumatic. In some cases families had worked for Olin for several generations. It had become an accepted way of life. Olin's explanation for the shutdown was economic but heavily emphasized the imposition of more rigid pollution standards by the Virginia Water Control Board.

A major concern is the impact of the shutdown on the community and the role of Olin during the shutdown and after its completion. Keith Davis argues that an individual business has responsibilities commensurate with its social powers.[1] Problems arise only because of the complexities involved in putting this concept into practice. On the other hand it may be argued that a business has only very limited responsibilities beyond its primary function of providing products or services at a profit.[2]

FOOTNOTES

[1] Keith Davis, "Can Business Afford to Ignore Social Responsibilities?" *California Management Review*, Spring 1960, p. 71.

[2] *Social Responsibilities of Business Corporations* (New York: Committee for Economic Development, June 1971), pp. 25–34. Lee E. Preston and James E. Post, *Private Management and Public Policy* (Englewood Cliffs, New Jersey: Prentice-Hall, Inc., 1975).

Olin's Pullout from Saltville:
A Company's Responsibility to the Community

Saltville, with a population of about 2500, is located in a beautiful high valley between the Blue Ridge and the Allegheny Mountains, in the southwestern part of Virginia. After years of relative obscurity, Saltville drew national attention in 1970, when Olin Corporation decided to close its local chemical operations and in the process eliminated approximately 800 jobs in a community where it had been the economic mainstay since 1892. The reason for the closing was attributed by the company to its inability to comply with newly enacted water quality standards and still operate the plant at a profit.

While the area around Saltville was known for its brine springs and salt deposits even in colonial times, and although Saltville proudly calls itself "the salt capital of the Confederacy," the town's history actually began in 1892, when Mathieson Alkali Works built its first plant beside the North Fork of the Holston River.[1] Since that time, Saltville has been umbilically tied to the big soda ash plant. Schools, water works, employees' homes, the town bank, the department store on Main Street, even the churches were owned by Mathieson for more than seven decades. Mathieson Alkali Works grew to become Mathieson Chemical Company. In 1954, it merged with Olin to form Olin Mathieson Chemical Corporation; the name was later shortened to Olin Corporation. Olin was a way of life and a means of existence. Saltville had its own municipal government, but "the plant" was the town's chief source of tax revenue. However, after World War II, Mathieson did begin to pursue a less paternalistic course. It sold its company houses to the workers and closed down the company store.[2]

However, the tradition of father-son employment at Olin continued. No one got rich this way, but life was secure, uncomplicated, and reasonably comfortable. For generations, fathers in Saltville simply took their sons down to the plant and taught them their jobs. Thus the pattern of dropping out of school in the early teens and passing on job skills through family developed in the town. This also resulted in a large number of residents without high school diplomas.

The Saltville works had expanded until it comprised a 1000 ton-per-day soda ash plant, a 290-ton-per-day mercury-cell chloralkali plant, a 250 ton-per-day dry ice plant, a large government-owned hydrazine plant, and a rubber-coating facility. Ammonia soda or soda ash was more or less the backbone of the installation, employing directly or indirectly over half the work force. Employment had reached a peak of 1500 in 1960; however, many of the facilities were old and, by today's standards, small and inefficient.[3]

In 1968 Olin embarked on an extensive modernization program in an attempt to increase productivity at the plant. An Olin official noted in 1971 after the changes had been completed that since 1968 production costs at Saltville had risen 35 percent for each unit of chlorine caustic. Employees also have indicated that the modernization somehow just did not pan out. There were no layoffs during this period but as people retired, died, or left for other reasons, they were not replaced. By early 1970, employment had leveled off at about 800 employees. Yet at that level the plant was still pumping $8 million per year into the area in payroll, plus $25 million more for supplies and services.[4]

About this time Olin policymakers invested what was described as millions of dollars in a new branch of the company—aluminum production. At that point, aluminum demand fell off sharply and Olin began to lose money. Officials commented that the company had fallen flat on its corporate face. With financial horizons bleak, Olin decided to tighten its belt. Executives called New York's top stock market people together and told them they were divesting the company of many of its weaker holdings. The next day, Olin stock reportedly began to rise.[5]

New Water Quality Standards

Olin's pollution problems arose primarily from the ammonia soda portion of its operations, which produced large quantities of sodium and calcium chlorides as waste products. The chlorides were not highly toxic but, because of their sheer volume, they created a very undesirable situation in the North Fork of the Holston River.

During the latter part of 1969, the Virginia Water Control Board announced that it would adopt strict water quality standards to conform with the guidelines set by the Federal Environmental Protection Agency. The new standards gradually increased chloride regulations to meet the agency's limit of 500 parts per million (p.p.m.) of chloride effluent as of June 1970. Production methods had met the 5000 p.p.m. standard previously set. However, Olin had to consider what it would do to comply with the new limits, knowing that compliance would require a $2 million expenditure.[6]

This had not been the first confrontation between Olin and the Virginia Water Control Board. In 1946 the board pressed Olin-Mathieson to reduce pollution of the Holston River caused by the Saltville plant. "We realized then that there would probably be no satisfactory solution in the long run," said Alfred Paessler, who has been executive secretary of the board since 1946. He added, "To have a really clean stream, Olin would have to build an evaporation plant to treat 1300 tons of industrial unusable waste (calcium and sodium chlorides) it dumps into the river everyday. It would cost several millions dollars a year to operate an evaporation plant, plus several million to install it. There is no question it can be done technologically. But the cost would probably run them out of business because soda ash is a low-value, high tonnage product. The profit margins just aren't high enough to justify an evaporation plant from the company's point of view." [7]

Since the Water Control Board did not make a final decision in the early 1950s—a decision that would probably have shut the plant down—the company did the only thing possible, according to Paessler. He continued, "We ordered them to parcel waste out to the North Fork so the impact on the main river would be as little as possible." [8]

Later, in 1963, the Saltville plant began using a waste control reservoir, called a sludge pond, to prevent further pollution of the river. Waste from the soda ash process was placed in the reservoir and held until the solids settled to the bottom of the sludge pond. When the water level in the river was high enough to dilute it, the water residue in the sludge pond was poured into the river and allowed to run off. In order to construct the 75-acre reservoir, a community of 60 homes was moved, a section of highway and a cemetery were relocated, and the entire riverbed was changed.

At the time the new standards were publicized, a variety of both opinions and facts about pollution in the Holston River emerged from several sources. Tate Buchanan, the Democratic candidate for Congress from the Saltville district and the former production manager at the plant, felt that the outcry over polluting the Holston River was vastly overstated. He pointed out that fish are living just 500 yards below the dumping point and observed this was the same waste that has been dumped in the river since 1895. He warned that a "helter-skelter approach is going to force the closing of many plants unnecessarily. We need a national commitment to solve pollution." Buchanan warned that a thorough research and development program must be maintained on the federal level. [9]

However, a study downstream revealed that salt deposits from Olin caused nearly $2 million in damages per year to the river. For instance, farmers near Saltville complained that their farm machinery became corroded from fording the river and stock had become ill from drinking the river water. Also, salt was found to flow at least 150 miles down the river. [10]

The North Fork of the Holston River begins at Sharon Springs in Bland County and winds through Saltville, through the rolling southwest Virginia terrain, until it joins the Holston River, near Kingsport, Tennessee. One of the major problems along this route has been the hardness of the water due to salt. It apparently did little harm to anyone in Saltville but industries and residents as far down the river as Knoxville, Tennessee contend that millions of dollars have been spent to soften the water and that discharge from the Saltville plant is the prime cause. [11]

Yet other statements by authorities seem to corroborate Buchanan's position that fish were not harmed by the pollution. Jack Hoffman, chief of the Fish Division of the Virginia Commission of Game and Inland Fisheries, noted that fish were knocked out at the plant but fully recovered by the time the stream reached

Scott County. He indicated in a statement early in July 1969 that the river was still a good smallmouth and rock bass stream. [12]

However, in September 1969, a report was made public that changed this assumption and upset residents along the river and throughout the area. Seventy miles of the river were ordered off limits to fishermen in a joint announcement by the Virginia and Tennessee Game and Fish Commissions. Mercury in extremely high levels had been found in the flesh of fish sampled in the 65 miles of river below the Saltville plant down to the Tennessee state line and for 5.1 miles from the line to the confluence with the South Fork of the Holston River at Rotherwood near Kingsport, Tennessee. Mercury pollution, unlike chloride pollution, is exceedingly toxic. [13]

According to officials at the company, the trend toward rising costs, the failure of the modernization move, and the new more demanding pollution standards in combination, forced Olin to announce in July 1970 that it would phase out the soda ash operation in Saltville. The announcement also indicated that a request was made that this phase out take place over a 2½-year period in order to give employees sufficient time to adjust to the change.

Under state and federal law, Olin could have asked the federal and state governments to reconsider jointly the new standards on grounds that pollution controls must give "consideration to the public interest and the equities of the case" at hand. If turned down on such an administrative review, the law permits an industry to appeal the case to a federal district court. Olin waived these rights and any right to appeal. [14]

This led several residents to argue that the company simply used pollution as an excuse to hide the fact that they were generating little profit from the Saltville plant. "This way the government gets all the blame and the company still has a good image," claims Sandy Price, one of many former employees. [15]

However, two factors were presented to lend credence to the company's claim that increased pollution standards were the principal cause of the shutdown.

First, while not desiring to be quoted on a specific figure, the plant manager, Charles Norris, felt that the complex was making extremely handsome profits prior to the problems in 1970. Furthermore, both Norris and Roger Allison of the *Saltville Progress*, agreed that the Saltville operation had been the "star performer" of the Olin Corporation during the 1960s. Thus, it would not seem that Olin's divestment would have been made had the regulations been less severe.

Finally, it was pointed out by Allison and Norris that extensive modernization had been carried out throughout the 1960s. Sixteen million dollars had been spent in 1968 alone. Olin had seemed to attempt to refurbish the complex and "stick it out." Furthermore, it may be considered unlikely that Olin would turn its back on such a large investment except only in an extremely adverse situation. [16]

This had been the first instance of a company in Virginia ever being forced to halt operations permanently because of water pollution problems.

The First Shutdowns at Saltville

Olin's request to the Virginia Water Control Board for a 2½-year extension in order to ensure an orderly shutdown was supported by the town government and was subsequently granted by the board. This meant an exemption until the end of 1972. Saltville then established an industrial development commission to attract new industry during the coming two years. Virginia Highlands Community College, located between Saltville and Abington, Virginia, established a retraining program to be conducted simultaneously with the shutdown. Also employees began putting away extra savings on the assumption that they would be out of work no earlier than mid-1972.

Added optimism about continued operation of the soda ash plant was generated by the settlement of a new 85 cent three-year contract with the Allied and Technical Workers Union. Regional 20 Director Karl Mowry commented that company spokesmen told the local bargaining committee that the successful results of negotiations would have a major bearing on the decision to continue soda ash operations beyond December 1972.[17]

In mid-June 1971, Olin abruptly announced it would close its soda ash operation at Saltville permanently on July 1, 1971 because its production was overflowing storage capacity even though the plant was operating at minimum output. Apparently as a result of knowledge of the impending shutdown, 16 of the firm's 18 largest customers found new long-term suppliers, and this caused the unexpected inventory buildup. William A. Oppold also noted, "In any continuous process plant, there is a minimum level of production that must be maintained for the process to sustain itself. . . . Right now our silos are full. Even scarce railroad cars are being used to contain the overflow soda ash." [18] The company did announce it would continue production of sodium bicarbonate, carbon dioxide, chlorine caustic, and hydrazine. The company would also continue to operate its rubber-coating facility at Saltville.

As a result of the shutdown on July 1, not only were more than 400 employees out of work but all the planning by the town, state employment experts, the community college, and Saltville families was thrown into confusion.

Other smaller layoffs followed as lesser areas of operation were phased out. Then, on November 18, 1971, the company announced the closing of its chlorine caustic soda plant on March 1, 1972. This shutdown would affect about 260 employees directly since the closing also meant the shutdown of the boiler plant and other supporting facilities. The operation was shut down for two major reasons according to company spokesmen. First, since 1968 production costs had risen 35 percent for each unit of chlorine caustic. Second, a plan to replace the present facility with a diaphragm cell plant was based on a preliminary cost estimate of $9 million, but the engineering contractor later demonstrated the actual cost would be more than $14 million. Thus it was no longer an economically viable project.[19]

Except for some 50 employees retained on a temporary basis to dismantle installations, the only remaining facility still operating by spring 1972 was the hydrazine plant. It employed approximately 100 people and its continued operation depended upon renewal of the government contract, which was to expire during the summer.

Reaction of Saltville to the Shutdown

The closing of the soda ash plant and other facilities at Saltville because of Olin's inability to meet new, more stringent pollution standards not only had a direct impact on approximately 600 jobs but indirectly affected about 3000 area residents. This included other communities in Smyth County such as Chilhowie and Rich Valley as well as people from Washington County located only a few miles from Saltville. The impact of the shutdown was amplified by the one-company status of the Saltville area. The only other industry in Saltville was the Kenrose garment factory established in 1969 and employing about 100 women. Expansion was possible at Kenrose but the company would still employ mainly women.

The magnitude of the shutdown revealed itself in several dimensions during the latter part of 1971 and spring of the following year. The familiar order of life based in large part on two and sometimes three generations of family employment at Olin had given way to unfamiliar anxiety and fright in the town. For instance, the day after the closing of the plant was announced men who had not missed a day's work in years called in sick with severe stomach distress and debilitating headaches.[20] Many families used federal food stamps for meals and, on Main Street, the stores offered 50 percent discounts for cash purchases. At the post office men and women lined up for unemployment checks that, in many cases, would run out shortly.

The town of Saltville was directly affected by the loss of a $6 million-per-year payroll and the county lost almost $192,000 in annual property taxes, most of which were returned to Saltville. The town also lost $15,000 in direct revenue from Olin. Appalachian Power Company lost more than $2 million and the Norfolk and Western Railroad lost around $1,275,000 in annual revenue from the plant, which in turn affected its employment rate.[21]

The closing also had an impact on property values including homes recently purchased from Olin by employees. For instance, a large house costing $16,000 prior to notification of the shutdown was sold afterwards for $7500.[22]

Adding another dimension, the Saltville town council directed its school board to approach Smyth County on the consolidating of Saltville's special school district. The major reasons for the move were the projected declines in enrollment in the Saltville area and uncertainty about the town's ability to furnish financial support.[23]

More precisely, comments from several residents demonstrated the range of reaction to the shutdown:

Harold Puckett, a 21-year Olin veteran, was among the luckier employees. He was assigned to the "rip-out" crew that dismantled the plant and thus was able to work longer than most. But he knew the day was not far away when he would be without a job. "This has hit people the hardest they ever been hit around here," he said. "It's just bad news to everybody. And it's not just the men out of work that's affected, either. This thing gets to the whole family. It even worries the children more than most people realize. I don't know what's gonna happen to us around here now. I just can't see much hope." [24]

"My wife was a lot more tore up about it than I was," said J. B. Price, an Olin foreman who lost his job. "And it wasn't just her. It was the whole town. You could see 'em standin' on the street corners talkin'. You see, despite what the company had said, none of 'em really believed it would ever go down." [25]

It was understandably difficult for a man who had lost, or was losing, his job to feel optimistic about the future of Saltville. Some of them figured the town would dry up and blow away. But many of the citizens not directly affected did not feel that way at all. In fact, the community as a whole exhibited a surprisingly bright outlook.

"When this thing first hit, I think most people felt like it was the end of the earth," said Bob McCoy, principal of Saltville's R. B. Worthy High School (named for a former superintendent of the Saltville plant). "But since then we've had time to take a more objective look at the situation, and we've come to realize this isn't the end. One thing that has helped in this respect is the simple fact that we haven't had a mass exodus of people. Before the shutdown, probably 50 percent of the children enrolled in our schools here were from Olin families. But despite that high proportion, we haven't lost more than 20 to 25 students this year from families moving away." [26]

As McCoy summed it up, "Saltville may be somewhat down, but it is definitely not out. Considering the magnitude of what has happened to the town, morale is very high. Saltville just doesn't look like a place that has lost the backbone of its economy. The streets are still busy. People on the sidewalks are smiling and talkative. Business places still appear to be thriving, and most of the merchants of the town say the shutdown has had surprisingly little effect on their revenues." [27]

"My first thought when I heard about the shutdown was that I'd better sell out and leave Saltville," stated Fred Singleton, owner of Singleton's Department Store. "But then I decided to wait and see what happened. And I'm glad I did. It just hasn't turned out to be as bad as everyone expected. Most of the merchants will tell you they haven't been affected all that much. I know in my business I actually had a slight increase last year." [28]

The optimism of businessmen such as Fred Singleton was shared by Saltville's mayor, W. J. Totten. He maintained that the majority of the people in the community feel the same way. And he presented some evidence to support his belief.

"We had a referendum on a bond issue for a new sewer system a while back," the mayor pointed out. "It passed by a whopping majority. I think that is a very good demonstration that our people still have faith in Saltville. Now I'm not denying that we've been hurt by this thing. Of course we have. But the way I look at it, over the long run, all this may turn out to be a blessing in disguise. I know that never again will our people be as dependent on one individual company as they have been in the past. And it's forced the town to stand on its own feet. We've changed from being strictly a company town and have become a community in our own right. And this was a transition we had to make if we were ever going to get anywhere." [29]

While many people expressed this kind of optimism, many recognized future difficulties. The fact that an estimated 50 percent of the displaced workers had found jobs in the general Saltville area had eased the burden of the shutdown. Those not finding jobs depended on unemployment checks but this source of income has already been exhausted for those caught in the initial layoff. Many businessmen also admit that the full impact of the closing has probably not yet been felt. Most feel the solution will come only through the creation of a large number of jobs.

Actions by the Community

Two organizations took action immediately after the first shutdown to minimize its impact. The Saltville Industrial Development Corporation formed under the auspices of the town's chamber of commerce had previously successfully negotiated the location of a Kenrose Manufacturing Company garment plant in Saltville. It now went to work in a cooperative effort with Olin in a search for other companies interested in locating in the area. Olin also donated land sites for use by companies wishing to move. [30]

Virginia Highlands Community College (VHCC) took seriously its mandate "to respond to the needs of the region"; the coordinator of the college learning laboratory developed a program to help prepare the laid-off workers for new jobs. VHCC convinced the Saltville town council of the merits of the plan and the council made available a 6-month-old, $250,000 building in the center of town. It had initially been built to house Olin's computer center and the company had donated it to Saltville at the time of the shutdown. The Job Preparedness Center opened its doors on July 19, 1971 and operated on a budget funded mainly by a $50,000 grant from Olin and additional funds from federal, state, and local sources. [31]

By the early summer of 1972, 228 students had enrolled, 27 had already earned their high school equivalency certification, and several more were ready to take the tests. Enrollees could also pursue programmed instruction courses in electronics, blueprint reading, fork-lift truck operation, typing, bookkeeping, and accounting. There was also shop craft instruction in welding. Many of these programs were filled and there were waiting lines for future courses. Saltville residents agreed that the center, practical benefits aside, provided a tremendous psychological boost for the unemployed workers. [32]

"When you've worked 20 years at a job," Mrs. Heath, director of instruction and a former Olin employee, pointed out, "it's a real shock not to have anything to do with your day. When the men first come, they're frustrated and bitter. But once they get into a routine again, their mood changes and they become happy again." She added, "You can train people and train them and train them. But if they can't go out then and find a job . . ." [33]

The Hydrazine Shutdown

After the initial shutdowns, the only Olin plant remaining in operation produced hydrazine under contract to the Air Force. The plant employed 125 people and was virtually the sole source of male employment remaining in the town. In early June 1972, the Air Force announced that it planned to close the hydrazine plant at Saltville on June 30 and purchase the fuel from the Lake Charles, Louisiana plant belonging to the Olin Corporation. A speed-up in production was also announced at this time in order to fill the quota of hydrazine ordered by the Air Force from the plant in fiscal year 1971–72 before the closing date. Olin's official position was that "it would be pleased in the interest of the people of Saltville to continue to operate a government-owned hydrazine plant on the basis of a reasonable contract with the Air Force." [34]

The Air Force stated it was closing out the operation for two major reasons. First, less than 10 percent of plant capacity had been utilized over the past two years with no anticipated increases in government hydrazine requirements in the future. Second, the Air Force pointed out that operating charges at Saltville had increased $700,000 per year as a result of the closing of Olin's chlor-alkali operation. [35]

The residents appealed to their elected officials to persuade the Air Force to retain the hydrazine plant in Saltville. United States Senators William B. Spong, Jr. (D-Va) and Harry F. Byrd (Ind-Va), U. S. Representative William C. Wampler (D-Va) and State Representative W. L. Lemmon (D-Va) used their influence to try to convince the Air Force to continue the Saltville operation. In telegrams to the Air Force and Olin on April 11, 1972, Senator Spong said that the shutdown of the soda ash and the chlor-alkali operations had already caused "a severe economic hardship on the community." He further noted, "Continued operation of the hydrazine plant hopefully will enable the community to attract other industries, thereby reducing an unemployment rate that is substantial." [36] Spong asked the Government Accounting Office (GAO) to review the Air Force's plans to close the Saltville plant. The Air Force contended that it would be more economical to close the Saltville plant. [37]

Senator Spong stated, "The Air Force has estimated that it can purchase hydrazine from Olin over the next three years at a price ranging from $1.40 to $1.60 per pound. Actual product cost was estimated by the Air Force to be approximately $1 per pound. The remainder included the cost of amortizing a plant expansion necessary at Lake Charles to accommodate Air Force needs. The cost of the expansion would be underwritten by the Air Force." [38]

The estimated cost per pound at Saltville over the upcoming three years had been figured by the Air Force at $2.84 per pound. [39]

The Senator's office had been informed verbally by representatives of Olin that the company sold hydrazine to commercial customers in 55-gallon drums containing 440 pounds each. Olin's production at Lake Charles was sold exclusively to non-government purchasers. In lots of one to four drums, Olin's price was $3.15 per pound. In lots of five drums or more, the price was $2.95 per pound. Both prices exceeded the estimated price at Saltville. Each price was FOB Lake Charles. In other words, the customer paid transportation costs. Olin also charged a deposit of $125 on each drum shipped from Lake Charles. [40]

Based on these data the Senator stated, "I question how Olin can sell hydrazine to the Air Force at an estimated price so far below its present commercial prices. The GAO should examine this." [41]

He further commented, "The study also indicates that it will cost the Air Force $2 million to install anti-pollution equipment necessary for the Saltville plant to meet Virginia's air and water quality standards. The Air Force figures that $750,000 of that total must be spent for water pollution control measures. However, I have been advised by the Virginia State Water Control Board that there is no water quality problem in the North Fork of the Holston River that is related to the hydrazine plant operation at Saltville. [42]

Despite the efforts of Senator Spong and others, the Air Force moved ahead with its plans and closed its hydrazine operation in Saltville on June 30, 1972. The Olin shutdown was now complete. About 100 men would be temporarily employed to complete the chore of decontaminating the hulks of noiseless machinery and empty buildings.

Olin's Contribution to Saltville

Olin took several steps during the time of the shutdowns to lessen the impact of the closings on individuals laid off and the town of Saltville.

The company had already instituted a generous corporate severance plan for "exempt" employees that provided up to 12 months' full salary. At the time of the closings, Olin voluntarily added another three months' salary to this figure. Similarly, severance pay for hourly workers—an item only recently included in the company union contract after additional negotiations with the union—was increased 50 percent over the previously negotiated amounts. [43]

Many of the employees were eligible for early retirement at age 55 with 20 years' service. Among the hourly employees, 121 of the group laid off at the time of the soda ash closing were immediately eligible. Also, the company and the union negotiated a three-year waiver; that is, if an employee were 52 years old or older, he would be entitled to benefits when he reached 55. According to Olin's Saltville personnel director, Harry Daugherty, basic payments under the early retirement plan amounted to between $50 and $150 per month. However, he pointed out, many workers elected the "social security option," which allowed them to draw almost twice the normal benefits until they reached 62, at which time they were eligible for social security. Practically all the workers also were entitled to unemployment compensation payments of 26 weeks, in addition to any benefits from Olin. Virginia has since extended the eligibility period an additional 13 weeks. [44]

Also at the time of the soda ash shutdown, Olin announced the establishment of relocation assistance service for the affected employees. Under this program, employees were informed of job opportunities in other Olin plants and were encouraged to transfer to fill these openings. The company announced that every Olin chemical plant would be prohibited from hiring outside employees until it established that openings could not be reasonably filled from Saltville.[45]

The last major decision that Olin had to make with respect to its Saltville holdings was what to do with the plant, property, and equipment after the operation had closed. The company had made several attempts in a cooperative effort with the town's Industrial Development Corporation to attract new industry to the area. According to Olin Vice President William A. Oppold in late 1971, "For more than a year, Olin has been trying to interest a number of companies in selecting Saltville as a site for new industry. Some companies have visited the area and studied its possibilities, but we know of no decisions yet to locate any new plant here. Efforts are continuing to interest other companies in the area." [46]

In late December 1972, Olin approached the town of Saltville with an offer to donate the plant, 3500 acres of property with mineral rights, and all remaining tangible personal property to the town. The company pointed out that the assets would further assist the community to attract industry to the area. The company also recognized that the transfer would eliminate the requirement to pay property taxes for another year.[47] All Olin asked was that it be given use of the buildings while completing its abandonment activities. This appeared to be a generous offer, but town officials pointed out that unless sufficient funds were available to hire experts to plan, develop, and rehabilitate the property, the donation would be of little real value. Therefore, at a cost of $30,000, Olin contracted the Boeing Aerospace Corporation to mark all of the equipment in the plant, and indicate to the town its use and probable market value.[48]

Accompanying this gift the Olin Corporation also contributed a $600,000 grant to the total package, which the town graciously accepted. The town attorney Jack White explained that $150,000 was to compensate the town for lost tax revenue over the next three years, and the remaining $450,000 would be used for planning, developing, and rehabilitating purposes over the next four years. The company required that a separate bank account be set up to handle the money and that a report be sent to Olin regarding use of the funds.[49]

The loss incurred in donating the property to the town was expected to be offset by "massive" tax write-offs. No one outside Olin was speculating on any figures, but one of the top mineral appraisers in the nation was called into the area by the company. Olin executives were understandably ready to fight the government to the wall for every nickel possible.[50]

According to Town Manager Henry Tuggle, only about 140 of the 3500 acres of land given to Saltville by Olin would be suitable as sites for location of new industry. Most of the land donated to the town was rolling hills suitable only for grazing land. The mineral rights, according to Olin officials, were no longer of value to the company.[51]

The town has not yet decided what to do with the plant itself. The hope, of course, is that new industry can be attracted to the area and, in that event, the plant and/or its facilities could be returned to use.

Olin management was reluctant to give information regarding the total value of the plant and all gifts to the town. But, it is worthwhile to note a comment made by an unidentified Olin official, "Saltville could be the richest town in Virginia if only it had proper town management of the assets donated to it by Olin." [52]

Pan-O-Rama

After the outrage and hopelessness that accompanied the end of the Olin era in Saltville decreased to a degree, the town began to examine alternatives to attracting outside industry. The gifts from Olin coupled with actions by the Industrial Development Corporation might eventually prove successful but the attraction of other companies to the area was taking considerable time. Many felt the survival of Saltville was at stake. Out of this realization grew the non-profit organization called Pan-O-Rama Incorporated. It represented one attempt to replace Olin with a new industry capable of providing employment, replenishing the tax base, and shoring up the local economy. The organization was made of citizens of the Saltville-Rich Valley area and was concerned with promoting the area through tourism. One of the natural advantages prompting members of the organization to opt for tourism was the discovery that approximately 150,000 people visit several state parks in close proximity to Saltville during the summer months. [53]

The organization's first attempt involved an expanded three-month program carried out during the summer of 1972. Activities during the summer covered the spectrum. The community exploited both its human and natural assets. Activities during summer weekends included such diverse events as slide presentations, tours of community historical sites, a circus, a "goat sacking" contest, a variety of theatrical entertainment, golf tournaments, horse shows, square dances, wrestling matches, fiddler conventions, a gun and coin show, and a real wagon train display.

Conclusions

The town of Saltville, Virginia has undergone a period of major upheaval and the final results are still not clear. Yet some footnotes are worth presenting.

About 400 of the Olin Corporation employees laid off during the first series of shutdowns during 1971 have found jobs, according to the industrial development coordinator at the Saltville Job Preparedness Center. However, about 30 percent of these workers are underemployed. [54]

Hardly 10 miles away in Chilhowie, the American Furniture Company of Martinsville, Virginia planned to employ 300 persons by the middle of 1973. This was accomplished, but the plant was shut down when demand fell off in 1974. The plant has since reopened and the company plans total employment of 275 by mid-1977. With the employment of approximately 300 at the American Furniture operation in Marion, Virginia, employment could reach 600 by the end of 1977.

FOOTNOTES

[1] Ward Worthy, "Saltville Rallies after Olin Shutdown," *Chemical and Engineering News*, March 13, 1972, p. 7.

[2] Carl Bernstein, "Saltville Tastes the Bitterness of Unemployment," *The Washington Post—Panorama*, November 4, 1971, p. Fl.

[3] Worthy, "Saltville Rallies," p. 7.

[4] *Ibid.*, pp. 7–8.

[5] John Doty, "Olin Gift Big Transfusion," *Bristol Herald Courier*, January 7, 1973, p. 131.

[6] Bernstein, "Saltville Tastes the Bitterness," p. F6.

[7] *Ibid.*

[8] *Ibid.*

[9] "Ecology-Crisis in Saltville," *District Fifty News*, August 10, 1970, p. 6.

[10] Wallace Coffey, "Olin: Meeting New Regulations Not Feasible," *Bristol Herald Courier*, July 7, 1970, p. 2.

[11] Jay Fields, "No Panic in Saltville," *Bristol Herald Courier*, July 22, 1970, p. 1.

[12] Coffey, "Olin: Meeting New Regulations," p. 2.

[13] *Ibid.*

[14] Bernstein, "Saltville Tastes the Bitterness," p. F6.

[15] *Ibid.*

[16] Interviews with Charles Norris, plant manager, Olin Corporation and Roger Allison of the *Saltville Progress*, Saltville, Virginia, November 16, 1973.

[17] "Saltville to Remain in Full Operation through 1972," *District Fifty News*, January 1971, p. 1.

[18] *Ibid.*

[19] "Olin Corporation Announces Shutdown by March," *Saltville Progress*, November 25, 1971, p. 4.

[20] Bernstein, "Saltville Tastes the Bitterness," p. Fl.

[21] Stan Benjamin, "It Hurts to be An Environmental Casualty," *Cleveland Daily Banner*, August 21, 1972, p. 10.

[22] *Ibid.*

[23] "Saltville Suggests Joint Schools," *Bristol Herald Courier*, December 16, 1971, p. 11-A.

[24] "Saltville: Caught in the Cleanup," *Tennessee Valley Perspective*, Summer 1972, p. 8.

[25] *Ibid.*, p. 6.

[26] *Ibid.*, p. 8.

[27] *Ibid.*

[28] *Ibid.*

[29] *Ibid.*, p. 9.

[30] *Ibid.*

[31] Worthy, "Saltville Rallies," p. 8.

[32] *Ibid.*

[33] *Ibid.*, p. 9.

[34] "Olin Would Be Pleased to Continue Hydrazine Operation," *Senator Spong Reports*, April 27, 1972.

[35] "GAO Will Review Plan to Close Saltville Plant," *Bristol Herald Courier*, June 4, 1972, p. B1.

[36] William B. Spong, telegram sent to John Senske, president of Chemicals Group, Olin Corporation, April 17, 1972.

[37] "Hydrazine Plant to Close Despite Efforts of Spong," *Saltville Progress*, June 15, 1972, p. 2.

[38] "GAO Will Review Plan to Close Saltville Plant," p. B1.

[39] *Ibid.*

[40] *Ibid.*

[41] *Ibid.*

[42] *Ibid.*

[43] Worthy, "Saltville Rallies," p. 8.

[44] *Ibid.*

[45] "Olin Corporation Announces Shutdown By March," p. 4.

[46] *Ibid.*

[47] Benjamin, "It Hurts," p. 10.

[48] Interview with Charles Norris, plant manager, Olin Corporation, Saltville, Virginia, November 16, 1973.

[49] John Doty, "Town Officials Hear Details," *Bristol Herald Courier*, December 28, 1972, p. 3.

[50] Doty, "Olin Gift Big Transfusion," p. B1.

[51] Mitchell Sandos, "Former Olin Property Toured By Newsmen," *Smyth County News*, January 4, 1973, p. 1.

[52] Interviews with Olin Corporation official, Saltville, Virginia, November 16, 1973.

[53] Paul Dellinger, "Saltville Trying Diversity, Development of Tourist Trade," *The Roanoke Times*, June 11, 1972, p. B-3.

[54] David Page, "Most Former Olin Workers Employed," *Bristol Herald Courier*, July 20, 1972, p. 1.

QUESTIONS

1. What factors appeared to shape Saltville's expectations of Olin's proper social role?
2. What appear to be Saltville's perceptions of underlying reasons for the shutdowns?
3. Did Olin have a responsibility to Saltville resulting from the shutdown?
4. How successful was the coping strategy invoked by Olin? From the perspective of the community? From the perspective of Olin?
5. What appear to be the policy reasons for the actions taken by Olin regarding Saltville during and after the shutdowns.
6. Olin's shutdown has social and political implications for Saltville as well as economic. Discuss the nature of these factors.
7. Did Olin have an alternative to shutting down its Saltville plants based on the information in the case?
8. What response should government (state and/or federal) make in such cases?

CHAPTER 6

COMMUNITY
AND
PUBLIC
SAFETY

CASE 4
A QUESTION OF RESPONSIBILITY

Classical economic thought portrayed the businessman as a profit maximizer. Under such conditions, the businessman by pursuing self-interest, also promoted the public good. Today the marketplace remains the principal means of promoting business and the public's interests, in part, because it has proven over time to be an efficient allocator of economic resources. However, government intervention has also become increasingly necessary to regulate conditions of competition as well as to guide economic activity toward public objectives as defined by the political process.

There is widespread recognition today among managers that corporate self-interest is inextricably tied to the well-being of society. It is also understood that the corporation is dependent on the goodwill of society, which can sustain or impair its existence through public pressure and government. It is further understood that essential resources and the goodwill of society are not naturally forthcoming to corporations. This understanding is the basis for the doctrine that it is in the "enlightened self-interest" of the corporation to promote the public welfare.

Often, a large corporation operating in several markets characterized by less-than-perfect competition, maintains a value system close to the austere model previously discussed. This view of social responsibility argues for behavior that leads to maximum profit to foster both the welfare of the owners of the corporation and the public good. Top management at the Pittston Company expressed values very similar to the austere model. Furthermore, managers appeared to experience little role strain despite the fact that this view of limited responsibility contributed to a major disaster for which the company then denied responsibility in the face of contrary conclusions arrived at by several investigations.

The Disaster at Buffalo Creek:
A Question of Responsibility for Survival

At 8:01 A.M., Saturday, February 26, 1972, a coal mine waste dam collapsed at the head of Buffalo Hollow in Logan County, West Virginia. The dam was built on company property of waste materials from coal mines owned by the Buffalo Mining Company, a subsidiary of the Pittston Company of New York City. A twenty-foot wall of water came crashing down the 17-mile-long hollow with a force equal to nearly a two-minute flow from Niagara Falls. Nothing could stand in its path. In its wake were left 125 dead and more than 1000 homes destroyed or damaged. Damages were estimated to exceed $50 million.[1]

Black Water and the Dam

In 1953, the state of West Virginia brought under its water pollution control program what people called "black water"—the discharge from preparation plants where coal is washed before shipping. The new, stricter conservation laws made it necessary for coal companies to cease dumping waste water from these plants into West Virginia streams. Water recycling systems cost from $0.5 million to $1 million.[2] A search by the coal companies for the "least expensive" method of treating the waste water turned up the idea of using mine waste or "gob"—fine coal, shale, clay, and mine rubbish—to build porous retaining dams. The sludge would settle behind the dam and the water would be clarified as it seeped through the porous structure. West Virginia's Governor Arch Moore would comment after the disaster that it seemed that such a dam provided a logical and constructive use.[3]

Along one side of the upper end of Buffalo Hollow was a gob pile 200 feet high and 1500 feet long, which had accumulated from 25 years of steady dumping by three different coal companies. Such gob piles ignite spontaneously and burn deep within the pile. These mounds also emit sulphur dioxide fumes which frequently cause illness among members of the coal mining communities.[4] The Lorado Coal Company started the dump in 1947 and continued dumping until it was bought out by the Buffalo Mining Company in 1964. The continued dumping by Buffalo Mining finally forced the residents of Middle Fork Hollow at the head of Buffalo Creek to move out.

The Buffalo Mining Company inherited two major problems from Lorado Coal Company. First, along with the mine, it acquired great quantities of waste water. Second, the company had to abide by state anti-pollution laws that prevented draining the black waste water into Buffalo Creek. At this time, the gob settling and filtration dam seemed feasible. Also, it appeared expedient to extend the existing gob pile across the mouth of the hollow in order to form such a dam. In 1966, because the impoundment was filled with sludge, a second dam was built farther up Middle Fork.

Meanwhile, in October 1966, in Aberfam, Wales, a major disaster occurred when a large hillside coal-refuse bank gave way, burying Aberfam schoolhouse and killing 144 children and adults.[5] As a direct result of this incident, the United States Department of the Interior, under Secretary Stewart Udall, had similar refuse dumps in the Appalachian coal fields inspected. Thirty-eight structures were inspected in West Virginia. Thirty were found to be unstable and four of them were judged to be critically dangerous. Buffalo Mining's dam No. 2 was inspected and found to be basically stable, although it "could be overtopped and breached" causing minor damage.[6]

As a result of these inspections in March 1967, Secretary Udall sent letters to all applicable government agencies, all West Virginia congressmen, and Governor Hulett Smith. The letter stated, "The Bureau of Mines will continue to observe mine dumps for possible critical conditions, and will receive counsel from the Geological Survey where unstable conditions that might endanger life are recognized."[7]

A few months later, in 1967, water from melting snow did in fact overtop both dams on Middle Fork, flooding yards and causing minor property damage in the town of Saunders. Residents, at that time, recalled a similar break the year before in a slag pile in Proctor Hollow, another offshoot of Buffalo Creek.[8] Mrs. Pearl Woodrum, a Buffalo Hollow resident, wrote a letter to Governor Smith warning of the dangerous situation and pleading for something to be done.

In 1968, Governor Smith received a second letter from Mrs. Woodrum attacking the dam in no uncertain terms. She wrote:

> Dear Sir, I live 3 miles above Lorado. I'm writing you about a big dam of water above us. The coal company has dumped a big pile of slate about 4 or 5 hundred feet high. The water behind it is about 400 feet high and it is like a river. It is endangering our homes and lives. There are over 20 families here and they own their homes. Please send someone here to see the water and see how dangerous it is. Everytime it rains it scares everyone to death. We are all afraid we will be washed away and drowned. They just keep dumping slate and slush in the water and making it more dangerous every day. Please let me hear from you at once and please for God's sake have the dump and water destroyed. Our lives are in danger.[9]

The West Virginia State Water Pollution Control Agency and the West Virginia Public Service Commission inspected the dam along with Steve Dasovich, the vice president and general foreman of Buffalo Mining. The above commission is required to license dams for construction after a thorough review of their design. In inter-agency letters and memoranda, it was acknowledged that the structure might slip and that the company had never sought the required license for building such a structure.[10] The Logan County prosecutor was made aware of the situation, but after the disaster on February 26, he insisted that the file on Buffalo Mining was sent "just for the record" and "that all they had done was pass the buck back and forth. They weren't interested in cracking down on Buffalo Mining—not by a long shot."[11]

The Pittston Company and the New Dam

By 1968, the pool behind the second dam was full, and Buffalo Mining decided to move farther up the hollow and build a dam big enough to hold all the water that would ever be required. The base of the structure was placed on the sludge and debris of the second dam. As with the first and second dams, it was a loose mixture of shale and low-grade coal irregularly compacted by a bulldozer, and again was built without state license.[12] In June 1970, at the time the dam was about one-half its eventual size, Buffalo Mining was sold to the Pittston Company, the fourth largest coal producer in the United States.

The Pittston Company is a conglomerate concentrating on the coal mining and oil distribution industries. The company, in 1971, operated 76 mines, eight at Buffalo Creek; owned an armored car protection service; operated a trucking company; and claimed to own more warehouse space than any other company in the world. The board of directors included Thurston Morton, former senator from Kentucky, former Republican national chairman, and brother to Rogers Morton, Secretary of Interior. The Department of Interior has jurisdiction over the Bureau of Mines.[13]

The philosophy of Pittston toward its subsidiaries, now including Buffalo Mining, was to provide as much independence as possible, with only the major decisions being made at the New York headquarters.

In early 1971, a front portion of the dam sloughed off, yet the company continued to dump refuse. During the same year, a water inspector continually noted in written reports to the company that the dam lacked an emergency spillway. Nothing was done.

In May 1971, the U. S. Bureau of Mines promulgated regulations effective July 1 under the 1969 Federal Coal Mine Health and Safety Act. "Refuse piles shall not be constructed so as to impede drainage or impound water," the regulations stated. "If failure of a water or silt retaining dam will create a hazard, it shall be of substantial construction and shall be inspected at least once a week." Inspection, however, was left up to the company.[14]

When completed, the dam stood approximately 60 feet high at the center of the hollow, was about 550 feet long, and about 400 feet thick. Sludge settled about 20 feet thick on the bottom and some 30 feet of water backed 1½ miles up the hollow stood above that. This amount of water was estimated at approximately 130 million gallons. This left ten feet of gob above the water level in normal times. No one seemed to think the dam would break and no warning system was installed.[15]

The Community and the Disaster

Before the flood, there were about 5000 people living in Buffalo Hollow along Buffalo Creek. The community was made up of 14 small towns. At the head of the hollow, just below the dam where three forks of Buffalo Creek converge, was the first small settlement of Three Forks. The other towns were Saunders, Pardee,

Lorado, Craneco, Lundale, Stowe, Crites, Latrobe, Robinette, Amherstdale, Brae-holm, Accoville, Crown, and Kestler. Buffalo Creek then flows by the town of Man and into the Guzandotte River. These small towns were not made up of company shacks normally associated with coal camps. Prospects for the coal industry looked good. In 1970, the industry had had its best year since 1947. Wages were high, and the Coal Mine Health and Safety Act of 1969 had successfully reduced accidents. [16] The houses and possessions of workers living along Buffalo Hollow reflected the better conditions.

This was newly acquired wealth, and the miners had not forgotten their childhood days in the coal fields. Such memories not only reminded miners of recent economic hard times, but also that they continued to work in the industry with the worst safety record in the United States. [17] In its 100-year history, coal mining had claimed 100,000 lives, and since 1930, there had been more than 1.5 million serious injuries. In addition, they now knew they faced an even more dangerous threat to their health—pneumoconiosis, or black lung. Anyone working underground for more than 10 years was almost certain to get it. [18]

Miners along Buffalo Creek not only lived in fear of a mine disaster, but also they and their families were constantly aware of the danger of the dam. It had been described by residents of the hollow as "a cocked pistol." [19] Many remembered the partial failure of dam No. 2 and during rainy weather, had spent entire nights on hillsides in tents or lean-tos for fear that the dam would collapse.

Mrs. Maxine Adkins was one who remembered the partial failure of dam No. 2. The night before the February 26 disaster had been the third day of rain, and flash flood warnings had been posted. During the three days, 3.7 inches had fallen, which might be expected on the average every two or three years. As a result of the rain, Mrs. Adkins and several others from Three Forks started to evacuate to the Lorado schoolhouse. Several men who had been up to the dam the night before watching the water creep to within a foot of the top went door to door pleading with friends and neighbors to leave. Many had received similar warnings in past years when nothing happened and, therefore, decided to stay. About 3:00 A.M., Mrs. Adkins phoned the sheriff's office to inform him of the situation. Jack Kent, superintendent of Buffalo Mining, called Steve Dasovich, his vice president and general foreman, to warn him of the possible danger. [20]

Sheriff Grimmett dispatched two deputies to alert the residents of the hollow and Dasovich went to inspect the dam himself. About 6:30 A.M., Dasovich met the two deputies at Lorado after visiting the dam and allegedly informed them that ". . . they had ditched around the heap and everything would be all right now." [21] One deputy went home and the other stayed on half-heartedly warning people. Dasovich maintained afterward that he had merely announced plans to ditch around the dam. Before the Senate labor subcommittee hearings after the disaster one deputy said, "I think myself and the other deputy and people there could have got everybody out." [22]

On the morning of February 26, 1972, at 8:01 A.M., the dam was breached and collapsed. Subsequent engineering studies revealed that during the night the dam became saturated and the particles of gob grew buoyant as the water climbed up its slope. The dam quite literally turned to slush and began to ooze forward, allowing the 132 million gallons of water to merge over the top, mingling with the sludge. The mass swept through the two lower dams, causing explosions in the smoldering bottom one, and crashed down on Saunders, destroying every dwelling. It picked up cars, trees, people, and even homes with whole familes clinging to them. Careening from side to side through the valley, the black mass skirted whole communities and leveled others. Had the flood come earlier, even more people would have died. But most were awake, and many saw the huge wave in time to run for the hills. It took the wave three hours to travel the seventeen miles to Man.[23]

A Department of Interior study showed 507 homes destroyed, 273 homes sustained major damage, 663 homes suffered minor damage, 30 trailers destroyed, 600 automobiles damaged or destroyed, at least 30 business establishments destroyed, 1000 injuries, and 125 deaths with 7 bodies unrecovered.[24] Four thousand persons were left homeless.[25] Seven million dollars in federal relief funds and $5.4 million in loans were made available to aid the flood victims.[26]

Interior Secretary Rogers Morton issued a press release saying that his department, which includes the Bureau of Mines, lacked the authority "to order the elimination of damages to public health and safety" posed by coal-refuse piles. The state investigative committee, however, would later conclude: "The U. S. Bureau of Mines indirectly has authority to prevent dams to be constructed from refuse piles."[27]

First Reactions to the Disaster

On February 29, a Pittston Company lawyer, Robert Reineke, stated that there was "potentially a great liability," and that the dam served a "functional" purpose— "to filter acid and fine coal and to back up the water." Ben Tudor, a general superintendent at Buffalo Mining, made the statement that "They were afraid of killing the trout. It was either the trout or the people, now they're both gone."[28] Yet, the most controversial statement was made by a Pittston Company official in New York. He was quoted as saying, "It was an act of God; the impoundment was incapable of holding the water which God poured into it."[29]

Not unexpectedly, the people of Buffalo Hollow reacted angrily. It appeared a direct affront to their deep religious feeling. "They're trying to blame it on God" was heard throughout the hollow.[30] Perhaps Mrs. Carl Taylor, a Buffalo Creek survivor, voiced the general consensus when she said, "You can blame the Almighty, all right—the almighty dollar."[31] Anger and bitterness increased. Many began to feel as did survivor Wager Hatfield, "They [the company] killed them people, just the same as if they'd shot 'em. It was pure murder, that's all it was."[32] Others began to question as did James and Tilda Miller, "They'd been watching that dam since midnight. They knew it was in trouble all the time. If they'd just leveled with us, I don't think anyone would have had to die."[33]

Ten days after the disaster Pittston's New York spokesmen were still claiming they didn't know who was in charge of the West Virginia operations. Their own explanation was "we let them run their own show." [34] Except for their initial statements and the preceding one, Pittston remained silent for two weeks following the flood.

On February 28, 1972, the Bureau of Mines chief coal mine health and safety enforcer, Donald P. Schlich, denied the bureau's responsibility by saying, "If it was a mine refuse pile, I think we might have jurisdiction, but if it was a dam, per se, I guess we don't" and disclaimed a responsibility for inspection since ". . . the question, as far as enforcement goes, now is whether anyone could have known it was a hazard until Saturday." [35] Assistant Secretary of Interior Hollis M. Dole reiterated this statement on March 16 and attributed the flood to heavy rainfall. [36]

Actions by the Pittston Company

On March 9, Pittston's headquarters in New York issued a statement to its company stockholders stating the company's sympathy to the families who had suffered loss and Pittston's efforts in making machinery and men available in the rescue operation. [37]

About a month after the flood, Pittston, carefully denying liability for the flood damages, nonetheless opened up two claims offices and announced plans to settle with survivors. This created another ordeal for the flood victims. For weeks they had queued up at various offices to get emergency loans, housing, unemployment benefits, medical help, welfare assistance, legal advice, and charity. Now Pittston was requiring receipts and proof of the date of purchase of all items being claimed. [38]

The immediate settlement had obvious advantages for the company. Dazed by their losses and eager for compensation, many filed claims without a thorough accounting of all that was gone. Not aware of the law, many did not place claims for all their losses, including physical and mental injuries. Most could not afford the two or three years it would take to sue and did not trust local lawyers, most of whom worked for coal companies. Finally, filing claims was arduous, for it often required three or four trips to the claims office to argue the worth of a house, a livingroom suite, a son's life. [39] Most people settled for the $10,000 maximum allowable penalty under West Virginia law for "wrongful" death. [40]

In a statement filed with the Securities and Exchange Commission on March 31, Pittston reported that while total claims could be substantial, it believed ". . . that ultimate effects of such claims should not be material in relation to its consolidated financial position." [41]

A $52 million damage suit was entered on behalf of more than 400 persons by the Washington, D.C. law firm of Arnold and Porter against Pittston; and the Clarksburg, West Virginia law firm of Steptoe and Johnson sought an injunction against Pittston to "prevent similar circumstances from occurring." [42] Nicholas Camicia, president of Pittston, referred to the lawsuit as "a nuisance" that would "take a lot of my time." [43]

On May 3, 1972, in Richmond, Virginia, Pittston had its annual stockholder's meeting, its first since the disaster. Forty-five bitter Buffalo Creek survivors boarded a chartered bus to take their grievances about claims handling before the meeting personally. They arrived the morning of the meeting but were barred from attendance. However, Pittston could not insulate the meeting from the events at Buffalo Creek. A month before the annual meeting, the New York based Field Foundation, which grants about $3 million annually to a wide range of social projects, several in Appalachia, discovered among its holdings 1000 shares of Pittston stock. Representatives of the Foundation came to the meeting and urged that something be done about the disaster. Field president Morris Abram explained, "As a participant in the total society [the Foundation does not want] to receive income from its investments and to spend the same income in allocating grants to redress the social distress attributable to that business investment. Moreover, the Field Foundation firmly believes that, in the long run, the safety of its investment in Pittston or any other company depends on the compatibility of that company's operation with the welfare of its workers and the conservation of the environment." [44]

Abram then proposed that the company submit a report on claim settlements by June 20, set up a citizens' committee to report on similar hazards at Pittston operations, and give ". . . forceful leadership in obtaining industry-allied attention to these problems." [45] The proposal was defeated by a vote of 12,000,000 shares to 1171 shares. [46] Camicia feared such a move would drive up the price of coal and disturb foreign markets. [47] Mr. Abram then amended his resolution to "urge" instead of "require" management action and it was adopted. [48]

Finally recognizing that the waiting West Virginians could no longer be ignored, Camicia agreed to meet with a delegation of seven. Camicia, the son of a coal miner, was raised in McDowell County, one county below Buffalo Creek. During the meeting he gave the delegation assurances that their claims would be promptly handled. One leader stated, "I'm satisfied Nick is going to do what he said. We have faith in the company." To reporters Camicia remarked: "I was born and raised in this very area. . . . These are my people. I assured them that our policy is to make restitution and to expedite the claims as rapidly as possible." [49]

Yet by early June, many victims hadn't received settlements or were dissatisfied with Pittston's offers. Thus, 3000 men staged a week-long strike protesting claims settlements and vowing to shut down all the company's mining subsidiaries if they were not paid back wages for the time lost because of the flood. The strike proved futile and the men returned to work. [50]

Investigations of the Disaster

The Department of Interior launched a full-scale investigation into the disaster. A joint task force, prepared by the U. S. Geological Survey and the U. S. Bureau of Mines, and composed of 22 technicians, was sent to Buffalo Creek to do a "flood profile" on the entire valley. This investigation determined that the flood could not be blamed on the weather and that basic engineering was apparently nonexistent. [51] Five causes of the failure were generally agreed upon. First, the dam was not constructed or designed to hold the potential amount of water that it could impound. Second, water level controls, such as spillways, were not included in the dam. Third, the dam was built on an inadequate foundation. Fourth, without engineered compaction of the gob, the structure thickness (400 feet) compared to its height (60 feet) led to the dam's reduced stability. Fifth, the dam was constructed of materials high in water soluble sulfates. The material was noncohesive and would not compact uniformly. The task force concluded that a safe economical dam could not be constructed from such materials alone.[52]

The Department of Interior commissioned Fred C. Walker, a civil engineer at Interior's Bureau of Reclamation, to perform another study into the cause of the dam failure. Walker's results coincided with those of the first study, but he further suspected ". . . that there was promotion of pollution control practices without a thorough evaluation of the side effects of the procedures adopted that produced these conditions, and it must share some of the responsibility for this disaster."[53]

On March 8, 1972, the U. S. Senate Labor Committee began an investigation. Harrison Williams, chairman of the Senate Labor Subcommittee, noted that Pittston had been cited more than any other company for violations of the Federal Coal Mining Health and Safety Act—5000 times carrying possible penalties of $1.1 million.[54] By appealing every fine as far as possible, Pittston had paid less than $300 in penalties.[55] Camicia, president of the company, responded that he was not aware of the situation, but that appeals were being filed to test the constitutionality of the Safety Act.[56]

The Army Corps of Engineers performed an in-depth analysis of the flood similar to that prepared by the Department of Interior's task force. Much the same conclusions were drawn. The report stated no other dams were observed in the area with conditions identical to those of the dam that failed. The others were ". . . significantly different—with better foundation conditions and generally better in method of construction."[57]

The state of West Virginia began its own investigation on March 2. Viewed by many as little more than a "whitewash," the nine member ad hoc commission surprisingly made some hard-nosed recommendations and conclusions. Pittston was blamed for the disaster. The commissioners called it, "flagrant disregard . . . for the safety of persons living on Buffalo Creek. . . . This attitude seems to be prevalent throughout much of the coal industry."[58] They also suggested that a Grand Jury probe be initiated to determine whether or not criminal charges should be brought against officials of Buffalo Mining and Pittston.[59]

The Logan County Grand Jury met in November. After three days of hearings, in which 30 witnesses were called, the Grand Jury concluded there had been no criminal law violations in the collapse of the dam.[60]

Two federal laws were violated: Interior regulation 77.200, which requires all mine structures to be in "good repair," and 77.216, which requires all hazardous conditions to be inspected by the company once per week.[61]

Now blame became the chief focus. West Virginia climatologist Robert Weedfall stated that, "If there'd been no dam, there'd have been no flood. It was not a naturally occurring flood." [62] The Army Corps of Engineers blamed the disaster on the failure of federal, state, and company officials to perform their legal responsibilities. [63] U. S. Geological Survey Geologist William Davies blamed the structure's failure in part on a last-minute alteration in the dam in an effort to increase its stability. [64] The Department of Interior's task force and the West Virginia ad hoc commission found many things other than the weather to be at fault; the only slag dam to fail in West Virginia—including others on Buffalo Creek—was Pittston's structure. [65] Many Pittston officials never ceased to assert that the weather caused the failure. [66]

Aftermath

Rebuilding got off to a slow start. Initially, some homes were condemned so that Highway 99 could be widened up to the hollow. Many felt its purpose was to service coal trucks and strip-mining operations. It seemed as though now that 100 percent federal disaster funding was available, plans for the highway formulated ten years ago were being dusted off. [67] However, by August, 483 mobile homes housing 633 people rent free for one year had been moved into the hollow by the federal government. [68]

Yet, social strategists have further complicated the hollow's future. They put forth a master plan for three "nodes" or subdevelopments of diversified housing in the $12,000 to $20,000 range, which was more than most people felt they could afford. Such concentrated housing, with no aid for private efforts, would leave the residents' property valueless. [69]

During the months following the disaster, the Pittston board of directors seemed preoccupied with the company's economic prospects. Apart from the flood, 1972 was a bad year. By October, net income was only $18.2 million compared with $34.9 million for the same period in 1971. Camicia and board chairman Joseph Routh blamed strip-mining restrictions and costly health and safety regulations, not the Buffalo Creek claims against which the company was insured. [70] Also in June 1972, the Price Commission accused Pittston of violating profit-margin guidelines and ordered them to reduce prices. [71]

For only a brief time, anger could be detected at Buffalo Creek. The mood soon changed to depression and uncertainty. A psychiatrist with the county mental health agency observed there exists "an extremely, almost paranoid, delusion of fear every time it begins to rain, especially with children." There are also guilt feelings among those who lived while so many died. Cases of extreme headaches, body aches, and hypochondria are common. A dozen elderly people, in whom the symptoms constituted acute neurosis, have been sent to a state mental hospital. [72]

FOOTNOTES

[1] Tom Nugent, *Death at Buffalo Creek*, (W. W. Norton and Company, Inc.: New York, 1973), p. 63.

[2] "After the Dam Broke, Cries for Controls," *Business Week*, March 11, 1972, p. 38.

[3] Ben A. Franklin, "Blame for Flood Is Hard to Fix," *New York Times*, February 28, 1972, p. 22.

[4] "Letter to the editor from Dr. I. E. Buff," *New York Times*, March 7, 1972, p. 38.

[5] Nugent, *Death at Buffalo Creek*, p. 33.

[6] *Ibid.*

[7] "After the Dam Broke, Cries for Controls," p. 38.

[8] Mary Walton, "After the Flood," *Harper's Magazine*, March 1973, p. 80.

[9] *Ibid.*

[10] *Ibid.*

[11] Nugent, *Death at Buffalo Creek*, p. 33.

[12] Walton, "After the Flood," p. 80.

[13] Nugent, *Death at Buffalo Creek*, p. 29.

[14] Walton, "After the Flood," p. 82.

[15] Nugent, *Death at Buffalo Creek*, pp. 28–29, 31.

[16] *Ibid.*, p. 35.

[17] *Ibid.*, p. 25.

[18] *Ibid.*

[19] Ben A. Franklin, "U.S. Warned West Virginia in 1967 that 30 Coal Waste Piles Were Unstable," *New York Times*, March 1, 1972.

[20] Nugent, *Death at Buffalo Creek*, p. 49.

[21] Franklin, "Blame for Flood Is Hard to Fix," p. 22.

[22] Walton, "After the Flood," p. 82.

[23] *Ibid.*

[24] Nugent, *Death at Buffalo Creek*, p. 146.

[25] *Ibid.*, p. 63.

[26] Harry M. Caudill, "Buffalo Creek Aftermath," *Saturday Review*, August 26, 1972, p. 16.

[27] Walton, "After the Flood," pp. 82–83.

[28] George Vecsey, "Homeless Thousands Await Future in Flooded Valley," *New York Times*, February 29, 1972, p. 1.

[29] Jack H. Morris, "After the Deluge, the Scapegoats," *The Wall Street Journal*, March 14, 1972, p. 24.

[30] Nugent, *Death at Buffalo Creek*, p. 156.

[31] Morris, "After the Deluge, the Scapegoats," p. 24.

[32] Nugent, *Death at Buffalo Creek*, p. 124.

[33] *Ibid.*, pp. 155–156.

[34] Morris, "After the Deluge, the Scapegoats," p. 24.

[35] Franklin, "Blame for Flood Is Hard to Fix," p. 22.

[36] "Agency Disclaims Tie to Dam Failure," *New York Times*, March 16, 1972, p. 25.

[37] Nugent, *Death at Buffalo Creek*, pp. 156–157.

[38] Walton, "After the Flood," p. 83.

[39] *Ibid.*

[40] George Vecsey, "Flood Survivors Seek Compensation," *New York Times*, April 1, 1972, p. 9.

[41] Caudill, "Buffalo Creek Aftermath," p. 16.

[42] "West Virginia Residents Are Suing for $52 Million From Pittston for Flood," *The Wall Street Journal*, September 11, 1972, p. 34.

[43] Walton, "After the Flood," p. 84.

[44] *Ibid.*, pp. 83–84.

[45] George Vecsey, "Pittston's Meeting Lively," *New York Times*, May 4, 1972, p. 65.

[46] Walton, "After the Flood," p. 84.

[47] Vecsey, "Pittston's Meeting Lively," p. 65.

[48] "Pittston's Shareholders Ask Mine-Tragedy Report," *The Wall Street Journal*, May 4, 1972, p. 24.

[49] Walton, "After the Flood," p. 84.

[50] *Ibid.*

[51] Nugent, *Death at Buffalo Creek*, pp. 159, 161.

[52] *Ibid.*, pp. 162–163.

[53] *Ibid.*, p. 164.

[54] Walton, "After the Flood," p. 84.

[55] Nugent, *Death at Buffalo Creek*, p. 170.

[56] Walton, "After the Flood," p. 84.

[57] Nugent, *Death at Buffalo Creek*, pp. 170, 173.

[58] *Ibid.*, pp. 179–180.

[59] *Ibid.*, p. 181.

[60] "Coal Dam Disaster Brings No Charges," *New York Times*, November 19, 1972, p. 43.

[61] George Vecsey, "U.S. Mine Bureau Scored on Flood," *New York Times*, March 19, 1972, p. 25.

[62] Walton, "After the Flood," p. 85.

[63] "Inspectors and Company Blamed in Dam Break," *New York Times*, May 30, 1972, p. 12.

[64] "After the Dam Broke, Cries for Controls," p. 38.

[65] Walton, "After the Flood," p. 85.

[66] *Ibid.*, p. 81.

[67] *Ibid.*, p. 85.

[68] Caudill, "Buffalo Creek Aftermath," p. 16.

[69] Walton, "After the Flood," p. 85.

[70] *Ibid.*, p. 84.

[71] "Price Cuts Ordered," *New York Times*, June 7, 1972, p. 90.

[72] Walton, "After the Flood," p. 85.

QUESTIONS

1. What appears to be the dominant value system operating in the Pittston Company, and what is its source?

2. What sanctions are leveled against Pittston as a result of its role in the Buffalo Creek disaster?

3. What role should the federal government have played in the events leading to the disas-

ter? Does your position differ from the actions actually taken by the government? What are reasons for differences, if any?

4. How would you characterize the managerial roles at Pittston?

5. What are the limits of Pittston's responsibility to the community, and what are the bases for such responsibilities?

6. What coping strategy did Pittston employ to respond to the reaction to the disaster?

7. What environmental factors seem to dictate reactions by the state of West Virginia?

8. Discuss the relationship between individual company value systems and social expectations.

9. What kinds of corporate power do you find Pittston employed in this case? Give examples.

10. In your opinion, what was the combination of forces that led to the disaster at Buffalo Creek?

11. Did Pittston act in accordance with social expectations? If not, what were the responses to this breach of legitimate business practices?

12. What methods can society employ to prevent the type of disaster that befell the people at Buffalo Creek?

CASE 5
AIRLINE SKYJACKING

The hijacking of a commercial aircraft normally involves a single or small number of individuals bent on forcing the crew of the aircraft to fly to a predetermined location for a variety of reasons, ranging from personal problems to criminal intent. In 1972 alone, 30 airlines from 14 countries were hijacked and 29 other hijacking attempts were made.[1] In addition to airline companies, hijackings have affected several other types of organizations, including industry associations, employee associations, government agencies, and individual countries. While the public's demand for safety is quite clear, these organizations often find themselves at cross purposes in their attempts to deal with the problem.

Airlines, both domestic and foreign, do not believe that they should have primary responsibility for preventing hijackings. The airlines' view is that governments are far better equipped to prevent hijackings and punish offenders than they. However, government involvement by necessity places hijacking in the political arena and adds a political perspective to the legal and humanitarian elements already present. For instance, several countries, including the United States, initially gave sanctuary or immunity from prosecution to hijackers, then later advocated extradition or prosecution.

Circumstances have been further complicated by the changing motives of hijackers. A shift from a simple demand for political asylum to terrorism has increased the potential for disaster to passengers and crew. The changed motives have resulted in different behavior patterns by hijackers and have dictated different coping strategies by organizations involved.

Airline hijackings have also posed new puzzles in determining airlines' liability to passengers. Cases arising from the hijacking of five airlines in September 1970 are expected to result in landmark rulings which, if found in favor of passengers, could result in sharply increased liability being thrust on international airlines that operate under the Warsaw Convention.[2]

FOOTNOTES

[1] H. D. S. Greenway, "U. S. Aids Cities' Toll of Terrorism Aloft," *Washington Post*, November 10, 1972.

[2] "Extent of Airline Industry Liability in Aerial Hijackings is Weighed," *Aviation Week & Space Technology*, April 9, 1973, p. 35.

The Airline Skyjacking Crisis: Business and Public Safety

History of Skyjacking

A basic teaching of guerrilla tactics is that the best targets are those of least defense and highest value. Nothing answers this description better than the commercial airline plane. It flies alone, unarmed, and carries the precious cargo of human lives. Since 1930, when the first hijacker commandeered a plane over Peru, over 250 aircraft have been hijacked, creating a large and delicate problem for both the airline industry and nations involved.

United States involvement with "skyjacking" began in 1948. A Czechoslovakian airliner was forced to land in the American zone of West Germany by thirty Czechs. On April 16, 1959, the United States granted political asylum to its first Cuban skyjacker. The precedent for political asylum had already been established by Turkey, Austria, the United States command in Germany, Italy, Greece, Yugoslavia, Denmark, West Germany, and North Korea. This "welcome" became a standard procedure for the next few years. At the time no one doubted that these acts were politically motivated and therefore justifiable.

By the end of 1961, President Kennedy noted twenty-five incidents of Cuban aircraft being diverted to the United States. To satisfy business claims against the property nationalized by the Castro government, the United States complicated these skyjackings by confiscating at least nine of the Cuban airplanes and selling them. Naturally these air piracies were politically embarrassing to Castro as well as being financially costly. To prevent further losses Castro added security guards to all commercial flights.

Then on May 1, 1965 the United States was stunned by the news of its first skyjacking to Cuba. Although Elperata Confrise was granted political asylum, the crew and passengers were released the same day. The skyjacking was still considered a freak incident. However, Castro decided to play the same game as the United

States and kept the airplane, an Eastern Airlines Electra. Over the ensuing uproar the country conveniently forgot that the United States had established these rules. Castro's point was well made because from that time on, the United States returned all aircraft subsequently skyjacked to the United States.

Also at this time Castro offered to enter into a bilateral agreement that included the return of both aircraft and the skyjacker. No one in the United States and certainly no one in the government believed that the problem was serious enough to warrant negotiations and so his offer was turned down. As a result a very effective means of dealing with both the potential and real skyjacker was ignored.

At first, the hijacking problem was dealt with by acquiescing to the demands of the pirate, flying him to his destination, and then moving to recover the aircraft and passengers. However, during the past several years, the increasing frequency of skyjackings for political purposes by militant groups has increased the danger to passengers, crew, and aircraft. These same skyjackings also have become an embarrassment to governments. Thus, earlier solutions have become inoperative yet little action was taken through 1968.

Problems faced by the airline industry were complicated further by the fact that, in most cases, air piracy created an international situation involving questions of extradition, political sanctuary, and the responsibilities of governments in the international community. Individual airlines took some actions aimed at preventing the hijacker from boarding the aircraft but were limited by desires not to delay customer boarding or antagonize the customer. International pilots' associations pushed for a multinational policy but were ineffective due mainly to a lack of unity.

The Airline Industry's Initial Reaction

Eleven hijackings in 1968 brought the air piracy issue squarely before the industry, catching it completely unprepared for the magnitude of the problems that were to follow. Most officials in both the industry and the government acknowledged a general state of helplessness in devising any clear-cut preventative for the forcible seizure of an aircraft in flight that would not endanger passengers and crew. A law enacted by Congress against air piracy carried a minimum penalty of 20 years' imprisonment or the death penalty on the recommendation of a jury. Yet the law's effect was minimal because of the country's inability to extradite an accused hijacker. An airline representative was quoted as saying, ". . . compliance with the hijacker is about the only thing we've been able to come up with." [1] Airlines and pilots were opposed to arming flight crews because of the potential dangers to the passengers. Also, arms are usually rendered ineffective since normally the pirate's first move is against a stewardess.

In 1970 air piracy exploded as a world problem with the hijackings of four airplanes by Arab guerrillas in the first week of September. A Boeing 747 was destroyed in Cairo, a Boeing 707, a McDonnell Douglas DC-8, and a BOAC Super VC-10 were forced into the Jordanian desert and destroyed. The governments of the five nations did not take any retaliatory action for fear of further inflaming the

Middle East crisis. Governments were caught up in the international complexities created by the political hijackings.

Some Economics of the Airline Industry

In 1968 most airline companies were having to face up to a serious profit squeeze as well as the realization that hijacking was not simply going to fade into the night. In fact their financial problems had lingered ever since the end of World War II. The ten years following the war were spent re-equipping their piston fleets. Companies had progressed to the long-range Lockheed Constellation and the Douglas DC-7 capable of nonstop transcontinental and transatlantic markets when the high yet hazardous promise of the far costlier jets seized them.

Conversion of commercial fleets to jets began at a time when the equity base of all major trunk line companies added up to only $865 million and aggregate large-term indebtedness was but $120 million less. With these rather meager assets and aggregate annual earnings of only $50 million, the carriers in 1958 committed themselves to purchase some $1.5 billion worth of jet equipment. Even this under-states the real value of the commitment. Many of the first generation jets were and are owned by and leased from banks, insurance companies, and other investors. The leases were long-term, typically for 15 years, and the payments were compara-ble to interest payments on long-term debt. The leases for the Big Four domestic trunks totaled close to $500 million.

In 1968 at the time skyjacking burst on the scene as an issue of some magni-tude, the average age of first generation jets was only 3½ years, yet these planes began to look outmoded. Commitments on second generation jets were made before prototypes had been flown. This generation included the "air buses"—Boe-ing 747, Lockheed L-1011, and McDonnell Douglas DC-10 and the supersonic Anglo-French Concorde scheduled for just beyond the subsonic airbuses.

Visible capital requirements of the twelve major trunks during the five-year span 1967–71 were estimated at $10.5 billion, according to a position paper laid before the Civil Aeronautics Board by the Air Transport Association, the trade group that represents the industry in Washington. Of this sum, about $8.8 billion would be used for new planes and flight equipment already on firm order. The other $1.7 billion would be used for ground-support gear and plant, additional ter-minal and cargo-handling facilities to serve the big new jets, expanded compu-terized reservation systems, more elaborate and more nearly automatic baggage-handling installations. However, several airline executives felt the real capital requirements of the twelve major carriers during 1967–71 for the big subsonic jets, more first generation jets, and ground support gear and plants would run 50 percent above the Air Transport Association's projection of $10.5 billion.[2]

In theory, investment in the wide-bodied jets could be recouped because of the planes' remarkable productivity. For instance the 747 was designed to operate at a seat-mile cost 32 percent below that of the 707, given comparable land factors.

However, matching these land factors would have been no easy task even if traffic had continued to grow at the pace of the early 1960s.[3]

When the new plane acquisitions were first planned, a general assumption was that perhaps three-quarters of the money to pay for them could be generated internally, primarily from cash flow from earnings and accelerated depreciation and sales of existing equipment. The rest was expected to come from borrowing, from leasing planes, or from sale of stock or convertible debentures. Earnings of major U.S. lines were off substantially from $371,500,000 in 1966 to $174,000,000 in 1969. Also a study during 1969 by the Air Transport Association conservatively projected a steady decline in cash flow over the next few years, together with growing cash requirements. The result was a projected need for some $10.3 billion in outside funds if the airlines were to meet debt repayment and rental and finance their orders, options, and plans for all the new aircrafts and ground facilities. It seemed obvious that all U. S. airlines would do well just to pay for the $4 billion worth of wide-bodied jets on firm order. Moreover, while interest rates in general climbed, for the airline industry generally they soared, with secured and unsecured borrowings often bringing 10 or 11 percent.[4]

For the twelve trunks as a whole, the debt ratio in 1968 was over 50 percent— versus ratios of 15 percent to 20 percent in typical manufacturing companies. Given the data available on funds likely to be generated by earnings and the investment tax credit, the Air Transport Association estimated the carriers would do no better than hold the existing ratio. In fact, the airline industry has a tradition of heavy dependence on leveraging. The borrowing has been encouraged over the years by assurances from the Civil Aeronautics Board (CAB) that it favors a 10 percent return on capital. Yet carriers have not achieved this return, partly because of CAB decisions creating an excess of carriers on particular routes. But since capital demands have always been high, leverage has obvious attractions, and indeed it is an institution in all the transportation industries; the airlines copied from the railroads and the steamship lines. The railroads and the ship companies, however, could make up for some debt costs in lean years by cutting back on such relatively nonessential expenses as refurbishing equipment and maintenance of right-of-way. These options were not open to airlines.[5]

Profit problems in 1969 were in part a function of the changing character of the airline industry. It was only 25 or so years ago that all an airline needed to make money was a fleet of planes and access to a public flying field. Today carriers look much more like railroads, in that their fixed or terminal costs are growing all out of proportion to their "line-haul" expenses (fuel, crew, and feeding). Terminal buildings alone are setting them back from $1 to $2 per passenger. The cost of putting a passenger on a plane, including sales, ticketing, checking, repairs, and maintenance, probably averages $8. So although the 747 was calculated to reduce line-haul or seat-mile expenses by at least 25 percent, rising terminal costs have eaten up a large part of the savings.[6]

Airlines in this country, even though well aware of the cyclical nature of the industry, have displayed a lack of caution in allowing growth rates in the most prosperous years to establish the slope of their future growth projections. This overoptimism, in part, led to the ordering of the new wide-bodied jets, which were no longer needed at time of delivery. In addition, a desire to increase market share has led the airlines to fly all available equipment, thus oversaturating their routes.[7]

Low yields on investment capital were due to other actions by the airlines. Some years ago the CAB sanctioned certain modest fare increases including a jet surcharge for the purpose of helping tide the carriers over the initial financing of first generation jets. In an attempt to hold these higher basic rates, which were especially profitable in the first-class section, the carriers began promoting a wide variety of special discount fares, such as the family plan, discover America packages, and off-day bargains. These inspired efforts to lure more people into the air met the desires of the price-minded CAB, which historically has held to the theory that the only way for the airlines to generate the mass market that will bring economic strength is to stimulate demand through lower fares. To the dismay of the carriers, however, the practical result of moving toward a mass market was to raise the coach and other discount fares fractions of the total revenues from only 65 percent in 1963 to more than 74 percent in 1968. To this extent, new business had been acquired at the cost of diluting the high-profit faction represented by business travelers, and even they moved frugally back to the coach section in increasing numbers.[8]

Airline troubles have developed not only because of their own actions but as a result of the decisions of the regulators. It is argued that regulators have legislated wasteful, ruinous overcompetition along air routes and then intervened unwisely to forestall the natural adjustments for overcompetition, such as mergers, statesmanlike agreements, or business failure.[9] An example of legislating overcompetition was the CAB's transpacific route award decision of 1969, which permitted five trunk lines to fly the Hawaii route in addition to the three lines already certified. Also a classic example of intervention was the CAB attempt to keep Northeast Airlines in business by allowing it to fly the New York-Miami route, a prime source of revenue for Eastern and National Airlines. The results not only failed to cure Northeast's ills, but reduced the profitability of the other two lines in the process.[10]

Thus, in addition to the obvious difficulties posed by the skyjackings, airline troubles by 1970 centered around empty seats, discounted fares, spiraling wage rates, depressed stock prices, disgruntled financial sources, and congested airways. The long-anticipated operating economies of the big new planes were more than offset by rising operating and interest costs.

ALPA and IFALPA

The 1968 skyjackings of Miami-bound flights to Cuba were the impetus for an unanimous decision by the board of directors of the Air Line Pilots Association (ALPA) to send messages to President Johnson and Transportation Secretary Alan S. Boyd requesting "immediate action" to stop skyjackings. The messages were sent in November of that year. The ALPA, which represents most of the U.S. commercial airline flight crews and a large proportion of cabin attendants, stated that hijackings were beginning to occur with "alarming regularity," and that they were "very damaging to the airline industry." In addition to inconveniencing the customers, the organization said that skyjacking "exposes airline pilots and passengers to excessive danger with possible injury and loss of life." [11]

In March 1969, the International Federation of Airline Pilots Associations (IFALPA) announced a possible worldwide pilot strike as a weapon in the campaign against skyjacking and other civil air transportation threats. The federation also threatened to boycott nations that harbored airline skyjackers. The reason for the strike was to focus world attention on the air piracy problem because governments of the international community were either unwilling or unable to stop what the organization considered its primary flight and ground safety problems. The primary officers of the federation were given the power to:

(1) send an official delegate for consultations with governments requesting them,
(2) use diplomatic channels to the maximum effect,
(3) coordinate with other organizations to restrict the movement of aircraft to the offending state and restrict the movement of cargo to and from the state, whether by surface or air (IFALPA has the support of the International Transportation Workers Federation in this action), and
(4) strike worldwide to focus attention on the threat to safety caused by skyjackings. [12]

The IFALPA approved exerting "every possible pressure" to ensure that no bilateral air transport agreements were concluded or renewed unless the governments of the nations involved gave firm commitment to apprehend hijackers who land in their countries. [13]

The August 29, 1969 skyjacking of a TWA Boeing 707 transport to Damascus, in which the plane was blown up minutes after the passengers left the craft, prompted the IFALPA to ask its member associations to ratify a call for a strike by September 8. The ratification empowered the federation to strike periodically to "get some kind of counteraction" against air piracy. [14] By this time the organization recognized that the problem had moved beyond a question of air safety to the political realm. The IFALPA also believed that responsibility for the problem rested with the United Nations Security Council, rather than with technical organizations. The organization was quoted as saying,

> This position is so serious that pilots all over the world feel that the safety of their passengers can be jeopardized at a moment's notice and, moreover they are now without the means fully to discharge their responsibility to deliver the passengers safely to their destination. [15]

The IFALPA began to apply pressure to several member states of the United Nations to bring the skyjacking of a TWA Boeing 707 to Syria on the agenda of the Security Council. It also completed a poll of member associations, revealing that all but Cuba and Syria would support a twenty-four-hour strike in September or October. The federation considered approaching the International Air Transport Association in an attempt to ban ticket sales to nations condoning air piracy or harboring skyjackers.[16]

The U.N. Security Council responded with the following statement:

> Members of the Security Council condemn and consider it necessary to put an end to acts that are directed against the safety of civil aviation and that are being perpetrated in various parts of the world, presenting serious obstacles to the normal use of air transportation. . .
>
> The Security Council calls upon States to take all appropriate measures within their jurisdiction to deter and prevent such acts and to take effective measures to deal with those who commit such acts.[17]

The Arab skyjacking of the four airplanes in September 1970, prompted the IFALPA to announce that it was ready to organize a boycott within twelve hours to be in full effect in twenty-four hours.[18] The industry noted that traditional freedom of the skies was threatened by skyjackers and government acts to prevent air piracy were not effective. Plans were made to place guards aboard aircraft. Also economic sanctions and boycotts were planned including provisions to suspend airline services to nations that refused to extradite air pirates. Officials of the airlines almost unanimously believed that the greatest deterrent to skyjacking would be the prosecution of offenders and imposition of the stiffest possible punishments.[19]

The last of September, however, marked IFALPA's special meeting to withdraw the call for a boycott. The organization announced that it was seeking instead to work with the International Transport Workers Federation to alleviate the problem.[20]

General indignation over escalating acts of air piracy prompted the American Air Line Pilots Association in June 1972 to direct all its pilots to implement a boycott of air service to all nations that aided skyjackers by granting asylum. During the same period, the federal government suggested arming flight crews and urged the airlines to drop their policy of nonresistance. The American ALPA was the first to recommend this boycott, and its president John O'Connell sought to secure the participation of IFALPA.[21] The boycott reflected the frustration of the pilots seeking relief from a problem in part rooted in political differences and disagreements over universal anti-skyjacking measures. A majority of the 51,000 members of IFALPA voiced full support for a twenty-four hour suspension of domestic and international air services throughout the world on June 19, 1972. Impatience and anger over the skyjack murder of a Czech pilot prompted the organization to make the decision despite a disposition for action to forestall skyjacking from the community of nations.[22] The purpose of the strike was to demonstrate that governments in the international community were dragging their heels in ratifying existing treaties on skyjacking.[23] Briefly, the three treaties state the following:

> *Tokyo Convention* of 1963. This pact calls for states involved in any way in crimes committed aboard aircraft to take all steps to restore control of the aircraft to its lawful commander or preserve control.

Hague Convention of 1970. In addition to returning the aircraft to its proper operator, this treaty calls for assistance to passengers and crew for continuation of their
journey and apprehension and prosecution or extradition of the hijacker. Each
contracting state agrees to make the offense punishable by severe penalties.

Montreal Convention of 1971. This prescribes severe punishment for attacks
against persons on aircraft and for such acts as sabotage and bombing that damage
aircraft or endanger flight safety.[24]

O'Donnell proposed that pilots learn hand-to-hand combat techniques and
crews on the flight deck be armed with non-lethal weapons. The pilots supported
a proposed Federal Aviation Administration rule requiring the installation of
locked armored bulkheads between the flight deck and passenger cabin, but the
airline industry management was skeptical of the project since armed threats against
stewardesses were just as effective as a gun against the pilot's head.[25]

The June 19th strike was weakened in the United States by court orders and dis-
sention within ALPA that enabled most American carriers to maintain normally
scheduled service. But the walk-out was quite effective in Western Europe, South
America, South Africa, Israel, and other areas of the world. As a result of the strike
top-level diplomatic and governmental groups pledged that action against air piracy
would be accelerated.[26]

In the United States, the Senate Commerce Committee ordered reported to the
floor a bill that would give the president the power to order unilateral suspension of
air service between the United States and countries that do not abide by the Hague
Convention. The bill would have also empowered the president to suspend service to the United States of any carrier whose government continued to provide
service to the offending country. The ALPA endorsed the legislation.[27]

One month later the ALPA called for a screening of all passengers and their
hand baggage on all flights. O'Donnell hinted that the airlines must accept more responsibility for combating air piracy, and also must be prepared to underwrite its
share of the bill.[28]

ATA and IATA

The Air Transport Association (ATA) represents the management of the airline
industry, and as such was at odds sometimes with the ALPA over which course of
action to pursue in combating air piracy. In January 1969, ATA reacted to the
skyjackings of eight aircraft during the month by polling its members to determine
whether industry agreement could be reached on posting a $25,000 reward for in-
formation leading to the arrest and conviction of skyjackers (ALPA reported to have
offered $20,000 for the same purpose). Head of the International Air Transport As-
sociation (IATA), Knut Hammarskjold made personal contact with the Cuban government to enlist its support.[29]

The August 29, 1969 skyjacking of a Boeing 707 to Damascus which prompted
the IFALPA to ask its members to ratify a strike call (later withdrawn) created one of
several conflicts with IATA. Hammarskjold remarked that the twenty-four hour

strikes would not serve any purpose except to focus world attention on the growing threat to commercial air transportation by unlawful seizure. The IATA charged that the responsibility to stop aircraft skyjacking rested with the governments and that tough punative laws should be passed as a deterrent to seizures.[30]

The IATA reacted to the September 1970 skyjackings of four aircraft to the Jordanian Desert by requesting that each nation take the initiative in adopting stiff laws to punish skyjackers. They further asked IFALPA to avoid, if possible, a threatened strike.[31]

Also during September 1970 a would-be skyjacker was shot during an attempted seizure of a TWA aircraft. After the shooting, a statement issued by IATA deplored the danger of vigilantism aboard aircraft, but it was withdrawn after TWA protested that the shooting was done by a Brinks courier working with the crew and the police. TWA reported that public reaction to passenger protection was favorable.[32] However, the airline industry continued to oppose the use of armed guards aboard aircraft.

Later that year, IATA charged that the unwillingness of governments to adopt tough punative measures sustained air piracy tension.[33] Hammarskjold remarked that the only way to stop hijacking ". . . is for all governments either to extradite skyjackers to the country of the airline concerned or to punish them severely at the point of landing."[34] Hammarskjold began personally pressing legislators to move their governments to adopt the following security measures:

(1) Protection of aircraft on the ground, as well as protection of installations (fencing of airports, surveillance of aircraft by closed circuit TV, etc.);
(2) The processing and protection of passengers, crew, and baggage through screening procedures;
(3) The inspection, screening, and isolation of unaccompanied baggage and cargo;
(4) The inspection and screening of airmail and parcel post;
(5) The development of standard procedure for actions in the event of unlawful seizure or in-flight explosion to be taken by air and ground crews.[35]

The June 19, 1972 strike by IFALPA was openly opposed by ATA. On June 16, ATA filed a request for enjoining the pilots from participating in the strike. John O'Donnell accused ATA of attempting "to destroy our efforts for economic reasons," and he termed that organization's action "unconscionable," adding ". . . any future violation (skyjacking or sabotage) is fully the responsibility of the ATA and the industry and its profit motives."[36] Hammarskjold stressed again that governments must provide the major defenses against skyjacking.[37]

As mentioned above, proposed legislation resulting from the June 19 work-stoppage gave the president the power to suspend air service unilaterally between the United States and countries not abiding by the Hague Convention. The proposal was endorsed by ALPA but objected to in part by ATA. ATA's criticism of the bill centered on the provisions for secondary boycotts, giving the president the authority to suspend service to the United States of any carrier whose government continued to provide service to an offending country. ATA feared retaliation by countries affected by the secondary boycott through suspension of operations of U.S. carriers to them.[38]

After keeping most U.S. pilots on the job during the June 19th work-stoppage by court action, ATA stiffened its anti-skyjacking image by endorsing resolutions calling on governments to take steps against states providing sanctuaries for air pirates. ATA also stated that it did not intend to pursue any contempt of court proceedings against on-duty pilots who did not work on June 19 in defiance of the court order.[39]

Speaking for the United States scheduled airlines, officials of ATA reported that airlines desired a greater federal and local law enforcement presence at airports, in order to shift some of the workload from airline agents and to avoid some of the stigma associated with passenger search.[40]

CAO and ICAO

Following a study on jurisdictional air rules initiated in June 1960, the International Civil Aviation Organization (ICAO), the repository for multilateral treaties on air transportation, drew up the Tokyo Convention in 1963 in order to establish continuity of jurisdiction over crimes committed on aircraft in international service. The convention drew strong industry support. The only criticism came in an article charging that the treaty was not thought to be broad enough in scope. There is a provision in the treaty for the safe conduct of passengers and crew following a skyjacking, and a call for the prompt return of the aircraft and cargo to the lawful owners. But there are no provisions for the apprehension of the skyjacker beyond the extradition laws of individual countries.[41]

The Tokyo Convention did establish a positive rule of international law between the contracting nations by providing that the country in which an aircraft is registered is competent to exercise jurisdiction over offenses committed in overseas or international flight. The agreement permitted the exercise of concurrent jurisdiction by other countries depending on their interest in the particular crime.[42] Thus, a contracting country that is not the nation of registration may try to prevent a criminal act if:

(1) the offense has effect on the territory of such a state,
(2) the offense has been committed by or against a national or permanent resident of the state,
(3) the offense is against the security of the state,
(4) the offense consists of a breach of any rules relating to the flight of aircraft in force in the state, and
(5) exercise of jurisdiction is necessary to ensure the obligation of the state under other multilateral agreements.[43]

Under the provisions of the treaty, a captain may take "reasonable" measures, including restraint, to protect the safety of the aircraft, maintain discipline on board, or deliver the offender to the proper authorities. He may require or authorize other crew members to assist him in restraining an offender. If necessary, he may authorize, but not require, passengers to give similar aid. This authority and power is recognized in most countries. A captain may turn over to authorities of any state party to the convention any person who he believes has committed a crime as defined by the penal law of his home country. Offenses committed in an aircraft will be treated as if they had occurred in the state of registration of the aircraft. The treaty adds, ". . . nothing in this convention shall be deemed to create an obligation to grant extradition."[44]

In February 1969, the United States formally proposed that the right of political asylum be denied to those persons who participate in an act of air piracy in the form of a protocol to the Tokyo Convention at the council of ICAO in Montreal. The U.S. proposal included provisions to:

(1) make skyjacking of commercial aircraft carrying passengers for hire a crime in all signatory states,
(2) require that skyjackers be returned to the state of registration of the skyjacked aircraft,
(3) grant absolute immunity to the skyjacker from prosecution for any crime other than that of air piracy.[45]

The proposed additional protocol met with stiff resistance from a majority of states, particularly Switzerland, who felt the principle of political asylum to be sacrosanct. Many states contended that the government of a nation retains the sole privilege of determining whether political asylum should be granted or not. The United States returned to the council of the ICAO in September 1969 with further proposals for the extradition of skyjackers. Its delegates were seeking bilateral or multinational agreements. At the same time, a draft treaty on the prosecution, punishment, and extradition of persons charged with air piracy, prepared by a special legal subcommittee of the ICAO, was circulated among the 116 member states.[46]

During June 1970, 91 member states of the ICAO attended a two-week session on unlawful interference with aircraft. With the exception of Cuba, they unanimously approved a comprehensive declaration to develop and implement a wide range of measures to prevent sabotage, skyjacking, and other illegal interference. The declaration, however, was morally binding but not legally so.[47]

The following September, the ICAO reacted to the four hijackings of American, Swiss, and British aircraft to the Jordanian desert, by reminding the member nations of the June agreement, and called for strong action against skyjackers.[48] In the United States, Chairman of the Board of the Civil Aviation Organization (CAO) Secor D. Browne suggested the following provisions be implemented:

(1) Training programs should be required for flight crews in the containment of a skyjacker once he reaches the cockpit.
(2) Ground crews consisting of airline and government personnel should be trained to take over immediate ground control of skyjacked aircraft.

(3) A task force of specialists, expert in aviation law and international relations, should be formed to ensure that a skyjacker is prosecuted to the fullest under varying laws covering air piracy throughout the world.[49]

At the same time, the ICAO was asked to convene a special meeting of its council to consider what steps could be taken to provide skyjacker security for international civil aviation. At the special meeting in Montreal, Secretary of Transportation John Volpe urged adoption of the following proposals:

(1) States in which a skyjacked aircraft lands have the obligation to permit passengers and crew to continue and to return the aircraft and cargo to its owners.
(2) The state to which a skyjacker has fled has the obligation to extradite or prosecute the skyjacker.
(3) Concentrated multilateral sanctions should be imposed against states which permit the detention of passengers, crew or aircraft, or which fail to extradite or prosecute persons responsible for unlawful seizure of aircraft.[50]

The thrust of the ICAO was strengthened November 14 when Russia became a member of the body and voiced strong support for international cooperation in prosecuting air pirates. The Soviet interest in securing an international agreement was heightened by the skyjacking of an Antonov AN-24 to Turkey, during which a stewardess was killed. Turkey granted the two skyjackers political asylum.[51]

The Hague Convention held in December 1970, produced a treaty signed by 50 of 77 participating member nations of the ICAO. The convention dealt with means of punishing aircraft skyjackers. The treaty called for either extradition or prosecution of air pirates and required that aircraft crews and passengers be allowed to continue onward without delay after control of the aircraft was returned to the crew. The treaty made much more difficult the use of a plea of political asylum. However, under the treaty, if a skyjacker is not extradited he may ask for political asylum after he has been tried and has served the punishment declared by the court. Universal jurisdiction was established requiring that jurisdiction over the skyjacker rest not only with the nation in which the pirated aircraft landed, or the nation in which the aircraft was registered, but also include a third country to which the skyjacker may have escaped. Cuba was invited to the convention, but did not attend, preferring to enter into bilateral agreements on extradition.[52]

By the time of the June 19, 1972 work-stoppage by IFALPA, only 49 nations had ratified the Tokyo Convention, only 15 had ratified the Hague Convention, and only one had ratified the Montreal Convention. The U.S. State Department established a task force to present to ICAO a document designed to encourage ratification of these three treaties. Board Chairman Browne of the CAO called for the formation of a single independent agency to cope with skyjacking, extortion, and sabotage. ALPA objected to the proposal, preferring the expertise of the FBI.[53] ICAO also adopted a resolution setting October 31, 1972 as the deadline for receipt of reports from member nations on security measures taken against skyjacking and sabotage. The resolution increased the pace of development of international standards that tightened security systems at airports, and reiterated the need for urgency in ratification of the three treaties concerned with air transportation interference.[54]

The Changing Impetus for Skyjacking and Its Response

The costs inflicted on an airline company by an act of air piracy were estimated by one industry spokesman to be between $15,000 and $25,000 per skyjacking in 1968. A Pan Am representative raised that range to between $35,000 and $50,000, while an officer with National Airlines put "out of pocket costs" at $4,000 to $5,000 plus "other expenses that would vary from plane to plane and what we intended to do with it." [55]

During 1969, the industry reported 33 successful skyjackings of U.S. aircraft, of which one was flown to Italy, one to Syria, and the remainder to Cuba. Industry management attributed piracy to leniency in the courts regarding sentencing, disparity of laws among nations, the lack of extradition authority, and the practices of political asylum.[56]

The skyjackings of four aircraft in September 1970 and their subsequent destruction by the commandos of the Popular Front for the Liberation of Palestine, greatly endangered peace in the Middle East. The commandos captured the planes in an attempt to free other commandos jailed in Britain, Switzerland, West Germany, and Israel, and vowed to continue such attacks. The skyjackings caused a redoubling of security procedures at major airports. They involved frisking overseas passengers, checking handbags and other carry-on baggage, and the use of electronic screening equipment. Immediate passenger reaction to the increased surveillance was favorable.[57] Prior to 1969, most skyjackings were considered to be politically motivated, but terrorism was not normally an ingredient. However, the motivation had shifted and had become a mixture of extortion and terrorism. A 3½ year study revealed that the instigating factors for air piracy assumed the following characteristics:

(1) Political asylum, which for the main part involved diversion of aircraft from domestic routes to Cuba.
(2) Mentally deranged persons, whose motivations seldom were clear.
(3) Palestinian guerrilla activity, in which terrorism served a key purpose.
(4) Extortion, which was more widely practiced in the United States than elsewhere.[58]

A court decision in March 1972, further complicated the problem of the airline industry. The New York State Supreme Court ruled that TWA was responsible for the mental as well as physical well-being of passengers involved in skyjacking. The court ruled that the passengers may recover for "fright and distress." [59]

Stiffer attitudes by both airline officials and law enforcement groups were demonstrated in July 1972 when two would-be skyjackers were shot and killed by FBI agents. However, during the shoot-out one passenger was killed and two others were wounded. Also in July 1972 the skyjacker of a Pan Am Boeing 747 was shot and killed by an armed passenger after the skyjacker had been overpowered by the captain.[60] In Washington, it was announced that to July 11, 1972, 210 persons had been involved in 153 skyjackings of U.S. aircraft. Of this group, 43 had been convicted of various charges associated with the act, while 109 were still classified as fugitives by the FAA.[61]

FAA Action

The flurry of skyjackings to Cuba in 1968 prompted increased use of the Federal Aviation Administration's (FAA) Sky Marshal program. The program consisted of specially trained FAA personnel who were assigned (at the request of the airline or the FBI) to ride aboard aircraft suspected of carrying a skyjacker. An airline official said the number of FAA personnel available was so small compared to the number of flights to Florida that the program was virtually meaningless.[62]

Armed federal guards were introduced aboard U.S. airline flights on international routes in addition to domestic flights as a response to the terrorist activities during the week of September 6, 1970. The success of armed guards aboard Israeli aircraft and the increased threat of destruction of aircraft and occupants by air pirates ended the industry's traditional opposition to force aboard the aircraft. The FAA's Sky Marshal program at this time drew personnel from the Defense Department, the U.S. Customs Department, the Secret Service, and the FBI as well as the FAA. All of these men were trained to operate within the aircraft with specific considerations for the vulnerable components of the plane. The Sky Marshals were under the command of the captain of the crew and were equipped with special ammunition to prevent damage to the aircraft skin.[63]

In mid-September 1970, Lt. Gen. Benjamin O. Davis (USAF, Ret.) was appointed director of the Transportation Department's Office of Civil Aviation Security, and the Sky Marshal program was made his responsibility. The training program for armed guards consisted of familiarization with cabin characteristics, courses dealing with the reaction of passengers to airflight maneuvers, indoctrination on the skyjacker behavioral profile system, and refresher courses on firearms and hand-to-hand combat. The program cost $28 million in 1971 and $50 million was appropriated in 1972.[64]

Transition of the U.S. Sky Marshal program from a temporary multi-agency status began with the graduation of the first class of officers on December 23, 1970. The school was scheduled to graduate 50 officers per week until a total of 2100 were graduated. By July 17, 1972, federal participation in anti-skyjacking included 1250 Customs Security Officers (including the Sky Marshals) and 230 U.S. Marshals. By this time few Sky Marshals were assigned to flights, but instead concentrated on preboarding screening activities.[65]

At this time during the anti-skyjacking campaign greater emphasis was placed on increasing airline security on the ground through the use of preboarding screening procedures consisting of electronic metal detection devices and the hijacker personality profile. Eastern Airlines was the first to employ preboarding screening effectively and the procedure cut the number of skyjackings from ten over the first three quarters of 1969 to a single instance for the remainder of the year. [66] General Davis, in November 1970, announced that the FAA was studying several new systems in hopes of increasing further ground security. The systems included a neutron activation system to detect explosives, a vapor detection device to detect explosives, a vapor detection apparatus designed for finding explosives in luggage and cargo, and the use of dogs to sniff out explosives. [67]

At the beginning of 1972, the FAA made preboarding passenger screening procedures mandatory and required that airlines develop the capacity to use the behavioral profile by February 6. They were required to spot check at least ten percent of the passengers on shuttle flights for proper identification. February 6 was also set as the date all airports were to display armed guards. In addition to these requirements, the FAA urged the airlines to purchase magnet meters, electronic metal detection devices. The FAA also began to rearrange the Customs Security Officer-Sky Marshal program to permit these officers to participate in the ground screening. However, Transportation Secretary John Volpe reiterated the administration's opposition to a federally financed airport police force and said that the cost of the new anti-skyjacking measures would ultimately be recovered by higher fares. Initially, though, the airports would have to absorb the expense of the luggage inspections and airport operations. The city and county governments would have to pay for the armed guards located at the boarding area.

On February 5, 1972, a federal judge, John Lewis Smith, Jr., ruled that the airlines could have a ten day extention to ready their armed police force. He stated that the type of emergency that existed did not require the "crash type" program the FAA had adopted. Many also felt the FAA had improperly shifted the burden of law enforcement to the public rather than allowing it to remain as a responsibility of the federal government.

Several skyjackings in July of that year prompted the FAA to tighten security rules, prohibiting the airlines from accepting passengers who met the skyjacker behavioral profile unless they were physically searched or a metal detector were used to ensure that they were not armed. Further, the FAA made available (to 20 major airports where a high probability of skyjacking existed) funds for portable X-ray units and for police dogs to sniff out explosives hidden in luggage. [68]

Congressional Action

Congress was slow to react to the initial flurry of skyjackings in 1968. At that time, Chairman of the House Committee on Interstate and Foreign Commerce, Rep. Hasley O. Staggers, indicated the committee was not committed to any action, but "there might be a day or two of hearings to clarify the situation." [69] The committee heard testimony in early 1969 on extradition treaties and possible methods of detecting potential skyjackers. In September of that year, the House introduced a resolution urging White House action, which included the use of economic sanctions, to protect U.S. aircraft from skyjackers. [70] The Ways and Means

Committee also completed legislation authorizing the armed guard program funds, provided for by increased passenger taxes.[71]

After the strike by the IFALPA on June 19, 1972, the House supported a resolution directing the President to cut economic or military aid to nations who would not cooperate in taking punative action against skyjackers and terrorists.[72]

At the beginning of August 1972, the Senate Commerce Committee approved an international anti-skyjacking measure permitting suspension of U.S. airline service to countries not abiding by the accords of the Hague Convention. It also empowered the President to halt service by non-U.S. carriers between the United States and any nation that continued to provide for or accept air service from any other nation that was encouraging skyjacking. Also, the Transportation Department Secretary could revoke or limit the operating authority of any non-U.S. air carrier whose government did not effectively maintain and administer adequate security measures. The bill expanded U.S. jurisdiction to include any aircraft landing in the United States with the skyjacker on board.[73]

White House Action

President Johnson signed the Tokyo Convention in 1969, and it was ratified by the Senate in the same year.

In September 1970, President Nixon signed a bill authorizing the government to extend war casualty insurance to U.S. airlines if they were unable to obtain it privately.[74] At the same time, he asked Congress for a $28 million appropriation for the Sky Marshal program and announced that anti-sabotage training would be made available to airline personnel. Also, the Departments of Transportation, Treasury, and Defense in addition to the CIA, FBI, and the Office of Science and Technology were directed to develop better security measures. The State Department was directed to consult with foreign governments and carriers about a full range of techniques to be employed to foil skyjacking attempts. Nixon's proposals called for extradition and full punishment of culprits and sanctions against nations giving them sanctuary. In fact, in both June 1972 and early 1973, Nixon urged retention of the death penalty as a possible punishment for skyjackers. The program adopted by the President represented a compromise in that it rejected measures that would equip the federal government with power to take unilateral action in all cases of skyjacking of U.S. aircraft.[75] The White House had held that the airlines have prime responsibility for deterring skyjacking, not the federal government.[76]

On February 15, 1972, the United States and Cuba signed an agreement to extradite or impose stiff penalties on skyjackers of planes and ships. The five-year agreement is an attempt to crack down on criminals and those persons who commit violence in the process of seeking asylum, yet it admits without penalty legitimate political refugees. Both countries have also agreed to return aircraft and vessels, any funds obtained by extortion or other means, and all innocent passengers and crew.

145

Aftermath

For the airlines, the newly demanded security checks were a financial drain. The precautions required would cost the airports at least $46 million per year, and some executives estimated a yearly cost of $300 million. Either figure would reduce, if not wipe out, estimated airline profits for the coming few years.

Ransom money was also beginning to pinch the airlines. Even if it were recovered, the airlines must borrow the money from banks at a high rate of interest. Often special arrangements had to be made with banks and race tracks in order to borrow the money on short notice over a weekend.

The passenger will probably end up paying most of the cost of this increased protection. The FAA has estimated that a boost averaging one dollar per ticket would raise about $180 million of the money required.

Epilogue

Senator Vance Hartke, (D-Ind), has repeatedly refused to be searched before boarding an aircraft. He claims that because of his congressional immunity, the search procedure is unconstitutional. Due to his actions, Delta Airlines has been fined $2000 by the FAA for permitting him to board a plane without going through preliminary security checks.

FOOTNOTES

[1] Harold D. Watkins, "Federal Action in Hijackings Urged," *Aviation Week and Space Technology*, December 2, 1968, pp. 24–25.

[2] Charles J. V. Murphy, "The Airlines' Turbulent New Economics," *Fortune*, March 1968, p. 117.

[3] Dan Cordtz, "Pan Am's Route Across the Sea of Red Ink," *Fortune*, January 1972, p. 80.

[4] Tom Alexander, "Is There Any Way to Run An Airline?" *Fortune*, September 1970, pp. 206, 211.

[5] Rush Loving, Jr., "How a Hotelman Got the Red Out of United Air Lines," *Fortune*, March 1972, p. 131.

[6] Gilbert Burck, "A New Flight Plan for the Airlines," *Fortune*, April 1969, pp. 99–100.

[7] Alexander, "Is There Any Way," p. 204.

[8] Murphy, "The Airlines' Turbulent New Economics," p. 117.

[9] Alexander, "Is There Any Way," p. 117.

[10] *Ibid.*, pp. 117, 204.

[11] Watkins, "Federal Action," pp. 24–25.

[12] "IFALPA Threatens Strike in Push Against Hijackings," *Aviation Week and Space Technology*, March 31, 1969, p. 31.

[13] *Ibid.*

[14] "IFALPA Mounts Anti-Hijack Drive," *Aviation Week and Space Technology*, September 8, 1969, p. 22.

[15] *Ibid.*

[16] Herbert J. Coleman, "IFALPA Pushing to Thrust Hijack Issue Before U.N.," *Aviation Week and Space Technology*, September 15, 1969, p. 39.

[17] "Security Council Hijacking Statement," *Aviation Week and Space Technology*, June 26, 1972, p. 180.

[18] "Arab Guerrillas Adopt Air Piracy as Tactic," *Aviation Week and Space Technology*, September 14, 1970, p. 33.

[19] Laurence Doty, "Anti-Hijacking Proposals Proliferate," *Aviation Week and Space Technology*, September 21, 1970, p. 26.

[20] Laurence Doty, "White House Drive Gains to Unify International Laws on Air Piracy," *Aviation Week and Space Technology*, September 28, 1970, p. 25.

[21] "Pilots' Hijack Action," *Aviation Week and Space Technology*, June 12, 1972, p. 27.

[22] "Hijacking Indignation Increases," *Aviation Week and Space Technology*, June 19, 1972, pp. 21–22.

[23] *Ibid.*

[24] "Treaties on Piracy," *Aviation Week and Space Technology*, June 19, 1972, pp. 21–22.

[25] "Hijacking Indignation Increases," pp. 21–22.

[26] Laurence Doty, "Pilots Press Anti-Hijacking Drive," *Aviation Week and Space Technology*, June 26, 1972, p. 180.

[27] "Anti-Hijacking Moves Accelerate In Wake of Pilots' Work Stoppage," *Aviation Week and Space Technology*, July 3, 1972, pp. 29–30.

[28] "Three Airlines Seal Ventral Doors on 727 as Deterrent to Hijacking," *Aviation Week and Space Technology*, July 24, 1972, p. 21.

[29] "Airlines, Government Accelerate Efforts at Hijacking Prevention," *Aviation Week and Space Technology*, January 27, 1969, p. 33.

[30] "IFALPA Mounts Anti-Hijack Drive," p. 22.

[31] "Arab Guerrillas Adopt Air Piracy as Tactic," p. 33.

[32] "Armed Courier Thwarts TWA Hijack Attempt," *Aviation Week and Space Technology*, September 21, 1970, p. 30.

[33] Doty, "White House Expands Hijack Talks," p. 28.

[34] "IATA, Official of Munich Airport Debate Over Anti-Hijacking Roles," *Aviation Week and Space Technology*, November 16, 1970, p. 29.

[35] Edward H. Kolcum, "IATA Chief Spurs Anti-Hijack Program," *Aviation Week and Space Technology*, December 7, 1970, p. 32.

[36] Laurence Doty, "Pilots Press Anti-Hijacking Drive," *Aviation Week and Space Technology*, June 26, 1972, pp. 180–181.

[37] "Hijacking Indignation Increases," p. 21.

[38] "Anti-Hijacking Moves Accelerate In Wake of Work Stoppage," p. 29.

[39] *Ibid.*, p. 30.

[40] Harold D. Watkins, "Anti-Hijacking Steps, Penalties Stiffens," *Aviation Week and Space Technology*, July 17, 1972, pp. 26–28.

[41] Laurence Doty, "Air Crimes Convention Supported Heavily," *Aviation Week and Space Technology*, November 18, 1968, p. 60.

[42] *Ibid.*

[43] *Ibid.*

[44] *Ibid.*

⁴⁵ "U.S. to Ask Denial of Asylum to Hijackers," *Aviation Week and Space Technology*, February 10, 1969, p. 27.

⁴⁶ "Extradition Delivered Air Piracy Cure," *Aviation Week and Space Technology*, September 8, 1969, p. 23.

⁴⁷ "ICAO Actions May Reduce Aircraft Violence Threat," *Aviation Week and Space Technology*, July 13, 1970, p. 21.

⁴⁸ "Arab Guerrillas Adopt Air Piracy As Tactic," p. 33.

⁴⁹ "Hijack Measures," *Aviation Week and Space Technology*, September 14, 1970, p. 32.

⁵⁰ Doty, "White House Drive Gains to Unify International Laws On Air Piracy," p. 25.

⁵¹ James P. Woolsey, "U.S. Sees Anti-Hijacking Support in Soviet's Membership in ICAO," *Aviation Week and Space Technology*, November 23, 1970, p. 26.

⁵² "Strong Anti-Hijack Treaty Signed: May Be Implemented by Mid-Year," *Aviation Week and Space Technology*, January 4, 1971, p. 26.

⁵³ "Hijacking Indignation Increases," p. 21.

⁵⁴ Doty, "Pilots Press Anti-Hijacking Drive," p. 180.

⁵⁵ "Hijacking Is No Joke for U.S. Airlines," *Business Week*, December 21, 1968, p. 65.

⁵⁶ "Airlines Demand Stiffer Hijack Penalties," *Aviation Week and Space Technology*, July 6, 1970, p. 32.

⁵⁷ Harold D. Watkins, "Hijacking Impact Swells Airline Problems," *Aviation Week and Space Technology*, September 21, 1970, p. 30.

⁵⁸ "Hijacking Indignation Increases," p. 21.

⁵⁹ "Passenger's Mental Well-Being Held to be TWA Responsibility," *Aviation Week and Space Technology*, March 27, 1972, p. 28.

⁶⁰ "Shootouts Thwart Attempted Hijackings," *Aviation Week and Space Technology*, July 19, 1972, p. 27.

⁶¹ "43 Convictions Obtained in Hijacking," *Aviation Week and Space Technology*, July 17, 1972, p. 24.

⁶² Watkins, "Federal Action in Hijackings Urged," p. 25.

⁶³ James P. Woolsey, "Prevention of Hijacking Switches from Passive to Active Measures," *Aviation Week and Space Technology*, September 21, 1970, p. 29.

⁶⁴ James P. Woolsey, "Cost of Anti-Hijacking Measures to be Borne Mainly by Airlines," *Aviation Week and Space Technology*, November 9, 1970, p. 29.

⁶⁵ Watkins, "Anti-Hijacking Step, Penalties Stiffen," p. 28.

⁶⁶ "Screening Success," *Aviation Week and Space Technology*, September 21, 1970, p. 30.

⁶⁷ Woolsey, "Cost of Anti-Hijacking Measures to be Borne Mainly by Airlines," p. 29.

⁶⁸ "$1-Million Hijack Tightens Security Roles," *Aviation Week and Space Technology*, August 7, 1972, p. 30.

⁶⁹ Watkins, "Federal Actions in Hijacking Urged," p. 24.

⁷⁰ "IFALPA Mounts Anti-Hijack Drives," p. 22.

⁷¹ "ICAO Actions May Reduce Aircraft Violence Threat," *Aviation Week and Space Technology*, July 13, 1970, p. 24.

⁷² "Hijacking Indignation Increases," p. 21.

⁷³ Charles E. Schneider, "Senate Unit Bulwarks Hague Bill," *Aviation Week and Space Technology*, July 13, 1970, p. 24.

⁷⁴ "The Airway War Escalates," *Business Week*, September 12, 1970, p. 21.

[75] Laurence Doty, "Stiffer Measures Rejected in Nixon Hijacking Plans," *Aviation Week and Space Technology*, October 5, 1970, p. 30.

[76] "Hijacking Indignation Increases," p. 21.

QUESTIONS

1. What were the major environmental factors affecting the nature of strategies proposed by the CAO?
2. Identify reasons for the changing perception of the U.S. government toward the proper response to airline hijacking?
3. What was the most commonly proposed coping strategy by participating organizations and governments?
4. In what manner did the shifting reasons for hijacking affect the response of the CAO?
5. How would you deal with the position that passenger screening is an encroachment on personal privacy?
6. In light of public demand, should preventative or corrective measures be more heavily emphasized? Who should bear responsibility for these measures?
7. What environmental factors dictate the proposed strategy of ALPA?
8. Businesses are typically profit-oriented. What are the limits of this orientation given this environmental threat?
9. Which of the coping strategies appear to be most responsive to the public demand for safety?
10. What is the nature of role strain to airline management created by hijackers?
11. Which involved organizations should have primary responsibility for deterring and correcting hijacking?
12. What were major factors causing the shifting roles of airlines and governments after 1972?
13. Discuss the nature of sanctions facing organizations affected by hijackings.

CHAPTER 7

THE
URBAN
CRISIS

CASE 6
SUBSTANDARD HOUSING

Many of our cities are decaying, and the impact of substandard housing is mainly on racial and ethnic minorities in the center city. During the mid-1960s, many metropolitan centers went through an upheaval in the form of violence to people and property. Part of the turmoil was blamed on social conditions in racial ghettos. Chicago provides one of many examples of the development of racial ghettos. As blacks expanded into Chicago's white areas, white workers left and industries unable to use unskilled black labor and not willing to train blacks moved to the suburbs. Since many of the new black families had less income than former residents, many stores also moved, abandoning their premises to storefront churches.

As local jobs declined, unemployment increased and, for those who had to take jobs out of the area, travel expenses increased the cost of holding a job. Most black workers in Chicago were dependent on public transportation. Today, even though blacks have moved into white areas closer to employment, the problem of housing, along with the problem of transportation, has not been solved.

In an attempt to solve the housing problem, the federal government introduced a subsidized housing program. However, a major problem was its susceptibility to fraud. For example: A speculator buys run-down houses at very low prices. A government appraiser establishes an appraisal price. The speculator does some cosmetic repairs on the dwellings and finds a buyer willing to pay the appraised price for the home. The speculator arranges for a mortgage company to make a government-insured loan to the buyer on the basis of either no down payment or a very low down payment. Soon the old house is found to be unsound, the roof may need to be replaced, the heating system may go bad, or the plumbing system may need major repair. The new owner, already financially squeezed by loan payments too large for his income, abandons the property, the loan is defaulted on and the Federal Housing Administration (FHA) pays off the mortgage and now owns the house.

The FHA recognized, after a variety of similar experiences coupled with rapidly decaying urban conditions, that it alone could not effectively contend with the urban housing problem. It believed that a solution would require the capabilities and unique skills of private industry. However, big business had realized for some time that involvement with low-income housing was both highly risky and not very profitable.

The Life Insurance Industry Pledge: Rebuilding the Ghetto

During the early and mid-1960s, violent upheavals racked many of the nation's metropolitan centers. Almost all of the violence flared up in black ghettos, and crowded, decaying housing was given much of the blame.

Addressing a conference of the National Association of Counties in New Orleans during mid-1966, Vice President Humphrey called for a national drive to wipe out slum housing. He argued that without rent supplements or rent subsidies for the poor:

> We will have open violence in every major city and county in America. It is time for the government officials to recognize the National Guard is no answer to the problems of slums. People will not live like animals, nor should they live in some of the filthy rotten housing that make up urban ghettos.[1]

First Reactions

Despite these warnings, formidable obstacles were apparently impeding efforts to improve housing for blacks by using urban renewal programs to tear down slums and relocate the residents in better dwellings. Cleveland, the scene of some of the worst violence and destruction, typified the problems encountered. A basic tenet of the urban renewal concept proclaims that uprooted slum dwellers should be relocated in decent housing. But, in Cleveland, urban renewal was stalled, and the major cause was failure to find adequate housing for uprooted families.

The dimensions of the relocation task grew as the federally sponsored urban renewal projects multiplied. By 1966, over 1600 projects were underway in more than 800 cities. At that time, more than 202,400 families had been evicted from their homes in the course of the slum clearance and redevelopment programs.[2]

Under these programs, cities buy run-down properties from private owners and clear the land. The cities then sell the land at low prices to private developers, who construct commercial buildings or middle- and upper-income apartments. The federal government makes up two-thirds to three-fourths of the losses on land sales and clearing costs, and states often help cities bear the rest of the expense. Since the housing built by developers is almost always out of the price range of the former slum residents, and since these so often are Negroes, civil rights leaders sometimes have applied the sarcastic label "Negro removal" to urban renewal.

The National Committee Against Discrimination in Housing contends that a majority of blacks desire to leave the ghetto. Here and there, urban renewal did lead to a measure of housing integration. Akron, Ohio, was cited by federal officials as an example. Large numbers of black homeowners in Akron were evicted from their single-family dwellings to make way for redevelopment projects. Instead of concentrating in one or two sections, and possibly causing a mass exodus of white homeowners, the blacks dispersed into several lower middle-income neighborhoods, and the white residents of those areas generally stayed. Elsewhere, however, city officials often relocated displaced blacks within ghetto areas. This has been the case in New York City, Philadelphia, and Chicago.

In early 1966, President Johnson offered a solution to the problems of the cities in the form of a proposed $2.3 billion plan spread over a six-year period and aimed at rebuilding entire slum neighborhoods. The President stated he believed that the program, if enacted, would help transform the congested and decaying cities of the present into "the masterpieces of our civilization." The plan was to go well beyond traditional forms of urban renewal by combining the physical rehabilitation of slum areas with the social rehabilitation of the people who live in them. The chief mechanism for achieving this was a "Demonstration Cities Program" under which 60 to 70 cities of various sizes would be selected for federal aid. The cities selected would be required to meet strict new requirements to prove they were "qualified" to use the federal funds with minimum waste and maximum coordination. It was confirmed that while the program would not significantly disturb established programs such as public housing and urban renewal, it would result in reduced funds for those programs in communities that qualified for the Demonstration Cities Program. Questions were quickly raised about the cost of the program, often from usually loyal Democrats from mainly rural areas.[3]

The tensions created by the riots also elicited other actions by the federal government. In order to implement federal programs more effectively, Congress replaced the Housing and Home Finance Agency with the new Department of Housing and Urban Development. During 1966, this department announced two major grants to relieve racial tensions. One dealt with making cheap bus service available to residents of Watts. The other involved the federal sharing of funds for neighborhood centers in such places as Masin City, California, the scene of rioting by blacks in late March 1966. In this case, the new center provided a library, facilities for vocational training, recreational space, and other services not then available to the community's residents.

The idea of a subsidized transportation system grew from a report by the McCone Commission appointed in 1965 to investigate the riots and their causes. The commission interviewed hundreds of black residents of the area and found they felt "landlocked" and cut off from the city and employment opportunities. This was punctuated by the fact that only 14 percent of the Watts area residents owned cars.

153

Still many technical problems required solution before the bus line could become a reality. Also, the bus lines serving Los Angeles had been critical of the notion of subsidized competition.[4]

As a result of the riots, the Senate Subcommittee on Executive Reorganization held hearings and looked into "the crisis of the cities." The first phase of the hearings was to end the last of August 1966, on a controversial note. President Johnson and many of his aides felt that while the hearings were proving useful for the identification of various city needs, they were also undercutting the President both politically and administratively. Mayor Samuel Yorty of Los Angeles went a step further and protested the hearings were politically motivated. That is, they were being used to promote Senator Robert Kennedy's campaign against the President.[5] To this charge the chairman of the subcommittee, Senator Abraham Ribicoff replied, "Nonsense." [6] When criticism of the administration continued to come from the hearings, the President struck back in a news conference by stating his administration had done more than any in history to help the cities.

At the end of the first phase, Senator Ribicoff stated he believed the hearings had pinpointed two basic needs: first, a tax increase to provide $10 billion in additional federal aid yearly to the cities; and second, greater coordination of urban aid programs.[7]

The subcommittee then reconvened for a period of three weeks during December 1966. The information acquired was voluminous, yet conclusions were tentative at best. However, most witnesses did agree that the problem of the city centered around the black ghetto. It was further believed the ideal solution would be dispersal of the ghetto's poor to the suburbs. But such integration was also viewed as many years away. Society, in the meantime, must concentrate its efforts on achieving enormous qualitative improvements in the ghetto itself.

The question of how to go about improving the slum neighborhoods was then examined. One remedy suggested by Daniel P. Moynihan, Whitney M. Young, Jr. (Director of the National Urban League), and Dr. Martin Luther King was a guaranteed annual family allowance for the poor. However, the prospects of implementing this concept were dim given estimated costs between $9 billion and $20 billion. A second suggestion included closer coordination of government programs, along with a reassessment of programs that were not working. The argument here was that some federal programs get caught in bureaucratic snarls and others "dehumanize" the intended beneficiary. The proponents advocated legislation aimed at giving the Department of Housing and Urban Development greater coordinating power over urban oriented programs. Finally, most witnesses agreed that none of the above recommendations would solve the problems of the cities without the cooperation of private enterprise. Here was felt to be the source of both technological capacity and the power to create jobs.[8] Yet, as several subcommittee members and interested parties pointed out, private industry is not going into the slums on its own. Few builders will engage in slum rehabilitation because there is no certainty anyone will rent or buy a place when it is finished. Banks will not lend builders mortgage money for the same reason. Thus, in order to entice private builders and mortgage money into the slums, it was argued that public housing authorities must guarantee the purchase of rehabilitated dwellings.

Suggestions offered to encourage private industry participation included tax incentives or a vast expansion of low-interest government mortgage insurance programs. Others saw a need for a nationwide, nonprofit corporation to arrange contracts with private industry and distribute the government money.[9]

A Departure from Tradition

As the reality of the tragedy occurring in the nation's major cities came more into focus during 1967, alternative solutions multiplied. During the year, 35 housing bills, of which approximately one-half dealt with the slum problem, were introduced in Congress. Two of the bills were authored by leading political figures and offered certain distinctive features. Following several months of study and active membership on the Senate Subcommittee on Executive Reorganization, which had been holding hearings on the problems in the cities, Senator Robert Kennedy presented a two-pronged proposal. The traditional approach, which usually consisted of specific cash grants to solve specific problems such as public housing for the poor and urban renewal for several purposes, was not employed. The cash grant approach involved business, but its role is limited by the amount of money Congress is willing to appropriate for each scheme. By contrast, Kennedy's program employed a new approach in that it sought to make business a continuous active partner in the slum rebuilding field. Government's role became supportive, rather than dominant. Business would supply much of the hard cash while government would provide guarantees, incentives, and backing to induce industry to supply capital in low-income, high-risk areas.[10]

Kennedy's proposal was aimed at creating more jobs for the ghetto poor, and building more and better low-rent housing. The housing proposal focused on rehabilitating or replacing up to 400,000 substandard dwelling units and would cost the Treasury no more than $50 million annually. The plan incorporated a combination of tax incentives and low-interest mortgages to achieve both low-rent housing for the poor and substantial return on investment for private entrepreneurs. One of the incentives to private industry was a system of long-term loans at low interest rates subsidized by the Treasury, payable at 2 percent annually over 50 years. Based on an estimated 300,000 to 400,000 units, the annual cost to the Treasury was estimated at $35 million. A second inducement was a set of tax incentives, the most important of which would be an investment tax credit of 3 percent to 22 percent of the cost of the project, depending on the amount of capital the builder was willing to invest. In this case the revenue loss was estimated at $15 million annually. Over the 50-year life of the mortgages, the total cost of the program would be about $2.5 billion. However, according to Kennedy, much of this would be recaptured by increased tax revenues the new construction would generate. The plan was designed to provide low monthly rentals for poor tenants ranging from $75 to $100, depending on the per unit cost of the project. At the same time, the plan would guarantee returns to investors of 13 percent to 15 percent on their own capital investment. As described above, the low rents were to be made possible by the long-term loans at 2 percent, while the high returns were to be made possible by the tax incentives.[11]

At approximately the same time, on the other side of the Senate aisle, Senator Charles Percy (R-Ill) presented a plan that also depended on private market capital. However, unlike the Kennedy proposal, this plan focused on expansion of home ownership by the poor. It proposed a federally chartered foundation that could sell up to $2 billion in government-backed bonds bearing commercial rates of interest. The fund would then be loaned at low rates of interest to low-income persons for the purchase of homes. The differences between the interest the foundation must pay to investors and the payments it would receive from the poor homeowner would be subsidized, through an elaborate coupon plan, by the government.[12]

During this same period, while testifying before the Housing Subcommittee of the Senate Banking and Currency Committee, the Secretary of Housing and Urban Development, Robert C. Weaver, warned against quick panaceas and said that it was a "snare and delusion" to give people in the slums the impression that their conditions could be changed "overnight." [13]

The Insurance Industry Steps Forward

Despite the much publicized concern at the federal level and the many bills presented by Congress, it still remained that the 400 or so federal government appropriations programs were not able to cope with the deterioration of housing and the community in broad areas of the cities. Apparently, government by itself was unable to solve these problems. In fact, the Report of the National Advisory Commission on Civil Disorders listed private enterprise first in stressing that:

> Private enterprise, labor unions, the churches, the foundations, the universities— all our urban institutions—must deepen their involvement in the life of the city and their commitment to its revival and welfare.[14]

In an addendum opinion to the report, the statement was made: "Business and industry are our last hope." [15]

Yet despite public exhortations, despite obvious private concern and real contributions, the leaders of the industrial establishment had never managed to come up with the dramatic program that might convince slum dwellers that U.S. business was serious about solving urban problems. However, industry certainly was aware of these problems. Since 1965, the Institute of Life Insurance had recommended that the life insurance industry should assume a greater role in the determination of solutions to the urban problems emerging at that time. In response, the Life Insurance Association of America and the American Life Convention appointed a Joint Committee on Urban Problems consisting of top executives from the various companies and under the chairmanship of Metropolitan's Board Chairman, Gilbert W. Fitzhugh. After much debate over the plight of the central cities, they concluded the life insurance business was particularly qualified to make a contribution in the area of financing, particularly in the fields of housing and job-creating facilities.[16]

Riots again swept through cities such as Detroit and Newark in the summer of 1967. Newark, with a population of 402,000, of which 52 percent were black, had the nation's highest crime and maternal mortality rates.[17] It was particularly hard hit. Insurance executive Orville Beal, president of Prudential Life Insurance, witnessed much of the rioting from his office atop the Prudential skyscraper headquarters just five blocks from the scene of the worst outbreaks. He mused, "I could look out of my window and see the fires, the smoke pouring from buildings and the helmets of the National Guard." [18]

Then on September 13, 1967, a group of seven insurance businessmen called on President Johnson with what might be considered an extraordinary proposal. Their plan was to divert $1 billion of investment funds from normal channels and apply them instead to upgrading real estate in hard-core urban slums. These were leaders in the industry; they represented three trade associations with 348 member corporations that had combined assets of $159 billion and normally invested around $17 billion annually. The pledge, then, represented about two-thirds of 1 percent of these assets and approximately 6 percent of yearly investable funds. It was hoped the bulk of the funds would be dispensed during the next year and be placed in mortgages for low-cost, low-income housing, particularly in housing built under the federal rent-supplement program. Most significantly, the insurance company's program marked the first major effort in this field by private enterprise. Yet despite the size of the insurance industry's commitment, virtually everyone agreed the problem was far more massive and Housing and Urban Development Secretary Weaver estimated that $300 billion would be needed for city housing in the next ten years.[19]

However, it was quite apparent that both the President and Secretary Weaver were quite pleased. After the initial meeting, the insurance men, led by their spokesman during the proceedings, Gilbert Fitzhugh, were ushered into the Fish Room in the White House for a press conference. During the exchange, some of the reporters appeared skeptical about the industry's ability to accomplish much, and most of them seemed a little confused about the mechanics of the proposal. At one point, a reporter asked, "What will be the criteria used to give away this money?" Fitzhugh replied tartly, "We are not giving away anything." [20]

In fact, neither the assumption explicit in the question nor the response was entirely correct. While contributions would not take the form of outright gifts and the $1 billion was to be invested in the slums to return a profit, the return would be less than alternative investment opportunities. The loans were to be made at 6 percent annually and were to be insured by the Federal Housing Administration.

In a *Fortune* article following the announcement, it was suggested that the difference in rates of return be considered a self-imposed "tax" designed to speed social progress. For instance, within a month of the announcement, the industry had committed $27,500,000 in mortgages in slum dwellings, which would yield just 6 percent interest in a mortgage market where it could easily acquire returns ranging from 6.75 percent to 7.5 percent. Further, these rates were tied to risks of real estate investment in the suburbs. The risks of investment in real estate in the blighted urban areas had driven rates as high as 25 percent, and even at this level little or no money was generally available. In recent years, and particularly after the riots, the private investment pattern in the slums was more often one of disinvestment.[21]

Again at the press conference in Washington, Fitzhugh was asked whether a company could still lose money on mortgages insured by the government. He answered, "Yes, we sure can. We hope not much." He was referring to the fact that loans made under Section 203(b) of the National Housing Act, which enables FHA to insure mortgages on one-to-four family homes, would be small ones and would typically involve high servicing charges. Thus, companies would be investing in residential mortgages in two ways: some money would be invested at less than market rates, with government insurance; some would be invested at market rates, but in high-risk markets where mortgage money has generally been unavailable. Finally, some of the $1 billion was to go into mortgages on commercial or industrial buildings in slums, to support companies that looked like good risks and might create a significant number of jobs. Because such businesses are normally not good risks, a new program by the Small Business Administration guarantees businessmen's lease rental payments in urban areas for as long as twenty years.[22]

President Johnson hailed the move as a "historic contribution to our country" and expressed the hope it would set a precedent for similar moves on the part of private industry.[23] However, others felt that Johnson's and Fitzhugh's announcement had all the earmarks of another political razzle-dazzle gimmick. It coincided with and upstaged hearings on the Robert Kennedy proposals, which were similar but broader, and the introduction of Senator Clark's (D-Penn.) bill to provide $2.5 billion for emergency jobs and urban redevelopment. Added skepticism resulted in mounting pressure on Congress to investigate life insurance firms.[24]

The Capital Market

The capital market climate at this time also indicated that the demand for funds would be strong. Factors contributing to this demand included: (1) The continuance of a high level of business spending for new plant, equipment, and inventories, (2) a sizable increase in family formations that would stimulate housing and durable goods markets, (3) the need to improve corporate liquidity, (4) the need to improve the liquidity of many financial institutions, (5) the prospect of increased spending at all government levels—federal, state, and local, and (6) rapidly rising asset prices which tend to increase the proportion of the purchase price that must be obtained externally.[25]

On the other hand, the supply of funds was also expected to be tight because of (1) a squeeze on personal saving due to a population mix with high proportions among older and younger people, who tend to spend rather than save, (2) a squeeze on corporate saving because of the wage cost-push effect on retained earnings and the tax increase, (3) the reluctance on the part of lenders to provide funds unless adequately compensated for expected inflation trends, and (4) a more restrictive monetary climate because of inflationary pressures and a persistent balance of payments and gold problem.[26]

Conclusions on the market were that capital markets would be tight with the advantages continuing on the side of suppliers rather than demanders.

Saving the Rent Supplement Program

Prior to the riots in 1967, the government had attempted to create investment channels back into the slums. The major channel through which most funds had been flowing was initiated in 1965. Congress at that time passed what had come to be known as the Rent Supplement Act. It was best known for the provision that enabled low-income families to obtain decent new or rehabilitated housing by helping pay the rent with federal subsidies. Renters paid 25 percent of their income and the government contributed the rest. Yet because the supply of adequate low-cost housing was so short, it was also necessary to encourage the building of more, and the Federal Housing Administration was the instrument chosen.

However, the act was already in trouble by the time it went into operation in late 1966. The problem was that the 6 percent mortgage return, which had seemed attractive when Congress acted, became unattractive because money rates had increased rapidly. The Federal National Mortgage Association became the only likely taker of rent-supplement mortgages. It was able to finance them under its "special assistance" program, which offers mortgages for projects deemed to be socially urgent but unattractive to private investors. However, an attempt to cover all the rent-supplement contracts would stretch its emergency funds uncomfortably.

The insurance companies' commitment undid this predicament and practically supplanted the Federal National Mortgage Association as buyer of rent-supplement mortgages. Then there arose the question as to whether Congress would vote added funds for the rent-supplement program. This might prove a limiting factor in estimating the amount insurance companies decided to put into these mortgages. If there were no limits at all, and the companies decided to put the entire $1 billion into rent-supplement mortgages, they could finance 80,000 housing units.[27]

Some Early Results of the Program

The insurance companies, at least initially, seemed rather vague about exactly how the $1 billion would be invested. For instance, an official at Metropolitan Life said the companies would not work directly in slum rehabilitation. When asked if tenants would have any measure of control in management of housing or social services, the industry was unable to say since they would hold only the first mortgage.[28]

Apparently, publication of the $1 billion commitment had been to this point the most explicit aspect of the program. Bankers Life Company of Des Moines, Iowa had bought several $7200-per-minute commercials on NBC television's

Today program, which had Hugh Downs congratulating the industry for "one of the finest examples of . . . social awareness and willingness to participate in the problems of society." Downs said, according to the script prepared for him:

> As just one of more than a million people carrying life insurance with Bankers Life Company of Des Moines, Iowa—I've had policies with them since 1954—I'm proud to let you know this morning that Bankers Life will be participating in this venture with millions of dollars of investment capital.

According to a Today official, the White House granted specific permission for use of President Johnson's name in Bankers Life commercials.[29]

Yet despite some skepticism on the part of the news media and slum residents, the program was not long getting under way. Funds were made available for a backlog of low-income rent supplement housing projects in urban areas for which Federal National Mortgage Association funds had been earmarked. These funds could now be released for other projects. While this provided an early start, the bulk of the program was being developed by individual companies seeking investment possibilities in cities throughout the nation.

By August 13, 1968, exactly eleven months after the $1 billion program was launched, the life insurance industry had made nearly $659 million in specific commitments and disbursements. The money had been committed to 215 cities all across the country. Housing at this point represented the largest share of the program. About 47,000 housing units would be financed by $517 million earmarked for this purpose. This amount was divided $286 million for one-to-four family houses and $231 million for multifamily units. The program's main thrust seemed to have three major areas: (1) 40-year mortgages on FHA-insured housing projects for low-income families, (2) insured mortgages on one-to-four family houses for low-to-moderate-income families, and (3) conventional loans on low-to-moderate-income housing projects, with shorter maturities than FHA loans.[30]

A variety of other investment opportunities was also pursued. Around $200,000 was committed in downtown Richmond, Virginia, in cooperation with the City Council Housing Committee to finance individual homes in order to rehouse lower-income families displaced by an expressway. In the Hough area of Cleveland, a six-building complex was initiated under the insurance industry program to house 94 low-income families with the aid of rent supplements. One insurance company participated with local banks and building and loan associations to provide financing of individual houses for low-income families through FHA-insured and VA-guaranteed mortgages. In Elizabeth, New Jersey, 40 families moved into a new apartment building conventionally financed under the program. The building provided housing for moderate-income minority families previously living in congested sections of the city.[31]

After 15 months, projects had been initiated in 227 cities in 42 states, the District of Columbia, and Puerto Rico. Approximately $622 million had been invested in housing for low- and moderate-income families, which provided 57,589 units.[32]

Efforts aimed at job creation in slum areas emphasized mortgage loans for industrial plants, warehouses or distribution terminals, and service facilities. Service facilities included hospitals, nursing homes, neighborhood shopping, and social service or educational facilities. Most monies for these purposes were without government guarantees. As of early 1969, $188 million had been devoted to these projects, which in turn had resulted in the creation of 26,436 permanent jobs, besides those created by the construction work.[33]

The Second Billion-Dollar Commitment

Despite encouragement generated by the initial $1 billion commitment by insurance companies, similar moves by other members of private industry did not take place. In April 1969, when the industry pledged a second $1 billion, twenty-eight fewer companies participated. In October 1968, at a top-level meeting in Harrison, New York, it was decided that there would be no further attempts to extend this industrywide pledge of investment funds. The industry was pulling out of the ghetto and the question was being asked: What had gone wrong? [34]

Tight money had posed a problem in the past according to Stanley Karson, director of the Institute of Life Insurance's Clearinghouse on Corporate Social Responsibility, but it was no longer a problem. [35]

It also was argued that the program was not continued because job-creating and service facilities offered few acceptable investment opportunities. However, the emphasis could be shifted more completely to housing, or the rate of use of funds might have been slowed down.

Also, a few projects had run into serious difficulties and there was some debate about how widespread these problems had become. One case of financial collapse was Prudential's Baber Village Apartments in Prince George's County, Maryland. The case was the subject of an article in the *Wall Street Journal* that many felt gave the impression, on the basis of one incident, that the entire program had been a disaster. [36] The following comments are based on the article's description of the project and its problems.

Baber Village consisted of 17 buildings, some of which almost immediately had been boarded up. Windows were broken and walls were knocked in. Sewers were sometimes backed up, filling bathtubs with raw waste. During its two-year life, there had been 10 resident managers, one of whom ran off with the rent money. In spring 1971, just three months before the article in the *Wall Street Journal*, the mortgage on Baber Village was assumed by the Department of Housing and Urban Development to avoid foreclosure. [37]

Apparently, the problems were quite diverse, and started with such simple matters as the inexperience of poverty-stricken tenants who took a garbage-disposal unit for a dishwasher or inadvertently sabotaged the plumbing by flushing discarded clothing down the toilet. Other problems involved substandard construction, vandalism, mismanagement, rent defaults, and outright fraud. [38]

As a result of experience with FHA, insurance companies have learned that such mortgage insurance is nothing like the surefire safety hedge it's cracked up to be. At several projects, including one in New York City, unhappy landlords had abandoned some one-to-four family buildings financed under the program and stopped making payments on their mortgages. The buildings were now run-down and needed rehabilitation. But Metropolitan Life Insurance Company, which owned the mortgages, still could not get paid by the FHA, because aside from natural reluctance to evict tenants, the company found that New York housing law made it extremely difficult in any case. But FHA cannot pay off a mortgage claim on a substandard building unless it is vacated or repaired.

Baber Village illustrates a lot of what went wrong with the program. It was officially owned by the Washington diocese of the African Methodist Episcopal Church. Yet like many other projects, Baber Village was the product of bigger money than the church was used to handling. As problems emerged, officials of the church said they never realized how burdensome the responsibilities would be when they joined the program.

For example, rental accounting became so disorderly that it was difficult to determine who wasn't paying rent. Each resident manager appeared to have left the books in worse shape than the previous manager. One manager disappeared with an estimated $3000 in rent money. As a last attempt to bring the project under financial control, an effort was made to evict 68 tenants accused of not paying rent. The tenants took the management to court and presented rent receipts showing payments that had apparently never been recorded. The court ruled against the eviction. However, if the rent money had been received, it was not used to pay off the mortgage.[39]

Finally, the article pointed out that the housing part of the insurance industries program had been the biggest disappointment. While Baber Village was an extreme example, it was by no means the only housing project in trouble. "I doubt that most will last out the full life of their 40-year mortgages," one insurance company official reportedly said.[40]

Another reason often put forth for the death of the program was the sharply diminishing returns on the publicity. The second billion-dollar pledge was announced from the White House but it was no longer front-page news. *The New York Times* carried the following story on page 44 of the late city edition only:

> Representatives of the life insurance industry told President Nixon at the White House today that they planned to spend $1-billion more in inner-city investments to create more jobs and furnish better housing in urban areas.
>
> The pledge was part of the industry's current program to direct investment funds into ghetto projects that, because of high risks involved, are normally financed by private investors.
>
> President Nixon said the pledge "demonstrates again the depth of their concern about the problems of our cities, and it will provide an effective way to bring more jobs and better housing to many Americans who need them."
>
> The program, begun in September 1967, has resulted so far in $1-billion going into low-cost housing and job-producing businesses in 227 cities, an industry spokesman said.[41]

Major news magazines and television networks gave the announcement of the second billion no coverage at all. To compensate for the lack of coverage, the Institute of Life Insurance ran large ads in 156 newspapers and 21 magazines. However, the media blackout was probably the major reason. As Stanley Karson of the Institute of Life Insurance pointed out, if a pledge of a third billion dollars were announced, the value in terms of social prestige would probably be negligible. People were still poor, but poverty had become a stale issue. [42]

Industry spokesmen indicate they haven't given up altogether. In a meeting held in December 1971, it was recommended that a clearinghouse be established to encourage individual companies to engage in socially responsible actions. These actions were to involve not only the ghetto, but minority employment, health, and environmental protection, among other areas, and were to be in the form of contributions as well as investments.

A few years after the decision to terminate the initial program, the following amount of the $2 billion pledged had been disbursed.

Urban Investment Program of the Life Insurance Business *
Status on January 1, 1972

Type of Investment		
Housing		
One- to Four-Family	50,901	$ 587,011,000
Multifamily	56,595	631,888,000
Securities	2,105	21,602,000
Total Housing	109,601	$1,240,501,000
	Number of Jobs Created	
Job-Creating and Service Facilities	*or Retained*	
Medical	25,362	$ 281,381,000
Industrial	19,489	110,366,000
Commercial	14,645	132,504,000
Social Services	2,581	69,167,000
Total Job-Creating and Service Facilities	62,077	$ 593,418,000
Total	—	$1,833,919,000

* *Life Insurance Fact Book 1972.* New York: Institute of Life Insurance, 1972, p. 10.

FOOTNOTES

[1] "Humphrey Warns of Slum Revolts," *The New York Times,* July 19, 1966, p. 19.

[2] Stanley Penn, "Drive for New Housing for Negroes in Slums Delayed in Many Cities," *The Wall Street Journal,* August 3, 1966, p. 1.

[3] Robert B. Semple, Jr., "Johnson Submits $2.3-Billion Plan to Rebuild Slums," *The New York Times,* January 27, 1966, pp. 1, 20.

[4] Robert B. Semple, Jr., "Direct Ghetto Aid Is Planned By U.S.," *The New York Times*, May 4, 1966, p. 28.

[5] Marjorie Hunter, "Urban Hearings Vex White House," *The New York Times*, August 29, 1966, p. 20.

[6] *Ibid.*

[7] *Ibid.*

[8] Robert B. Semple, Jr., "Prescriptions for Slums," *The New York Times*, December 19, 1966, p. 32.

[9] *Ibid.*

[10] "Riot Prevention Urged by Weaver," *The New York Times*, July 18, 1967, p. 24.

[11] Robert B. Semple, Jr., "Kennedy Outlines Slum Plan Costs," *The New York Times*, July 14, 1967, p. 13.

[12] Robert B. Semple, Jr., "The Target Is the Slum," *The New York Times*, July 9, 1967, p. 4E.

[13] "Riot Prevention Urged by Weaver," p. 24.

[14] Report of the National Advisory Commission on Civil Disorders, Washington, D.C., March 1, 1968, p. 230.

[15] *Ibid.*, p. 313.

[16] Charles Moeller, Jr., "Economic Implications of the Life Insurance Industry's Investment Program in the Central Cities," *The Journal of Risk and Insurance*, March 1969, p. 97.

[17] John F. Lyons, "Prudential Allocates Loans, Meets With Radical Blacks, Works Quietly at City Hall," *The Wall Street Journal*, March 20, 1968, p. 1.

[18] "Slum Housing: A Billion-Dollar Baby," *Newsweek*, September 25, 1967, p. 81.

[19] *Ibid.*

[20] Walter McQuade, "Mortgages for the Slums," *Fortune*, January 1968, p. 162.

[21] *Ibid.*

[22] *Ibid.*, p. 163.

[23] "Slum Housing: A Billion-Dollar Baby," p. 81.

[24] "Billion Dollar Bubble," *Commonweal*, September 29, 1967, p. 598.

[25] Moeller, Jr., "Economic Implications," p. 94.

[26] *Ibid.*

[27] McQuade, "Mortgages for the Slums," pp. 162–163.

[28] "Insurance in the Slums," *New Republic*, September 30, 1967, p. 8.

[29] *Ibid.*

[30] Moeller, Jr., "Economic Implications," p. 99.

[31] *Ibid.*, pp. 99–100.

[32] "News of Realty: Slum Investment," *The New York Times*, January 2, 1969, p. 52.

[33] *Ibid.*

[34] Eugene Epstein, "The Insurance Industry's Quiet Retreat," *Business and Society Review*, Summer 1972, p. 40.

[35] *Ibid.*

[36] *Ibid.*

[37] Priscilla S. Meyer, "Life Insurers' Program to Fund Big Projects Hits Plenty of Snags," *The Wall Street Journal*, July 21, 1971, p. 1.

[38] *Ibid.*

[39] *Ibid.*, pp. 1, 27.

[40] Ibid., p. 1.

[41] "Insurance Industry to Spend $1-Billion More in Slums," *The New York Times*, April 16, 1969, p. 44.

[42] Epstein, "The Insurance Industry's Quiet Retreat," p. 41.

QUESTIONS

1. Substandard housing is a part of what larger social problem?
2. What appears to be the primary reasons for the life insurance industry's channeling of the $1 billion?
3. What is the nature of the coping strategy embarked on by the government and the life insurance industry?
4. Why had the competitive market system not effectively dealt with the urban crisis since it was, in part, economic in nature?
5. How successful was the release of the $2 billion from the standpoint of the life insurance industry and from the standpoint of society?
6. What seemed to be the underlying causes of the problems occurring at Baber Village?
7. How effectively did private industry add its particular talents to the solution of the urban crisis in this case?
8. In light of social expectations, why was there a lack of interest in the project after the second year by the life insurance industry?
9. What actions might have been taken to improve the effective use of the $2 billion contribution by the insurance industry?
10. Based on the results of the partnership, what has been learned about the most effective way to perform the complementary roles of the two major participants?

CHAPTER 8

DISCRIMINATION
IN
INDUSTRY

CASE 7
RACIAL DISCRIMINATION

Discrimination in the United States has been widespread and includes many minority groups, however, the labor force problems of blacks deserve special consideration.

First, statistically, blacks compose about 90 percent of all the nonwhite population in the United States.[1] They account for 10 percent of the labor force, 20 percent of total unemployment, and 30 percent of long-term unemployment.[2]

Second, blacks have suffered a more brutal and continuous form of discrimination than any other minority group; such discrimination has its roots in the cultural mores that justified and perpetuated slavery. A black businessman several years ago in a speech before the National Association of Manufacturers' Congress of American Industry concluded that blacks have failed to progress with other elements of society mainly because of their own lack of initiative, courage, integrity, loyalty, and wisdom. Charles Silberman argues that in a sense this indictment is correct. "Many Negroes do lack ambition, initiative, courage, and wisdom. But this itself should be no comfort to white businessmen or to other white citizens. If these charges are correct, it is because for 350 years we whites have maintained a system in the United States which was designed to destroy ambition, initiative, and courage among Negroes, to penalize them for displaying such qualities and, in fact, to prevent the accumulation of wisdom."[3]

Third, blacks, by way of the civil rights movement of the fifties and sixties, have forced the larger society to focus attention on their plight with the explicit goal of improving their situation.

Fourth, blacks have a dominant physical characteristic which is easily identifiable and hence readily used to perpetuate discrimination.

Only recently has a concerted attempt been made to remedy racial discrimination in the labor force. Following a number of massive anti-black demonstrations in the South in 1963, President Kennedy reaffirmed his view that social discrimination was a moral issue and asked Congress to pass a Civil Rights Act, which it did in 1964. Title VII of this act prohibits discrimination by race or sex in hiring and clearly outlaws the type of economic discrimination in business that has so long existed for blacks.[4]

The Duke Power Company became one of the first companies taken to court under the act when on November 1966, 13 blacks in the firm's labor department at its Dan River Plant filed suit charging discrimination.

FOOTNOTES

[1] U.S. Bureau of the Census, *The Social and Economic Status of Negroes in the United States, 1970*, Current Population Report, Series P-23, No. 38, BLS Report No. 394 (Washington, D.C.: U.S. Government Printing Office, 1971), p. iv.

[2] Charles E. Silberman, "The Economics of the Negro Problem," in Eli Ginzberg, (Ed.), *The Negro Challenge to the Business Community* (New York: McGraw-Hill Book Company, 1964), p. 16.

[3] Silberman, "The Economics of the Negro Problem," p. 17.

[4] George A. Steiner, *Business and Society* (New York: Random House, 1971), p. 204.

Duke Power Company and Race Relations: Was There Cultural Bias of Testing Procedures?

The 1964 Civil Rights Act makes it unlawful for an employer to deprive any person of employment opportunities or otherwise adversely affect his status as an employee because of the individual's race. However, under the law an employer, when hiring and promoting workers, may utilize any professionally developed ability test provided the test isn't designed or used to discriminate against blacks. The law also permits employers to apply different standards of employment among workers, provided there is no intentional discrimination.

Duke Power Company: The Dan River Plant

The Duke Power Company is an electric utility engaged in the generation, transmission, and distribution of electric power to the general public and industry in both North Carolina and South Carolina. The company was incorporated in North Carolina in June 1964 as a successor to a company of the same name originally incorporated in New Jersey on May 1, 1917 as Wateree Electric Company. The name was changed to Duke Power Company in November 1924. By 1965, Duke employed approximately 6000 persons.[1]

The Dan River Plant is one of several company power stations and was constructed in 1949. The plant is located at Draper, North Carolina and employed 95 persons in 1965.

The Dan River Plant was organized for operational purposes into the following departments: (1) operations; (2) maintenance; (3) laboratory and tests; (4) coal handling; and (5) labor. Jobs that are classified as watchman, clerk, and storekeeper are included in a miscellaneous category. Each department also possesses specialized job classifications and these are presented in Exhibit 1.

Members of the operations department are responsible for the operation of the station's generating equipment, including boilers, turbines, auxiliary and control equipment, and the electrical substation. They also handle interconnections between the station, the company's power system, and the systems of other power companies.[2]

Workers in the coal handling department unload, weigh, sample, crush, and transport coal received from the mines. In the process they operate diesel and electrical equipment, bulldozers, conveyer belts, crushes, as well as other kinds of heavy equipment. In order to carry out their functions these employees must be able to read and understand manuals relating to the machinery and equipment.[3]

EXHIBIT 1 Job Classifications within Departments

Power Station Operators	*Labor*
Control Operator	Labor Foreman
Pump Operator	Auxiliary Serviceman
Utility Operator	Laborer (Semi-skilled)
Learner	Laborer (Common)
Coal and Material Handling	*Miscellaneous*
Coal Handling Foreman	Watchman
Coal Equipment Operator	Clerk
Coal Handling Operator	Chief Clerk
Helper	Storekeeper
Learner	
	Supervisors
Maintenance	Superintendent
Machinist	Assistant Superintendent
Electrician—Welder	Plant Engineer
Mechanic A	Assistant Plant Engineer
Mechanic B	Chemist
Repairman	Test Supervisor
Learner	Maintenance Supervisor
	Assistant Maintenance Supervisor
Test and Laboratory	Shift Supervisor
Testman—Labman	Junior Engineer
Lab and Test Technician	
Lab and Test Assistant	

Source: Griggs v. Duke Power, 292 F. Supp. 243 (1968), p. 245.

Technicians in the laboratory department analyze water to determine its fitness for use in the boilers and run analyses of coal samples to ascertain the quality of the coal for use as fuel in the power station. Test department personnel are responsible for the performance of the station and accomplish this by maintaining the accuracy of instrument gauges and control devices.[4]

The maintenance department, as demonstrated in Exhibit 1, is comprised of machinists, electrician-welders, mechanics, repairmen, and learners. The department is responsible for maintenance of all the mechanical and electrical equipment and machinery in the plant.[5]

The labor department acts as a service group for all other departments and is responsible generally for the janitorial services in the plant. Its employees mix mortar, collect garbage, help construct forms, clean bolts, and provide the necessary labor involved in performing other miscellaneous jobs. Workers in this department receive the lowest wages at the station. In 1965, the maximum wage for a member of the labor department was $1.565 per hour while the minimum wage for an employee in any other department was $1.705 per hour. Maximum wages paid employees in other departments ranged from $3.18 per hour to $3.65 per hour.[6]

Dan River Hiring and Promotion Policies

In 1955, Duke Power initiated a policy that required a high school education or its equivalent for all new employees, except those hired for the labor department. An employee already a member of the department had to have a high school education or its equivalent before he could be considered for advancement from the department to coal handling, operations, or maintenance or advancement from coal handling to operations or maintenance.[7]

The line of progression for employee advancement at Dan River was based on job classifications within each department. Normally promotions were made as vacancies occurred. The senior man in the classification directly below the vacancy was promoted, if qualified to do the job. There was no formal training program directed at achieving promotable employees within departments, although some on-the-job training was carried out. When an employee moved from one department to another, he was normally transferred at the entry level; however, at Dan River, an employee was often able to move into another department above the entry level, depending on his qualifications.[8]

In July 1965, the effective date of the Civil Rights Act of 1964, Duke Power instituted some changes in its employment and transfer policies. Prior to this time, the company had made a practice of hiring and restricting blacks only to the labor department. It was no secret that the company had been openly discriminating on the basis of race in the hiring and assigning of employees at the Dan River plant.[9] After the 1965 effective date men being hired for employment in the labor department were required to make a satisfactory score on the Revised Bata Test. In all other departments and classifications, applicants were required to have a high school education and register satisfactory scores on two professionally prepared aptitude tests—the Wonderlic Personnel Test, which purports to measure general intelligence, and the Bennett Mechanical Aptitude Test.[10]

In September 1965, the company's promotion and transfer policies were also amended. Prior to this date a high school education was required for transfer to the more desirable departments including operations, maintenance and laboratory. However, now the company began to permit employees on the payroll prior to September 1, 1965, without high school educations or their equivalent to become eligible for transfer or promotion from the coal and material handling department and labor department to more desirable departments by satisfactorily passing the Wonderlic and Bennett tests.[11] The requisite scores used for both initial hiring and transfer approximated the national median for high school graduates.[12]

The change in transfer policy came in response to requests from members of the coal and material handling department. They stated they wanted a means of escaping from that department. In granting this opportunity, the company also provided the same chance to employees in the labor department.

Tests Used by Duke Power

The minimum acceptable score used by Duke was approximately that achieved by the average high school graduate. A score of 20 was acceptable on the Wonderlic Personnel Test, and the average high school graduate scored 21.9. On the Bennett Mechanical Comprehension Test a score of 39 was acceptable; this was the same score achieved by the average high school graduate.[13] The standardized aptitude test is designed to predict future ability by testing the accumulation of acquired knowledge. Neither test used by Duke was intended to measure the ability to learn to perform a particular job or category of jobs.[14]

One criticism often leveled at such standardized tests is that they are culture bound—the contents may draw too heavily on common knowledge and skills acquired within the majority culture. In one instance, it was found that 58 percent of whites could pass a battery of standardized tests, while only 6 percent of the blacks were successful. Among the tests included in this battery were the Wonderlic and Bennett tests.[15] According to the research, one reason for the discrepancy in scores is that blacks are more likely to have lived in different and poorer sections of a city, to have gone to inferior schools, and to have had less encouragement to continue their education than whites.[16] Researchers point to the following questions taken from the tests used by Duke as examples of this bias:

Does B.C. mean "before Christ?"
Do "adopt" and "adept" have similar meanings? [17]

The predictive ability of standardized tests has also been questioned. In one study, it was found that although for some industrial occupations tests do give accurate predictions, the overall trend was one of low validity.[18] In a second study, 15 black workers were hired and employed on an assembly line. No tests were given during the hiring process. After six months, the workers were given the Wonderlic battery of tests. Although prior to the examination all workers were rated satisfactory by their supervisors, no one passed the test.[19]

Reaction of Black Employees at Dan River

Although Duke officials claim that there had never been a company policy of hiring blacks only in the labor department and only whites in the other departments, all 14 blacks employed at Dan River worked in the labor department until 1966. Also, in 1966 qualifications of members of most operating departments demonstrated conflict with stated policy. Three of the 14 blacks in the labor department had high school educations while only three of the nine whites in the coal handling department had high school diplomas. Only eight of the 17 white employees in the maintenance department had diplomas. Among supervisors, two white shift supervisors in the power plant had less than high school educations; two coal handling foremen had less than high school educations; and the labor foreman had no high school diploma.[20]

On August 8, 1966, Jesse Martin, a member of the labor department since 1953 and the senior black with a high school education in that department, was promoted to learner in the coal handling department. The promotion came five months after charges of discriminatory employment practices had been filed with the Equal Employment Opportunity Commission (EEOC) by the workers in the labor department.[21]

In November 1966, the 13 blacks remaining in the labor department filed suit against Duke Power Company. The workers claimed that Duke's educational and testing requirements were both discriminatory and invalid. They argued that there was no evidence showing a business need for the requirements, that Duke Power had not conducted any studies to discern whether or not such requirements were related to an employee's ability to perform duties, and that the tests were not job related.[22] The plaintiffs also claimed that prior to the effective date of the Civil Rights Act, blacks had been relegated to the lowest paying department at Dan River and had been deprived of access to other more favorable departments on the basis of racial discrimination.[23] They believed the educational and testing requirements established by Duke preserved and continued the effects of past racial discrimination and therefore violated the Civil Rights Act.[24]

The plaintiffs also stated that centuries of cultural and educational discrimination have placed blacks at a disadvantage when competing with whites for positions measured in terms of an educational or testing standing. Further, Duke merely seized upon such requirements as a means of discrimination without a business purpose in mind.[25] For instance, the North Carolina census statistics show, as of 1960, 34 percent of white males had graduated from high school while only 12 percent of black males had achieved the same success. Thus, on one level, use of the high school diploma requirement would favor whites by a ratio of approximately 3 to 1. Black employees also pointed out that observation of Duke's policies in practice demonstrates that white employees without a high school education were eligible for job openings in the more lucrative departments while black employees with the same qualifications were restricted to job classifications in the lower paying labor department.[26] Finally, the plaintiffs claimed that Duke discriminated on the basis of race in the allocation of overtime work at the Dan River plant.

The plaintiffs, in their court battle with Duke Power, sought injunctive relief rather than monetary awards.

Duke's Response to the Charges

Duke responded to the charges of the 13 blacks by admitting that when it initiated the requirements no formal studies were carried out to determine the relationship such requirements would bear to its employees' ability to perform their duties. A job-related validity study at the Dan River plant was initiated in 1966, but had not been completed at the time the case came to trial. Officers with the company argued the policy was employed because its business was becoming more complex and it had employees who simply weren't able to cope with the changing situation. These were men who were unable to read or reason out simple problems and did not have the intelligence to enable them to progress through the company's line of advancement.[27] At the time of the charges, the company employed an intracompany promotion policy and trained its own employees for supervisory positions rather than hiring supervisory personnel from outside. Duke claimed that it initiated the high school education requirement to provide some reasonable assurance that its employees would be able to advance into supervisory positions. The company argued that its educational and testing requirements were valid because they possessed a legitimate business purpose. Officials further pointed out the tests were professionally developed ability tests, as sanctioned under Section 703(h) of the Civil Rights Act.

The company also hired a psychologist in the field of industrial and personnel testing, Dr. Dannie Moffie, to observe operations at the Dan River plant. After observing personnel in the performance of jobs, studying written summaries of job duties, and spending several days with company representatives discussing job content, Dr. Moffie concluded that a high school education would provide the training, ability, and judgment necessary to perform tasks at the higher skill classifications.[28] However, Duke realized there were limitations to the applicability of the high school requirement. One executive stated, "There is nothing magic about it, and it doesn't work all the time, because you can have a man who graduated from high school, who is certainly incompetent to go on up, but we felt this was a reasonable requirement." [29]

Duke was aware of the adverse effect the educational requirement had on black employees in the labor department, but pointed out that the white employees appointed watchmen or employed in the coal handling department were also affected. In order to assist these employees with less than a high school education, Duke had initiated a policy of paying most of the expenses incurred by an employee who wished to return to school to achieve a high school diploma or its equivalent.

Section 703(h) of Title VII

That part of the 1964 Civil Rights Act that underlies Duke's plight is Section 703(h) of Title VII. It states in part:

Sec. 703(a) It shall be an unlawful employment practice for an employer—

(2) to limit, segregate, or classify his employees in any way which would deprive or tend to deprive any individual of employment opportunities or otherwise adversely affect his status as an employee, because of such individual's race, color, religion, sex, or national origin.

(h) Notwithstanding any other provision of this Title, it shall not be an unlawful employment practice for an employer . . . to give and to act upon the results of any professionally developed ability test provided that such a test, its administration or action upon the results is not designed, intended, or used to discriminate because of race, color, religion, sex, or national origin . . .

This particular part of Section 703 was included in the act mainly because of an amendment by Senator John Tower (R-Tex). When proposing the original amendment, Senator Tower stated:

It is an effort to protect the system whereby employers give general ability and intelligence tests to determine the trainability of prospective employees. The amendment arises from my concern about what happened in the Motorola FEPC Case.[30]

Senator Tower's concern was based on a then-recent finding by a hearing examiner for the Illinois Fair Employment Practice Commission in a case involving Motorola, Inc. The examiner found that a pre-employment general intelligence test which Motorola had given to a black applicant had apparently denied the applicant an equal employment opportunity because blacks were found to be a culturally deprived or disadvantaged group.[31] Senator Tower was quite concerned about the impact of these findings on the character of Title VII of the Civil Rights Act. Regarding this concern he commented:

Let me say, only, in view of the findings in the Motorola case, that the Equal Employment Opportunity Commission, which would be set up by the Act, operating in pursuance of Title VII, might attempt to regulate the use of tests by employers.[32]

He further argued:

If we should fail to adopt language of this kind, there could be an Equal Employment Opportunity Commission ruling which would in effect invalidate tests of various kinds of employees by both private business and Government to determine the professional competence or ability or trainability or suitability of a person to do a job.[33]

Several members of Congress opposed Senator Tower's original amendment because, they argued, as written, it would permit an employer to give any test, whether it was effective or not, so long as it was professionally designed. Under such conditions discrimination could exist under the guise of compliance with the statute. As a result of these criticisms the amendment was defeated. Two days later Senator Tower offered a substitute amendment which was subsequently adopted verbatim and therefore became Section 703(h) of Title VII.[34]

Senator Hubert Humphrey (D-Minn) had opposed the first amendment but supported the second. He stated, "Senators on both sides of the aisle who were deeply interested in Title VII have examined the text of this amendment and have found it to be in accord with the intent and purpose of that Title." [35] In an interpretive memorandum, Senators Joseph Clark (D-Penn) and Clifford Case (R-NJ) stated:

> There is no requirement in Title VII that employers abandon bona fide qualification tests where, because of differences in background and education, members of some groups are able to perform better on these tests than members of other groups. An employer may set his qualifications as high as he likes, he may test to determine which applicants have these qualifications, and he may hire, assign, and promote on the basis of test performance.[36]

Interpretation of Title VII by the Equal Employment Opportunity Commission

The Equal Employment Opportunity Commission's interpretation of Title VII is set forth in *Guidelines on Employment Testing Procedures*. It states that a test can be a "professionally developed ability test" only if it:

> fairly measures the knowledge or skills required by the particular job or class of jobs which the applicant seeks, or which fairly affords the employer a chance to measure the applicant's ability to perform a particular job or class of jobs. The fact that a test was prepared by an individual or organization claiming expertise in test preparation does not, without more, justify its use within the meaning of Title VII.[37]

Both the Justice Department and the EEOC argued that any interpretation of Title VII that does not restrict tests to those directly related to job requirements "invites the use of a wide array of tests and other qualifying devices which operate unjustly to limit employment opportunities for Negroes." [38]

With regard to the applicability of EEOC rulings, the Supeme Court has held that:

> When faced with a problem of statutory construction, this Court shows great deference to the interpretation given the statute by officers or agency charged with its administration. Particularly is this respect due when the administration practice at stake involves a contemporaneous construction of a statute by the men charged with the responsibility of setting its machinery in motion; of making the parts work efficiently and smoothly while they are yet untried and new! [39]

District Court Decision

The Federal District Court held that the two tests used by the defendant were never intended to measure accurately the ability of an employee to perform the particular job available. However, the court continued:

> A test which measures the level of general intelligence, but is unrelated to the job to be performed is just as reasonable a prerequisite to hiring or promotion as is a high school diploma. In fact, a general intelligence test is probably more accurate and uniform in application than is the high school education requirement.[40]

Thus, the court refused to give weight to the EEOC ruling that a test must be job related. Addressing itself to that ruling, the court stated, "Nowhere does the act require the use of only one type of test to the exclusion of other non-discriminatory tests."[41]

Consistent with its ruling on tests, the court found no evidence of discrimination in the allocation of overtime. Each employee at the Dan River plant was allotted eight hours of overtime every four weeks. All other overtime had been referred to as "emergency overtime." Exhibit 2 sets forth overtime by department as a percentage of total hours worked.

The court's argument in support of its position on the allocation of overtime states:

> The high percentage of overtime worked by employees in Coal Handling was due to erratic deliveries of coal and the difficulty in handling frozen coal during winter months. As a general rule, overtime work is done by the employees of the department which would ordinarily do the work. But occasionally in coal handling, the work load becomes so great that employees from other departments are called in to help. The jist of plaintiffs contention is that Negroes are denied overtime work in coal handling and so are discriminated against in the allocation of overtime. The evidence does not support this contention.

> The percentage of overtime worked in each department with the exception of coal handling, are very similar. The higher percentage in the maintenance department appears to have been due to overtime work in repairing equipment and not in overtime in the coal handling operations. Further, the evidence is that Negroes in the labor department assigned to work in coal handling do not work the same overtime as employees in the coal handling department because of the danger involved in doing their work at night while the coal handling operations are going on.

> It is concluded that the difference between allocation of overtime to employees is not the result of discriminatory practices and is not in violation of the Act.[42]

The court, after examination, also disapproved the plaintiffs' contention that the high school education requirement continued the effects of past discrimination. The court argued, "Congress intended the Act to be given prospective application only. Any discriminatory employment practices occuring before the effective date of the Act, July 2, 1965, are not remedial under the Act."[43]

The district court found that while the company had previously followed a policy of overt racial discrimination in a period prior to the Act, such conduct had ceased. Thus the court found that no relief was appropriate to the plaintiffs. While not discouraged, the employees of the labor department appealed.

Appeals Court Decision

The case then went to the Fourth Circuit Court of Appeals in Richmond, Virginia, which then was confronted with the task of determining the meaning of Title VII. After careful analysis, a majority of the court concluded that a subjective test of the employer's intent should govern, particularly in a close case, and that in this case there was no indication of a discriminatory purpose in the adoption of the diploma and testing requirements. The court also found there was no discrimination in administration and scoring of the tests and that the tests were professionally developed.[44]

The court took the position that Duke's requirement that employees have a high school education or successfully pass a battery of tests for advancement from lowest-paying departments had a genuine business purpose. Addressing itself specifically to the question of the tests used by Duke the court stated, "An amendment requiring direct relation between a test and a particular position was proposed in May 1968, but was defeated. We agree with the District Court that a test does not have to be job-related in order to be valid under Section 703(h)." [45] Therefore since the court found no discrimination was intended against black employees hired after adoption of the educational and test requirements, the four blacks without high school educations hired after the requirements were initiated were denied relief.

However, the Court of Appeals reversed the District Court in part, rejecting the position that residual discrimination arising from prior employment practices was insulated from remedial action. The court's disagreement with the District Court over the prospective virtue of the Civil Rights Act was based on the case of *Quarles v. Phillip Morris, Inc.* in which it was directly held that present and continuing consequences of past discrimination are covered by the Act. The court stated that Congress did not intend to freeze an entire generation of black employees into discriminatory patterns that existed before the act.[46]

Thus, the court found that the six employees without high school educations

EXHIBIT 2 Percentage of Total Working Hours in Overtime

Coal Handling Department	10.39%
Maintenance	7.84
Operations	5.39
Labor	5.22
Other	5.19

Source: Griggs v. Duke Power, 292 F. Supp. 243 (1968), p. 251.

who were hired prior to the adoption of education and test requirements were entitled to relief. These employees had been racially discriminated against at the time of hiring and placed in the plant's lowest paying department. They were then required to pass tests with scores equivalent to those achieved by average high school graduates to be eligible for advancement. Yet white employees without high school diplomas were not required to take the tests. Since the court had ruled that the high school diploma requirement was discriminatory for the six blacks hired prior to its initiation and the tests were being used as an approximate equivalent for advancement purposes, the court also ruled the tests were discriminatory. The adoption of such requirements simply locked the black employees into the labor department. The court therefore directed that the six plaintiffs were entitled to nondiscriminating consideration for advancement to other departments if and when job openings occurred.[47] However, the court also ruled that if following a reasonable period of time after a black was promoted to a job in one of the better departments it could be determined that he was unable to perform the duties of the job, the company was justified in returning him to his previous position or placing him elsewhere.

Where relief was provided, the court decided that seniority rights should also be altered. The court argued:

> When strict departmental seniority could result in continuation of defects of past discrimination against Negroes wherever one of the employees discriminated against was considered in the future for advancement to vacant jobs in competition with a white employee who had already gained departmental seniority as a result of past discriminatory hiring practices, seniority rights of such Negro employees should be considered on plant wide rather than departmental basis.[48]

The court stated the case was moot regarding two black plaintiffs who had high school educations and had been promoted and Willie Boyd, who had acquired the equivalent of a high school education and was eligible for advancement. H. E. Martin, one of the high school graduates, was promoted to watchman, on March 19, 1968, and subsequently to learner in the coal handling department. R. A. Jumper, the last black with a high school education to leave the labor department, was promoted to watchman and then to trainee for test assistant on May 7, 1968.

The Fourth Circuit Court of Appeals had held that, in the absence of a discriminatory purpose, use of the education and test requirements was permitted by the Civil Rights Act. In doing so, the court rejected the claim that because these two requirements operated to render ineligible a markedly disproportionate number of blacks, they were unlawful under Title VII unless shown to be job-related. It was on these claims that the Supreme Court granted review of the appellate ruling.[49]

EEOC Rules on Tests

In 1970, the EEOC issued new guidelines on employment testing procedures. The ruling enlarged upon the *Guidelines on Employment Testing Procedures* set forth on August 24, 1966. The commission defined "tests" as follows:

The term "tests" included all formal, scored, qualified or standardized techniques of assessing job suitability including, in addition to the above, specific qualifying or disqualifying personnel history or background requirements, scored interviews, biographical information blanks, interviewers' rating scales, scored application forms, etc. . . .[50]

The EEOC ruling requires that each organization using tests to select from candidates for a position or for membership must have available for inspection evidence that the tests are being used in a manner that does not adversely affect hiring, promotion, or any other employment or membership opportunity of classes protected by Title VII.[51] Also, empirical data must be provided as evidence of a test's validity. The evidence should demonstrate that the test is significantly correlated with important elements of work behavior relevant to the job or jobs for which the candidate is being evaluated.[52]

Supreme Court Decision

After the Court of Appeals ruling, the plaintiffs, with the support of the Justice Department, sought the Supreme Court review. The Justice Department urged the Court to accept the Duke Power Case, on the grounds that the issue was of great importance because use of employment criteria of the kind employed by Duke was widespread in many parts of the country.[53] The Supreme Court granted review of the case in order to resolve the question of whether an employer is prohibited by the Civil Rights Act of 1964, Title VII, from requiring a high school education or passing a standardized intelligence test as a condition of employment or transfer when (a) neither standard is shown to be significantly related to successful job performance, (b) both requirements operate to disqualify blacks at a substantially higher rate than white applicants, and (c) the jobs in question formerly had been filled only by white employees as part of a long-standing practice of giving preference to whites.[54]

During the case, Duke contended that its general intelligence tests were specifically permitted by Section 703(h) of the act. On the other hand, lawyers for the NAACP Legal Defense Fund argued that black laborers, because of poor schooling, never passed the company's tests, and thus were frozen into the lowest rung on the job ladder.

The Supreme Court opinion placed heavy emphasis on the intent of Congress. It has already been observed that the EEOC had issued guidelines interpreting Section 703(h) to permit only the use of job-related tests. Justice Burger's opinion observed that because the act and its legislative history support the EEOC construction this affords good reason to treat the guidelines as expressing the will of Congress. The Chief Justice further stated, "From the sum of the legislative history relevant to this case, the conclusion is inescapable that EEOC's construction of Section 703(h) to require that employment tests be job-related comports with congressional intent." [55]

The Court found that neither the high school completion requirements nor the general intelligence test is shown to bear a demonstrable relationship to successful performance of the job for which it was used. The evidence suggested that employees who had not completed high school or taken the tests had continued to perform satisfactorily and made progress in departments for which the high school and test criteria were being used. The Court emphasized:

> History is filled with examples of men and women who rendered highly effective performance without the conventional badges of accomplishment in terms of certificates, diplomas, or degrees. Diplomas and tests are useful servants, but Congress has mandated the common sense proposition that they are not to become masters of reality.[56]

In its 8–0 opinion the Supreme Court observed that the Fourth Circuit had argued that Duke Power had adopted the diploma and test requirements without intent to discriminate. While the Chief Justice believed neither the District Court nor Court of Appeals erred in its examination of Duke's intent, he further wrote, "But good intent or absence of discriminatory intent does not redeem employment procedures or testing mechanisms that operate as 'built-in headwinds' for minority groups and are unrelated to measuring job capacity." [57] Under the Civil Rights Act, "practice, procedures, or tests neutral on their face, and even neutral in terms of intent, cannot be maintained if they operate to freeze the status quo of prior discriminatory employment practices." [58]

The Court further clarified its position on congressional intent in the following statements:

> Congress has not commanded that the less qualified be preferred over the better qualified simply because of minority origins. Far from disparaging job qualifications as such, Congress has made such qualifications the controlling factors, so that race, religion, nationality, and sex became irrelevant. What Congress has commanded is that any tests used must measure the person for the job and not the person in abstract.[59]

> . . . Congress has placed on the employer the burden of showing that any given requirement must have a manifest relationship to the employment in question.[60]

> Nothing in the Act precludes the use of testing or measuring procedures; obviously they are useful. What Congress has forbidden is giving these devices and mechanisms controlling force unless they are demonstrably a reasonable measure of job performance.[61]

> What is required by Congress is the removal of artificial, arbitrary, and unnecessary barriers to employment when the barriers operate individually to discriminate on the basis of racial or other impermissible classifications.[62]

Epilogue

The Supreme Court by its actions had struck down specific educational requirements as a job qualification if such requisites worked to deprive some people of a chance and could not be shown to relate to on-the-job performance. However, the Court left open the question of whether testing requirements that take into account capacity for the next succeeding position or related future promotion might be utilized if shown that such long-range requirements fulfill a genuine business need.[63]

Reactions to the Court's decision were swift and varied. Generally company personnel departments across the country recognized that personnel tests and degree requirements used in hiring or promoting would now have to demonstrate a connection with the job in question.

Test marketers began holding meetings with client company personnel and lawyers in order to assess the impact of the Court's decision on this particular segment of the $55 million educational testing market. Certainly such tests were still useful but apparently subject to questions of discrimination unless roughly the same percentage of blacks and whites, men and women, and English-speaking and Spanish-speaking applicants passed them.[64]

Herbert Hill, the NAACP national labor director, commented after the decision, "We've been waiting for this for years." [65] "We are now ready to proceed with scores of cases involving many thousands of workers who have been denied jobs or promotions because of nonjob-related tests which have come into widespread use since passage [of the 1964 Civil Rights Act]." [66]

On the other hand the U.S. Chamber of Commerce reacted by filing with the Court a brief concerning the legal weight to be given employment statistics in racial issues. It said that if such statistics alone are evidence of illegal job discrimination a countless variety of long-standing racially neutral employment policies will be open to attack.[67]

FOOTNOTES

[1] *Moody's Public Utility Manual* (New York: Moody's Investors Service, Inc., 1972), p. 58.

[2] Griggs v. Duke Power, 420 F. 2d. 1225 (1970), p. 1228.

[3] *Ibid.*

[4] *Ibid.*

[5] *Ibid.*

[6] *Ibid.*

[7] *Ibid.*, p. 1229.

[8] *Ibid.*, p. 1228.

[9] James C. McBrearty, "Legality of Employment Tests: The Impact of Duke Power Co.," *Labor Law Journal*, July 1971, p. 388.

[10] Griggs v. Duke Power, 292 F. Supp. 243 (1968, p. 246).

[11] Griggs, 420 F. 2d., p. 1229.

[12] McBrearty, "Legality of Employment Tests," p. 389.

[13] Griggs, 420 F. 2d., p. 1233.

[14] Griggs v. Duke Power, 91 S. Ct. 849 (1971), p. 852.

[15] Griggs, 420 F. 2d., p. 1239.

[16] *Manpower Report of the President*, U.S. Department of Labor (Washington, D.C.: U.S. Government Printing Office, 1969), p. 107.

[17] "Court Forbids Job Tests That Screen Out Negroes," *The New York Times*, March 9, 1971, p. 21.

[18] E. E. Ghisselli, *The Validity of Occupational Aptitude Tests* (New York: J. Wiley & Sons, 1966), p. 127.

[19] T. A. Fermen, *The Negro and Equal Employment Opportunities* (New York: Frederick A. Praeger, 1968), p. 47.

[20] Griggs, 292 F. Supp., p. 247.

[21] Griggs, 91 S. Ct., p. 851.

[22] Griggs, 420 F. 2d., p. 1231.

[23] *Ibid.*, p. 1226.

[24] *Ibid.*

[25] *Ibid.*, p. 1232.

[26] Griggs, 292 F. 2d., p. 247.

[27] Griggs, 420 F. 2d., p. 1231.

[28] *Ibid.*

[29] *Ibid.*, p. 1244.

[30] *Ibid.*, p. 1241.

[31] *Ibid.*, p. 1234.

[32] *Ibid.*

[33] *Ibid.*

[34] Griggs, 915 Ct., pp. 855–856.

[35] *Ibid.*

[36] Griggs, 420 F 2d., p. 1242.

[37] Griggs, 915 Ct., p. 855.

[38] "Educational Requirements for Jobs Face High Court Review Under Civil Rights Act," *The Wall Street Journal*, June 30, 1970, p. 3.

[39] Griggs, 420 F. 2d., pp. 1240–1241.

[40] Griggs, 292 F. Supp., p. 250.

[41] *Ibid.*

[42] *Ibid.*, p. 251.

[43] *Ibid.*, p. 247.

[44] Griggs, 420 F. 2d., p. 1233.

[45] *Ibid.*, p. 1235.

[46] *Ibid.*, p. 1230.

[47] *Ibid.*, p. 1231.

[48] *Ibid.*, p. 1227.

[49] McBrearty, "Legality of Employment Tests," pp. 389–390.

[50] "Guidelines on Employment Selection Procedures," *Federal Register*, August 1, 1970, p. 12334.

[51] *Ibid.*

[52] *Ibid.*

[53] "Educational Requirements for Jobs Face High Court Review Under Civil Rights Act," p. 3.

[54] Griggs, 91 S. Ct., p. 851.

[55] McBrearty, "Legality of Employment Tests," p. 390.

[56] Griggs, 91 S. Ct., p. 854.

[57] *Ibid.*

[58] *Ibid.*, p. 853.

[59] *Ibid.*, p. 856.

[60] McBrearty, "Legality of Employment Tests," p. 390.

[61] *Ibid.*

[62] Griggs, 91 S. Ct., p. 853.

[63] McBrearty, "Legality of Employment Tests," p. 391.

[64] "Stricter Standards for Personnel Tests," *Business Week*, March 20, 1971, p. 34.

[65] *Ibid.*

[66] "Supreme Court Bars Employment Tests That Result in Anti-Negro Discrimination," *The Wall Street Journal*, March 9, 1971, p. 4.

[67] *Ibid.*

QUESTIONS

1. What should be government's role in achieving equality of economic opportunity?
2. After the 1964 Civil Rights Act was passed, how should the Duke Power Company have gone about establishing a coping strategy to deal with that part of its environment?
3. What were the reasons why Duke Power took the position leading to the initial action by black employees?
4. Identify legitimate business-related reasons for employing the tests after the 1965 effective date of the Civil Rights Act.
5. Discuss the distinctions between "trainable" and "qualifiable" and their relationship to the case situation.
6. What are the personnel implications of the appeals court requirement that in some circumstances plantwide seniority should be a basis for promotion?
7. What are some of the implications of the Supreme Court decision on promotion practices?
8. Define discrimination and discuss your view of the proper role of private business organizations in an environment in which discrimination has existed for some time.
9. Does it appear that discrimination pays from the standpoint of the employer?

CASE 8
PREGNANCY LEAVE

One of the most generally accepted objectives of our society today must be the achievement of equal opportunity for all. To achieve this end the federal government enacted the Civil Rights Act of 1964 to forbid discrimination in employment. The act established the Equal Employment Opportunity Commission (EEOC) to enforce compliance. In 1972 the EEOC was given power to sue for compliance in its own name. However most of the actions taken as a result of this legislation have been in the form of suits directed at eliminating discrimination against ethnic minority groups. Since 1964 business has become increasingly involved with other groups of individuals who find themselves at a disadvantage in the labor market. Title VII of the 1964 act deals with equal employment opportunities not only regardless of race, color, religion, and natural origin but also regardless of sex. Under the act, employers, unions, and employment agencies are prohibited from discriminating on the basis of sex in wages, fringe benefits, promotions or assignments, use of facilities, training or retraining, hiring and firing, and terms of employment. An employer discriminating against a person on grounds of sex has the burden of proving that sex is a *bona fide* occupational qualification reasonably necessary to the normal operation of the job. The periodic filing of suits under the act has allowed the courts to spell out congressional intent more clearly.[1]

Despite such legislation it appears that treatment of women at work continues to be unequal. Some see this inequality as unjust and are taking employers to court under the Civil Rights Act. Others see the inequality as a function of particular group attributes that, if ignored, would create a drop in national productivity. For instance, female employees are often identified as having an average lower productivity on the job than males and higher turnover, and greater absenteeism than male employees.[2] Frequently these factors result in little motivation by the employer to either train or promote females. This in turn tends to limit female employees to predominantly unskilled, less well-paid jobs with little hope of reaching positions high in the organization.

However if the data supporting the existence of the above-mentioned female group attributes are valid then there may be a strong economic argument for distinguishing between the sexes in industry. The question must be raised if females are relatively more expensive to employ than males because of differing long-run levels of productivity, then should the Civil Rights Act allow firms to compensate for this by offering females lower wage rates. In order for a factor to be a *bona fide* occupational qualification, an employer must prove reasonable cause to believe—based on some factual evidence—that all or substantially all women would be unable to perform the duties of the job safely and efficiently. If the above group attributes are not recognized as occupational qualifications, one must assume that the intent of the legislation is that differences in net cost of employment between the sexes should not be legitimate grounds for discrimination.

In the following case the General Electric Company finds itself accused of sex discrimination because it did not pay illness and accident benefits to women employees during pregnancy and childbirth.

FOOTNOTES

[1] B. Chaplin and P. J. Sloane, "Equal Employment Opportunities for Women," *Industrial Relations Journal*, vol. 6, Autumn 1975, p. 26.

[2] *Ibid.*, pp. 21–24.

Sex Discrimination: A Look at Fringe Benefits at General Electric

On March 15, 1972, a discrimination suit against the General Electric Corporation (GE) was filed in Richmond Federal Court by the International Union of Electrical, Radio and Machine Workers (IUEW). The chairman of the IUEW-GE

Conference Board in New York City, John Shambo, said that the suit was filed on behalf of seven female employees of the Salem, Virginia plant but would set a precedent for female employees at other GI locations and in other industries. He further stated that the basis of the suit was GE's refusal to pay weekly sickness and accident benefits when an employee could not work because of pregnancy.[1] Shambo commented that the seven women were out the previous year and were members of the Salem Local 161.

According to the suit, GE paid male employees sickness and accident benefits but refused to pay female employees for any absence caused by disabilities arising from or related to pregnancies or childbirths. Shambo also stated that the benefits amounted to approximately 60 percent of the weekly wage. At least one-third of the GE work force were women and, under the law, the suit would be retroactive to October 1, 1971. According to a union spokesman, "It is the first suit of its kind involving pregnancy and work benefits, and the court's decision would set a precedent." [2]

The Salem Plant

The GE plant in Salem, Virginia contains two departments, the Industry Control Products Department and the Drive Systems Product Department. Current total employment is approximately 3500 people of which one-third are women.

Products produced by the Industry Control Department can be divided into five general classifications: (1) motor starters; (2) components, which include brakes, resistors and rheostats, contractors and relays, and specialized limit switches; (3) electric vehicle controls; (4) automation products; and (5) plastic molding controls. The Drive Systems Product Department evolved from the Industry Control Department and builds controls that regulate oil pumping equipment, the manufacturing process in steel mills, gas turbine generators, gas line pumpers, unmanned engine rooms of merchant and naval ships, and the production processes in certain paper and mining industries. The production of this type of electrical equipment requires a labor force that can perform specialized and skilled functions. Thus, training is an important prerequisite which is both time consuming and costly to GE.

GE's Focus on Current Social Issues

General Electric's true beginnings date not from its moment of incorporation but from the formation of the company that, in 1878, was established to finance Thomas A. Edison's development of the incandescent lamp. On that basis, GE is 97 years old instead of merely 83, the date when it was incorporated. From that time GE has been a leader in electrical and allied technologies.[3] The company also has been frequently involved in programs and projects that only indirectly relate to its primary economic function. For instance, candidates for President, Congress, governor, and hundreds of state and local offices come to GE plants and offices in record numbers during election years as a result of GE's Constructive Citizenship Programs.

Also, according to management, GE takes a great deal of pride in its activities in the field of career development for both youth and minority groups. The company has developed a pre-engineering curriculum designed to provide special assistance to minority youth entering college, with the anticipation of multiplying graduates ten times. Deans and faculty from black colleges, engineering schools, and universities are invited to participate in workshops and in-service training programs. A developmental program for minority professionals fresh from college has been established to aid these individuals by acquainting them with the opportunities open to them in industry. As a part of the annual business review process, all GE managers must now fill out a lengthy questionnaire dealing with minority and female employment. This system calls for preferential treatment to make possible accelerated promotion of minorities. GE has called for a large-scale effort to attract more blacks to engineering schools.

Occasionally GE sponsors four-day seminars for teenagers to orient them to the social uses of technology. They ask private and public high schools to nominate students on the bases of leadership potential and interest in science. About half the group is usually girls and about one-fourth are racial minority group members.

Regarding women, GE's premise is that effective use of womanpower is good business—it means giving women options and the opportunity to pursue them.

GE Foundation awards are given to employees whose volunteer service has aided disadvantaged people and youth. These awards are made available as an incentive for GE employees to become socially involved either through service clubs within the organization or outside GE.

According to management, GE is deeply involved in environmental protection, in research, in exploration, in entertainment (especially TV), in home services, and in expanding opportunities for women and minority employees without diminishing progress. As stated by management, a major thrust over the past few years has been:

> To achieve progress in providing equal employment and career opportunities for women . . . and to do so consistent with social and legal norms, but without diminishing progress in providing full opportunities to minority employees.[4]

Management further points out that there are opportunites for women in management, in research, in engineering, in computer science, in sales and home demonstration, as well as advertising and limitless other fields. GE's long-range objective is to ensure that race, sex, religion, national origin, age, and other nonjob related factors are ignored in considering people to hire, fire, promote, demote, or for other terms and conditions of employment. According to GE's Equal Employment Opportunity for Women (EEOW) program the goals are:

1. To be responsive to the government's requirements;
2. To use womanpower effectively;
3. To establish goals, priorities, and measurements for management;
4. To gain men's and women's understanding and awareness of the problems both face in overcoming existing patterns of thought and action.[5]

According to an article, "Expanding Opportunities for Women," some GE women have broken new ground. They have made progress in management, as supervisors, welders, security patrol guards; there are women on the traveling auditor staff, a female underwater environmental lab director, a test pilot, and a vice president of Tomorrow Entertainment. On the corporate staff are women consultants in marketing, management development, employee benefits, business planning and employee relations, and investment securities analysis. Scores of women have joined the company on the financial, employee relations, engineering, marketing, and other management development programs. [6]

Again according to management, GE's philosophy about women and minorities and equal opportunities and fair treatment might be summed up as follows:

> The passage of the Civil Rights Act in 1964 marked a moment in history when this nation became aware that the discriminatory practices of the past would no longer be tolerated. Subsequent events, beginning with the thrust for improved minority opportunity and the current added focus on women, have sparked changes few predicted a decade ago. Civil rights and women's rights stem from the same historical roots and emerge from the same human needs—the universal quest for equality. As members of a corporation, we must recognize that the best interests of all our constituencies—employees, management, customers, share owners—will be best served by our commitment to equal opportunity. [7]

The Discrimination Suit

Lawyers for the union contended that GE's failure to pay the sickness benefits to the women constituted sex discrimination as interpreted under the 1964 Federal Civil Rights Act. At that time the Equal Employment Opportunity Commission (EEOC) had not yet received permission to bring suit but had ruled that women should receive sickness and accident benefits for pregnancy. Thus, the EEOC did grant permission to the IUEW to bring suit. [8]

A second reason for the union's filing of the suit, according to its general counsel, was that the union was trying to protect its own interests. Conceivably union members could sue the IUEW jointly with GE or with any other company with which it had a similar contract. To head this off the IUEW urged all locals to file grievances on the maternity disability issue. [9]

The union contended that GE in Salem was notifed of the pending suit the first week in March; but the employee relations director for the Salem GE plant said that he first knew of the suit on March 15, 1972. In any case GE was given 20 days from the date that official notification of the suit was received to file an answer. The employee relations director stated that "General Electric is paying benefits to all employees strictly in accordance with a mutually agreed upon contract between GE and the IUEW and pregnancy is treated as an illness and the employees received full reimbursement for medical costs." He also said that "expenses incurred in the course of pregnancy for physicians, hospitalization, and drugs are paid for under GE insurance policies the same as any other illness." [10]

In the complaint, the IUEW made the point that GE paid male employees disability benefits for every kind and type of sickness and accident but refused to pay "any female employee for any absence due to disability arising from or related to pregnancy or childbirth." [11] For this reason, the suit asked the court to enter an injunction directing GE to pay the benefits referred to, both to the seven plaintiffs and to other women employed by GE. Also requested were damages, court costs, and attorney fees.

Plaintiff Charges

The plaintiffs charged that GE arbitrarily began leaves after six months of pregnancy and directed female employees to return to work within eight weeks of termination of pregnancy. The plaintiffs contended that this action constituted discrimination because of sex in compensation, terms, conditions, and privileges of employment in violation of the Civil Rights Act of 1964. The union did not specify the amount of the benefits requested, but its contract provided for sickness and accident payments of 60 percent of a worker's straight time weekly pay or a maximum of $150 for up to 26 weeks per disability. These benefits were not paid when a woman left her job to have a child. GE did pay medical benefits to some 5000 pregnant women employees in 1971; according to a GE spokesman, "assuming an average eligibility of $90 disability payments, 26 weeks of payments would have cost the insurance company $12.7 million. It also would have cost GE a substantial increased in insurance premiums." [12] According to one plaintiff, "I think the company did us wrong. . . . It's a good place to work for and all that, and the company has been good to me . . . they do pay the best money for women in this area." [13] Another plaintiff charged that she was hospitalized during pregnancy and wasn't paid for the loss of work. She returned to work and became ill again and was not allowed to return when she was able as she had passed the six-month cutoff period. Like GE, many companies do not pay benefits during job absences stemming from pregnancy or childbirth, and at least one grievance is on file already—at General Motors' Delco Products Division in Rochester, N.Y. GM pays six weeks of benefits for maternity-related absences, compared with varying, seniority-linked periods for other absences. [14]

The plaintiffs in the GE suit were Martha V. Gilbert, Sharon E. Godfrey, Barbara Hall, Alberta B. Smith, Johnnie Taylor, Doris B. Wiley, and Mary R. Williams. According to Mary Williams, "sickness benefits for being pregnant aren't any different from a male falling and hurting a leg and losing time from work." [15] Another plaintiff claimed that a woman couldn't work during delivery and should, therefore, be given the same consideration as one who is hospitalized for an operation or accident.

When questioned why the union filed the charge in Richmond rather than Roanoke, which has geographical jurisdiction for the Salem plant, the union spokesman, John Shambo, indicated that it was thought that they would have a better opportunity for a favorable decision under Judge Robert Merhige in Richmond.

Merhige had received national attention from labor lawyers when he ruled that the Chesterfield County School Board could not force a teacher to quit in her fifth month of pregnancy when she was able to continue teaching.[16]

GE's Defense

From the company viewpoint, the initial defense rebuttal was twofold. The first argument was that during the negotiation sessions for the preceding labor contracts, it was agreed upon by the union and GE that sickness and accident benefits would not be paid to women during their pregnancy leaves. This policy had, in fact, become a type of precedent during the bargaining sessions. As a result, a company spokesman replied that GE was "paying benefits to all employees strictly in accordance with the mutually agreed IUEW-GE contract covering insurance payments and other employee benefits." [17]

The second argument, which was related to the first, was that GE refused to pay illness benefits to pregnant workers on the grounds that pregnancy was not considered as an illness under the terms of the company's sickness and accident insurance program. The union did make several unsuccessful attempts to negotiate for a modified plan for sickness benefits for pregnant women employees but the company resisted and would not agree to negotiate on the grounds that such negotiations are normally tied to contract agreements, and the three-year IUEW-GE contract negotiations were not due to start for several months.

General Electric contended that pregnancy is a special kind of disability because it is incurred voluntarily. Management further claimed that GE was paying all expenses incurred in the course of pregnancy for physicians, hospitalization, and drugs the same as any other illness. GE argued that pregnancy benefits would award women greater economic benefits than men and cause a sharp increase in insurance benefits industrywide. Judge Merhige's reply to this defense was "if it be viewed as a greater economic benefit to women, then this is a simple recognition of women's biologically more burdensome place in the scheme of human existence." [18]

Other Discrimination Suits in 1972

This was the third sex discrimination suit filed by IUEW against GE during 1972. The previous cases challenged GE's 5-foot, 7-inch height rule for employment at the Tyler, Texas plant and the Equal Pay Act suit filed against the Fort Wayne, Indiana plant.

In the Fort Wayne, Indiana suit, women were paid an estimated $300,000 in back pay in settlement of a suit filed under the Equal Pay Act. The payment was made to 350 women as an adjustment for comparable or nearly comparable work in 21 different job categories in which the women had been paid less than men. This was said to be the biggest settlement ever in a private equal-pay suit.[19]

In the Tyler, Texas plant, the union cited a survey by the Department of Health, Education, and Welfare that indicated that the 5-foot, 7-inch requirement for employment eliminated more than 94 percent of all females aged 18 to 79. The women and the union also sued the employment commission alleging that it cooperated with GE by declining to send applicants under 5-foot, 7-inches to the plant for prospective employment. At the time a GE spokesman said, "We're surprised by this turn of events; we haven't had a chance to review the charges and can't comment." [20]

Women's Rights Debate

The Equal Rights Amendment in the Senate awaiting debate is expected to be affected by some of the recent court decisions that women have lost as well as the victories. Advocates of the amendment say that the victories and losses taken together show that progress toward equal treatment of the sexes is so slow and inconsistent that a constitutional amendment is the only way to achieve equality. The amendment would invalidate all laws—federal, state, or local—that require or sanction discrimination based on sex. [21]

One of the cases that feminists regard as discouraging is *Schattman v. Texas Employment Commission*. This is the first case to reach the appeals court level which challenges a state law requiring a woman to quit her job at a certain point in pregnancy, regardless of her desire to continue working and her doctor's opinion that she could do so without harm. The Court of Appeals upheld the law in favor of the Texas Employment Commission and ruled that the commission was not in violation of the requirement of the 14th Amendment that all citizens receive the equal protection of the laws. The loss of this case was regarded by feminists as a severe blow. [22]

However, a significant victory was won by feminists in the area of laws covering pregnancy when the attorney general of the state of Michigan issued an opinion invalidating a Michigan law that prohibited a woman from collecting unemployment benefits beginning 10 weeks before an expected date of delivery and for six weeks after delivery. The attorney general said that the 14th Amendment prohibits such "arbitrary" rules and requires pregnancy to be treated just like any other temporary physical disability. He stated that "The test of eligibility for unemployment benefits for a woman, as for a man, must be simply whether she is 'available for work.' " [23] This was the first such ruling by a state official.

Question of Trial Site

On May 11, 1972, the following Richmond news release was carried in the *World-News*:

> U. S. District Judge Robert R. Merhige, Jr. has ordered a sex discrimination suit against the General Electric plant at Salem transferred from federal court here to the U. S. Western District Court in Roanoke.
>
> The company had sought the change of venue on the grounds that all poten-

tial witnesses and employment records are located in Salem, that the alleged discriminatory acts occurred in Salem, and that all the plaintiffs reside there.

Further, GE contended that the plaintiffs, represented by the International Union of Electrical Workers, had gone "forum or judge shopping" in filing the suit here.

A union official was quoted to the effect that the suit was filed in Merhige's court because a "favorable" ruling was more likely.

Seven female employees of the plant claim discrimination because the company's health insurance plan does not include maternity benefits. [24]

Another release in the *Roanoke Times* on the same day stated that Richmond was "clearly not the appropriate district to maintain this action." [25]

In July 1972, the union petitioned Judge Merhige to retain the suit in Richmond. This petition followed the order for the case to be transferred to the U. S. District Court in Roanoke. Merhige was directed by the Fourth U.S. Circuit Court of Appeals to hold a hearing on the plea for returning the suit to Richmond.

The hearing brought the contention from the IUEW that plaintiffs in civil rights suits should be permitted to avoid unfriendly judiciary. Ruth Weyand, IUEW's associate general counsel, said that "the 1964 Civil Rights Act specifies that persons who feel discriminated against may file suit in 'any district in the state' where the alleged discrimination occurs." [26] She further contended that IUEW was seeking to add the names of 25 eastern Virginia women who worked at GE to the list of plaintiffs. This seemed to be an apparent effort to blunt GE's contention that the suit should be heard in Roanoke because it was where the plaintiffs, company records, and potential witnesses were located. An attorney for GE argued that there was nothing in the appeals court ruling that indicated that Merhige was wrong in granting GE's request for a switch in the trial site, only that he should have had a hearing first. [27] GE indicated that the July 24, 1972 hearing had qualified that ruling.

During the hearing Merhige commented further on GE's contention that the union was "forum or judge shopping" when they originally filed suit in Richmond. In response to the charge he stated, "You all do it. They (IUEW) were just honest enough to admit it." [28]

As a result of the hearing arguments, on September 26, 1972, Judge Merhige reversed his earlier ruling, thus denying GE's motion for a change in trial site from Richmond to Roanoke.

Suit Expanded

At the time the suit was first initiated, in early 1972, the seven plaintiffs elected to sue on behalf of all present and former female employees of GE at all its facilities. Thus a class action on behalf of over 100,000 women was sought.

On May 1, 1973, Judge Merhige ordered that the more than 100,000 women workers at an estimated 125 GE plants and offices across the country be included as plaintiffs in the suit. The suit, originally scheduled for trial on May 8, 1972 in

Richmond, was postponed in order to give the women workers the opportunity to object to being included in the suit even though they would not be individually named as plaintiffs. Fourteen months had passed since the original suit was filed by the plaintiffs (IUEW and seven women at the Salem plant). The union had made four unsuccessful efforts to obtain a modified plan for sickness benefits for pregnant women employees prior to the filing of the suit. [29]

On May 8, 1973, lawyers for GE filed a motion with Judge Merhige to include unions that represent the women as third parties in the suit. They contended that the unions would be indispensable and necessary to the complete adjudication of the action suit as they had been engaged in collective bargaining negotiations for GE's women workers. [30] No ruling was made on the motion by Judge Merhige since additional documents were to be filed before the trial date of July 24, 1973.

Trial Testimonies

In the first day of testimony eight plaintiff's witnesses testified in U. S. District Court before Judge Robert R. Merhige, Jr. Two of the women testified that GE told them they would have to quit work. The third woman said her doctor told her to quit, and that during her pregnancy, she was "in the bed or on the couch most of the time," so she couldn't work anyplace else. The three women said that GE did pay their medical and hospital bills as a result of their pregnancies. One woman stated that she had filed two claims for sick pay. GE didn't accept one; the second claim was accepted, but denied. [31]

A Richmond doctor testified that about "50 to 60 percent" of his patients with their first pregnancy work. He stated that he generally advises his patients to continue working as long as they feel able even up to labor, barring complications. He further pointed out that patients who work seemingly tolerate their pregnancy better than those who don't; he saw no medical reason why a normal healthy pregnant woman should stop working before the onset of labor. [32]

The doctor was then asked if most of his patients were covered by medical insurance, with pregnancy benefits. He said, "I would say the majority are . . . most are covered by their husband's insurance." [33]

During the trial, Judge Merhige permitted The Women's Equity Action League, Human Rights for Women, and the National Organization for Women to join the case as "friends of the court."

A Washington-based actuary, Paul H. Jackson, testified on behalf of GE as a representative of the Wyatt Co. He related that most all short-term disability policies offer maternity benefits, but they are separate from sickness and accident benefits, thus separating the two. Jackson said that he had never seen a disability income policy that included pregnancy benefits. He contended that this type of coverage would be difficult to control and funds from other benefits would have to be channeled to pay for the maternity benefits. [34] Another witness, Dr. Andre E. Hellegers, director of the Georgetown University Center for Study of Human Reproduction, indicated that it was a myth for women to have to claim disability benefits and not work for six weeks following delivery.

Thomas F. Hilbert, Jr., labor relations counsel for GE testified that GE's women employees were absent longer and more frequently than men workers. "About 40 per cent of our women employees who become pregnant don't return to work. About 3,000 GE employees become pregnant annually." [35] He continued, "women make up about one-third of GE's work force. It would cost GE between $3 and $12 million a year to give pregnant workers disability pay." [36]

It was further argued that the final results of the case could have a significant impact, particularly on the insurance industry. Some estimates were that annual costs to the industry for pregnancy pay alone would reach at least $1.3 billion. Judge Merhige maintained serious doubts whether costs mean anything when compared with discrimination. [37]

GE Loses Case

Judge Merhige ruled on April 15, 1974, that General Electric's policy of with-holding sickness and accident benefits from pregnant women employees was delib-erate and intentional discrimination and violated the Civil Rights Act of 1964. [38] In making his judgment Merhige said that "in his opinion male and female employees should be treated the same; and while pregnancy is unique to women, parenthood is common to both sexes. No such consequences would befall a male employee who chose to subject himself to a selective operation, such as a vasectomy or cosmetic surgery." [39] The ruling affected some 100,000 women employees at GE plants throughout the nation. Since the ruling specified GE policy constituted sexual dis-crimination, Judge Merhige barred GE from withholding weekly disability benefits from employees absent for pregnancy-related causes. Monetary judgments in favor of the women employees who had been denied the benefits were scheduled to be entered at a later date. A GE spokesman announced that the ruling would be ap-pealed. Until the case could be heard and ruled upon in the Fourth Circuit Court of Appeals, the company stated that women employees who became pregnant might elect to take maternity leave as they had in the past. [40]

The women plaintiffs expressed the feeling that they did not consider them-selves activists and admitted that they would never have become involved in the suit if the union had not backed them. Union representatives saw the ruling as a victory and an important step toward bringing women the first-class citizenship to which they are entitled. [41] Of the seven women who originally filed the suit, two later quit work at GE. The remaining five still work for the company. Union leaders do not deny that they encouraged the women to become involved. The five women still working at the plant joke that "the children of those pregnancies that took them to court in 1971 will be in school and grown up before it is over." [42]

Many employers throughout the country quickly realized that the outcome of the GE appeal could have significant ramifications for them as well as the principal parties. The statement of appeal from GE caused employers to watch closely and nervously. If GE should fail to overturn the federal court order, group insurance costs could rise substantially for all employers with large numbers of women employees. According to GE, the decision in Richmond threatened to "raise substantially the costs of the GE insurance plan, and ultimately affect group insurance rates for employers all across the country." [43] The company also argued that allowing benefits for pregnancy would give women a disproportionate share of benefits.

While not necessarily agreeing with GE, the president of Local 161 at the Salem plant estimated that if the court ruling were upheld it could cost the company from $1400 to $1800 in pay for women employees who are off from four to five months during a pregnancy. [44] GE cited several cases that set the precedent for its appeal. In a similar suit, involving Delta Airlines, the judge ruled there was no discrimination against a woman denied benefits in a pregnancy. [45] In Illinois a union has now gone to court against such a ruling. In this case the company required women to go on leave at the beginning of the sixth month of pregnancy, paid only six weeks of benefits, and required the women to continue to contribute to the insurance fund while on maternity leave. Some companies have signed labor contracts with conditional clauses on pregnancy to be put into effect if GE should finally lose its case. [46]

On January 8, 1975 GE asked the appeals court to vacate the lower court's decision to make the case a class action and asked that the complaint be dismissed. By this time the case had attracted not only the attention of several feminist rights organizations but also a major feminist-oriented law firm in New York. On the other hand, American Telephone and Telegraph filed a support petition favoring GE's position. [47] "Pregnancy is neither a sickness nor an accident, but is voluntary and subject to planning," said one of GE's attorneys. He further stated that it was the "considered judgment generally that such pregnancy pay exclusions are a rational reasonable business practice. . . ." [48]

The court dismissed GE's argument that denial of disability benefits was justified because pregnancy is voluntary and on June 30, 1975, ruled that pregnant workers are entitled to disability pay under company insurance programs. Thus, the appeals court in Richmond affirmed the lower court ruling of 1974 that found GE guilty of sex discrimination in denying benefits to its female workers. The appeals court opinion stated that a program compensating employees absent from work because of disability becomes less comprehensive for women than for men when benefits are denied if the disability is caused by childbirth or a complication of pregnancy. Even if the sex discrimination were unintended, the consequences would not be negated. [49]

General Electric declined to comment on the ruling except to note that a similar case involving Liberty Mutual Insurance Company, Boston, was pending before the Supreme Court. Management indicated that GE had previously asked the Supreme Court to hear its case along with that involving Liberty Mutual. [50]

Supreme Court Willing to Review Ruling

On October 6, 1975, the Supreme Court agreed to review the lower court decision that GE violated the federal Civil Rights Act by excluding pregnancy from its disability insurance program along with the Liberty Mutual case. The major difference between the two cases is that the Liberty Mutual case was decided by a summary judgment midway in the trial, but the GE case was decided after all the evidence was in. In fact attorneys for the parties in the GE case have argued, "We believe that the completeness of the record in this case could be of great assistance to the court in deciding a question as important as that presented." [51]

On January 19, 1976 attorneys for GE presented their case to the Supreme Court. The company's arguments before the Court were more directed to the cost issues involved than the earlier presentation. GE told the court that the company refused to pay disability benefits for pregnancy for sound and solid business reasons and not because it discriminates against women. Furthermore, the company stated that it is the practice of the insurance industry to cover the unexpected and that pregnancy can now be planned in today's "contraceptive society." [52]

The GE attorney also argued that the underlying reason for excluding pregnancy payments from the GE benefit plan was that the company found it "appropriate not to cover this type of income maintenance." Since 40 percent of the women who left GE plants because of pregnancy never returned, disability payments would be a form of severance pay. Also, more than 90 percent of the women who left for other health reasons returned. In addition, the median absence for men for health reasons was two weeks, while it was thirteen weeks for women. Chief Justice Warren Burger stated that the court, in considering the case, would take judicial notice of the higher cost of annuities for women. [53]

The following day associate general counsel for the IUEW attempted to counter GE's cost argument by presenting additional data. Counsel stated that based on 1971 employment figures, the disability benefits for six weeks per pregnancy leave would have cost GE $1,157,000. This contrasted with $200 million spent by GE for all insurance plans in 1972. Moreover, it was pointed out that a wage increase of 10 percent an hour would amount to a $60 million expense for GE. [54]

Counsel further argued that since pregnancy is unique to women to discriminate because of it is to discriminate on the basis of sex. Title VII of the 1964 Civil Rights Act forbids depriving women of their rights. It was also argued that women had to get other jobs and, in some cases, seek welfare aid because of the lack of income during pregnancy. When a woman was forced to seek other work while on pregnancy leave from GE, it tended to interfere with her "permanence on the job" and tended to make her a "transient worker." [55]

On December 7, 1976, the Supreme Court by a 6-3 decision ruled that employers are not required to pay pregnancy benefits. In its ruling, the Court stated GE employees had failed to prove lack of pregnancy benefits was "designed to effect an invidious discrimination against the members of one sex or the other." [56]

FOOTNOTES

[1] "Union Sues GE for Birth Benefits," *The World-News*, March 15, 1972, p. 23.

[2] *Ibid.*

[3] "A Capsule History of GE," *General Electric Monogram*, 1972, p. 2.

[4] "Expanding Opportunities for Women," *General Electric Monogram*, May–June 1974, pp. 27–30.

[5] *Ibid.*, p. 27.

[6] "Women and the Top Jobs," *General Electric Monogram*, July–August 1970, pp. 10–13.

[7] "Expanding Opportunities," pp. 27–30.

[8] George Kegley, "Seven Women File Against GE," *The Roanoke Times*, March 16, 1972, p. 31.

[9] "Women Press for Maternity Benefits," *Business Week*, March 25, 1972, p. 26.

[10] "Suit Filed Against GE for Pregnancy Benefits," *Salem Times-Register*, March 16, 1972, p. 1.

[11] *Ibid.*

[12] "Women Press for Maternity Benefits," p. 26.

[13] "Benefits Sought During Pregnancy," *The Roanoke Times*, March 16, 1972, p. 2.

[14] "Women Press for Maternity Benefits," p. 26.

[15] "Job Benefits Due During Pregnancy, Women Say," *The Roanoke Times*, March 16, 1972, p. 1.

[16] "Hearing Held on Shift of Suit Against GE," *The Roanoke Times*, July 25, 1972, p. 16.

[17] "7 Women File Suit Against GE," *The Roanoke Times*, March 16, 1972, p. 31.

[18] "Company Performance Roundup," *Business and Society Review*, Summer 1974, p. 98.

[19] "Women at GE Plant Win Higher Wages in Bias Suit," *The Wall Street Journal*, July 9, 1973, p. 12.

[20] "GE, Texas Job Agency Draw Sex-Bias Suit Over a Height Rule," *The Wall Street Journal*, February 15, 1972, p. 12.

[21] "Women's Rights to Be Debated," *The Roanoke Times*, March 20, 1972, p. 4.

[22] *Ibid.*

[23] *Ibid.*

[24] "GE Sex Suit Transferred to Roanoke," *The World-News*, May 11, 1972.

[25] "Suit Against GE Moved to Roanoke," *The Roanoke Times*, May 12, 1972, p. 28.

[26] "Hearing Held on Shift of Suit Against GE," *The Roanoke Times*, July 25, 1972, p. 16.

[27] *Ibid.*

[28] *Ibid.*

[29] "Judge Expands Suit Against GE," *The Roanoke Times*, May 2, 1973, p. 17.

[30] "Union's Suit Against GE Will Be Heard on July 24," *The Roanoke Times*, May 9, 1973, p. 7.

[31] "Roanoke Women Testify Against GE Pregnancy Policy," *The Roanoke Times*, July 25, 1973, p. 17.

[32] "Unique GE Trial Gets Under Way," *The World-News*, July 24, 1973, p. 17.

[33] *Ibid.*

[34] "Actuarial Data Given Court in GE Case," *The Roanoke Times,* July 26, 1973, p. 17.

[35] *Ibid.*

[36] "Absenteeism of Women High, GE Says," *The Roanoke Times,* July 27, 1973, p. 25.

[37] *Ibid.*

[38] "GE Loses Case in Pregnancies," *The World-News,* April 15, 1974.

[39] *Ibid.*

[40] "GE to Appeal Maternity Rule," *The Roanoke Times,* April 16, 1974, p. 17.

[41] *Ibid.*

[42] "Mothers in GE Lawsuit Don't Feel Like Activisits," *The Roanoke Times,* April 22, 1974, p. 10.

[43] "GE to Appeal Maternity Rule," p. 17.

[44] "Seeking Pay for Maternity Leave," *Business Week,* May 18, 1974, p. 74.

[45] *Ibid.*

[46] *Ibid.*

[47] "GE Gives Court Pregnancy Plea," *The World-News,* January 8, 1975, p. 1.

[48] "Pregnancy Not Illness, GE Insists in Defense," *The Roanoke Times,* January 9, 1975, p. 23.

[49] "Pregnant Workers Are Entitled to Collect Disability Pay, Court Rules in GE Appeal," *The Wall Street Journal,* June 30, 1975.

[50] *Ibid.,* p. 13.

[51] "High Court to Review GE Pregnancy Decision," *The Roanoke Times,* October 7, 1975, p. 16.

[52] "Policy Not Biased, GE Tells Court," *The Roanoke Times,* January 20, 1976, p. 1.

[53] *Ibid.*

[54] "GE Pregnancy Costs Small, Union Claims," *The Roanoke Times,* January 21, 1976, p. 1.

[55] *Ibid.*

[56] George Kegley. "GE Wins Pregnancy Suit," *The Roanoke Times,* December 8, 1976, p. 1.

QUESTIONS

1. Explain the nature of the coping strategy employed by General Electric. Explain the rationale for such a strategy in light of the 1964 Civil Rights Act.
2. Are there legitimate business-related reasons for including pregnancy leave as a part of the sickness and accident benefits?
3. Explain why a company such as General Electric, which has a fine record of little or no employment discrimination, suddenly found itself in a discrimination suit.
4. Discuss the character of the role performed by the IUEW in this case. Can it be described as a traditional union role? Explain.
5. How would you characterize management's perception of its role at General Electric?
6. Identify social expectations of General Electric by its relevant publics.
7. What social values might General Electric internalize as a basis for more effectively relating to its environment?
8. Discuss the sensitivity of General Electric's responsiveness to social expectations.
9. Discuss the concept of cost/benefit analysis and how such an analysis could be applied to the circumstances in this case.

10. What appear to be the implications of court actions opposing General Electric's position?
11. A company's role normally evolves as a result of the changing expectations of its environment. Discuss the contingency nature of General Electric's perceived social role.

CHAPTER 9

BUSINESS
AND
LABOR

CASE 9
THE LORDSTOWN EXPERIMENT

One means of segmenting the automobile market is by the size of the car, often measured in terms of the wheelbase. U.S. manufacturers have traditionally concentrated on the production of full- and medium-size cars and have left the production of compact and subcompact cars to foreign manufacturers. With the possible exception of American Motors Corporation, occasional forays into this segment of the market by U. S. manufacturers have not proven particularly successful. Low price and, in some cases, quality have been the principal bases for marketing the compact car.

Since U. S. manufacturers have always believed that demand in this country is greatest for the full-size car, little effort has been made to compete with foreign manufacturers. As a result, these manufacturers have gained a foothold in the U. S. market. The compact car has become a second car in many two-car families and the principal car for young economy-minded singles and newly married couples.

In the late sixties and early seventies a combination of factors changed the attitude of U.S. manufacturers. Ecology, congestion, increasing costs, and, most important, the energy crisis increased significantly the appeal of the compact and subcompact car. Domestic companies recognized the need to compete for this increasingly important segment of the automobile market.

The General Motors Corporation (GM) is the largest industrial organization and manufacturer of automobiles in the world. GM believed that in order to compete effectively with foreign compacts, it would have to reduce the costs and improve quality over the imported cars. To achieve these goals, the company built the Lordstown, Ohio production plant and shifted supervision of the assembly operation to General Motors Assembly Division (GMAD).

The new plant is much more highly automated than the traditional assembly line, and was supposed to relieve the back-breaking drudgery on the assembly line while improving manufacturing, efficiency, and product quality. Yet in March 1972, the GM Chevy Vega plant in Lordstown went on strike, not for higher wages or fringe benefits, but for something workers called the dehumanization of the work environment.

The Lordstown Experiment: The Zone of Acceptance of Young Workers

Nick Scherodnic, a repair welder at the huge GM plant at Lordstown, Ohio, drove to Reuther Hall, the local union headquarters, at 5 A.M. on February 1, 1972 to be one of the first to vote in favor of a strike over a labor dispute that raised issues that have left the auto industry shaking.

He was lucky that he dragged himself out of bed before daylight, because one hour after he cast his ballot, workers arriving in cars found a line more than a mile long in either direction on the road in front of Reuther Hall. It was the heaviest turnout for any vote in the history of Local 1112 of the United Auto Workers (UAW). A spokesman for the local said that 97 percent of the 6556 employees who had voted supported the strike. This was out of a total of 7900 eligible to vote.[1]

By 2 A.M. on March 4, 1972, the start of the working day at Lordstown, GM's only Chevrolet Vega plant, the temperature had dropped to three degrees. Bystanders wondered if there was really going to be a strike; in spite of the lung-shattering, lip-splitting cold no one had brought portable heaters. It was obvious that Local 1112 was not a strike-oriented body, yet it struck anyway. Kept warm by only its internal anger, the union made it clear that it truly believed in the righteousness of the strike.[2]

Lordstown Plant

Lordstown is actually two plants. One is a metal fabricating plant operated by Fisher Body Division. Fisher stamps out sheet metal and does much of the subassembly work on body parts such as doors, deck lids, and fenders.

A second facility, where cars are assembled, is about one city block away from the Fisher plant. This plant is operated jointly by Fisher and Chevrolet. Both plants devote total production to Chevrolet's compact car, the Vega. The main assembly plant has a single production line, off of which GM can produce Vegas of four different styles—sedans, fastbacks, wagons, and panel trucks.

The two plants are connected by a covered conveyor line. Finished sheet metal can be shipped off the end of the line at the Fisher factory to the appropriate station in the assembly plant without being exposed to the elements. There is no waiting for parts to be trundled from one plant to another, no tie-ups because trains or trucks can't travel, no risk of parts being damaged in handling or transit, no panicked phone calls back and forth between feeder and mother plants. Except for the Vega engine, which is manufactured at Tonawanda, New York, Lordstown is a self-contained operation.[3]

Because of continuously increasing wages the Lordstown plant is highly automated. It appears to be a giant step toward the car manufacturer's ideal plant —one that produces cars untouched by human hands. Because of this the number of assembly-line workers has been cut drastically. Ideally the line will produce 100 cars per hour. This means that each function must be performed by each worker in about 36 seconds.

Since the Vega is competing against a host of small foreign cars produced at much cheaper labor rates, high speed production is not enough in itself to make the Vega competitive. To minimize costs, Chevrolet

1. decreased the number of body parts from 996 in the average car to 578. Most of these parts are interchangeable for the four models. The hood, fenders, engine compartment, and front-end panels of all models are identical.
2. simplified assembly through careful choice of materials. Plastics were used liberally. For example, the one-piece interior roof eliminates cutting and sewing fabric and makes installation easier.
3. pulled some of the detailed assembly work off the main body and vehicle lines. This increases the number of major sub-assemblies capable of being automated by machines.
4. adjusted the height of the 1¼-mile vehicle conveyor in order to give each worker the most comfortable working height.
5. installed a line of Unimation's programmable robots, which make 95 percent of the spot welds on the car. One two-stage robot on this line bangs out 130 welds in just 4½ seconds.[4]

A computer is used to keep the various sections of the line in balance in order to equalize the work loads and give each worker the time needed to do each job right. The computer also attempts to pinpoint prospective lemons. Quality control inspectors at the checking stations record their observations by marking boxes on cards and feeding the cards to an optical scanner. The computer checks them against tolerances and, if necessary, sounds an alarm.

The computer's contribution to the Vega started well before any metal was cut for the car. GM worked out mathematical models for the assembly operations and used the computer to test production planning. James R. Seegret, quality control engineer for Chevrolet, stated "The individual components, critical systems, and, in effect, the entire vehicles were assembled thousands of times in the computer."[5] Among other things, the computer showed GM that it should change the position of the instrument panel and find a better way to insert the engine and rear axle. Savings in time and money were substantial.

The computer also slashed thousands of man-hours from design engineering and tooling. An electronic scanner picked off the contours from clay models, and generated perforated tape to run numerically controlled drafting machines and cutting tools. The automatic cutting tools produce the wood molds for the tooling dies and the templates used to check them.

The robots used in the Lordstown plant are called Unimates, after the name of the company, Unimation, Inc., which produces them. The Vega plant has at least 26 Unimates and probably a few more spares, which gives it the largest crew of industrial robots in a single plant in the United States.

> The Unimate robot is a mechanical arm controlled by a solid-state memory system. Five separate articulations provide up-down, in-out, and rotary motion from a central pivot point and at the outer arm, a bending and swiveling motion. The arm can pick up an 80-pound item and move it anywhere within a 350-cubic foot working area with an accuracy of 0.050 inches. It can reach from three and a half to seven and a half feet and rotate 220 degrees.
>
> The Unimate is taught a job by leading it manually through the required motions, establishing the work program in the machine's memory. The work program can also be fed into the machine via paper tape. Up to 180 sequential commands can be employed in a program. The memory receives information from machinery as it works and makes limited decisions based on incoming information. It can also issue commands and control operation of other machines.[6]

According to *Popular Mechanics:* "Unimate . . . can be fitted with a practically endless variety of hands, fingers and gripping surfaces for grasping and holding objects. Power tools can be substituted for fingers without dismantling the unit's 'hands.' . . . The GM robots are incapable of turning out an inferior job."[7]

Originally GM did not use these machines anywhere near their full capacities or capabilities. Robert Lund, after an unofficial trip to Lordstown, stated that GM "appears to be feeling its way with its benign Frankensteins. What can they do? How reliable are they? How will the union react?"[8]

General Motors Assembly Division

In October 1971, General Motors Assembly Division, which had been described by UAW president, Leonard Woodcock, as "probably the roughest, toughest division at GM," was put in charge of the Vega plant at Lordstown.[9] Due to a sharp increase of 43 percent in industrial compensation and only a 13 percent increase in productivity, GM's profit margins dropped from 10 percent to 7 percent five years ago.[10] GM's top man, Richard Gerstenberg, stated "We've got to temper something else to offset those things (cost increases). We want to keep these cars within the reach of the masses."[11]

Gerstenberg stated in December 1971 that he planned to restore GM profits to the 10 percent level and one way to do this was to reduce absenteeism. "GM is attempting to improve worker attitudes under a joint program with the UAW. Another profit booster would be automation. GM's Lordstown assembly plant, which builds 100 Chevrolet Vegas an hour, is the premier automated domestic assembly plant. The company wants to extend this capability to other facilities."[12]

Since 1968, GMAD had taken over nearly all 22 of GM's car-assembly plants.

GMAD made bold efforts to cut costs and raise productivity. At the time Lordstown was taken over, both the Fisher Body plant and the assembly plant were consolidated under one management and GMAD's continuous computerized system of grading and ranking was installed.

Under this highly sophisticated reporting system, Joseph Godfrey, GMAD's general manager, receives a daily performance rating on each GMAD plant. At the end of each month, each plant is ranked according to efficiency and quality. Those in the lower third of the ranks get special attention including a visit from the boss "to talk things over," if no improvement has occurred in succeeding months. The ranking system is endless since improvement in one plant pushes another down the scale. There are no final goals.

Godfrey states this open-endedness puts continuous pressure on the management of each plant to reduce costs. He agrees this is a hard practice but sums up his feelings by pointing out "this is competition." [13]

Godfrey is not awed by strikes. In the year following GMAD's takeover of its first six plants in 1968, there were strikes in each of the plants. Regardless of unions and contracts, Godfrey feels GMAD has the right to reorganize the jobs anyway it wishes in order to increase efficiency. He says, "Within reason and without endangering their health, if we can occupy a man for 60 minutes, we have that right." [14]

GMAD has always held that when it takes over a plant, local agreements between the union and other GM divisions are no longer in force. The UAW claims that GMAD uses this point to slash employment ruthlessly and to force the remaining workers to build more cars than ever. The company says that it has only eliminated excess manpower.

GMAD's operational techniques, while tougher, are not unusually different from standard techniques used in the rest of the auto industry. Work standards engineers determine the number of seconds required to perform an operation and foremen are given the manpower calculated to perform at that rate. If any employee fails to perform, the cars go down the line incomplete, the repair shop lot is filled, and management sends the entire workforce home. The idea is that those serious workers who need the money will put pressure on the troublemakers to find some other method to show their discontent.

Today's Young Worker at Lordstown

Whatever its aim, GMAD did not befriend the workers. With only two 23-minute breaks and a half hour for lunch to relieve the monotony of the assembly line, the workers did not welcome GMAD's added pressure for speed and efficiency. According to Gary Bryner, president of Local 1112 at Lordstown: "We had 100 or so grievances before the new management (GMAD) at Lordstown came last October. Now we have over 5,000." [15] This is even more surprising since GM carefully screened all applicants in an attempt to get the better workers for the automated Vega plant. It sought out young white workers with a better than average education.

There were less than 500 women and only 100 blacks at the plant.[16] Wages averaged about $36 per day not counting fringe benefits and, according to a GM brochure issued to all workers, this places even the lowest paid hourly employee in the top third of the U.S. income spectrum.[17]

Management felt it could identify several reasons why workers were not content. Earl Bramblett, GM's vice president for personnel, stated absenteeism occurred not because the jobs were dull, but because of the nation's economic abundance and increased security.[18] He felt the younger workers should show appreciation for what they had and not keep demanding more. UAW Vice President Douglas Fraser countered with the accusation that "in some cases high absenteeism has been caused almost exclusively by high overtime. The young workers won't accept the same old kind of discipline their fathers did." [19]

Although they may have disagreed on the exact problems both GM and the UAW appear to agree that the young workers' ideas about work were the cause. Ken Bannon, a UAW vice president said "New and younger workers will be less attracted to repetition and uninteresting or physically arduous routine tasks. The traditional concept that hard work is a virtue and a duty, which older workers have adhered to, is not applicable to young workers, and the concepts of the younger labor force must be taken into account." [20] Gary Bryner felt that GM had to face the fact that "the guys want to feel like they are making real contributions. They don't want to feel like part of the machines. . . . The management concern is for productivity and profits. Ours is for the employee. There's got to be a blending." [21]

Reese Orlosky, one of the young workers at the Lordstown plant, felt the company never understood why he didn't want to work overtime. He believed money was, of course, important but to the new generation of factory workers it was no longer overwhelming. On the other hand, Reese Orlosky's 58-year-old father, Tom, argued, "These kids who come up today want to sit on their fantails eight hours a day. They think the plant owes them a living. When I was young you put in a day's work. No question about it." [22]

A GM consultant argued, "You can't take a young man, and subject him to the dreadful, dismal future of a production line." [23]

Problems at Lordstown

During the summer of 1971 the Vega assembly plant was consolidated with the local Fisher Body plant and over 10 percent of the 8000 workforce was laid off.[24] At this time the number of grievances rose astronomically. Noting some resistance, GM instituted informal talks with the workers in an effort to resolve some of the opposition; but union officials pointed out that management either did not understand the UAW system of grievance committeemen or stewards, or simply ignored them.

Initially, management did little about grievances but pressure mounted as the number of damaged cars increased. Although the company hesitated to level any charges of industrial sabotage, most officials were convinced this was what was happening. During October 1972, somebody deliberately set fire to an assembly-line control box shed, causing the line to shut down. Autos regularly rolled off the line with slit upholstery, scratched paint, dented bodies, bent gear shift levers, cut ignition wires, and loose or missing bolts. In some cars the trunk keys were broken off in the trunk lock, thereby jamming the lock and forcing replacement. As time passed and tensions grew, it became more and more common to have the 2000 car capacity repair lot completely filled.[25]

For about three months management fought back by shifting personnel, shutting down the line, and sending shifts home early when too many defective cars came off the line. In addition workers were also fined pay for not properly performing their jobs.[26] Finally in January 1971, after repeated instances of incomplete assembly the company made public charges of sabotage.[27]

In mid-January, UAW Local 1112 leaked a story to the press that GM was shipping defective Vegas to dealers, a charge which GM vehemently denied. Gary Bryner cracked afterwards, "We warned them that we were going to get our story out if they wouldn't work with us." [28] By the end of January, management estimated it had lost production of 12,000 cars and 4000 trucks and that workers had lost more than $3.3 million in wages. Management also estimated that since the trouble began in October, lost production had cost them approximately $50 million.[29]

During a National Automobile Dealers convention held in Detroit on February 19, 1972, several Chevrolet dealers were asked about the effects of Lordstown. Some dealers said they had noticed a decline in quality in the Vega; but an overwhelming majority of dealers stated they had not noticed any new problems.

A spokesman for Chevrolet again emphasized that there was very little likelihood of defective cars reaching customers since dealers make a thorough check of each car delivered before it goes in the showroom. He also said that there had not been any increase in warranty claims by dealers selling Vegas.[30]

Thus, on February 1, 1972, at the union hall, beginning early in the morning, a record 97 percent of the members of Local 1112 turned out to vote to strike the Lordstown complex.[31] During the third week of February the informal climate of discussion at Lordstown changed as serious negotiations were begun by both sides.

The union's discontent resulted from actions initiated by GMAD that Irving Bluestone of the UAW summarized as "reducing manpower, disciplining workers in wholesale numbers," and taking away agreements previously negotiated. The initial actions taken by GMAD were viewed by the workers as an old-fashioned "speedup." The union contended that after laying off over 700 workers, extra tasks were assigned to the remaining workers in addition to their regular jobs. The union stated that the men on the line just didn't have enough time and that the extra tasks violated the 1970 GM-UAW contract. The 1970 contract described in great detail the duties assigned to each person's job.

Workers felt GM must return all lost jobs and allow employees to keep seniority rights already negotiated. Workers also believed GM must include the issue of probability of future lay offs in the negotiations. In addition, UAW objected to the tactics used by GMAD when the production problems peaked. The union felt the wholesale disciplining of workers, by sending entire shifts home, was unjust. They also objected to mandatory overtime, used by GM on good production days to regain lost production.

All the above issues had been discussed before at bargaining sessions but one new issue did arise. This was the problem of job monotony and boredom associated with repetitive assembly work. What these workers wanted was relief from what they called "dehumanizing" conditions of work. A six-year veteran of the line stated, "It's going to take something, somewhere to change that (the repetitive, boring nature of the assembly line), where a guy can take an interest in the job." [32]

One car comes down the assembly line every 36 seconds in the Vega plant. To keep up with the never-ending line of cars, the worker's task must be simple—one he can perform within the 36-second time span allowed. He completes his task over and over for eight hours every day, and some days he puts in overtime. By the time their shifts are up, some workers are ready to scream. [33]

The need for change was particularly emphasized by the younger employees. A 27-year-old worker said, "You don't let people tell you things have always been done this way. . . . When my parents told me to do something, I did it, but I kept asking questions." [34] When the question is how to fight boredom, another 27-year-old employee stated, "There's no way to beat it. You just try not to think about it or you can go insane. You just sort of get numb." [35]

Workers felt part of the boredom was due to the speed of the line. They wanted time to talk to a friend, stretch an arm, wander a few feet from the line and take a few puffs on their cigarettes. Some also felt there should be something else to do on their eight-hour shifts beside their tasks on the line, lunch or supper, and their two 23-minute breaks.

On the other hand management felt all their moves were necessary. Management contended that when the Fisher Body and Chevrolet Assembly plants were merged many duplicate jobs were created. They argued that the assembly line very rarely reached its designed operating level and production goals were not being reached. They further stressed that foreign competition made such cutbacks and/or changes necessary in order to return a profit to the company.

Regarding wholesale disciplinary actions and overtime charges, management stated it could not afford to pay workers for partial assembly of cars or, in some cases, sabotage of production. Since production was down and sporadic, management felt that on good producing days overtime was the only means of reaching production needs. It also allowed good workers the chance to make up any losses in their salaries caused by the shutdowns. [36]

On February 21, 1972, the UAW notified GM that the 11,900 members of its union planned to strike at the Lordstown plant and the Wilmington, Delaware plant. This notification was given twelve days in advance rather than the normal five, required by the GM/UAW "crisis situations" agreement. [37]

Neither side wanted a long strike. For GM a prolonged strike would cut off supply of the Vega. Dealers had about a thirty days' supply of cars, but GM would lose production of about 1500 cars per day. [38] For the UAW a long strike would put an added burden on the union strike fund. The union was still heavily in debt from the last strike against GM in 1970. Thus, the International Board told local leaders that strike benefits would not be available for too long.[39]

The Strike

On March 4, 1972, the UAW struck the big complex at Lordstown, idling about 10,000 employees and shutting down GM's only Vega assembly line. Some of the workers took personal tools with them when the strike began indicating they expected a long walkout.[40] About 50 workers patrolled the plant gates. Other plants forced to reduce production were the foundry plant at Massena, New York, the engine plant at Tonawanda, New York, and the axle plant in Buffalo, New York. A GM spokesman estimated that up to 8000 workers in nine Vega parts plants in New York, New Jersey, Michigan, and Ohio would face layoffs if the strike continued.[41]

Since the strike started after the last shift of the week, management hoped to settle the dispute before Monday morning and thus avoid any production loss. Both sides began intense continuous negotiations at 11 A.M., Saturday, March 4. On Sunday Gary Bryner, the local president, said in an interview that most of the conflict over elimination of jobs had been resolved.

Top negotiators for both sides assisted with the bargaining. George Morris, the head of labor relations at GM represented the company and Irving Bluestone, chief of UAW, General Motors Department, represented the union. As the talks continued hopes were high for a quick settlement; however, neither side seemed anxious to give in regardless of the high stakes.

Throughout the weekend small groups of pickets huddled around oil drums filled with burning logs, outside the plant gates. Saturday morning, some pickets tried to prevent some non-union staff workers from entering the plant but were dissuaded by union leaders. In fact, for a time it appeared that even the management team would be denied passage to attend the settlement session.[42]

There was a last minute drive by both union and management Sunday night to settle the dispute but hopes declined when the union presented a new "package deal" late in the evening. At 3:30 A.M. the two sides deadlocked, the union broke off talks saying that "further movement toward a settlement appeared remote in the present climate of bargaining."[43]

Morris pointed out in a statement that the 39-hour marathon bargaining session had made "very significant progress. However, it appeared that the local was merely concerned with exerting its muscle instead of continuing for a responsible settlement." However striking workers seemed ready for a long fight despite a lack of union funds. William Washington, a car test-driver, stated, "You could see this coming six months ago, so I put a little away. There'll be some time for the kids and then I've got some work to do on the home. I'm not too worried."[44] Many of the workers in the local were single and had few responsibilities and, therefore, would not suffer a great deal during the strike.

Neither side would give details of the package proposal, but it was reported the remaining issues were seniority rights and shift preference. The number of grievances had been cut from about 5000 to several hundred and management had indicated that it would restore some of the eliminated jobs. Mr. Bluestone said that before the strike GM had agreed to take back only 20 men; however, by the time negotiations broke down, he stated, "considerable additional progress had been made," though he asserted that "the manpower issue still isn't put completely to bed." [45]

Within hours of the breakdown the top bargainers from both sides, Bluestone and Morris, returned to Detroit. Upon arrival in Detroit, Bluestone went directly to a previously scheduled education conference for UAW representatives from GM around the country. Though the meeting was closed to reporters, it was learned that he delivered a ten-minute report on the Lordstown situation. He reportedly confirmed initial progress but said talks were cancelled as "hopeless" when GM bargainers rejected the late-hour union "package proposal," aimed at resolving major issues. [46]

"I don't know at this point how long the Lordstown strike will go on," he reportedly told the delegates. In his report, Bluestone said he and top GM officials, including retired GM chairman, James Roche, and current chairman, Richard Gerstenberg, had held a "regular stream" of meetings beginning in July 1971 to discuss potential labor difficulties in GMAD plants. Bluestone asserted he had "cautioned" GM about the tough management methods of GMAD, which he felt had precipitated labor disputes in the past. [47]

Bluestone also told delegates that UAW's International Headquarters had proposed to GM a method for settling labor tension in Lordstown during January but indicated that the local union officials would not go along. The plan, applied by the UAW and GM in similar disputes, called for the separate settlement of worker grievances stemming from disciplinary action and other grievances tied to overwork complaints. Bluestone did not criticize the local union leadership for not adopting the plan. However, in reference to the plan GM's Morris said, "It is unfortunate that this local cannot go along with agreements that other GM-UAW locals have used to settle comparable disputes." [48]

Monday morning, March 6, pickets blocked off the three gates to the plant and would not let the salaried personnel pass. When a car moved up to the main gate, the men stood in front of logs they had placed in the gate and shouted "Go home, go home!". At the local headquarters, Reuther Hall, about 400 workers waited to sign up for strike benefits under which a single worker could get $30 per week, a married worker $35 per week, and a married worker with children $40 per week. [49]

After a threat by GM to close down a third facility, a fabricating plant employing 2200 workers, by Friday, talks resumed on Wednesday, March 8.

On Tuesday, March 22, GM corporation was charged by the regional office of the National Labor Relations Board (NLRB) in Detroit with engaging in unfair labor practices in bargaining at the GM Lordstown and Norwood plants. The board cited refusal of GM to disclose the exact size of cutbacks at Norwood and Lordstown as the problem. GM flatly denied the charges. A key issue at both plants had been the reduction of the workforce by GMAD. The NLRB office charged that GM had repeatedly refused to tell the union by exactly how much it had reduced the work-force at each of the plants. The NLRB contended that such information was needed by the union as a basis for negotiating a settlement to the production standards disputes.

The NLRB regional director, Jerome Brooks, argued in his complaint against GM that by refusing to provide the information sought by the union, GM was not bargaining collectively with its employees. Brooks's charge was based on a complaint on the ground that there was "reasonable cause to believe" an unfair labor practice occurred. GM denied the allegations saying: "The UAW charges were based on a demand for information they already had in their possession." [50]

The complaint allowed GM 10 days (until April 3) to file a formal answer. A hearing date was set for April 18. However, Brooks stated a negotiated settlement might be arranged prior to the hearing.

On March 24, the UAW and GM announced that an agreement had been reached to end the Lordstown strike. On Sunday, March 26, the workers were to vote on the agreement and, if passed, the Lordstown plant would begin operation the next day.

At the time the agreement was being announced, Gary Bryner made a statement to clear up a few of the disputed facts. He admitted that the accusation that 800 men were laid off by GMAD since October was a little inflated. It was much closer to the 400 or so GMAD had claimed all along. Bryner also felt the union had won several major concessions. He said, "We're back where we started in October as far as jobs. . . . 240 jobs have been restored and that 130 men would be laid off. Most of these men have less than 90 days on the job [no seniority]." [51] GMAD, however, claimed that only about 150 of the 400 were rehired. [52]

Workers who were sent home because they did not keep up with GMAD's work standards were to receive back pay in cases where the standard had been changed by the settlement. "That involves tens of thousands of dollars," said Bryner. [53] Even with the settlement, however, several hundred local grievances were still to be resolved at Lordstown.

Monday, March 26, Local 1112 ended its strike by ratifying the new settlement contract. But the voting was light. Only 2940 of 7700 members voted and 900 or approximately 30 percent of the voters turned the contract down. About 300 dissident skilled workers walked out of the union ratification meeting, contending they had been denied their right to an exclusive vote on issues involving only their positions. The dissidents later held their own meeting and decided to stay off the job as a protest against the local's ratification. [54]

A GM spokesman said that approximately 50 skilled tradesmen were called in Sunday night to begin start-up operations. Management did not state how many showed up. There were only about 600 skilled tradesmen at the Lordstown plant capable of preparing the assembly line for resumption of production. GM also announced that workers would return to their jobs Monday afternoon and that full production would resume Tuesday morning.

On Monday, March 25, 1972, workers returned as scheduled and Vegas were again rolling off the assembly line, but it was common knowledge that the labor strike had not completely ended. The poor voter turn out, the significant number of negative votes, and the pressure of dissidents, all pointed to continued dissatisfaction. Not only were some major issues left unresolved but added strain was put on labor-management relations. As William O'Connel, a picket said, "Before this we had respect for each other. I used to go out with the foreman for a drink. Now, I wouldn't do it anymore. It wasn't his fault that I can't do it anymore after this." [55] Bryner stated that an important result of the struggle was that it had changed the young workforce. Many were indifferent to the union; but now had become strongly committed to the UAW. "They (GM) built more unionism than we ever could," he continued.[56]

However, a number of young workers including Resse Orlosky saw the union playing a changing role. They believed the union should be an instrument of social progress, and they were not satisfied that this role had been fulfilled by UAW Local 1112 during the strike.[57]

Once the Lordstown complex was back in production, GM stated they might take future steps to improve the plant's efficiency. Initial experience with extensive use of high production machinery had not created significant cost savings. Yet, if future cost savings involved labor, new problems would likely occur.[58] Some auto industry officials believed failure at Lordstown could mean a step toward ending production in the United States of vehicles designed to compete with imports. Three major car manufacturers began importing cars and trucks from Japan and selling them under familiar American name plates.[59] The same companies were also looking to other countries for the manufacture of larger cars.

Epilogue

A recent nationwide Department of Labor survey suggests that the American worker insists most that his job be interesting. Earlier workers disliked "speed-ups" but, in general, accepted such tactics as part of their jobs. Today's young workers have different ideas. Job monotony has become a critical issue and the young worker places the problem with management. "Automobiles are still being made the same way they've always been made," states John Grix, an executive at Lordstown. "Automation makes the work easier, but it is still monotonous. It always was monotonous." [60] However, Gary Bryner argues that workers are no longer willing to put up with job monotony. "Five years ago the union didn't even discuss it." [61]

Whatever is done, says GM's director of employee research, Delmar L. Landen Jr., it must be remembered that absenteeism and allied production problems are only symptoms of the trouble. For too long the automobile industry has "assumed economic man was served if the pay was okay," says Landen, who has a doctorate in industrial psychology and fourteen years experience with GM, "It didn't matter if the job was fulfilling. Once the pay is good, though, higher values come into play." Other satisfactions are required. "One thing is sure: if they won't come in for $32.40 a day, they won't come in for a monogrammed glass." In Landen's view, a greater sense of participation must be built into the job; he does not know just how. He is currently completing a major survey of foremen to learn the exact dimensions of, and the basic reasons for, low worker morale. The study has been in preparation for more than a year. From the findings, he will develop specific recommendations. At this point he is surprisingly optimistic. "We are having very vital, critical changes in our society," he says. "And the question is how we can exploit the forces of change and profit from them." [62]

After interviewing both sides at Lordstown, Edwin Reingold, Detroit bureau chief for *Time* magazine, reported, "There has been much talk of 'job enrichment' —assigning a worker more tasks in order to give him a sense of fulfillment. But some union leaders charge that enriching a worker's job by making him do two jobs each 30 times an hour instead of one job 60 times an hour is a 'con.' At Lordstown the workers want more time to do their single, simple job." [63]

FOOTNOTES

[1] Agis Salpukas, "Extra Work Prompts Vote to Strike at GM Plant, *The New York Times*, February 3, 1972, p. 38.

[2] Kyle Given, "The Unmaking of the Vega," *Motor Trend*, May 1972, p. 48.

[3] Robert Lund, "Made in Ohio by Robots," *Popular Mechanics*, September 1970, p. 82.

[4] "GM's Mini: The Very Model of Automation," *Business Week*, August 8, 1970, p. 26.

[5] *Ibid.*

[6] Lund, "Made in Ohio by Robots," pp. 83,204.

[7] *Ibid.*, p. 204.

[8] "GM's Mini: The Very Model of Automation," p. 26.

[9] B. J. Widick, "The Men Won't Toe the Vega Line," *The Nation*, March 27, 1972, pp. 403–404.

[10] "Can GM's New Top Team Cope With the Seventies?" *Business Week*, December 11, 1971, p. 71.

[11] *Ibid.*

[12] *Ibid.*

[13] Agis Salpukas, "GM's Toughest Division," *New York Times*, April 16, 1972, p. 1.

[14] *Ibid.*

[15] Russel W. Gibbons, "Showdown at Lordstown," *Commonwealth*, March 3, 1972, pp. 523–524.

[16] Widick, "The Men Won't Toe the Vega Line," p. 403.

[17] Judson Gooding, "Blue-Collar Blues on the Assembly Line," *Fortune*, July 1970, p. 71.

[18] *Ibid.*

[19] "The Spreading Lordstown Syndrome," *Business Week*, March 4, 1972, p. 70.

[20] *Ibid.*, p. 69.

[21] "Job Monotony Becomes Critical," *Business Week*, September 9, 1972, p. 108.

[22] Michael Mauney, "Boredom Spells Trouble on the Line," *Life*, September 1, 1972, p. 36.

23 Widick, "The Men Won't Toe the Vega Line," p. 404.

24 Gibbons, "Showdown at Lordstown," p. 524.

25 "Sabotage at Lordstown?" *Time*, February 7, 1972, p. 36. Reprinted by permission from *Time*, The Weekly Newsmagazine; Copyright Time Inc.

26 Agis Salpukas, "Talks Show Gain in GM Ohio Strike," *New York Times*, March 6, 1972, p. 65.

27 Agis Salpukas, "Dealers Minimizing Defect Rate in Vegas," *New York Times*, February 20, 1972, p. 28.

28 "Sabotage at Lordstown?" p. 36.

29 Salpukas, "Dealers Minimizing Defect Rate in Vegas," p. 28.

30 *Ibid.*

31 Salpukas, "Extra Work Prompts Vote to Strike at GM Plant," p. 38.

32 Salpukas, "Dealers Minimizing Defect Rate in Vegas," p. 28.

33 "What Is Work?" *Senior Scholastic*, November 6, 1972, p. 6.

34 "Union Strikes GM Facility in Work Methods Dispute," *New York Times*, March 5, 1972, p. 36.

35 "Revolt of the Robots," *New York Times*, March 7, 1972, p. 38.

36 Salpukas, "Extra Work Prompts Vote to Strike at GM," p. 38.

37 "U.A.W. Notifies GM 11,900 Members at Two Plants Plan Strike," *The Wall Street Journal*, February 22, 1972, p. 3.

38 *Ibid.*

39 Salpukas, "Talks Show Gain in GM Ohio Strike," p. 65.

40 "Revolt of the Robots," p. 38.

41 "Auto Firms Schedule 1.4% Drop in Output This Week From 1971," *The Wall Street Journal*, March 7, 1972, p. 14.

42 Salpukas, "Talks Show Gain in GM Ohio Strike," p. 65.

43 "Revolt of the Robots," p. 38.

44 *Ibid.*

45 "Auto Firms Schedule 1.4% Drop in Output This Week From 1971," p. 14.

46 *Ibid.*

47 *Ibid.*

48 *Ibid.*

49 Agis Salpukas, "GM's Vega Plant Closed by Strike," *New York Times*, March 7, 1972, p. 42.

50 "NLRB Files Complaint Against GM Charging Unfair Labor Practice," *The Wall Street Journal*, March 23, 1972, p. 19.

51 "The Lordstown Syndrome Spreads," *Business Week*, April 1, 1972, p. 64.

52 "Vega Strike Ends, But the Issue Still Boils," *Business Week*, April 1, 1972, p. 23.

53 Agis Salpukas, "GM Plant in Ohio is Producing Again," *New York Times*, March 28, 1972, p. 33.

54 "Dissidents Imperil Vega Plant Accord," *New York Times*, March 27, 1972, p. 38.

55 *Ibid.*

56 *Ibid.*

57 Michael Mauney, "Boredom Spells Trouble on the Line," p. 36.

58 "GM Resuming Output at Lordstown, Ohio as Striking U.A.W. Local Ratifies Accord," *The Wall Street Journal*, March 27, 1972, p. 2.

59 Jerry M. Flint, "GM Plant in Ohio is Producing Again," *New York Times*, March 25, 1972, p. 63.

[60] "The Will to Work and Some Ways to Increase It," *Life*, September 1, 1971, p. 38.
[61] "Job Monotony Becomes Critical," *Business Week*, September 9, 1972, p. 108.
[62] Gooding, "Blue-Collar Blues on the Assembly Line," p. 117.
[63] "Sabotage at Lordstown?" p. 36.

QUESTIONS

1. What were the dominant factors in GM's environment fostering the Lordstown experiment?
2. Discuss your perception of GMAD's concept of human nature.
3. What was the coping strategy employed by GM to deal with the foreign compact cars?
4. Why would GM, certainly knowledgeable of contributions of the behavioral sciences, employ the assembly line and incentive system found at Lordstown?
5. Would you expect GM to view its coping strategy as unsuccessful after what happened at Lordstown? Explain your answer.
6. Why was the response of younger workers different from that of the older employees?
7. Discuss the circumstances under which GM's Lordstown experiment may be viewed as appropriate.
8. How did the younger employees view the proper role of the UAW?
9. Discuss the appropriateness of GM's strategy in both the short and long run.
10. What are alternative means of coping with human problems on the assembly line?
11. What appear to be the underlying reasons for the nature of the strategy employed by GM?
12. What factors determine the limits of GM's responsibilities to its employees?

CHAPTER 10

THE
MILITARY-INDUSTRIAL
COMPLEX

CASE 10
THE WEAPONS-SYSTEMS CONTRACTOR

While our national heritage has made us suspicious of the power inherent in a standing army, we have seen fit to integrate the military and private industry in order to maintain a permanent military posture since our entry into World War I. This merging of the military and corporations in the private sector was called the military-industrial complex by President Eisenhower during his farewell address:

> . . . This conjunction of an immense military establishment and a large arms industry is new in the American experience. The total influence—economic, political, even spiritual—is felt in every city, every state house, every office of the Federal government. We recognize the imperative need for this development. Yet we must not fail to comprehend its grave implications. Our toil, resources, and livelihood are all involved; so the very structure of our society.
>
> We must never let the weight of this combination endanger our liberties or democratic processes. We should take nothing for granted. Only an alert and knowledgeable citizenry can compel the proper meshing of the huge industrial and military machinery of defense with our peaceful methods and goals so that security and liberty may prosper together.[1]

One method of judging the increasing importance of the defense establishment is to look at the value of its property. In 1971, Defense Department property was valued at $214.6 billion.[2] In comparison, the two largest corporations in the United States—General Motors and Standard Oil of New Jersey—have combined assets of less than $40 billion.[3] Another comparison that indicates the economic importance of defense expenditures is a comparison of defense-related employment with total U. S. employment. Civilian and armed forces personnel (employed in defense agencies in 1971) totaled nearly 3.9 million. This is down from a high in 1968 at the height of our action in Vietnam when approximately 4.8 million people were involved in defense agencies. Most of the reduction has come through a decrease in the armed forces. Civilian defense employees made up about 1.3 percent of the civilian labor force in 1971, and if armed forces personnel, are included employment in defense agencies totaled 4.7 percent of the labor force.[4]

These statistics underestimate the impact of defense expenditures on the labor market. The U. S. Department of Labor estimates that total defense-generated employment in fiscal 1970 amounted to approximately 3.7 million jobs, excluding the armed forces; of this total, 1.1 million were employees of federal, state, and local governments, but nearly 2.6 million jobs in the private sector were generated by defense expenditures. In 1970, one out of every twenty jobs was dependent upon defense spending.[5]

The Lockheed Corporation is one of the largest defense contractors in the country and a long-standing member of the military-industrial complex. The company is certainly not a newcomer to the defense industry and its top management has had many years' experience attempting to survive in its turbulent environment. Despite this kind of experience, the company immediately ran into substantial cost overruns on the C-5A, a system supposedly not requiring new technology.

Because of the many instances of substantial overruns within companies in the defense industry, critics allege that the character of the military-industrial complex encourages production inefficiencies, rapidly increasing defense costs, and the production of weapons systems that quickly become obsolete. This indictment takes on added significance when it is realized that under present conditions the United States has no alternative but to maintain a strong defense establishment.

FOOTNOTES

[1] Dwight D. Eisenhower, "President Eisenhower's Farewell to the Nation," *The Department of State Bulletin*, February 6, 1961, pp. 180–181.

[2] *The American Almanac* (New York: Grosset and Dunlap, 1971), p. 253.

[3] "The 500 Largest U. S. Industrial Corporations," *Fortune*, May 1972.

[4] *The Statistical Abstract of the United States*, 1972, p. 248.

[5] Richard Dempsey and Douglas Schmude, "Occupational Impact on Defense Expenditures," *Monthy Labor Review*, December 1971, pp. 12–15.

Lockheed's Problems with the C-5A: The Military-Industrial Complex

The End of an Era at Lockheed

The Lockheed Aircraft Corporation has been one of the largest defense contractors in the country during the last decade and, in fact, became the largest contractor during 1969. Despite the need to deal with economic, political, and techological risks unique to the defense weapon systems industry, until the late 1960s Lockheed had been able to grow and prosper. Much of this success was achieved by effectively exploring technological frontiers. Lockheed's board chairman, Daniel J. Haughton, has characterized his company by saying, "We're in the business of taking risks— the business of developing new systems. Engineering is not an exact science, and we have to invent as we go along." [1]

Haughton's election to chairman of the board in 1967 marked the end of an era for Lockheed. From 1937 until the election, the company was led by one or the other of the Gross brothers, Robert and Courtlandt. After Robert's death in 1961, his brother became chairman and Haughton moved to the presidency. As a young man, the new president had worked in a coal mine in northwestern Alabama. Because of family financial needs, Haughton was late starting school, but very quickly proved to be a superior student. When Courtlandt retired at age sixty-two, he did so with confidence that Haughton was ready to bear the full load.

Courtlandt felt confident that Haughton had managerial and leadership qualities, loyalty, and very good judgment. After some time on the job, it also became apparent that he had sales and planning abilities. As he progressed through the operating levels and later to administration, Haughton proved himself a good man on every assignment. He was always willing to subordinate himself to the overall good of the company.

Indeed, Haughton appeared to be a man of boundless energy. Four or five hours of sleep at his home in the Hollywood Hills was a good night's rest for him, and 6:00 A.M. normally found him at his office desk. Often, he would return to the Lockheed-run Burbank Airport after a night flight from the east coast in his Lockheed Jetstar, visit his home fifteen minutes away for a quick shave and shower, then drive directly to his office across from the Burbank passenger terminal. There, at 3:00 A.M. or 4:00 A.M., he would settle down in his gold-carpeted office to begin the day's work.

One of Lockheed's largest divisions, Lockheed-Georgia, located at Marietta, Georgia, is the largest industrial enterprise in the Southeast. From the mid-1950s until the mid-1960s this plant produced the C-130 Hercules and the C-141 Starlifter, two of the company's biggest money makers. Since the first C-130—an unlovely prop jet cargo carrier—was delivered in 1956, some 1067 were sold, 56 during the 1968–69 period.

However, Lockheed's success during this time was limited to government contracts. For instance, the special virtues that made the C-130 a highly successful military aircraft limited its potential commercial market. Also, the contract for the C-141 was won in 1960; before Lockheed could make a commercial version, Boeing and Douglas designed cheaper commercial cargo versions of their biggest passenger jets. Recognizing its dependence on the military market, Lockheed made strong efforts to enter the commercial market. According to the *New York Times Magazine*, Lockheed had not had a major entry in the commercial aircraft market since its Constellations were phased out by the airlines in the late 1950s. During this time Lockheed developed the Turboprop Electra in hopes that the airlines were not yet ready to plunge into straight jet aircraft. The company guessed wrong and the airlines ordered the straight jet 707s from Boeing and DC-8s from Douglas.[2]

C-5A

In 1962, the idea of an extremely large cargo plane with certain unique characteristics was being developed by Robert McNamara's Pentagon. The military wanted a cargo plane that would give the United States the ability to deploy fully equipped forces worldwide on minimum notice, thereby reducing the necessity for so many overseas bases. It was also felt by its proponents that the aircraft would cut defense costs, help combat the balance-of-payments deficit, and at the same time add to the options open to an American President responding to emergencies abroad.

The aircraft was envisioned as the largest plane ever built and was expected to carry every piece of equipment required by an army division from tanks to helicopters, up to 265,000 pounds of payload at a time—the equivalent of nearly 10 railroad box cars fully loaded with household appliances. Specifically, the plane was designed to carry a 100,000-pound payload 2875 miles to an unprepared, surfaced (dirt) runway, then load and take off over a 50-foot obstacle in less than 4000 feet on a hot day, returning to base without refueling. The plane's navigational and guidance systems were to be very precise allowing the aircraft to fly with only a 50-foot ceiling and 700-foot visibility for landing, even in a combat zone.[3]

After inception of the idea in the early 1960s, the Pentagon decided to go ahead with plans for the C-5A in 1964. In December 1964, the Air Force issued a detailed request for bids on the gigantic aircraft. At the time the Pentagon's internal estimate of all costs on 115 air planes, including research, development, and production, was $2.2 billion for the air frame and $577 million for the engines, for a total of approximately $2.8 billion. The field of prospective bidders was narrowed down to only three companies because of the awesome financial, physical, and technological capabilities required for such an aircraft. In April 1965, the final bids were submitted for the 115-plane contract plus five experimental models. Boeing was high bidder with a target figure of $2.3 billion, Douglas was next at $2.0 billion and Lockheed was a surprising low at $1.9 billion. However, price was only one factor in determining a proposal and the evaluation team found some flaws in Lockheed's design. For instance, it did not meet specifications for short field takeoff and landing. The company changed the wing and flap design and made the plane larger but did not change the price.[4] General Electric and United Aircraft's Pratt and Whitney division bid on the engines. When the bids were opened, GE won the contract for the engines with a bid of $624 million, slightly above the 1964 Air Force estimate.

The bidders on the C-5A contract were quite aware that the stakes were appreciably greater than the program itself. The winner might legitimately expect to get a corner on the commercial market with a plane that promised eventually to become a standard workhorse of the air-transport business. The fortunate company also would be financed by the Defense Department while it developed the engineering and manufacturing experience to produce a potentially far more profitable commercial version. [5]

Berkeley Rice of the *New York Times* felt that Lockheed had more to lose than its competitors by not acquiring the contract.

> Lockheed needed the C-5A contract much more than either Boeing or Douglas. Lockheed-Georgia, the division that builds Lockheed's military aircraft, was nearing the end of production on the C-141 Starlifter, the predecessor to the C-5A, and there were no other major contracts in sight. Under such pressures, Lockheed submitted the low bid of $1.9-billion for the C-5A airframe-assembly contract. Boeing was high with a bid of $2.3 billion. Since Boeing executives later conceded that even their bid was a trifle "optimistic," and since the Air Force itself had been estimating the cost of the work at $2.2 billion, many Pentagon officials and Congressional critics contend that Lockheed deliberately tried to "buy in" with an unreasonably low bid, assuming that later contract changes would boost the final price enough to provide a comfortable margin of profit. [6]

Though this assumption is bold there is precedent for such behavior. Many of the military contracts let during this time had cost overruns estimated at a minimum of 50 percent.

Lockheed was awarded the contract because of its previous excellent record of producing military cargo aircraft and the substantial savings to the government promised by the low bid. However, the Air Force Source Selection Board had originally chosen Boeing because of its design superiority. The board feared that Lockheed's version would cause schedule delays and cost increases. When Lockheed won the C-5A contract in 1965, many felt this gave the company a good chance to break into the commercial market. However, immediate competition was to come from Boeing, which modified the design it had submitted for the C-5A and produced the 747. Boeing also designed a cargo version of the 747.

Also in 1965, the Air Force, in an attempt to reduce waste in its military procurement programs, hired Arthur E. Fitzgerald as Deputy to the Assistant Secretary of the Air Forces for Management Systems. His job was to find waste and reduce costs. One of the programs in which he was to become deeply involved was the C-5A.

The C-5A Contract

When the decision to build the C-5A was made the Air Force employed a new kind of contract called "total package procurement," (TPP). The principal creator of the concept was Robert H. Charles. Appointed assistant secretary of the Air Force for installations and logistics by President Kennedy in 1963, Charles had previously served eighteen years with McDonnell Aircraft, seven of them as executive vice president. He went to the Pentagon with the conviction that military procurement was in urgent need of drastic reform. Under the previous contract system there was real competition only for initial research and development awards. The winner generally became the sole source for the product and enjoyed an advantage over the government when the time came to negotiate the price of a production contract.[7] Because research and development typically accounts for only about 20 percent of a defense project's total cost, Charles argued that competition ended far too early in the project cycle. He believed that the government could save money and obtain better products by making contractors compete for a total package—research and development, testing, evaluation, and production under a single contract that would clearly define price, schedule, and performance commitments. Also, the contractor would share added costs or profits with the government determined by an intricate formula involving target and ceiling prices. To prevent windfall profits or disastrous losses for the contractor, the production phase would be split into segments, with the price of the latter segments to be determined by the actual costs encountered.

Under the contract, Lockheed's commitment was divided into three principal parts. The company was first required to design, develop, test, and evaluate five plans. Then it was to produce a "Run A" of 53 planes. Next, depending on the Air Force's exercise of certain options, 24 months before scheduled delivery of the planes there would be a "Run B" of 57 aircraft, plus spare parts for the five test airplanes and some ground support equipment. Another option, not covered by the original bid prices, provided for a "Run C" of up to 85 C-5As.

The bid of $1.9 billion on the air frame contract represented the target price, which included profit, research and development, testing, evaluation of the five prototypes, and production of Runs A and B. There was also a ceiling price of $2.3 billion on the air frame with the government to pay 70 percent and Lockheed 30 percent of the cost between the target and ceiling prices. The contract also set forth a separate price for Run B, along with a formula for adjusting the overall price of the contract should actual costs in Run A exceed 130 percent of the Run A target cost. The adjusted contract price had no provision for profit, which under the cost-sharing features would have been eaten up in offsetting the costs of Run A.

The repricing formula on Run B was worked out by a computer and was quite complex. If actual audited costs of Run A should exceed 140.5 percent of the Run A target cost, the excess percentage over 130 percent was to be multiplied by two. The resulting percentage figure was then used to multiply the target cost of Run B as established in the original contract back in 1965. The result set the new target cost and ceiling price of the contract.

During its life the most widely criticized part of the C-5A contract was the repricing provision. The *Washington Post* habitually referred to the price-adjustment formula as a "golden handshake." Senator Proxmire charged that it set up a "reverse incentive" for the contractor to pack costs into Run A in order to get a higher price on Run B. On the other hand, the Air Force contended that an element of reverse incentive on Run A could enter in only if the contractors were certain that all of the Run B option would be picked up. To counter this, the Air Force authorized a "buy" of only 23 planes on Run B when the first option deadline rolled around. Even these 23 were subject to the appropriation of additional funds by Congress.[8]

Cost Overrun

Soon after work began on the C-5A in 1965, unexpectedly severe inflation and stubborn technical problems coupled with shortages of skilled workers and essential materials threw cost and schedule estimates out of kilter. Lockheed reestimated and projected a cost to the government of $3.2 billion for the 115 air frames through Run B with the company absorbing a loss of some $13 million. The overrun of $1.3 billion would be about 68 percent of Lockheed's original target cost. However, with the effect of inflation—about $627 million—taken out, Lockheed's overrun on the C-5A promised to be a truly remarkable 35 percent of the original bid. Air Force estimates placed the final cost to the government of the C-5A air frames about where Lockheed said it was.[9]

Lockheed officials stated that the overruns resulted from the required use of "advanced technology" even though in awarding the contract the Pentagon specifically maintained that the job did not require any major technological advances. These same cost overruns continued during 1966 and 1967. Lockheed, from time to time, requested "additional funding" from the Air Force and the Air Force revised the C-5A budget and the overrun disappeared.[10]

After several news leaks concern mounted regarding the overruns. The *New York Times Magazine* stated:

> A few Air Force officers tried without success to call attention to the growing overrun. One of them was transferred to Vietnam, another was suddenly found qualified to become air attache to the U.S. Embassy in Addis Ababa. In November, 1968, long frustrated by the apparent unwillingness of his superiors to try to hold costs down on the C-5A, Ernest Fitzgerald, an Air Force civilian cost-control expert, disclosed before Senator William Proxmire's subcommittee on Economy in Government that the program would cost more than $5 billion—$2 billion more than the official Air Force estimates at this time. For his audacity, Fitzgerald was stripped of most his duties and later fired.[11]

The Fitzgerald Incident

A major source of controversy about the overruns at this time came from within the Pentagon. Arthur E. Fitzgerald had been hired by the Air Force in 1965 to reduce waste. Robert H. Charles, a former Assistant Secretary of the Air Force in charge of procurement, figured the C-5A overrun at only $882 million. Fitzgerald countered that the real cost overrun probably totaled closer to $2 billion.

Air Force Secretary Robert C. Seamans, Jr. said the truth probably lay somewhere between $1 billion and $1.5 billion. It depended, he insisted, on which of several early estimates of the cost of the C-5A was used as a base and also the extent to which the cost of spare parts was included.[12]

Fitzgerald's association with the C-5A program began with the emergence of the project in 1965. Because of his monitoring of the program, Fitzgerald was present at many of the monthly progress reviews and high level presentations on the total C-5A system. At one program review presented by the Air Force Systems Command, a complete system overview was given.[13] In an attempt to clarify some of the Vu-graphs, Fitzgerald questioned several areas of concern and apparent conflicting information. In the next several days he persisted in calling and questioning various Air Force staff personnel. His primary questions to the Air Force staff were, "Why was there one billion dollars extra for the C-5A? Doesn't the TPP contract put all odds and ends on which the contractor traditionally gets fat into the one pot?" The response from the Air Force was, "Not really, the contract does commit the contractor to a price on the first production run, but not on all the aerospace ground equipment and spares. We have reached an agreement (verbal between the Air Force Systems Command and Lockheed) on how these items would be defined and priced later on, but its the same old cost-plus-percentage-of-cost contracting for the aerospace ground equipment and spares when you cut all the rhetoric away." The Vu-graph depicting aerospace ground equipment and spares indicated only in footnotes that these items on the "What we bought " list were provided for. At this point in December 1965, Fitzgerald asked for a complete copy of the contract for the C-5A.[14]

The following year Fitzgerald was still very deeply involved in the C-5A program management areas. Lockheed presented a program review on December 16, 1966. It was described by Fitzgerald as follows: "The second briefing was very much like seeing a rerun of an old movie, the plot still has drama and suspense, the script was excellent, the acting superb, but the outcome will be the same as it was the first, second, or thousandth time it was shown. The contract cost will be exceeded." Regarding the C-5As "magic" contract, he wrote, "The provisions of the contract will not act as a brake on cost increases, in fact, the contract almost guarantees increases. The coming cost increase will be more than justified, supported, rationalized and explained by the contractor. His position will be supported by the Air Force. The costs, whatever they are, will duly be entered into data banks, to prove beyond any doubt that they are true costs. Who can argue that they should or could have been different?" [15]

From January 1967 to January 1969, very little was published about the problems encountered by the C-5A program. However, both Senator Proxmire and the House Armed Services Committee became interested during this period, as a result of congressional testimony and money requests that demonstrated considerable disparity between the original selling price of the C-5A and its estimated price at the time.

During hearings carried out by the Armed Services Committee in 1969, General Jeffrey of the Air Force Systems Command was questioned both during and after his testimony concerning the C-5A. His statements focused on some of the past estimates of the airplanes' costs. He stated that in October 1965, the cost estimate for the TPP, less support, was $3.116 billion. In October 1968, the estimate as to the ceiling on the program was $4.338 billion, or a difference of $1.223 billion.[16]

It was calculated that $500 million of this figure represented inflation during this period. The Air Force did not consider this to be a part of the cost overrun or an error on anyone's part. It might be noted here that the procurement pricing practices of the Department of Defense are controlled by Congress in that budget requests for a total program may not include "expected" inflation but only present costs of the program.

Also, the aircraft emerged heavier by 83,000 pounds than original estimates. This translated into a $350 million increase in cost. The Air Force did not consider this an error on anyone's part either.[17] The Air Force then argued that the remaining $372 million making up the $1.223 billion difference between the 1965 and the 1968 estimates was a result of technical difficulties that the contractor ran into during development and initial production. The Air Force attributed this to Lockheed's underestimate of the magnitude of the task involved.[18]

Fitzgerald then was called to appear before the committee hearings concerning the C-5A, and he testified to the facts as he saw them. He had data to support his position, but much of it was altered by the Pentagon prior to its submission for the record to the Committee. Fitzgerald testified that a variety of techniques were used by the Air Force to cover up cost overruns. The cost of spare C-5A parts had been deleted from both the original cost estimates and from 1969 cost projections. Also, some figures were arbitrarily cut in half. He felt the greatest deviations were achieved by raising the amount of the original estimates in order to make the overrun look smaller. This was accomplished by substituting the original C-5A estimate for a later estimate.[19]

During this time in 1969, a project headed by Brigadier General Joseph Cappucci, the director of the Air Force Office of Special Investigations, focused on determining anything that would discredit Fitzgerald. Fitzgerald was informed of the activities by a friend who knew the personnel involved in the investigation. According to the secret sympathizer, the big contractor, whom Fitzgerald had bruised, was jubilant. At long last, in concert with the Department of Defense, they were finally going to "get Ernie." The investigation was aimed at establishing his (1) relationship with women other than his wife, (2) overuse of alcohol, (3) use of drugs, and (4) homosexual contacts. Later it was learned that the investigation number was HOD 24-12052—the prefix 24 denotes "Special Inquiry." The investigators found no facts to discredit Fitzgerald. Ted Marks, of the Times-Mirror Corporation in Los Angeles, said to some of the investigators, as he threw them out of his office, "If this gets out, it's only going to hurt the Air Force." [20]

After a long and frustrating series of attempts to isolate the data on overruns and in the process receiving abusive treatment from both co-workers and associates, Fitzgerald was accused by Seamans of giving classified information to Congress. The accusations were made during the closing hearings before the Armed Services Committee and Chairman Mendel Rivers commented, "If I had a fellow like that working in my office, he would have been long gone. You don't need to be afraid about firing him." [21]

Fitzgerald had written several letters to his immediate superior concerning the accusers and requested an audience with the accusers to defend himself, but he was ignored. Then Fitzgerald, who was nominated by the Air Force in 1967 for a Distinguished Service Award, was placed in Pentagon purgatory. His civil service status, routinely given any appointee at his level after three years of service, was revoked because of "a computer error." He also believed his mail was being opened. One letter even bore the initials and stamp of the "action officer" who had opened it. He still works at the Pentagon but instead of monitoring the costs of the multibillion dollar C-5A and F-111, he spends his time evaluating relative minor projects. His first assignment was to review contractors of a bowling alley in Thailand. His finding: a $100,000 overrun.[22]

The Air Force Cuts Its Order

There was no question that Lockheed would take its lumps over the C-5A in Seaman's judgment. It appeared, he told the Senate Committee, that Lockheed would lose a "catastrophic" $671 million on the five research and development planes and 53 Run A production planes when work was completed. But under the reprising formula that came into play for the 57 planes making up Run B, the company's loss would be cut to $285 million. The Air Force had contracted for all of the 58 Run A planes but Seamans indicated that the program would be cut to 81 airplanes or only 23 in Run B. The Air Force estimated this would cut total cost from $4.831 billion to around $4 billion. In 1971 this estimate would be revised upward by the Air Force to $4.5 billion. Even with the cutback to 81 planes the program would cost more than the original estimate for all 115 planes. Lockheed protested and took the dispute to the Armed Services Board of Contract Appeals for settlement. Lockheed argued that the Air Force had exercised its option to buy all 115 planes. Because the settlement threatened to take several years, the Pentagon, in order to ease the cutback, allowed Lockheed to stretch out the program by producing only two planes per month instead of three. This meant a year's delay in delivery and added as much as $75 million to the cost of the program.[23]

The Need for Additional Funds

The Armed Services Committee continued to explore the C-5A's cost problems because it had to pass on the Air Force's budget request of $1 billion, which included money for the 23 planes of Run B. Should Congress refuse, the government's contractual responsibility would be limited to the initial 58 planes. In late 1969 the Armed Services Committee sent to the Senate a recommendation of $1 billion for the C-5A without giving any consideration to the controversy over the C-5A costs or even the need for the airplane.[24]

Financial crises were further augmented by development problems. According to an Air Force general, several of the plane's complex systems were performing with "lower than desired reliability." He also stated that there were "structural fatigue problems." These involved cracks that developed in the wing. Lockheed estimated in January 1970 that the cost to fix these in all 81 planes would be $6.5

million. By February 1, 1971, the cost was $28 million. Because of these and other problems, by 1971 the overall cost of each plane grew from $23 million to around $60 million.

Berkeley Rice claimed that most of the investment for the program was being made by the government.

> To cover Lockheed's expenses on the C-5A program, the Air Force made regular "progress payments," weekly checks that amounted to more than 90 percent of the company's current outlays. In addition, the company received a number of special "milestone payments," or bonuses, though the program was far behind schedule. The progress and milestone payments and the fact that much of the plant and machinery at Lockheed-Georgia are owned by the Defense Department mean that most of the investment for the C-5A program was being made by the Government.[25]

Because of the cost overruns Lockheed ran out of enough funds to run the program. In March 1970, Dan Haughton wrote the Pentagon requesting an additional $435–500 million. He stated that Lockheed could not wait for the settlement of the contract suit. Lockheed blamed inflation for more than $500 million of the overrun even though the contract specifically allowed for $300 million. It also blamed financial troubles in part on other military contracts such as the Cheyenne helicopter for the Army, the short-range attack missile (SRAM), and nine ships for the Navy. In his message to the Pentagon, Haughton stated the requested money was essential to the future of the C-5A. Defense officials stated that Lockheed would go bankrupt without the extra money. Since Lockheed produced the Polaris and Poseidon missiles and dozens of other weapons systems, the Defense Department claimed that Lockheed's collapse would dangerously weaken the nation's defense. Because of this, Congress passed a contingency fund of $200 million. After the loan from Congress, banks agreed to lend Lockheed $150 million more. This arrangement also included $100 million in accelerated advance payments by Lockheed's three major customers for the commercial versions of the C-5A: Trans World Airlines, Delta, and Eastern. The airlines had already given large sums as down payments for the commercial version and they did not want to see their investments lost due to financial troubles with the C-5A.[26]

Haughton reluctantly accepted a settlement that brought Lockheed's losses on the disputed defense contracts to $400 million (before taxes), all but $190 million of which it had already written off. That gave the company an apparent after-tax loss for 1970 of $80 million, instead of a previously reported profit of about $10 million, and its net worth declined from $331 million to $240 million. Many felt this was a very tough settlement for Lockheed. One presidential assistant said, "The Defense Department negotiated these guys out of $350 million."[27]

Looking back now, Haughton admits that Lockheed was too optimistic about what it would cost to develop and build the big aircraft. But he stoutly insists that unexpected pressures—not poor management—caused the cost overruns.

The Commercial Market and the L-1011 TriStar

Lockheed for some time had wanted to return to the commercial market. With this in mind the company had utilized the technology and production techniques developed for the C-5A to begin planning the L-1011, a wide-bodied, medium-range trijet passenger liner. The market for such a plane was estimated to be enormous. For the planes' engines, Lockheed accepted bids from Rolls-Royce Ltd., General Electric, and Pratt and Whitney. Lockheed awarded the $489 million contract to Rolls-Royce for 550 engines because of its low bid and superior design. [28]

When the RB.211 was chosen for the TriStar in 1968, all Britain celebrated. David Huddie, then managing director of Rolls' Aero Engine Division, was knighted by the Queen for his contribution to the nation's balance of trade, and the British government agreed to pay 70 percent of the then-estimated cost of developing the RB.211. The government's contribution was to be repaid out of sales of the engine.

Because McDonnell-Douglas had also designed almost the same plane, the DC-10, orders and options for the L-1011 did not come in early enough or fast enough to cover Lockheed's development costs of about $500 million. As a result of this and C-5A cost problems, the company was desperately short of cash. In the summer of 1969, Lockheed arranged a $440 million loan from a consortium of 24 banks. However, by March 1970, when the C-5A crisis reached a peak, Lockheed had already drawn $300 million of the loan and still was desperately short of cash. [29]

Lockheed was plagued with other problems that threatened the success of the L-1011. In September 1970, both Lockheed and McDonnell-Douglas rolled out their first test models, but McDonnell-Douglas was well ahead in orders. The company had orders and options on 241 planes ($3.6 billion) while Lockheed only had orders and options on 173 planes ($2.6 billion). McDonnell-Douglas appeared to be ahead mainly because of its use of GE engines. "With tremendous financial resources of its own, GE has been able to help DC-10 buyers finance their orders." [30] During this same time, Rolls was also experiencing problems. For a long time no one found much cause for concern, though by the end of 1969 the company's debt had risen sharply. Rolls-Royce owed some $150 million to creditors, some of whom had to wait six months or more to be paid. Other debts in the form of bank overdrafts, short-term papers, and debentures totaled $266 million. No one seemed really alarmed, however, until Rolls reported a $115 million loss for the first half of 1970. This was, in large part, due to Rolls' executives' gross underestimate of technical problems involved in the development of the RB.211 engine. [31]

Even then the alarm was slight because of the belief that Rolls could always turn to the government. In fact, in the spring of 1970, Rolls did receive a $24 million loan and the promise of another $24 million in 1971 from the Industrial Reorganization Corporation, a government agency. In return for the aid, Rolls was required to put two new members on its board of directors. Further study revealed the need for more money. The Heath government agreed to provide $101 million and Rolls' banks supplied $43 million. There was, however, a price for this help.

Sir Denning Pearson was replaced as chairman by Lord Cole, who had recently retired as chairman of Unilever. A four-man committee, headed by one of the newly appointed board members, took over Pearson's chief executive functions. The money promised by the government and banks was then withheld pending an audit. The new management soon concluded that the cost of bringing the new engines into production would increase from the 1968 estimate of $156 million to more than $600 million.[32]

Bankruptcy of Rolls-Royce Ltd.

Over its long life, Rolls-Royce Ltd. had earned an outstanding reputation of technical excellence and reliability. These virtues were further demonstrated when Rolls assigned 22,000 employees to the research and development of the engine it hoped to put in Lockheed's L-1011 TriStar. From this effort came the RB.211 engine. The engine possessed 20 percent fewer rotating parts than other engines and had a huge fan and two compressor sections that revolved independently on concentric drive shafts. These characteristics gave the pilot more flexibility in controlling power in landing and made the RB.211 an unusually quiet and clean engine.

With the advanced RB.211 engine and a final settlement with the Pentagon over the C-5A completed, Haughton appeared to have some breathing space. Such tranquility was short-lived, however, for on February 2, 1971, over luncheon with Lord Cole he learned of the bleak realities and dire prospects for Rolls. Development was behind schedule, the engine was not performing as expected, and Rolls was unable to attain additional funds from the government. As a result Rolls was forced to declare bankruptcy. This would make it impossible for Lockheed to deliver the 10 planes scheduled for the fall and at the same time place significant strains on the company's financial resources, particularly after the Pentagon settlement over the C-5A required the company to take a $200 million loss.[33]

At this point, only the British government could supply the funds necessary for Rolls to continue with the RB.211. This the government was not willing to risk without assurance from the U.S. government that Lockheed would survive. Now Lockheed calculated that regardless of whether the engines were British or American it would require another $350 million of outside financing from banks and customers to put TriStar in full production. The banks also were not willing to make such a loan without some form of guarantee from the U.S. government. This would require congressional action. Haughton was now trying to negotiate with 2 governments, 9 customers, and 24 banks.[34]

The only alternatives left to Lockheed were to renegotiate a contract with bankrupted Rolls or use General Electric or Pratt and Whitney engines. The use of GE or Pratt and Whitney engines would result in major drawbacks. The cost for the new engines would add at least $100,000 more to the Rolls' contract price and they would require at least $100 million more to redesign the L-1011. This would cause a delay in delivery of at least six months. The costs would have to be passed on to the airlines, and this would hurt Lockheed's competitive position in relation to Mc-

Donnell-Douglas. These factors coupled with continued favorable response of the airlines to the RB.211 despite political uncertainties caused Lockheed to again stick with the British company. But, since the British government would not take over this division of Rolls, Haughton would have to negotiate a new contract.[35]

After additional studies by the British government to determine if Rolls could be saved it was calculated that another $288 million would be enough to complete engine development. Based on this information, Lord Carrington, the Minister of Defense, presented an offer to Haughton in March 1971. The price of the engines would be increased to $1,180,000 from $840,000. The government would put up $144 million toward development and Lockheed would provide the remaining $144 million. Haughton rejected the offer saying that Lockheed did not want to add Rolls' problems to its own and that the $288 million calculation was twice its own estimate. Minor changes were made in the offer, but it became clear that the core requirement had to be U.S. government guarantee of loans Lockheed required from its banks. Obviously, some form of government participation had become essential.[36]

A recognition of the need for U.S. government participation, the continued favorable response of the airlines, and the British government's decision to save the RB.211 intensified negotiations for a new contract. Late in March a contract calling for the production of 555 engines was signed. The British government agreed to pay all further development costs (estimated at $240 million) and to subsidize production costs if necessary. Lockheed agreed to an increased price of the engine of around $1,020,000 apiece. Now Haughton had to get his customers to agree to the new price and a $103,000 increase in the price of each air frame, resulting from production delays. However, the added total cost of $643,000 was less than had there been a change in engines. The chief condition for the agreement between Haughton and Lord Carrington was assurance to the British that TriStar production would continue.[37]

The agreement sent Haughton to John Connally, Secretary of the Treasury, to arrange U.S. government backing on an additional $250 million in bank loans, which were to cover all foreseeable contingencies. After a meeting between Connally and President Nixon on May 6, 1971, an announcement was made indicating the loan guarantee legislation would be sent to Congress. At the time Connally stated, "The health of an aircraft industry is essential to the nation's commerce, employment, technological development and protection. We do not anticipate any cost to the taxpayer from this loan guarantee." [38] The legislation, which did not specifically name Lockheed, contained a number of restrictions and safeguards. *Fortune* magazine stated:

> . . . the Secretary of the Treasury would be given full access to Lockheed's books, with the company to pay the government's out-of-pocket surveillance costs. All the guaranteed $250 million in loans would be repaid ahead of the $400 million in earlier loans advanced by the banks, and before Lockheed can resume the dividends that it last paid in the fourth quarter of 1969. In the event of Lock-

heed's bankruptcy, the government's claims would have precedence over those of other creditors. [39]

Support for the Loan Guarantee

One basic position was stated in a *Fortune* editorial. It argued that the case for the Lockheed guarantee rested on the fact that it was an exceptional measure and dealt with an unusual emergency that befell a corporation especially vulnerable to circumstances beyond its control. While certainly not the only factor, the editorial also hinted that an element of bad management may have contributed to Lockheed's predicament. [40]

It also argued that the bankruptcy of Lockheed would be detrimental to the national economy:

> Lockheed claims that a total of $1.4 billion in U.S. investments would be threatened if the L-1011 should be cancelled. This includes investments of $400 million by Lockheed's 24 banks, $270 million by its airline customers, $350 million by L-1011 subcontractors and the rest in earlier investments by Lockheed in buildings and tooling for the L-1011. Chances of substantial portions of the investment being recovered should the company go into receivership are minimal, according to Lockheed, which estimates its net worth has slipped from $371 million in 1968 to $240 million now because of pre-tax losses estimated at $500 million on four defense programs. [41]

An estimated 30,000 jobs in the United States would also be affected by elimination of the L-1011 program. "As of January 31, 1971, Lockheed says, 17,700 employees were assigned to the L-1011, with another 14,000 employed by first tier subcontractors in 35 states. Although 8,000 have been laid off since the Rolls-Royce crisis, Lockheed maintains some of these would be recalled if the guarantees are approved and the L-1011 continues." [42] Because Trans World Airlines had invested $101.3 million and since it was already deeply in the red, speculation on Wall Street was that if Lockheed toppled, TWA may not be far behind. *Fortune* magazine felt:

> . . . the government itself bears some responsibility for the company's present plight. During the early 1960's, for high-minded reasons, the Pentagon adopted a new form of defense contracting that proved to be unworkable. It called for firm commitments years in advance to produce weaponry that had yet to be invented. In trying to anticipate the unforeseeable, the Pentagon wrote contracts so intricate that they lend themselves to misunderstanding and legal disputes. Lockheed was unlucky—or perhaps unwise—enough to win several of those contracts, and is now paying for its success. [43]

In addition, *Fortune* felt that there would be a real cost to the taxpayers in terms of income taxes no longer collected, as well as payments for unemployment compensation, retraining programs, and other government efforts to minimize the impact on individuals and the economy. [44]

Connally, in the course of debate, was asked if such aid to Lockheed would set a precedent, or if the government had done this before. Connally answered:

> Sure the Government has done it before . . . they did it in the days of RFC [Reconstruction Finance Corp.]; in defense contracts now; in 1967, a $75 million V loan was made available to Douglas Aircraft prior to its merger with McDonnell. We do it through the FDIC, we guarantee bank deposits and savings and loan deposits and through export-import loans. We are now guaranteeing investment in the market. We guarantee a lot of things. [45]

Ian MacGregor, chairman and chief executive officer of American Metal Climax, Inc. stated: "If Lockheed were allowed to go bankrupt now, it would be worse than the bankruptcy of Penn Central last year. Now we are expecting the economy to recover. A Lockheed bankruptcy would be like a hard frost hitting the spring flowers." [46]

Finally, the Nixon administration was solidly behind the legislation. It pushed it hard arguing that risk to the taxpayer was nominal and Lockheed's collapse would put 60,000 workers out of jobs. [47]

Opposition to the Loan Guarantee

Opponents of the legislation argued for weeks that the bill's passage would set a bad precedent encouraging many other beleaguered companies to go to Washington for financial help. *Time* magazine stated:

> The Government would set a precedent of propping up a poorly managed company at the expense of its more efficient rivals, giving Lockheed and Rolls-Royce special competitive privileges in markets that may well be better—and more cheaply—served by McDonnell-Douglas, Boeing, General Electric and Pratt and Whitney. By contending that Lockheed is too important to be allowed to fail as the result of a commercial project, the Government gives itself vast new powers to determine just which firms are "important" enough to survive. Should military contractors be given precedence over civilian companies? Should big firms be favored over small? For an administration that champions free enterprise, there is yet another question: How deeply can the Government intrude in the marketplace without bending the whole system out of shape? [48]

On the same subject, Milton Friedman, a noted economist, stated:

> I am opposed to the Government guarantee of the Lockheed loan because I believe it is an undesirable interference with free enterprise. A free enterprise system is a profit-and-loss system, and the loss part is at least as important as the profit part. What provides and assures the proper use of resources in a free eneterprise system is that if a firm doesn't use resources properly, it goes broke. And, if you say that every time it goes broke, it is going to be bailed out by the Government, then there is no effective mechanism for the weeding out of inefficient enterprise. [49]

Economist J. Kenneth Galbraith does not often find himself on the same side of an argument with Milton Friedman, but in this case, both agreed on Lockheed's future. Testifying before the Senate Banking Committee, Galbraith stated, "In 30 years of testimony on various bills it is both philosophically and practically the most nearly indefensible measure that I have encountered." [50] Galbraith, who once proposed nationalization of the defense industry, went on to state that if the bill were enacted, it would prove that the military-industrial complex is alive and well in Washington. [51]

Critics also stated that financial repercussions would not be as serious as proponents had suggested. Even if Lockheed went bankrupt much would be saved. Except for the L-1011, almost every other project would survive. Though Lockheed's assets were lower than before and would decrease further after liquidation, a percentage would eventually pass to the banks and airlines. Shareholders would definitely take a loss. With regard to employment, there would very likely be additional hiring by Boeing, McDonnell-Douglas, and their engine manufacturers, Pratt and Whitney and General Electric. Thus, Lockheed's demise would cause unemployment in some parts of the country but would probably create jobs in other parts.

It was also believed that the British government failed to support its own industry and, by passing the loan guarantee, both Rolls-Royce and Lockheed would achieve undeserved survival. [52]

Lockheed did not get much support from the aerospace industry. Officials of General Electric, Aerojet-General, and McDonnell-Douglas urged Congress to disapprove the loan guarantees for Lockheed. Jack Vollbrecht, president of Aerojet-General Corp. said: "It is wrong to protect an environment in which a company makes a bad bid and is not forced to live with the consequences of it." [53] *Fortune* commented: "Any company that can lose huge sums on four defense contracts at the same time must be doing something wrong." [54]

The Decision by Congress

By a one-vote margin, the Senate passed and sent to the White House a bill authorizing up to $250 million of federal loan guarantees for Lockheed Aircraft Corporation. The bill established an emergency loan guarantee board headed by the Treasury secretary with the chairman of the Federal Reserve Board and the chairman of the Securities and Exchange Commission as members. The board has the authority to guarantee federal loans up to $250 million after finding that the loan is needed to enable the borrower to continue to furnish goods and services, and failure to meet this need would adversely and seriously affect the economy. [55]

President Nixon said he had received news of the Senate's vote with "gratitude and deep satisfaction." He said "the bill's passage would save tens of thousands of jobs that would otherwise have been eliminated." [56]

A Lockheed spokesman at Burbank said that the company expected certification and formal delivery of the first L-1011 by April, 1972. Four of the aircraft are completed, and three are in the flight test program. That program, he said, is on schedule and the L-1011 has performed many of the tasks laid out for it, including speed and altitude tests. Currently, Lockheed has 178 orders for the L-1011. [57]

FOOTNOTES

¹ Harold B. Meyers, "For Lockheed Everything's Coming Up Unk-Unks," *Fortune*, August 1, 1969, p. 77.

² Berkeley Rice, "C-5A + L-1011 = Lockheed's Financial Crisis," *New York Times Magazine*, May 9, 1971, p. 87.

³ Meyers, "For Lockheed, Everything's Coming Up Unk-Unks," pp. 81, 131.

⁴ Arthur E. Fitzgerald, *The High Priest of Waste* (New York: W. W. Norton and Company, Inc., 1972), pp. 233–236.

⁵ Rice, "C-5A + L-1011 = Lockheed's Financial Crisis," p. 85.

⁶ *Ibid.*

⁷ Meyers, "For Lockheed, Everything's Coming Up Unk-Unks," p. 131.

⁸ *Ibid.*, pp. 132–133.

⁹ *Ibid.*, p. 133.

¹⁰ Fitzgerald, *The High Priest of Waste*, p. 107.

¹¹ Rice, "C-5A + L-1011 = Lockheed's Financial Crisis," p. 85.

¹² "Lockheed's Ledger on the C-5A," *Business Week*, June 7, 1969, p. 35.

¹³ Fitzgerald, *The High Priest of Waste*, pp. 48–54.

¹⁴ *Ibid.*, p. 53.

¹⁵ *Ibid.*, p. 107.

¹⁶ "Hearings on Military Posture," p. 2325.

¹⁷ Berkeley Rice, *The C-5A Scandal* (Boston: Houghton-Mifflin Company, 1971), p. 30.

¹⁸ "Hearings on Military Posture," p. 2325.

¹⁹ *Ibid.*, p. 2339.

²⁰ "Jack Anderson's Special Report," *San Francisco Chronicle*, December 26, 1969, p. 3.

²¹ "Hearings on Military Posture," p. 2340.

²² "Defense," *Time*, July 11, 1969, p. 17.

²³ Rice, "C-5A + L-1011 = Lockheed's Financial Crisis," p. 86.

²⁴ "Lockheed's Ledger on the C-5A," p. 35.

²⁵ Rice, "C-5A + L-1011 = Lockheed's Financial Crisis," p. 86.

²⁶ *Ibid.*

²⁷ Harold B. Meyers, "The Salvage of the Lockheed 1011," *Fortune*, June 1971, p. 69.

²⁸ Rice, "C-5A + L-1011 = Lockheed's Financial Crisis," p. 87.

²⁹ *Ibid.*

³⁰ *Ibid.*, p. 88.

³¹ Meyers, "The Salvage of the Lockheed 1011," p. 71.

³² *Ibid.*

³³ *Ibid.*, pp. 67–68.

³⁴ *Ibid.*, p. 68.

³⁵ *Ibid.*, p. 67.

³⁶ *Ibid.*, p. 156.

³⁷ *Ibid.*, p. 159.

³⁸ *Ibid.*, p. 160.

³⁹ *Ibid.*

⁴⁰ "Give Lockheed a Second Chance," *Fortune*, June 1971, pp. 63–64.

[41] James P. Woolsey, "Lockheed Says Guarantee Means Saving U.S. Jobs, Investments," *Aviation Week and Space Technology*, May 24, 1971, p. 15.

[42] *Ibid.*

[43] "Give Lockheed a Second Chance," p. 63.

[44] *Ibid.*

[45] "Why the Drive to Bail Out Businesses in Trouble," *U.S. News and World Report*, May 24, 1971, p. 41.

[46] "The Case for Helping Lockheed," *Business Week*, May 15, 1971, p. 41.

[47] "Senate Votes Lockheed Aid, 49 to 48; $250 Million Measure Is Nixon Victory," *The Wall Street Journal*, August 3, 1971, p. 3.

[48] "Should Lockheed be Saved?" *Time*, May 31, 1971, p. 79. Reprinted by permission from *Time*, The Weekly Newsmagazine; Copyright Time Inc.

[49] "Milton Friedman Responds: A Business and Society Review Interview," *Business and Society Review*, Spring 1972, p. 12.

[50] "Aid for Lockheed Opposed by Galbraith," *The New York Times*, July 9, 1971, p. 39.

[51] *Ibid.*

[52] "Should Lockheed be Saved?" p. 79.

[53] "The Case for Helping Lockheed," p. 41.

[54] Rice, "C-5A + L-1011 = Lockheed's Financial Crisis, p. 86.

[55] Eileen Shanahan, "Senate Backs Lockheed, 49–48," *The New York Times*, August 3, 1971, p. 1.

[56] *Ibid.*

[57] "Senate Votes Lockheed Aid, 49 to 48; $250 Million Measure Is Nixon Victory," p. 3.

QUESTIONS

1. Discuss arguments for, as well as against, continuation of the military-industrial complex.
2. Identify the major factors comprising Lockheed's environment.
3. Do the constraints of competition play a role at any point during the contract, development, or manufacturing phase of the operation of a defense contractor?
4. Are sanctions normally imposed by the market imposed on the defense contractor by other environmental factors? If so, identify.
5. What are major constraints on the military-industrial complex?
6. What are the advantages and disadvantages of nationalizing firms in the military-industrial complex?
7. What appeared to be the major reasons for cost overruns on the C-5A?
8. What was the nature of coping strategies used by Lockheed? Were they successful?
9. What appears to be the basis for allocation of resources in the military-industrial complex?
10. Discuss the argument that Lockheed should be saved because of the economic impact its loss would have on the economy.
11. What type of risks and sanctions are unique to the defense contractor?
12. Explain what "model" of responsible behavior best fits Lockheed.

CHAPTER 11

BUSINESS
AND
POLITICS

CASE 11
A CONCEPT OF CORPORATE POWER

At the time of this case International Telephone and Telegraph (ITT) was listed ninth among *Fortune's* 500 largest industrial corporations. ITT is an international conglomerate with a large number of subsidiaries in unrelated industries. Despite its size its president Harold Geneen set out to achieve additional domestic growth by launching an acquisition and internal expansion campaign to increase domestic earnings as a percent of total income. Behavior of this kind by one of the largest and therefore most powerful members of the private sector typically evokes an environmental response. In light of our traditional suspicions of size one might expect the response to be to suppress further growth to foster competition.

The market has traditionally been singled out as the most effective means of controlling abuses that could result from the concentration of power in the private sector. Yet controversy continues over the effectiveness of competition, particularly among very large corporations, to control abuses of power. To Ralph Nader, competition is probably best measured by the number of small competitors in a market. To General Motors retired chairman James Roche, competition is the vigorous year-in, year-out fight to win buyers from another large and capable company. The distinction is fundamental. Populists, like Nader, worry about a corporation's power—how much there is and what it could do. The businessman is concerned with a company's performance and how power affects profits. A company may engage in no overt anti-competitive acts and still be "anti-competitive," by virtue of its size or position in a line of business.

The federal government is also likely to respond when a giant such as ITT makes a move to grow larger. It has intervened frequently in recent years in attempts to regulate competition and guide economic activity toward public objectives. The range of relationships between corporations and government is extreme. At least part of the spectrum of interrelationships is found in the controversy in this case between ITT and the executive branch of the federal government. However, actions by government may stem from many sources including the courts, public pressures, private pressure, political realities, and the administrative process. Government action to control concentration of economic power and restrain abuse of its exercise is often a function of the impact of many sources.

ITT and Limits of Lobbying: Big Business and Politics

When Harold Geneen moved into the executive suite at ITT in 1959, he demanded of his vice presidents: Why do we have such a low price/earnings ratio? The reply: We're too vulnerable overseas.[1] Geneen then launched an acquisition campaign that pushed ITT's domestic earnings from 20 percent to around 50 percent of total. He neglected neither side of the business, however, and ITT truly became international and multinational.

If a consumer were to become annoyed with ITT he would have difficulty boycotting the company. He could not rent an Avis car, buy a Levitt house, sleep in a Sheraton Hotel, park in an APCOA garage, use Scott fertilizer or seed, eat Wonder Bread or Morton frozen foods. He would have to avoid advertising posters in commuter trains and buses for ITT owns TDI, the company that rents advertising space. He could not have watched televised reports of President Nixon's visit to China for ITT World Communications coordinated all of the transmissions.[2]

However in 1971 an antitrust consent decree finally limited Geneen's acquisition splurge. At the behest of the Justice Department, ITT agreed to divest itself of six important companies. Subject to court approval, the parts to be severed were the Canteen Corp., acquired in 1969; Grinnell Corp.'s fire protection division, acquired in the fall of 1969; Avis Rent-a-Car Inc.; ITT-Levitt home builders, acquired in 1968; and the Hamilton and ITT life insurance companies. Geneen had two years to dispose of the first two firms and three years for the rest.

However, as a result of actions by the contesting parties, one of the most crucial ambiguities in antitrust law was left unsolved: Does the Clayton Act, a keystone of the nation's antitrust policy for more than five decades, apply to conglomerates? The act clearly bans major acquisitions that "substantially lessen competition." It has been applied to horizontal mergers of directly competing firms and to vertical mergers of companies that have customer-supplier relationships. But it does not specifically forbid the kind of mergers that form conglomerates: those involving firms offering apparently unrelated goods or services. The Justice Department's three suits against ITT's Canteen Corp., Grinnell Corp., and Hartford Fire were intended to clear up the issue by bringing it before the U.S. Supreme Court. But to avoid lengthy litigation that would delay divesture for years, Justice Department attorneys agreed to settle the suits out of court.

The question of just how competition should be measured is focused most sharply in the attacks on conglomerates. These multi-line companies dominate no individual markets and raise none of the traditional objections to big mergers. Instead the cases appear to be rooted in the American tradition, which deeply distrusts big institutions and argues that sheer size can constitute a social ill. In the case of ITT, Richard W. McLaren, assistant attorney general and chief of the Antitrust Division, argued that would-be competitors stayed out of the way of ITT simply because they were afraid of taking on such a giant.[3]

Management and Corporate Background

By 1971 Harold Geneen, at 63, was the highest paid corporate executive in the United States ($812,494) and just four years short of mandatory retirement. An accountant by training, the chief executive officer was known for possessing the constitution of a concrete block, the dedication of a hangman paid by piecework, and a motivational force that must have been genetic in such men as Alexander the Great, Napoleon, and General Patton.

Geneen was brought into ITT with a mandate to acquire new companies and expand its domestic revenues. At this time 80 percent of its revenue was produced abroad even though all of the company's stockholders were Americans. With his appointment, Geneen all but perfected the techniques of going into unrelated businesses for the sole purpose of growth. Yet the development of the conglomerate may have been assisted by the coincidence that between 1965 and 1968 the Antitrust Division was headed by a Harvard law professor, Donald T. Turner. He took the position that conglomerate mergers should be dealt with, if at all, by special legislation rather than by antitrust enforcement. Turner neither sought legislation nor filed complaints in conglomerate cases.

On performance, as measured by generally accepted auditing principles, the ITT record would be difficult to match. For 54 consecutive quarters, Geneen reported substantial gains in revenues, assets, profits, and earnings per share. For over a decade, ITT had outstripped the U.S. economy in rate of growth and the company was expected to continue to grow at a rate of 10 percent to 12 percent annually. According to a survey of 2300 chief executives made by *Dun's Review*, ITT was among the ten best-managed companies in the United States and was singled out for its excellence in financial acumen and keen insight.

Forbes magazine once referred to ITT as Geneen U. from which "graduates" of Hal's hazardous school emerged to populate the management levels of industry. Many of those who did not break under the strain profited immensely from Geneen's tutelage.[4]

In 13 years under Geneen's command ITT catapulted from a corporation worth $680 million in annual revenues to a multinational corporation that approached $8.5 billion in 1972. It had become an acquisition-oriented operation acquiring 700 to 800 enterprises in 80 countries. It employed nearly 400,000 people, more than half of them abroad. In particular the acquisition by ITT of Hartford, with assets of $1.5 billion took place in 1971 in contradiction to—and some said in clear violation of—the laws of Connecticut and the clearly defined policy of the U.S. Department of Justice.[5]

When Geneen began to move in on the Connecticut insurance giant, which was protected—or so the state legislature intended—from acquisition by Public Act 444 of that state, some of his more daring underlings cautioned against it: "Hal, don't do Hartford," one executive pleaded.[6]

It would have been difficult to imagine a few years back that Hartford Fire would ever look like such a sweet proposition. The property and casualty insurance business was then considered a clinker, incapable of making money on its basic underwriting business. Geneen, though he began moving ITT into the life insurance business in the mid-1960s, wanted no part of the casualty business, believing it to be unstable. The man who changed his mind was Felix G. Rohatyn, director of ITT, a partner in Lazard Freres and a headliner in the 1972 Senate hearings on Richard Kleindienst. Geneen came to feel that casualty insurance was really two businesses: first an underwriting business which was indeed erratic although, in Geneen's opinion, subject to some improvement; and an investment business, capable of producing a steady flow of profits from its stock and bond portfolio.[7]

At the rate Hartford was growing it would, in a few years, lack the capital to support its premium growth and ITT would then expect to pump it up with additional capital. This might be very desirable strategy in light of the fact that during the merger preliminaries the company was persistently assailed by critics who believed that it was ITT's intention to scavenge Hartford's wealth rather than aggressively build its business. On the other hand, it should be mentioned that Hartford's wealth, in the form of a debt-free balance sheet, did a lot for ITT's debt ratio. Within months after the Hartford acquisition the bond-rating services moved ITT up from a Baa rating to an A rating.[8] A veteran executive at ITT, who knew Geneen for years, put the following excerpts on tape.

> Hell, Geneen didn't even need Hartford. It was an ego trip. He wanted to see if he could get away with it. These government agencies and their lawyers are no match for Geneen. He confounds them. He works men to death. He is amoral, immune to persuasion, incapable of knowing right from wrong. But the antitrust department doesn't seem to know right from wrong either—not on any rational basis. And that's where Geneen multiplies his strength . . . He tells them 'you do what I tell you, but don't do anything wrong.' This is impossible. Some of the inner circle had to do wrong, they had to participate in corruption to accomplish what they were directed to do.
>
> Geneen wanted to become the highest paid management executive on earth. He wanted to run the biggest operation on earth. He wanted the most power. He cannot stand the presence of anyone else who wants power. Money he will give them. Power, no.
>
> He's not so much above as beyond the law. All law, especially antitrust, is something to overcome.
>
> . . . He reacts to restraint by cranking out more energy to overcome them.

That's what he did in the Hartford case. I know Geneen has this fantastic genius. I also know he is a nut.[9]

The Suits

In 1969 the Department of Justice brought three anti-merger cases against ITT. On April 28, 1969 the United States filed action in the U.S. District Court for the Northern District of Illinois charging that the effects of ITT's acquisition of the Canteen Corporation stock might be to lessen competition substantially, and thus the acquisition was a violation of Section 7 of the Clayton Act. On August 1, 1969, the Justice Department filed an action challenging ITT's proposed merger with Hartford and another action challenging ITT's proposed acquisition of the stock of Grinnell. The complaints in both of the latter actions were filed in the U.S. District Court for the District of Connecticut.[10]

In the complaint challenging the proposed merger of ITT with Hartford, it was alleged that ITT entered the life insurance business through a series of acquisitions. The complaint stated that, as a result of its extensive business operations, ITT was a large purchaser of insurance; that it had channeled its insurance business to its own subsidiaries where feasible, but since its current capacity to handle this business was limited, ITT had paid substantial premiums ($33 million in 1968) to outside insurance firms. The complaint alleged that ITT set up group insurance policies for its employees and channeled the premiums to insurance companies that it selected; and that ITT's Levitt operation arranged, along with mortgage financing, the placement of property and liability insurance on the homes it sold.[11]

Hartford was a leading writer of property and liability insurance, ranking fourth among domestic property and liability insurance companies operating under the American Agency System and sixth among all domestic property and liability insurance companies. Hartford also had available $400 million in excess of its required surplus to use in an active expansion and diversification program.

In the Hartford complaint, the government alleged that ITT's proposed merger with Hartford would violate Section 7 in several ways. It was thought that reciprocity power and its effect in favor of Hartford in the realm of insurance would be substantially increased. Also actual and potential competitors of Hartford might be foreclosed from competing for the insurance purchases of ITT. Actual and potential competition by ITT and Hartford might be eliminated or diminished in numerous markets. It was believed likely that competitive advantages would accrue to ITT and Hartford, leading firms in several industries, thus raising barriers to entry and discouraging smaller firms from competing in those industries. The merger also might trigger mergers by companies seeking protection or similar advantages. Finally the acquisition of Hartford and Grinnell might enable ITT to use its insurance business to promote and increase Grinnell's sales of automatic sprinkling systems, thus further entrenching Grinnell's dominant position in that market and raising barriers to entry.[12]

Action by the Courts

Between the time the complaints were filed and the judgments entered, the ITT cases were actively prosecuted. The government moved for preliminary injunctions in the Hartford and Grinnell cases. Its motions were denied. Later the Grinnell case was tried. The government lost and filed an appeal. The Canteen case was tried and the government lost again.

Federal District Judge Richard B. Austin, in his decision in the Canteen case, found that ITT actually spurred competition in the food business by applying time-and-motion studies to vending machine repairs and cost analysis to cafeteria menu planning. He lauded the "vigor, enthusiasm, and motivation" that ITT engendered in Canteen employees. [13]

Actions by the Government

The government moved in August 1969 for injunctions that would preliminarily enjoin the acquisition by ITT of the stock of Grinnell and the merger of ITT with Hartford. The Federal District Court at New Haven, Connecticut with Chief Judge William H. Timbers presiding held evidentiary hearings, and denied both motions. The court held that the government did not sustain its burden of establishing a reasonable probability of success in proving that either the Grinnell acquisition or the Hartford merger would result in substantial anti-competitive effects.

An ITT statement on the hearings said, "The proposed litigation appears to be part of the announced effort by the Justice Department to bend the antitrust law to stop mergers among large companies regardless of the fact that there isn't discernible adverse impacts upon competition." The conglomerate added that in its opinion, "the merger would be pro-competitive and in the public interest." [14]

Harold Geneen believed he had his own company under control and it irked him that the whole country wasn't in hand as well. "Our . . Government is about to run the country down the drain," he said, losing his temper for a moment. He felt the antitrust laws were hopelessly out of date and he resented what he considered was government's hostile attitude toward business at a time when foreign governments were working hand-in-glove with their national business interests. [15]

Judge Timbers also said:

> . . . alleged adverse effect of economic concentration brought about by merger activity, especially merger activity of large diversified corporations such as ITT arguably may be such that as a result of social and economic policy, the standard by which the legality of the merger should be measured under the antitrust laws is the degree to which it may increase economic concentration—not merely the degree to which it may lessen competition. If the standard is to be changed, however, in the opinion of this court, it is fundamental under our system of government that the determinate be made by Congress and not by the courts. [16]

The court's refusal to issue a preliminary injunction against the Hartford merger was based on its ruling that the government failed to sustain its claims of anti-competitive effects of the merger. The government's primary contention was that the ITT-Hartford merger would create a market structure conducive to reciprocal dealing, in that ITT suppliers would tend to switch their insurance business to Hartford. But the court stated that an oligopolistic or concentrated market with dull price competition was essential for creating an opportunity for reciprocal dealing; and the record was largely silent on this point. Also, the court argued that because of ITT's anti-reciprocity policy it could not conclude that reciprocity was likely to occur. [17]

The government's evidence showed that Hartford had approximately $400 million in excess surplus and contended that the proposed merger would give ITT subsidiaries access to those monies for use in financing ITT's expansion plans. Levitt and Sons, a leading home builder, was cited by the government as an ITT subsidiary that would gain significant competitive advantage through such access. The argument wasn't sustained.

The government also contended that purchases of insurance from Hartford by ITT and its subsidiaries would result in illegal foreclosure. The court found that only 1/25 of 1 percent of total property and liability insurance premiums paid to domestic insurers were represented by ITT's property and liability insurance premiums. This, the court said, was insignificant.

Several of ITT's subsidiaries wrote life insurance, as did Hartford. The court found that the combined market position of ITT and Hartford was less than 3/10 of 1 percent and that this was minimal. Therefore, no elimination of actual and potential competition could be proven.

The government contended that Hartford would be in a position to bolster Grinnell's sales by recommending Grinnell's sprinkler systems to its fire insurance customers. The court said that the evidence did not establish that Hartford would have the opportunity to make such recommendations or that such recommendations would be likely to help Grinnell secure business from a substantial share of the market. [18]

The motion for preliminary injunction was denied on October 21, 1969. The trial of the Hartford case was later assigned to begin September 21, 1971. The case never came to trial. It was settled by consent judgment entered September 24, 1971.

Connecticut Action

In December 1969 Commissioner William Cotter of the Connecticut Insurance Commission barred the merger of Hartford Fire Insurance Company and ITT. His decision was followed immediately by a revised offer by ITT designed to meet his objections.

Both Harold Geneen and Harry V. Williams, president and chairman of Hartford, stated they would appeal the decision in Connecticut courts. In effect then, the two companies indicated that they would pursue the fight to merge through the original plan and also through the newly developed public tender offer. This offer was made, according to Geneen, in the belief that all of Mr. Cotter's expressed concerns would be satisfied if ITT proceeded by way of a voluntary exchange rather than through a merger.[19]

The commissioner's nine-page rejection was based on his opinion that the transaction was not in the best interest of Hartford shareholders. Yet the shareholders had previously approved the merger by a significant majority. The commissioner gave four main reasons for his ruling:

1. ITT would gain more benefit than would Hartford Fire;
2. Some officials of the insurer could gain about $3 million if the deal were consummated;
3. The tender offer approach should have been used to preserve the rights of minority stockholders;
4. Hartford Fire's only advantage in merging would be limited to ITT's guidance, counsel, and knowledge of foreign commerce.

The action to block the merger drew criticism from a group of executives of leading investment brokerage houses and from shareholders owning 1.5 percent of the 22 million Hartford shares outstanding.[20]

Mr. Pomerantz, New York attorney representing the shareholders, stated that the Cotter verdict was incomprehensible and that the rejection threatened Hartford shareholders with the loss of $600 million. His estimate was based on a settlement by Chief Judge Timbers who cited this figure as the premium over-the-market value of Hartford stock that would result from the merger. Judge Timbers's estimate was made in his ruling denying a temporary injunction to the Justice Department.

Then during the last days of May 1970, Commissioner Cotter approved the merger of Hartford and ITT. His approval was a result of ITT's acceptance of specifications to protect the insurer, its thousands of employees, and the city of Hartford. Cotter's directives, subject to enforcement by Connecticut's attorney general, were:

1. the insurer's headquarters must remain in Hartford for ten years;
2. the employee level of Hartford Fire must not be substantially reduced for at least ten years;
3. for ten years, Hartford Fire could not transmit in any one year funds to ITT in excess of the insurer's earnings;
4. no changes adverse to the insurer's employees were to be made in their pension rights or other fringe benefits;
5. the insurer could not invest in any ITT company without approval by the Connecticut Department of Insurance;
6. for at least five years, ITT would not reduce the amount of insurance Hartford sold in any one line below the average of the years 1964–1969;
7. the insurer would not curtail the current scope of involvements in its personnel

and the level of the company's financial and other participation in the civic and charitable activities of the city of Hartford and other local communities.[21]

For the transaction to be tax free, 80 percent of Hartford stock must be tendered to ITT. In a previous merger vote, shareholders of both companies overwhelmingly favored the move. After Cotter's decision ITT stated it was proceeding with its take-over of Hartford Fire despite a new attempt by Ralph Nader, consumer advocate, to block the merger. Nader and Reuben Robertson, Washington attorney and a Hartford policyholder, filed an appeal in Hartford Superior Court after Commissioner William Cotter rejected a petition by Nader and his associate for a rehearing. Later a U.S. court rejected Nader's bid to reopen the Hartford-ITT case.[22]

At this point Nader demanded Cotter's resignation, charging that his campaign for Congress had placed the Connecticut Insurance Commissioner "in a conflict of interest and allegiance" in approving the tender offer of ITT to acquire control of the Hartford Insurance Group. Nader also urged Governor John Dempsey of Connecticut to disqualify Commissioner Cotter from "any further participation in the ITT-Hartford case."[23]

"It's quite clear that Mr. Cotter, in handling the duties of his office while at the same time promoting his political career, did not display minimal recognition of the requisites of insurance law and order," Nader stated in his letter to Governor Dempsey. "His disqualification from further involvement in the ITT case is essential to protect the public interest as well as that of stockholders and policyholders. The people of Connecticut and the nation deserve better."[24]

Nader also wrote Cotter that his resignation

. . . would also free the insurance department from the inhibitions imposed on it by your candidacy. Your resignation . . . at this time would relieve Connecticut taxpayers of having to pay your salary to subsidize your political endeavors, and would alleviate the necessity for the governor having to deal with this problem.[25]

The Settlement

On July 31, 1971, the Justice Department announced that it had reached agreement in principle with ITT for settlement of the three law suits and it announced the terms of the proposed settlement. A settlement in such a case is subject to court approval, and under Department of Justice practice the terms of settlement, in the form of a proposed judgment, must be filed with the court 30 days prior to the court's action upon it. On September 24, 1971, Judge Blumenfield approved and entered final judgments in *Grinnell* and *Hartford*, and shortly thereafter, on the same day, Judge Austin in Chicago approved and entered the final judgment in *Canteen*.

The consent judgments required ITT to divest Canteen, the Fire Protection Division of Grinnell, Hajoca Corporation, and either (a) Levitt, Avis, Hamilton Life and ITT Life, or (b) Hartford. For ten years, the judgments prohibit the use of reciprocity power and the maintenance of any statistics that would facilitate its use, and they mandated detailed steps that would tend to eliminate reciprocity effect, including the issuance of no-reciprocity statements to employers and customers and suppliers. For ten years or until ITT divested itself of Hartford, whichever was sooner, ITT and Hartford must not discriminate in favor of one another in the purchase and sale of ITT's insurance requirements. For the same period ITT was enjoined from acquiring 1 percent or more of the voting stock of any company described or assets thereof, unless it first obtained the consent of the government or approval of the court upon ITT's establishing by a preponderance of the evidence that the acquisition would not lessen competition or tend to create a monopoly in any line of commerce in any section of the country. [26]

At the time that the Justice Department announced the settlement, ITT announced that it would elect to retain Hartford.

Subject to the above, ITT was prohibited from acquiring: (a) any domestic company having book assets of more than $100 million; (b) any domestic company having sales of more than $25 million and accounting for more than 15 percent of sales in any market in which total sales exceeded $100 million and in which any four companies accounted for more than 50 percent of total sales; (c) any domestic company engaged in the manufacture, fabrication, installation, or sale of automatic sprinkler devices or systems; and (d) any domestic company engaged in the domestic insurance business with insurance assets of more than $10 million. [27]

To ITT insiders, however, the decision was no surprise. Geneen chose to sell; the alternative was a costly antitrust battle with the Justice Department that would have tied up his company in courts for years and might still have ended in divestiture. [28]

However, the limitations placed by the court on ITT's domestic activities did not apply to foreign ventures. In return for the U.S. companies that had to be given up ITT would receive approximately $600 million. ITT could now go looking for bargains abroad with a rather large bank account. In fact during the time since the consent decree ITT had acquired about twelve European companies in the automobile parts, cosmetics, and toiletries industries and had extended its very profitable telecommunications business.

Of course the decree did allow ITT the option to acquire small U.S. companies. In the nine months following the consent decree ITT acquired about twenty companies, most of them manufacturers, with an estimated total of $100 million in sales. [29]

Thus, the U.S. Justice Department's action to bar ITT's moves at home forced the company to return to expansion abroad, which proved a financial boon.

ITT had acquired 99.8% of the common stock of Hartford Fire, which, together with its subsidiaries, was engaged in the business of writing fire, marine, casualty, health, and life and accident insurance as well as annuity contracts, surety bonds and in the investment and reinvestment of their assets.

The long-term outlook for fire and casualty insurance in 1972 was strong, reflecting the nation's increasing wealth as well as the spiraling costs of inflation. From 1967 to 1971 net premiums written had advanced from $819 million to $1.2

billion, or at an average annual rate of 14 percent. Hartford's expense ratio had declined from 32.8% in June 1967 to 30.5% for the 12 months ending in June 1971.

More intensive computerization of operations, a downward adjustment in some commission rates and the trend toward "no fault" auto insurance produced a further reduction of the expense ratio. A decline in the frequency of claims for bodily injuries and collisions in the important automobile line helped cut the company's loss ratio.[30]

The Justice Department and the Antitrust Division

Back in February 1969, Assistant Attorney General Richard W. McLaren came into office as chief of the Justice Department's Antitrust Division preceeded by a formidable reputation. Unlike his predecessors under the Johnson Administration, McLaren believed that existing antitrust legislation prohibited conglomerate mergers of companies in different lines of business, and he was determined to enforce the law. He had no doubt that Congress had intended that the antitrust laws should be applied to all classes of mergers, including conglomerates, and he was convinced that the Supreme Court would agree if it were provided the opportunity. He promptly gave Attorney General Mitchell a speech to deliver that contained the following warnings:

> The danger that super-concentration poses to our economic, political and social structure cannot be overestimated. . . . The Department of Justice may very well oppose any merger among the top 200 manufacturing firms . . . (or) by one of the top 200 manufacturing firms of any leading producer in any concentrated industry.[31]

Within his first year he had filed five major suits against expanding conglomerates, including three against new acquisitions by the ITT Corporation. In testimony concerning ITT McLaren stated he had been determined to take the company to court, "regardless of economic or financial hardship pleas" from the company.[32] Since then, McLaren has been "promoted" to a federal judgeship in Illinois.

By McLaren's account several arguments convinced him to settle for less than complete divestiture. Felix Rohatyn made the key argument on April 29 before McLaren, Kleindienst, and several other Justice Department antitrust lawyers. In sum, he stated that taking Hartford away from ITT might cause the company to fold, might throw the stock market into chaos, depress the economy, and hurt the U.S. balance of payments. McLaren claimed he hadn't really considered these possibilities before.[33]

McLaren blew up at questions about whether others had influenced his decision to settle. "I was not pressured or influenced by anyone in any way! I think it's absolutely outrageous the way these committee proceedings are going. There was no hanky-panky about it." Yet McLaren, too, had refreshed his memory since the week before. He conceded that he had talked to the chief White House troubleshooter on relations with corporations, Peter Flanigan. "Mr. Flanigan was simply a conduit," McLaren said. Flanigan obtained a report on the financial impact that ITT would sustain if it were required to divest itself of Hartford Fire Insurance Co., as McLaren had been insisting it must. The analysis helped change McLaren's mind. "I read the report and found it persuasive," McLaren said.[34]

The report had been prepared by Richard Ramsden who spent two days analyzing the $7 billion per year conglomerate, was paid $242—and delivered his report to Flanigan rather than the Justice Department. California Democrat John Tunney asked whether the fact that Ramsden's firm manages some 200,000 shares of ITT stock would affect Ramsden's objectivity. "No," replied McLaren, "it would not bother me a bit." But could not a negative report by Ramsden have adversely affected the stock's value? "I have no comment," replied McLaren. The angry McLaren attributed his reversal to this report, his own antitrust experience, and consultation with the Treasury Department. But he conceded under questioning that the Treasury involvement consisted of one brief telephone call.[35]

The Dita Beard Memo

Things settled down for some months during preparation for divestiture. Then on February 28, 1972, Jack Anderson, a Washington D.C. columnist, disclosed the following memo:

Personal and Confidential
Date: June 25, 1971

To: W. R. Merriam
From: D. D. Beard
Subject: San Diego Convention

I just had a long talk with EJG [E. J. Gerrity, ITT's public relations chief]. I'm so sorry that we got that call from the White House. I thought you and I had agreed very thoroughly that under no circumstances would anyone in this office discuss with anyone our participation in the Convention including me. Other than permitting John Mitchell, [Calif. Lt. Gov.] Ed Reinecke, Bob Haldeman and Nixon (besides Wilson, of course) no one has known from whom that 400 thousand commitment had come. You can't imagine how many queries I've had from "friends" about this situation and I have in each and every case denied knowledge of any kind. It would be wise for all of us here to continue to do that, regardless of from whom any questions come; White House or whoever. John Mitchell has certainly kept it on the higher level only. We should be able to do the same.

I was afraid the discussion about the three hundred/four hundred thousand commitment would come up soon. If you remember, I suggested that we all stay out of that, other than the fact that I told you I had heard Hal [Harold Geneen, ITT president] up the original amount.

Now I understand from Ned that both he and you are upset about the decision to make it four hundred in services. Believe me, this is not what Hal said. Just after I talked with Ned, Wilson called me, to report on his meeting with Hal. Hal at no time told Wilson that our donation would be in services ONLY. In fact, quite the contrary. There would be very little cash involved, but certainly some. I am convinced, because of several conversations with Louie [former Kentucky Gov. Nunn] re Mitchell, that our noble commitment has gone a long way toward our negotiations on the mergers eventually coming out as Hal wants them. Certainly the President has told Mitchell to see that things are worked out fairly. It is still only [Antitrust chief Richard] McLaren's mickey-mouse we are suffering.

We all know Hal and his big mouth! But this is one time he cannot tell you and Ned one thing and Wilson (and me) another!

I hope, dear Bill, that all of this can be reconciled—between Hal and Wilson—if all of us in this office remain totally ignorant of any commitment ITT has made to anyone. If it gets too much publicity, you can believe our negotiations with Justice will wind up shot down. Mitchell is definitely helping us, but cannot let it be known. Please destroy this, huh? [36]

The memo had been dated June 25, 1971, a month before the Justice Department made the out-of-court settlement with ITT, and addressed by Dita Beard, a company lobbyist, to her boss, William Merriam, a vice president in charge of local operations. The memo implied, and Anderson concluded, that there had been a favorable settlement between the highest officials in the Justice Department and ITT, in return for a contribution ranging from $200,000 to $400,000 to the Republican Convention.[37] But from her hospital bed in Denver, Dita Beard claimed that the memo attributed to her was actually a forgery and a hoax.

On March 1, 1972, the Dita Beard memo was presented to the Senate Judicial Subcommittee Hearings by Jack Anderson. The purpose of the hearings were to approve the appointment of Kleindienst as Attorney General of the United States. Kleindienst had been acting Attorney General during the incident with ITT.

Anderson found a motive in Beard's belated denial. "She's at the economic mercy of ITT." He did not appear shaken by the repudiation. "She's clearly lying," he said. "She's committing perjury if she says this under oath." Anderson recalled that Beard had vouched for the memorandum's authenticity when his assistant, Brit Hume, visited her on February 23 and 24. Hume had testified that he had shown her the memorandum at her office in the presence of two ITT public-relations men. She acknowledged that the initial at the top of the memorandum was hers, but told him the office was not a good place to talk about it. They met the next evening at her Arlington, Virginia home where, according to Hume, she acknowledged: "You know I wrote it. Of course I wrote it." [38]

On March 2, 1972, Kleindienst testified, "I set in motion a series of events by which McLaren became persuaded that he ought to come off his position against the settlement." [39] Kleindienst also testified that he did not take part in the negotiations. In response to questions about the $400,000 contribution to the Republican Convention in San Diego, he told the subcommittee that he had been unaware until late November or December that the ITT subsidiary had pledged the money to help underwrite the convention.[40]

At that time, Senator Edward Kennedy (D-Mass) produced two letters that he said would prove that Kleindienst knew of the commitment two months before he had testified that he did. The first letter was from Reuben B. Robertson III, an associate of Ralph Nader. It was dated September 22, 1971 and asked about rumors of the link between the settlement with ITT and the $400,000 pledge to the Republican Convention. The second letter was a reply to the first. It was written by McLaren and denied any link between the two events.[41]

In other testimony that day, Anderson testified that Edgar Gillenwater, assistant to the Lt. Governor of California and Lt. Governor Ed Reinecke had met Attorney General John Mitchell in his office in mid-May and that they told him that ITT had offered to put up as much as $400,000 to support the convention in San Diego.[42] This testimony conflicted with Mitchell's testimony the previous day in which he had stated that he "did not know as of that time and still don't know what arrangements the Republican Party had with San Diego or anyone else."[43]

Because Kleindienst, during the hearing, was adamant that there had been no impropriety, at least two committee members began to wonder what he would consider improper. Senator Birch Bayh (D-Ind) read aloud a section of the U.S. Corrupt Practices Act that makes it unlawful "for any corporation whatever" to make any contribution or expenditure "in connection with any primary election, political convention or caucus held to select candidates" for federal office. Did Kleindienst think it would be wrong for a corporation under prosecution by the Justice Department to spend $400,000 on a party's national convention? Kleindienst said he didn't have the "specific facts" but that his "horseback opinion" was no, there would be no violation.[44]

On March 4, 1972, ITT issued a statement attempting to clarify intent. It pointed out that the contribution by Sheraton (Hotel) of America, an ITT subsidiary, to the San Diego Convention was "in no sense a political payment," but a means of attracting business to the new Sheraton. The amount according to the statement was $100,000 with a possible addition of $100,000 at a later date. Geneen called the underwriting of the San Diego Republican Convention a "damn good business investment" to promote the new San Diego hotel.[45]

On March 11, 1972, Jack Anderson again took the stand. Anderson accused Mitchell of lying when he denied knowledge of financial commitment by the subsidiary of ITT to the convention. Anderson said, "It will be one of the most arrogant displays of perjury this committee has ever heard."[46]

On March 14, 1972, Mitchell admitted talking to Geneen for about 35 minutes during a 1970 meeting but he said that he refused to discuss the case.[47]

Watergate Hearings

Additional information about the ITT incident surfaced later during the Watergate investigation. On June 14, 1973, Charles Colson, a White House aide, stated that he had directed E. Howard Hunt, one of the Watergate burglars, to go to Denver and interview Beard about the memo. Colson explained that the task force investigating the Beard memo had become suspicious that the name was not authentic.[48]

On July 11, 1973, John Mitchell was called to testify before the Senate Watergate hearings. He stated that he withheld information about activities including "horror stories . . and the spiriting out of Washington of Dita Beard, a controversial lobbyist for ITT." [49]

In response to pressure generated by the Watergate hearings, President Nixon appointed a special prosecutor, Archibald Cox, on May 25, 1973. On November 1, 1973, a news leak to the *New York Times* stated that President Nixon was directly involved in the ITT settlement. The leak was traced to Special Prosecutor Cox and according to the White House justified his being fired.[50]

The following day, Attorney General Kleindienst, who had approached Cox with the information because he feared prosecution for perjury in the 1972 Judicial Committee Hearings, issued the following statement:

Three weeks ago I had a conversation at the Special Prosecutor's office with Mr. Cox and two of his assistants concerning the handling of the I.T.T. antitrust case during my tenure as Deputy Attorney General. A story in The New York Times yesterday, which was repeated on the networks and in newspapers around the country, contained a very specific report of one part of that conversation.

As a result of the leak to the Times, I have been accused on national television of having given false information to the Senate Judicial Committee at the time of my nomination as Attorney General. That accusation is false.

My conversation with Professor Cox was held under strict assurances of confidentiality, and as Professor Cox has stated, was a serious breach of faith on the part of the Special Prosecutor. I continue to regard my conversation with Professor Cox as confidential, but because of the distorted and misleading accounts of my conduct that have appeared in the press, I feel compelled at this time to relate an important aspect of the event which was not leaked.

On Monday afternoon, April 19th, 1971, Mr. Ehrlichman abruptly called and stated that the President directed me not to file the appeal in the Grinnell case. That was the last day in which that appeal could be taken. I informed him that we had determined to take that appeal, and that he should so inform the President. Minutes later the President called me and without any discussion ordered me to drop the appeal. Immediately thereafter, I sent word to the President that if he persisted in this direction I would be compelled to submit my resignation. Because that was the last day in which the appeal could be perfected, I obtained an extension of time from the Supreme Court to enable the President to consider my position.

The President changed his mind and the appeal was filed 30 days later in the exact form it would have been filed one month earlier. Thus, but for my threat to resign, the Grinnell case would never have been appealed and we would never have been able to obtain what even Professor Cox has characterized as a settlement highly advantageous to the United States.

At the time of my testimony before the Senate Judiciary Committee, I was not asked whether I had had any contacts with the White House at the time of this decision and I did not deny any such contacts.

The focus of the hearings dealing with the I.T.T. affair was the negotiations in May, June and July of 1971 leading to settlement of the pending cases on July 31. I was questioned at length concerning these negotiations and particularly with reference to any conversations or meetings I might have had with Mr. Peter Flanigan of the White House staff. It was in the context of those questions that I made the statement quoted on C.B.S. news last evening as follows:

> In the discharge of my responsibilities as the Acting Attorney General in these cases, I was not interfered with by anybody at the White House; I was not importuned; I was not pressured; I was not directed.

It was also in response to a question by Senator Fong concerning Mr. Flanigan that I made the other statement quoted by C.B.S. as follows:

> . . . . I would have had a vivid recollection if someone at the White House had called me up and said, 'Look, Kleindienst, this is the way we are going to handle that case.' People who know me, I don't think would talk to me that way, but if anybody did it would be a very sharp impact on my mind because I believe I know how I would have responded. No such conversation occurred.

Both of these statements, taken in the context in which they were made, were completely accurate.

In short, I did not perjure myself or give false information to the Senate Judiciary Committee. A fair and objective reading of the transcript of my testimony will so indicate.

I deeply regret the circumstances which have compelled me to make this statement. However, in view of the serious breach of faith by the Special Prosecutor and the distorted treatment of my testimony in the press, I have no other choice. I have done no wrong.[51]

FOOTNOTES

[1] "Two Ways to Do It," *Forbes*, January 1, 1972, pp. 24–5.

[2] "ITT's Big Conglomerate of Troubles," *Time*, May 1, 1972, p. 72.

[3] "The Views on Bigness are Contradictory," *Business Week*, August 7, 1971, pp. 58–63.

[4] "ITT's Geneen; How to Succeed in Business by Really Trying," *Ramparts*, March 1973, pp. 30–34.

[5] *Ibid.*

[6] *Ibid.*

[7] Carol J. Loomis, "Harold Geneen's Moneymaking Machine is Still Humming," *Fortune*, September 1972, p. 212.

[8] *Ibid.*, p. 216.

[9] "ITT's Geneen: How to Succeed in Business by Really Trying," p. 56.

[10] Eleanor M. Fox, "The ITT Antimerger Cases," *Conference Board Record*, June 1972, pp. 34–44.

[11] *Ibid.*

[12] *Ibid.*

[13] "The Views on Bigness are Contradictory," pp. 58–63.

[14] "Justice Department to File Suit Against ITT-Hartford Tie," *The National Underwriter* (Life Ed.), June 28, 1969, p. 1.

[15] "Geneen of ITT," *Forbes*, May 15, 1971, pp. 186–190.

[16] "U.S. Court Denies Injunction Against Hartford-ITT Merger," *The National Underwriters* (Life Ed.), October 25, 1969, p. 1.

[17] *Ibid.*

[18] *Ibid.*

[19] "Hartford Fire, ITT Merger Rejected by Cotter of Connecticut," *The National Underwriter* (Life Ed.), December 20, 1969, p. 1.

[20] *Ibid.*

[21] "Cotter Approves ITT Takeover of Hartford Fire," *The National Underwriter* (Life Ed.), May 30, 1970, p. 1.

[22] "U.S. Court Rejects Nader Bid to Open Hartford-ITT Case," *The National Underwriter* (Property Ed.), September 15, 1972, p. 1.

[23] "Nader Urges Cotter to Resign, Also Asks Ouster," *The National Underwriter* (Life Ed.), June 6, 1970, p. 28.

[24] *Ibid.*

[25] *Ibid.*

[26] Fox, "The ITT Antimerger Cases," pp. 34-44.

[27] *Ibid.*

[28] "ITT's Bigger Push in Europe," *Time*, December 20, 1971, p. 70.

[29] *Ibid.*

[30] "ITT's Geneen; How to Succeed in Business by Really Trying," pp. 30–34+.

[31] H. M. Blake, "Beyond the ITT Case," *Harper's*, June 1972, p. 75.

[32] "ITT Scandal," *New Republic*, March 18, 1972, pp. 5–7.

[33] *Ibid.*·

[34] "Slugging It Out Over the ITT Affair," *Time*, March 20, 1972, pp. 12–15. Reprinted by permission from *Time*, The Weekly Newsmagazine; Copyright Time Inc.

[35] *Ibid.*

[36] "Columnist Releases ITT Memo," *Washington Post*, March 2, 1972, p. A-5.

[37] "Know-Nothing Mitchell; Hearing on the ITT Scandal," *New Republic*, March 25, 1972, p. 5.

[38] "Fake? Hearing on the ITT Affair," *Newsweek*, March 27, 1972, p. 28.

[39] Fred Graham, "Kleindienst Says He Set Up Talks on ITT," *New York Times*, March 3, 1972, p. 20.

[40] Fred Graham, "Role in ITT Suit is Laid on Nixon," *New York Times*, March 10, 1972, p. 1.

[41] *Ibid.*

[42] Fred Graham, "Witness Disputes Mitchell Denial," *New York Times*, March 11, 1972, p. 13.

[43] *Ibid.*

[44] "ITT Scandal," pp. 5–7.

[45] "Fake? Hearing on the ITT Affair," p. 28.

[46] Graham, "Witness Disputes Mitchell Denial," p. 13.

[47] Fred Graham, "Mitchell Denies Discussing 3 Cases With ITT Chief," *New York Times*, March 15, 1972, p. 1.

[48] E. W. Kenworthy, "Colson Says He Put Hunt on ITT Job," *New York Times*, June 15, 1973, p. 21.

[49] James M. Naughton, "Mitchell Says He Concealed Watergate From Nixon to Prevent Election Damage; Charges Magruder Lied Disputes Dean," *New York Times*, July 11, 1973, p. 1.

[50] Nicholas Gage, "Nixon Reported to Have Ordered ITT Settlement," *The New York Times*, October 30, 1973, p. 1.

[51] "Text of Kleindienst Statement on ITT," *The New York Times*, November 1, 1973, p. 33.

QUESTIONS

1. Does the information in the case demonstrate the existence of a power elite in this country, free to act with few constraints?
2. Does the case demonstrate that conglomerates add to or reinforce oligopolistic behavior?
3. What role did size play, if any, in the behavior of ITT during the incidents depicted in the case?
4. Discuss the decisions by the courts regarding ITT, based on Section 7 of the Clayton Act.
5. What are the traditional bases for the control of economic power?
6. What appears to be the source of the power employed by ITT?
7. Which managerial type is Geneen? Explain.
8. Certainly a company the size of ITT possesses a significant amount of power. Based on the occurrences in the case, did ITT use its power in a legitimate manner? Explain the reasoning for your position.
9. Explain alternative reasons for actions of the Justice Department.
10. We have argued that when a company's role is viewed as contrary to societal expectations, sanctions are normally imposed. Discuss the ITT case from this perspective.
11. Explain the nature of ITT's environment.
12. In your view is this firm acting in a socially responsible manner?

CASE 12
FOREIGN BRIBES

Businessmen today often find themselves in what might best be called a moral quandary, stemming from the fact that often there is no single clear standard of approved moral action available to them to use in making specific operational decisions.[1] There appears to be several reasons for this condition.[2] First, a diversity of cultural patterns has created a certain amount of moral diversity. This is particularly significant for multinational companies operating in a variety of diverse cultural settings.

Second, society's view of what is right and wrong often changes from one generation to another. The accelerated pace of social and technological change in today's society has further condensed the time necessary to bring about changes in moral attitudes. These changes are also complicated by the fact that individuals and groups within society have differing ideas of what is right and wrong.

Third, despite changes in moral attitudes in society there still may be a consensus on underlying values. However, when specific actions want approval the consensus often disintegrates, thus allowing different, sometimes contrary actions to find sources of approval.

This lack of clarity has contributed to a growing doubt in the mind of the businessman as to what is and what is not moral behavior. Many areas of business practice are still not defined by law or are so vaguely defined as to give considerable discretion to the decision maker. One such moral issue has become increasingly important during the last few years and has affected some of the country's largest and most prominent multinational companies.

Apparently some companies feel that bribes to foreign representatives, often high government officials, are a necessary practice if the company is going to compete abroad. From one perspective these bribes may be seen as clearly contrary to social mores. On the other hand, the same practice may be interpreted as a commission. In certain countries, this "fee" is expected and if a company wishes to do business there it must go along with the payment of high commissions. Currently the uncertainty over what constitutes a fair commission abroad has become very troublesome to many U.S. businessmen. While the bribing of a foreign official is not a crime in the United States, the act when made public has created a variety of undesirable repercussions for the management, the company, and its owners.[3]

The Securities and Exchange Commission (SEC) has found itself in somewhat of a quandary over this same issue. It has been searching for a long-term policy on which to base its disclosure requirements. While the SEC has no authority to bring suit for foreign bribes, it does have the power to require public disclosure of important business and financial information to enable the investor to make decisions. Certainly when large sums of money are used for mysterious purposes, questions are raised about what the company is doing, which further contributes to questions of the quality of management and integrity of financial accounts and reporting. Yet the SEC recognizes that efforts to force disclosure of such activities to protect the investor may cause the reverse to occur. For instance, the forced disclosure of a bribe may result in nationalization by a disgruntled foreign government or the loss of substantial business in a highly competitive foreign market. The question then arises of just how far the SEC should push disclosure. Is Congress asking the agency to make a moral judgment? [4]

The United Brands Company is one of this country's leading producers and distributors of bananas and one of the company's major sources of supply is its banana plantations in Honduras. Actions taken by United Brands have led to quite severe moral as well as social, political, and economic ramifications, both in the United States and in Honduras.

FOOTNOTES

[1] George Steiner, *Business and Society* (New York: Random House, 1971), pp. 217–221.
[2] *Ibid.*
[3] Alan Riding, "Honduras Eyes Banana Take-over," *The New York Times*, July 29, 1975, p. 38.
[4] Kenneth Bacon, "Fall Disclosure Push by SEC on Companies Worries Some Critics," *The Wall Street Journal*, May 15, 1975, pp. 1, 22.

Payments to Honduran Officials by United Brands

United Brands Company is a multinational organization engaged in the food products business through its Agrimark Division, one of the world's largest producers and marketers of bananas. The subsidiary is engaged in floriculture operations in the United States and Honduras. Through its subsidiary, John Morrell & Company, United Brands is also a major meat packer in the United States. Through its Diversified Group, United Brands is involved in food processing, food services, domestic agriculture, plastics, and communications. United Brands Company employs approximately 50,000 people and had 1974 sales of over $2 billion.[1]

United Brands was formed in 1970 by the merger of AMK Corporation and United Fruit Company. The merger was engineered by AMK's chairman Eli Black who became United Brand's new chairman. Mr. Black ran the company with what colleagues and observers believed was a strong authoritarian bent but is credited with almost single-handedly building United Brands into what it is today.[2]

At 8:20 A.M., Monday, February 3, 1975, Eli Black (53 years old) locked his office doors on the 44th floor of the Pan Am Building in mid-Manhattan, smashed his attache case through his office window, and jumped to his death.[3]

What had caused Eli Black to take his own life? Nineteen hundred and seventy-four had been an extremely difficult year for United Brands. The company had been shaken by a huge financial loss, a hurricane that destroyed much of its banana crop, increased competition from its two chief rivals—Castle & Cooke, and Del Monte—and bitter strife within the boardroom. Financially it had reported a 9-month loss of $40.2 million, contrasted with a $16.5 million profit a year before, and had omitted preferred stock dividends in December. Ironically, however, most United Brands executives felt that the worst for the company was over. "The great tragedy of Eli Black's death at this time is that under his leadership the company was on its way to overcoming several crises," Edward Gelsthorpe, executive vice president stated. "We were convinced the traumatic period was behind us." [4]

The SEC has a rule: when the chief executive of a public company commits suicide, investigate. [5] This investigation led to the admission by United Brands that they had made a payoff of $1.25 million "to an official" of Honduras as part of "an understanding with the official concerned." They also admitted to having made "certain other payments in countries outside the Western Hemisphere" of about $750,000. [6]

Events Leading to the Payoff

The situation that led to the Honduras bribe began to build in 1973 when seven Latin American countries formed a Union of Banana Exporting Countries and called for a $1 tax on every 40-pound box of bananas exported from their countries. The banana taxes were recommended in order to offset the higher fuel costs caused by the Arab oil embargo. That same year a windstorm swept through Honduras, completely stopping for a time the company's production. After the storm United Brands sharply increased its exports of bananas from Honduras to the United States, as did its major competitors. These factors combined to create an oversupply, which severely depressed banana prices. The original tax plan died because of the glut on the world banana market and the refusal of Ecuador, the leading producer, to enact the tax.

However, in March 1974 the countries again announced intentions of increasing taxes from 1 to 2½ cents per pound, to offset rising fuel costs. The tax was not to affect the price of bananas to the consumer significantly while raising $160 million per year for the exporting countries. However, the commodity business is prone to wild fluctuations in price and profits. For instance, United Brands in 1972 reported pre-tax income of $35 million on sales of $451 million in bananas and related products. In 1971, the same level of shipments generated only $398 million in sales and $11 million in earnings. [7]

The effort to impose these taxes began what is referred to as "the banana war," between the countries and the three major banana companies (United Brands, Castle & Cooke, Del Monte), which bring 110 million 40-pound boxes of bananas into North America each year. The banana companies quickly protested the taxes, and the war was reduced to skirmishes involving three of the countries (Panama, Costa Rica, and Honduras), which went ahead with the taxes. [8]

In April 1974, Honduras, the world's third largest banana-producing country, imposed a tax of 50 cents on each 40-pound box of bananas. It deferred payment on this tax, however, until June. United Brands was heavily dependent on Honduras, owning 28,000 acres of banana properties that supplied 35 percent of their bananas. United Brands officials felt the tax would have to be passed on to consumers and feared people would simply stop buying "Chiquita" bananas, United Brands' best-known brand. [9]

During June 1974, Eli Black met with the president of Honduras, General

Oswaldo Lopez, and proposed to him that the company make a payment to him personally in return for a reduction of the tax. General Lopez rejected the proposal. However, in July, Harvey Johnson, United Brands' vice president in charge of banana operations, was allegedly approached by the Honduran minister of the economy, Abraham Bennaton. At a Miami meeting Bennaton indicated the banana tax could be reduced if the company was willing to pay $5 million. Johnson reported the offer to Eli Black who told him to report the offer to his immediate superior, John Taylor, a United Brands senior vice president. Taylor was then said to have told Black that he would "take care of it." [10]

Accounts of how the payments were made and to whom are fuzzy. United Brands acknowledged authorization of a $2.5 million payment by Black. Taylor allegedly took care of the details, which included a $1.25 million payment and the promise of another $1.25 million payment at a later time. The initial payment was made in September 1974, when money was transferred from United Brands' European operations into Swiss bank accounts. United Brands sent the following telegram to the Paris branch of Chase Manhattan Bank: "Please transfer today, by cable, to Swiss Credit Bank, Paradeplatz, Zurich, $1.25 million value, 4 September, in favor of Abraham Bennaton, care of Joseph Schildklecht. Confirm code number, signed (Promes)." Schildklecht is a Swiss banker but the signature was unexplained. The second payment was never made. [11] The payment was listed on company books as "the cost of European sales." According to one United Brands official, this book entry "was very clumsily handled. The entry stuck out like a sore thumb." [12]

In August 1974, Black wrote a letter to United Brands' shareholders in which he said that the Panamanian tax of $1 per box, the Costa Rican tax of 25 cents per box, and the Honduran tax of 50 cents per box "violated and breached the provisions of existing agreements with these countries." But he also wrote that "the company realized the countries' need for additional revenue" and said "he intended to negotiate with them to attempt to arrive at a reasonable formula." [13]

In late August, United Brands announced it had reached an "understanding" with Honduras for a tax of 25 cents per box—instead of 50 cents—with yearly increases beginning in 1975, depending in part on the banana market at the time. At the time of the payoff, few company officials besides Black, Taylor, and Johnson knew of the matter. However, in November at least two additional United Brands officials did have some knowledge. Robert Gallop, senior vice president, general counsel, and a director of United Brands, said he was informed of the payment by Edward Gelsthorpe.

A month after the announced understanding on the tax with Honduras, Hurricane Fifi swept through Honduras knocking out some 75 percent of the company's plantation operation. Houston Lacombe, general manager of United Brands in Honduras, said of the company's 28,000 acres of banana plantation 24,000 had been destroyed and only 4000 could be partly saved. Also 11 million boxes of bananas worth $44 million, which were ready for shipping, had been destroyed in the warehouses. The net loss of insurance came to around $20 million. [14]

Eli Black, who had predicted 1974 would be a banner year for United Brands now faced disastrous losses due to the hurricane, increased export taxes, and increased cost of cattle feed for its John Morrell subsidiary. The price of the company's common stock dropped from $12 a share in 1973 to $4 per share. Black took this as a personal defeat. As one United Brands executive said, "Eli assumed too much responsibility; as the company grew and its fortunes sank, he felt the responsibility even more keenly. His expectations of himself were too much." [15]

Actions Taken to Improve United Brands' Financial Condition

In order to cover losses and to infuse some working capital into United Brands, Black sold, at a hefty profit, the company's 62 percent interest in Foster Grant, Inc., a sunglasses and plastics producer. His decision to sell the profitable interest triggered industry rumors of discontent within United Brands ranks with Black's authoritarian direction. Black denied any management turmoil. [16]

On December 19, 1974 United Brands and Panama entered into an agreement, negotiated by Mr. Gelsthorpe, which provided over a three-year period that United Brands would sell all of its banana-producing and related properties in Panama to the government. The first Black heard of this was at the board meeting on December 27 when the agreement was on the agenda for approval. According to one close associate of Black, "Eli felt that Gelsthorpe had sold the company down the river in order to build up his own reputation." [17]

Shift in Control at United Brands

Apparently personal feuding and corporate infighting during the height of the "banana war" further added to the stress on Black. At first, the relationship between Black and Gelsthorpe, the executive vice president, was one of mutual admiration. However, Gelsthorpe built a power base at United Brands' Boston office and tried to arrogate more and more responsibility from Black. According to Gelsthorpe, Black threatened to fire him several times for not "getting in line." Other company officers stated there were frequent clashes due to Black's authoritarian philosophy and his willingness to play one executive off against another. Gelsthorpe also won the allegiance of many United Brands employees because Black's New York AMK Corporation had merged with United Fruit Company, an old-line Boston firm and moved corporate headquarters to New York. [18]

Knowledge of the sale of properties in Panama was Eli Black's first feeling of losing control. His power was further shaken at the company's January 10 board meeting. George Gardner turned to Taylor and asked him if he wanted to discuss the Honduran situation. At this time the matter of payments came out, but full discussion was cut off because it was not on the agenda. However the mention of the payoff by a director he had no reason to believe knew of the matter greatly concerned Black. "He felt vulnerable," Allen Nadler, Black's son-in-law said.

"He felt the Honduras payment could possibly be used against him if there were a power struggle." [19]

Over the next few weeks, Black became convinced that Gelsthorpe, Gardner, and Taylor were planning to throw him out of his own company. According to Gallop, a close friend of Black's for 20 years, "Eli felt they were going to oust him. I tried to convince him that nobody could oust him unless he wanted to be removed but he felt his control was dissipating." [20]

Eli Black jumped to his death on February 3. His suicide left no one clearly in charge of the company. Most outside observers felt Edward Gelsthorpe would be named immediately to the post of chief executive officer. But most members of the board knew of Black's feelings about his chief operating officer and were determined to block his appointment. On February 6 the board met to work out a solution. After some disputes an interim solution was reached where Gelsthorpe would continue as executive vice president and chief operating officer and would report to a management committee, headed by J. E. Goldman, an outside director.

Events Leading to Public Disclosure of the Payoff

At the February 6 board meeting, Gelsthorpe and Taylor also explained the specifics of the Honduras arrangement. At this time Price Waterhouse and Company, the company's independent auditor, had been examining the books. Some people close to the company suspected someone tipped the accountants off. Price Waterhouse said that "the matter came to our attention during the audit." [21] At the board meeting the accounting firm suggested the board hire outside counsel. Therefore, the firm of Covington and Burling was hired.

Shortly after being hired Covington and Burling brought the matter to the Securities and Exchange Commission. The SEC investigation had started with Black's death and had been helped by information passed on to it by the State Department. According to a top level State Department officer, the U. S. embassy in Tegucigalpa, capital of Honduras, had developed some information regarding alleged payoffs by United Brands to the president of Honduras. The embassy passed this information along to Washington, which in turn passed it on to the SEC.

In March Covington and Burling along with Price Waterhouse's lawyers asked the SEC not to disclose the details of the payoff and applied for confidential treatment under an SEC rule that allows a company to request that sensitive information remain private. United Brands felt disclosure could hurt the company and its stockholders, jeopardize its dealings in Honduras, and cause diplomatic problems as well.

The State Department was therefore asked to intervene on the grounds that disclosure could harm U. S. relations with Honduras. However, the State Department rebuffed the request when William D. Rogers, Assistant Secretary of State for Inter-American Affairs, replied that multinational corporations "must respect the laws of the nations in which they operate and conduct themselves as good corporate citizens of those nations, refraining from improper interference in their internal affairs." [22]

The matter did remain a secret until April. During this period Price Waterhouse discovered payments of $750,000 that had been made to Italian officials over the last five years to prevent restriction on United Brands' banana exports to that country. Nobody seemed to know, however, who authorized the payments.

United Brands filed its annual financial report, Form 10-K, with the SEC on April 1 but didn't disclose the payment. However, the company did disclose it was under SEC investigation, without saying why. Price Waterhouse's audit letter, filed with the SEC as part of the required 10-K report referred the reader to the section on "Risk of Foreign Operations." The section having to do with United Brands' tax troubles in Panama, Costa Rica, and Honduras, concluded as follows: "Certain information has been omitted from this Annual Report on Form 10-K and is being filed separately with the Securities and Exchange Commission, together with an application to the Commission for a determination that such information be kept confidential." [23]

If Price Waterhouse had qualified its opinion because of the bribe on the confidentiality request, an explicit mention of this in its audit letter would have been required. Usually an auditor qualifies an opinion because of important uncertainties or contingencies that could affect the company. A Price Waterhouse official described the audit firm's decision as "a judgement call" involving many factors, but said the decisive point was concern that disclosure would hurt the company by provoking the Honduran government. [24]

The SEC's enforcement division studied the matter and sent an account of its findings to the five-member commission on April 7. The division believed United Brands violated the reporting provisions of federal securities law by failing to disclose the payoff in its financial statements. The SEC does not have jurisdiction over the crime of bribery itself. Rather, it is instructed by the 1933 act to patrol the full disclosure of "material" information by corporations that issue stocks and other securities for investment by the public. The SEC is often able to use this rule as a lever to pry out information about shady dealings. [25]

Public disclosure of important business and financial information to allow investors to make informed decisions has always been the basis of federal securities law. However, recently some corporations are discovering that disclosure can be painful. With more large multinational companies feeling such pain as a result of the SEC proceedings, corporate lawyers and some government officials are complaining that the SEC may be going too far in requiring certain disclosures. They argue this may be damaging the public interest. [26]

In explaining the commission's use of disclosure rules to illuminate hidden corners of corporate activity, one SEC member declared, "We're not engaged in some sort of campaign to blacken people or moralize the world. We're just trying to force disclosure" of important facts. The SEC contends that the agency has not expanded its view of what constitutes material information that must be disclosed.

Rather the controversies have erupted because the SEC has applied its normal disclosure standards to cases that, it developed, have abnormal implications.[27]

Finally, on April 8, the *Wall Street Journal* queried United Brands about payments to a Honduran official, and in response the company publicly admitted the bribe. The secret was out.[28]

Actions by the SEC

As a result of the admission, the SEC suspended stock market trading in United Brands' securities on April 8. The stock had closed at $6 per share that day. The action was taken to give investors an opportunity to evaluate the news.

In a statement issued by United Brands, the board of directors stated the payoffs were made without their knowledge and were authorized by the late Eli Black. Furthermore the statement said, "the board . . . has determined that this additional payment ($1.25 million) shall not be made. This action and disclosure. . . could result in a material reduction in future earnings and a loss of substantial corporate assets which in turn, could affect the continuity of operations of the Company." [29] The company also indicated in the statement that it would name a special committee to investigate the circumstances.

The next day, April 9, the SEC announced the filing of a complaint in the U. S. District Court for the District of Columbia against United Brands. The complaint alleged that United Brands violated the anti-fraud and reporting provisions of the securities laws by filing reports with the SEC without disclosing that United Brands had affected improper cash payments to officials of certain foreign governments.[30]

More specifically the complaint alleged that United Brands failed to disclose a method of doing business whereby an arrangement was entered into, in which United Brands agreed to pay $2.5 million to high government officials of the Republic of Honduras in exchange for favorable government action benefiting United Brands. Additionally United Brands' filing failed to disclose that the company deposited $1.25 million in a Swiss bank account of designated government officials of the Republic of Honduras in September 1974 and had agreed to pay an additional $1.25 million in the spring of 1975.[31]

The complaint further alleged that United Brands, by making false entries on the books and records of United Brands, caused to be disbursed approximately $750,000 in corporate funds over a five-year period to officials of a foreign government in Europe.[32]

In its complaint, the SEC requested a permanent injunction enjoining further violations of the provisions of the securities laws and the appointment of a special master to examine the books and records of United Brands and to submit a report to the court, the SEC, and shareholders of United Brands regarding any improper payments by United Brands to government officials.[33]

The Initiation of Stockholder Suits

On April 10 the U. S. Attorney's office in the Southern District of New York began its own investigation into whether United Brands or its officials violated any criminal laws.[34]

The same day United Brands called in Price Waterhouse to amend the 10-K annual report that had been submitted to the SEC less than two weeks before.

In U. S. District Court, Southern District of New York, a United Brands share-holder filed a derivative and class action suit against the company, charging mis-management of corporate assets as well as violation of the Securities Exchange Act of 1934. The suit brought by Henry Neugarten named as defendants United Brands, 12 of the 14 directors, two United Brands officers, and the estate of Eli Black.

Count I of the suit charged that United Brands' bribe to a Honduras official constituted a wrongful co-version and spoilation of the assets of the company. This part of the suit is a derivative action that is brought by a shareholder for the benefit of the corporation rather than for himself. If damages are assessed, they are awarded to the corporation.[35]

Count II, a class action suit, charged the defendants made untrue statements and failed to state material facts, which had the effect of inflating the price of the company's stock and therefore damages were claimed from the defendants for this loss by Neugarten and members of the class described in the complaint. These were the people who purchased common stock during the period from on or about April 1974 to on or about April 8, 1975.[36]

A United Brands company spokesman said "the concern hasn't any comment on the suit until it has time to study it." [37] Lawyers for United Brands expected other similar suits to follow.

They didn't have long to wait. The next day, April 11, a suit was filed in the same court by two more shareholders, Joan and Jesse Brooklyn. The suit charged the company and 15 officers and directors with adopting "a policy and practice of bribing foreign officials" and failing to disclose such practices to the investors. They asked for the recovery of the bribes and a court order to void all company elections of board members since 1971.[38]

A Sequence of Maneuvers by United Brands and the Government

The Senate Foreign Relations Subcommittee on Multinational Corporations began a quiet investigation of United Brands before deciding whether or not to call full hearings.

On April 12 the SEC was given a lengthy series of amendments to Form 10-K. The amended report deleted the reference to the attempted confidential treatment and disclosed the payments. Price Waterhouse made its acceptance of the company's financial figures "subject to any adverse impact resulting from the disclosure by the company that it made a payment to a government official in Honduras and payments in other foreign countries.[39] United Brands also announced the amended form was available to shareholders upon request.

Trading was resumed on United Brands securities on April 14. However, on the New York Stock Exchange, trading was delayed until 1:00 P.M., due to a heavy imbalance of orders, when 10,800 shares crossed the ticker tape at $5 a share, down $1 from its closing price just before suspension of trading. Remarking on the price level, a company official said, "not too bad." [40]

On the same day the United Brands board of directors had a long meeting. The board discussed whether the company should try to fight the SEC or settle the case on the best terms it could get. If the company decided to fight it ran the risk that more details, including names, would become public and further endanger company relations with Honduras.[41]

The next day, the directors issued a statement announcing the postponement of their annual meeting to sometime in the late summer. The meeting was originally scheduled for May 14, but the board said that disclosure of the foreign payments had taken up "the attention of management and directors." The board also announced that the quarterly dividends on the preferred stock would again be omitted.[42]

The Senate Foreign Relations subcommittee on multinational corporations on April 16 announced it would call full hearings, on United Brands payoffs, within three weeks.[43]

On April 17 United Brands and the SEC opened preliminary negotiations in order to reach an out-of-court settlement of the government's charges. Officials familiar with the case voiced hope that a mutually acceptable solution would be found "very soon." [44]

On April 22 United Brands reported a $4 million loss for the first quarter of 1975.

The SEC on April 24 submitted a proposal of terms for settlement to United Brands, whereby the company would agree to a court order barring it from future violations of anti-fraud and reporting violations. Also the company must agree to the appointment of a special master to examine corporate records and give the SEC and stockholders a report "detailing all corporate funds which may have been used for improper payment to government officials foreign or domestic, or for other improper purposes.[45] United Brands postponed a decision on the proposed terms until April 29. After the meeting held to consider the terms, United Brands rejected as too severe the SEC's proposal for settlement of the suit. United Brands lawyers said the company did not feel it had violated any security laws and that it would propose a settlement with milder terms, but did not elaborate.[46]

On May 2 Wallace W. Booth was elected president and chief executive officer of United Brands. His election ended the power struggle between the directors supporting Gelsthorpe and those opposing him because of Eli Black's feelings. Max M. Fisher was also elected acting chairman.

Two days after the election of Booth the Senate Foreign Relations subcommittee on multinational corporations started full hearings on United Brands' payoffs.

United Brands filed a motion on May 14 in U.S. District Court for the District of Columbia, asking that the SEC's investigation of the company be held up until the U.S. Attorney's office in New York completed its criminal investigation. United Brands complained that providing depositions to both investigating staffs would tie up and burden corporate officials, if the investigations were allowed to proceed simultaneously.[47]

It was disclosed in the court records that the U.S. Attorney's office had turned the investigation over to a federal grand jury in New York to weigh possible criminal charges against United Brands and its officers and directors. It was also disclosed that the U.S. Attorney's office had subpoenaed documents relating to possible payoffs in Italy, West Germany, Panama, and Costa Rica, as well as Honduras.[48]

United Brands' special committee investigating payoffs announced on May 15 that it was investigating payments made to Italian officials. This was the first mention of the country's identity since April 8 when United Brands admitted the $750,000 payment to a European country. The committee also stated that no payments had been made to Costa Rica, Panama, or West Germany.[49]

The SEC filed a motion on May 21 in the U.S. District Court for the District of Columbia to block United Brands' appeal for a stay of the SEC civil suit. The motion charged United Brands with a continuing effort to conceal "the true scope and extent" of its payments to foreign officials. "The true purpose of the company's request for a stay is to further prevent disclosure of the full facts and circumstances surrounding its payments of monies to government officials in Italy and Honduras," according to the SEC.[50]

The papers accompanying the SEC countermove confirmed for the first time that the $750,000 mentioned in the original complaint had been paid to Italian government officials.

A judge from the U.S. District Court for the District of Columbia ruled on July 20 that the SEC could continue to prosecute its suits against United Brands.

On August 12 the SEC subpoenaed 17 United Brands officials and partners from Price Waterhouse. In addition, Price Waterhouse was ordered to produce documents describing payments to foreign officials by United Brands and the manner in which the payments appeared in the company's accounting.[51]

United Brands in Central America

The old United Fruit Company had a tradition of paternalism and exploitation—i.e., low wages, few benefits, company control of the community—in Central America. It exerted such an influence on the affairs of Central America that the term "banana republic" entered the language. The company was then derisively known as "el pulpo," the octopus, and was the largest private employer and landowner in a number of Latin countries. It overturned unfriendly governments as easily as it picked its Chiquitas, according to business lore.[52]

However, when United Brands was formed, it was evident to Eli Black that something had to be done. He believed it imperative that the company's image be changed from that of the Yankee exploiter. In Honduras and elsewhere, United Brands began supplying free housing and electricity for its employees. For those workers who didn't want to live in company houses, United Brands built houses which it sold to them below cost. The company furnished schools, hospitals, and other public facilities. At the same time, it raised wages for its agricultural workers to nearly six times the level that other companies were paying. In Honduras the average annual income is $275 but United Brands workers averaged $2400 per year.[53]

Eli Black believed that he could straddle the two worlds successfully by combining business with a social conscience and sensitivity. He explained: "Besides believing in the necessity of multinational corporations behaving responsibly, we are also aware that improved conditions lead to greater productivity on the part of employees, thus increasing the profits of the company."[54]

Speaking of United Brands' efforts in Central America, the *Boston Globe* reported in 1972, that they "may well be the most socially conscious American company in the hemisphere."[55]

Economic, Social, and Political Problems in Honduras

At the time the payoffs were made public in the United States, Honduras was suffering from the aftermath of Hurricane Fifi. As a result of the storm five thousand people died, 10,000 homes were destroyed, and damage to crops, public property, and private industry was estimated at $250 million. United Brands attempted to ease the crises by using its own helicopters to carry aid to survivors in rural areas.

Banana exports, which accounted for about 39 percent of the country's total 1973 exports of $242 million plummeted dramatically because of storm damage. Banana exports for 1975 were projected to be only 9 percent of an estimated $192 million in total exports. This decline was certain to contribute to the unemployment rate.[56]

Some of the banana companies were negotiating with the government to sell their land. They felt it was not economically feasible to rehabilitate the storm-damaged acreage. However Honduras had neither the money nor the technical know-how to continue to run an increasingly technological operation. The leader of the militant banana union was convinced that these apparent attempts at sale were merely a means of trying to get the banana tax abolished. He accused the banana companies of trying to topple the regime of President Oswaldo Lopez. The allegations were strongly denied by the companies.[57]

Because of lack of social reform under Lopez, a group of young reform-minded lieutenant colonels had gradually been pushing its way into control of the machinery of government. On March 31, the government stripped President Lopez of most of his power and his role as chief of the armed forces. His replacement, Colonel Melgar Castro argued this would let President Lopez devote more of his time to the country's problems. It was generally felt that Lopez was on his way out.[58]

When the payoff first became public neither the United Brands statement, nor the SEC complaint named the Honduran official or officials to whom the company made the $1.25 million payment. However, sources close to the investigation alleged the payment was destined for President Lopez.[59]

President Lopez's Denial and the Establishment of a Fact-Finding Commission

On April 9 President Lopez called an urgent meeting of government officials to prepare a "statement of clarification." President Lopez did not make a public statement; however, a military spokesman did state that reports of his involvement were "completely false." Abraham Bennaton called the charges totally unacceptable and said the President was "free of sin." [60]

At the same time the Council of Ministers named a seven-man commission, with ambassadorial status and immunity from prosecution, to investigate the bribery charges and to report to the council. It appropriated $50,000 initially for the commission to begin work. The commission was headed by the rector of the national university, Jorge Arturo Reina.

The commission began holding meetings April 10 behind closed doors. Enrique Balboa, senior vice president of United Brands, and Houston Lacombe, manager of the Tela Railroad—a United Brands subsidiary—were closely interrogated for 11 hours over two days. The executives were said to have "collaborated fully." [61]

The commission prohibited all high-and middle-level government officials and employees of United Brands from leaving the country.

Meanwhile there was mounting public pressure for a convincing investigation. Newspapers in Tegucigalpa expressed strong doubt about the commission's ability to expose any high officials. In editorials the papers demanded the commission report "the full truth." Also newspapers were highly critical of President Lopez. One paper carried a front page cartoon showing the chief of state slipping on a banana skin.[62]

Honduran officers at United Brands started running ads in local newspapers disclaiming any participation by the Honduran office.

Meanwhile leaders of Honduran student groups and labor unions demanded that the country nationalize United Brands' properties in Honduras and boost the banana tax to $1.00 per box.

The commission conceded that there was some validity to charges that top officials had taken bribes from United Brands. Reina said, "Up to now, everything points to the fact that there are some guilty individuals. We have rational indications [of bribery]." [63]

The commission questioned President Lopez at length at the Casa Presidencial. Reina declined to discuss the nature of the president's replies only saying he "responded frankly to all questions." [64] President Lopez had still not made a public statement regarding the payoff.

The commission on April 21 announced that all members of the government except President Lopez had granted it legal authority to investigate their foreign bank accounts. The commission stated that the refusal was "a limitation and obstacle to the work of the commission." [65] After rejecting the commission's request President Lopez was overthrown in a bloodless coup by the Honduran military. He was replaced by Colonel Melgar Castro, the Commander in Chief of the armed forces. The new president was believed to be considerably more conservative than the young lieutenant colonels that appointed him.

The broadcast announcing the takeover also stated that the military government would remain in power until further notice. The announcement further indicated that the new government would press on with the controversial agrarian reform program. This program was supposed to distribute 1.5 million acres of land to 120,000 peasant families over the next 5 years. It was also expected to affect significantly United Brands' vast holdings of land in Honduras. [66]

Observers in Honduras described the country as "calm and tranquil" with government and private business activities proceeding "normally." [67]

The Commission Comes to the United States

An hour before the coup the commission left for the United States where it was planning to interview officials of United Brands as well as members of the SEC. Upon arrival in the United States the commission immediately met with enforcement officers of the SEC for 2½ hours. It also met with Manuel Cohen, a lawyer representing the outside directors of United Brands. After these meetings the commission announced in Washington that it "had not yet sufficient evidence to say that the deposed President personally benefited from the $1.25 million deposited by United Brands last September in a numbered Swiss bank account." Reina said, "I won't say who got the money until I see the deposit slips with my own eyes." [68]

In Honduras a spokesman for the new government announced, "We're going to prepare the country for true democracy, but we're not going to hand the country back to the traditional conservative parties that exploit the poor and illiterate. We'll stay in office as long as necessary, perhaps five or ten years. There is opposition to the agrarian reform program but we know that if the government doesn't promote social change, there will be a bloody revolution in Honduras." [69]

Also Colonel Castro, the new Chief of State, announced his cabinet. He retained only three members of the ousted regime. Among those gone was Abraham Bennaton, the minister of the economy, who was mentioned in the scandal. The *Wall Street Journal* reported that Abraham Bennaton had met with Harvey Johnson, United Brands' vice president of banana operations, in Miami, sometime in July 1974. Bennaton supposedly had demanded $5 million to lower the banana tax. [70] Bennaton denied he demanded money from United Brands in order to lower the banana tax. He admitted having the meeting with Johnson but not for that purpose. However he would not give details of the meeting. [71]

The commission verified that United Brands had made a payoff to a Honduran official. It did not identify the official. Yet, it did announce that Abraham Bennaton, after authorizing the commission to examine his foreign bank accounts, had withdrawn his authorization on the grounds that it had been obtained under duress. [72]

Finally, in a nationwide radio address on May 15, Reina announced that Abraham Bennaton was the official who took the bribe. He said John Taylor, United Brands vice president, had paid the money to Mr. Bennaton at a meeting September 3–4, 1974 in Zurich, Switzerland. The commission came to this conclusion based on three telegrams tracing the bribe. Reina said ex-president Lopez apparently was kept in the dark by Bennaton. "The commission however, was unable to find whether Lopez was involved in the case because he refused to authorize the commission to check his account." [73] However, Reina went on to say that both the SEC and United Brands had "agreed in pointing at former chief of state Lopez as the person to whom the bribery proposal was originally made." [74]

Criminal Charges Filed

As a result of the commission's investigation both in Honduras and the United States the Honduran government filed criminal charges against the United Brands company's subsidiary Tela Railroad Company for the alleged bribes. In addition, Attorney General Serupio Hernandez Castellances urged the nationalization of United Brands' holdings. [75] The first step toward nationalization would probably involve government takeover of the railroads and docks owned by the company. The equivalent of a grand jury began an investigation of Bennaton's involvements in the whole affair. Proceedings were also started against Bennaton for perjury, tax fraud, bribery, and offending the dignity of the nation. Approximately two weeks after proceedings were initiated Bennaton was released from custody on $825 bail. Shortly thereafter he was declared innocent of the tax fraud charges.

Internal Events Believed Sparked by the United Brands Affair

In Honduras 70 percent of the inhabitants are classified as peasants and the per capita income is less than $300 per year. These conditions prompted the new government to continue the controversial agrarian reform under which uncultivated properties were appropriated and distributed to landless farmers. There was opposition to the plan from conservatives. However, they also realized that if the government didn't promote social change, there was likely to be a revolution. Conservatives believed there must be "some Socialist-type reforms in order to avoid Communism." [76]

Two months after the new government was formed, the 38,000-member National Peasant Union in a move to accelerate the agrarian reform program invaded and occupied 128 private and state landholdings. They withdrew when the government threatened to expel them by force. However, the following month, militant landless peasants, on a "hunger" march to demonstrate support for the agrarian reform program, were assaulted by government soldiers and a small group of cattle farmers in the town of Juticalpa, 35 miles north of the capital city. Five of the peasants were killed. The same day nine more of the demonstrators disappeared from Juticalpa, including an American priest. Their mutilated bodies were found several weeks later in a dynamited well on the ranch of a wealthy landowner. The new government now faced growing tension between the landless peasants demanding agrarian reform and the powerful Honduran Cattle Farmers Federation who were violently against the reform program.[77]

Shortly thereafter, a Special Banana Advisory Commission, set up by President Castro, unanimously recommended that the Honduran government take action to nationalize concessions and property owned by United Brands and Castle & Cooke in order to increase Honduran participation in banana exporting.

On August 17 the government of Honduras announced the cancellation of a series of special privileges accorded the large banana companies. The privileges to be revoked on September 15 included certain tax and tariff exemptions. Also announced was the government's intentions to buy out the operating facilities of United Brands' Tela Railroad Company. President Castro accused United Brands of "committing immoral acts" by continuing to enjoy these "unjustified" privileges. However, a government official said there "won't be any outright nationalization or expropriation." [78]

The Annual Stockholders Meeting

At the time of the annual meeting on August 18, 1975, the future of United Brands was clouded. At least seven stockholder lawsuits had been filed; and in addition to the U. S. Attorney's office in New York, the SEC and a Senate subcommittee were investigating the company. Despite the clouds, Wallace Booth, the company's new president, assured stockholders the company was "going to stay in the business of raising and exporting bananas." [79] In response to the announcement of the previous day, that the Honduran government intended to suspend the concessions under which United Brands operated, he said, "this was not a move to nationalize the company's banana-production facilities there. Rather this action is a reflection of the government's previously expressed desire to replace the existing concessions with a more modern working arrangement." [80] Furthermore, Booth said "the Government has indicated that it will pay the fair value for [United Brands] facilities." [81]

Epilogue

Just what the final results of the bribery scandal will be only time will tell. Since Honduras is dependent on the United States for aid and a market for its products it appears unlikely the country will take any drastic actions against United Brands. However, common themes in commentaries emerging from Honduras and other Latin American countries demonstrate strong resentment of multinational companies. They also call for much tighter controls. But one Honduran professional put the blame closer to home: "Who is responsible for all this? It is us, the people, always with our heads down." [82]

FOOTNOTES

[1] Annual Report 1974, *United Brands Company*, p. 1.

[2] "United Brands Paid Bribe to President of Honduras, It's Said," *The Wall Street Journal*, April 9, 1975, p. 1.

[3] Mary Bralove, "Was Eli Black's Suicide Caused by the Tensions of Conflicting Worlds?" *The Wall Street Journal*, February 14, 1975, p. 1.

[4] Mary Bralove, "United Brands' Chairman, Eli M. Black, Plunges to His Death in Apparent Suicide," *The Wall Street Journal*, April 11, 1975, p. 15.

[5] "Banana Bribes," *The Economist*, April 19, 1975, p. 74.

[6] Mary Bralove, "United Brands Named in Suit Filed by Holder," *The Wall Street Journal*, April 11, 1975, p. 4.

[7] "At War with Chiquita Banana," *Business Week*, June 16, 1973, p. 59.

[8] "United Brands Paid Bribe to President of Honduras, It's Said," p. 1.

[9] Mary Bralove, "At United Brands Co., Fight for Control Came After Honduran Payoff," *The Wall Street Journal*, May 7, 1975, p. 1.

[10] Robert J. Cole, "Direct Bribe Bid is Laid to Black," *The New York Times*, May 17, 1975, p. 33.

[11] Robert J. Cole, "Honduras Gets Bribe Telegrams," *The New York Times*, May 21, 1975, p. 61.

[12] Bralove, "At United Brands Co., Fight for Control Came After Honduran Payoff," p. 1.

[13] "United Brands Paid Bribe to President of Honduras, It's Said," p. 1.

[14] "United Brands Says Hurricane's Damage to Bananas to Cut Net," *The Wall Street Journal*, November 24, 1974, p. 8.

[15] Bralove, "United Brands' Chairman, Eli M. Black, Plunges to His Death in Apparent Suicide," p. 15.

[16] *Ibid.*, p. 4.

[17] Bralove, "At United Brands Co., Fight for Control Came After Honduran Payoff," p. 1.

[18] *Ibid.*

[19] *Ibid.*

[20] *Ibid.*

[21] *Ibid.*

[22] Robert E. Mooney, "Foiling Corporate Cover-Ups," *The New York Times*, April 13, 1975, p. 33.

[23] Bralove, "United Brands Named in Suit Filed by Holder," p. 4.

[24] *Ibid.*

[25] "United Brands Paid Bribe to President of Honduras, It's Said," p. 4.

[26] Kenneth Bacon, "Full Disclosure Push by S.E.C. on Companies Worries Some Critics," *The Wall Street Journal*, May 15, 1975, p. 1.

[27] *Ibid.*

[28] Kenneth Bacon and Mary Bralove, "United Brands Co. Also Made Payoff in Europe, S.E.C. Says," *The Wall Street Journal*, April 10, 1975, p. 1.

[29] Robert J. Cole, "Stock Trading Halted," *The New York Times*, April 10, 1975, p. 59.

[30] "Complaint Names United Brand Company," *S.E.C. Digest*, Issue 75-50, April 10, 1975, p. 1.

[31] *Ibid.*

[32] *Ibid.*

[33] *Ibid.*

[34] Kenneth H. Bacon, "U. S. Looks for Possible Criminal Charges in United Brands' Payment in Honduras," *The Wall Street Journal*, April 16, 1975, p. 3.

[35] Bralove, "United Brands Named in Suit Filed by Holder," p. 4.

[36] Annual Report 1974, *United Brands Company*, p. 24.

[37] Bralove, "United Brands Named in Suit Filed by Holder," p. 4.

[38] Robert J. Cole, "More Stockholders Suing United Brands on Bribery," *The New York Times*, April 12, 1975, p. 33.

[39] Robert J. Cole, "S.E.C. is Tentative on United Brands," *The New York Times*, April 14, 1975, p. 5.

[40] Robert J. Cole, "No United Brands Fight on S.E.C. Charges Seen," *The New York Times*, April 15, 1975, p. 47.

[41] *Ibid.*

[42] Bacon, "U. S. Looks for Possible Criminal Charges in United Brands Payment in Honduras," p. 3.

[43] "Senate May Call Hearing on United Brands," *The New York Times*, April 14, 1975, p. 67.

[44] Robert J. Cole, "Honduran Panel Concedes Signs of Banana Bribery," *The New York Times*, April 18, 1975, p. 45.

[45] "S.E.C. Files Charge on United Brands," *The New York Times*, May 22, 1975, p. 65.

[46] "United Brands Company Rejects S.E.C. Terms of Settlement Offer," *The Wall Street Journal*, May 15, 1975, p. 18.

[47] "Honduran Official Named in United Brands Bribe," *The New York Times*, May 16, 1975, p. 53.

[48] "New Top Banana," *Time*, May 26, 1975, p. 72.

[49] "United Brands Checks to See if Payments Went to Italian Aides," *The Wall Street Journal*, May 16, 1975, p. 7.

[50] "S.E.C. Files Charge on United Brands," p. 65.

[51] "United Brands Officials' Auditor Subpoenaed by S.E.C. in Bribery Suit," *The Wall Street Journal*, August 13, 1975, p. 6.

[52] Stephen Sansweet and Mike Tharp, "Calm on the Surface, Hondurans Are Ready for Political Turmoil," *The Wall Street Journal*, April 14, 1975, p. 1.

[53] Bralove, "Was Eli Black's Suicide Caused by the Tensions of Conflicting Worlds?" p. 1.

[54] Paul Romero, "United Brands Polishes Its Image in Latin America," *Management Review*, March 1975, p. 28.

[55] Bralove, "Was Eli Black's Suicide Caused by the Tensions of Conflicting Worlds?" p. 1.

[56] Sansweet and Tharp, "Calm on the Surface, Hondurans Are Ready for Political Turmoil," p. 1.

[57] *Ibid.*

[58] *Ibid.*

[59] Bralove, "United Brands Named in Suit Filed by Holder," p. 4.

[60] Cole, "Stock Trading Halted," p. 59.

[61] Cole, "S.E.C. is Tentative on United Brands," p. 5.

[62] *Ibid.*

[63] Cole, "Honduran Panel Concedes Signs of Banana Bribery," p. 45.

[64] *Ibid.*

[65] Alan Riding, "Honduran Army Ousts Leader Named in Bribery Case in U. S.," *The New York Times*, April 25, 1975, p. 2.

[66] Alan Riding, "Hondurans Pledge to Democracy," *The New York Times*, April 25, 1975, p. 6.

[67] "Honduran President Ousted by Military In Bloodless Coup; Successor Is Named," *The Wall Street Journal*, April 23, 1975, p. 38.

[68] Robert J. Cole, "Hondurans in U. S. for Bribe Inquiry, Say They Still Lack Proof of Lopez Tie," *The New York Times*, April 24, 1975, p. 3.

[69] Riding, "Hondurans Pledge to Democracy," p. 2.

[70] "At United Brands Company, Fight for Control Came After Honduran Payoff," p. 1. *cit.*, p. 1.

[71] "Honduran Ex-Minister Denies He Demanded Brands Payoff," *The Wall Street Journal*, May 9, 1975, p. 10.

[72] Cole, "Honduras Gets Bribe Telegrams," p. 1.

[73] "Honduran Official Named in United Brands Bribe," p. 1.

[74] Cole, "Honduras Gets Bribe Telegrams," p. 69.

[75] Cole, "Direct Bribe Bid is Laid to Black," p. 40.

[76] Riding, "Hondurans Pledge to Democracy," p. 2.

[77] Alan Riding, "Discontent of Peasants in Honduras Leads to Violence and Death," *The New York Times*, July 22, 1975, p. 8.

[78] Mary Bralove, "United Brands Says Committee Studying Foreign Payments Plans Code of Conduct," *The Wall Street Journal*, August 19; 1975, p. 7.

[79] Ann Crittenden, "United Brands Sees Hope in Panama," *The New York Times*, August 19, 1975, p. 1.

[80] Bralove, "United Brands Says Committee Studying Foreign Payments Plans Code of Conduct," p. 7.

[81] Crittenden, "United Brands Sees Hope in Panama," p. 1.

[82] Sansweet and Tharp, "Calm on the Surface, Hondurans Are Ready for Political Turmoil," p. 16.

QUESTIONS

1. Discuss the nature and significance of environmental forces impinging on United Brands at the time the bribe was made to the Honduran official.
2. Explain the nature of the moral content of decisions leading up to and culminating in the decision to accept the $1.25 million.
3. Identify and discuss the concept of role conflict as applied to United Brands in this case.
4. Identify and discuss the concept of role conflicts as applied to the Securities and Exchange Commission in this case.
5. Since at the time the $1.25 million payment was made it was not against the law in the United States, was United Brands acting in accord with broad social trends in this country?
6. Describe in detail the coping strategy employed by United Brands under Eli Black. Explain the contingency nature of such a strategy.
7. Did social expectations of United Brands' role differ between the United States and Honduras in this case? Explain.
8. Identify United Brands' relevant publics and explain the manner in which the company related to each. Would you have established priorities differently?
9. Would the use of social values as a coping mechanism have been an effective way for United Brands to relate to its environment?
10. If it is true that a business organization has a limited moral responsibility, in your opinion where does that limit exist in the United Brands case?

CASE 13
POLITICAL CONTRIBUTIONS

It is difficult to understand business, or business-societal relationships, without some knowledge of the moral problems facing businessmen and what society thinks is the state of business morality compared to what society expects from business.[1]

Some social observers see improvement in business morality. For instance, as a part of the aftermath of the electrical price fixing conspiracy indictments, the U. S. Secretary of Commerce convened in 1961 a Business Ethics Advisory Council to encourage voluntary improvement in business conduct. Surveys of businessmen conducted at that time indicated an awareness of social issues and a concern that business practices had not kept up with social standards of conduct.[2] At that time, companies were achieving greater public visibility and engendering increased public interest in business morality. Today it is reported by observers of the business scene that the standards of morality in American business are at an all-time high but that this still leave room for improvement.[3]

The businessman currently finds himself in a moral quandary. While society may view standards of morality in business at an all-time high, the businessman apparently harbors some doubt as to what is and what is not moral behavior. Several of the factors described in the introduction to the section on foreign bribes contribute to this condition. Certainly one reason for this condition during the last few years is the rapidly changing character of our physical environment and accompanying values. In turn, the increasing size and pervasiveness of modern business organizations have also added to such change. This has resulted in companies impinging on additional dimensions of their environment and, in turn, being affected by new and different environmental elements. Awareness of these new interrelationships has been described as a form of socialization, a process by which a company recognizes that it possesses relevant publics beyond its traditional market relationships.[4] Pressures often brought to bear by these publics on the company may have a moral dimension. A company then must establish a set of priorities by which it can effectively relate to these often conflicting demands. Priorities may differ between the organization as an entity and individuals within the organization. Also, decisions viewed as moral by one relevant public may be viewed differently by others. That is, a businessman often thinks he is acting morally but his behavior is not considered moral by observers.

One apparent example of such circumstances came during the 1972 presidential election campaign. A law governing campaign contributions was broken time and again by many of this country's largest companies and industry associations. This was dramatically brought to public attention during the Watergate investigations. The number of companies was large enough that a set procedure emerged for disclosure by companies and actions by the courts.

Several of these companies emphasized that a great amount of pressure was placed on them by election campaign organizations to make the contributions. Of course, with such large contributions, pressures may also be brought in the other direction by the business organization making the donation.

The Gulf Oil Corporation was one of the companies that made illegal contributions during the 1972 presidential election.

FOOTNOTES

[1] George Steiner, *Business and Society* (New York: Random House, 1971), pp. 218–219.

[2] Keith Davis and Robert Blomstrom, *Business and Society: Environment and Responsibility* (New York: McGraw-Hill Book Company, 1975), p. 172.

[3] Steiner, *Business and Society*, p. 221.

[4] Lee Preston and James Post, *Private Management and Public Policy* (Englewood Cliffs, New Jersey: Prentice-Hall, Inc., 1975), pp. 43–54.

Illegal Political Contributions by Gulf Oil Corporation

Gulf Oil Corporation was incorporated in Pennsylvania on August 9, 1922 and since that time has acquired the business and properties of various subsidiaries. These acquisitions have resulted in the company becoming the sixth largest industrial company by sales in the United States.[1] Gulf Oil is engaged primarily in the purchase, production, transportation, refining, and sale of crude petroleum and products derived from that basic raw material. The company also is involved heavily in exploratory and development work in order to provide for future oil requirements. Refined products consist principally of gasoline, residual fuel oil, distillate fuel oil, lubricating oils, industrial naphtha, kerosene, petrolatum, and wax. The company also produces such auxiliary products as natural gas, chemicals, tires, and batteries. In addition, Gulf has established itself in the nuclear energy field by uranium exploration and mining, high temperature gas production, cooled reactor production, and nuclear fuel manufacture and reclamation. [2]

Election Campaign Contributions

On August 13, 1973, the *Wall Street Journal* reported that Gulf Oil Corporation joined the growing list of major corporations disclosing illegal contributions to President Nixon's reelection campaign. [3] The information was made public as a result of a lawsuit filed by Common Cause, a public interest lobbying group, which forced the White House to release a list showing Gulf's contribution. Gulf acknowledged a contribution of $100,000 but said the money was later returned by the Finance Committee to Reelect the President. The acknowledgement followed a statement, by the office of special Watergate prosecutor Archibald Cox, that the investigation into illegal campaign financing would be stepped up in the coming week.

As the investigation accelerated, a pattern of corporate disclosure seemed to be emerging:

> —The major corporations are deciding to disclose such gifts, apparently in hopes of protecting their officers from jail sentences.
>
> —The corporations, however, are insisting and have obtained the agreement of the special prosecutor's office, that they be allowed to handle the disclosures in their own way. This means disclosure from corporate headquarters rather than from Washington and, so the pattern has been, on late Friday after the stock market closes and when their action will be reported in the poorly read Saturday newspapers.
>
> —The disclosure procedure, in many cases, takes the form of a request for a refund of the illegal contributions from the Finance Committee to Re-elect the President, which has adopted the practice of granting the request promptly. In the Gulf case, the committee issued a statement declaring that it hadn't known that the money came from corporate funds.
>
> —The Cox office puts out a stock statement offering 'mitigating circumstances' to those who voluntarily disclose illegal contributions. In the Gulf disclosure, however, the Cox office further defined its offer to apply only to those who volunteer disclosure in good faith. 'If a corporation's offices disclose illegal corporate contributions only after our investigation focused on that particular corporation,' a spokesman said, 'one might question how voluntary that decision is.' [4]

Gulf Oil did willingly report that it contributed $100,000 of corporate funds to Nixon's campaign, without either the knowledge or approval of its board, because, and here they emphasized the fact, there was a tremendous amount of political pressure. According to B. R. Dorsey, Gulf chairman of the board, the pressure was intense and, at the time, it was thought to be irresistible by the company's Washington representative. The Gulf contributions were made in the name of the company's Washington representative and his wife, Mr. and Mrs. Claude C. Wild, Jr., and were delivered in two installments of $50,000 in 1971 and early 1972. Dorsey further stated that the company wasn't seeking any favors and didn't have any corporate activity under government scrutiny.[5]

James E. Lee, Gulf's president, stated he was on assignment in London as head of Gulf's eastern hemisphere operations at the time of the illegal contribution. He did not know about it and said he did not want to know about it. Lee believed that the contribution came to light as a result of the investigation following the Watergate affair and he was very surprised that such a thing could have happened to Gulf.[6]

Gulf Pleads Guilty

On November 14, 1973 Gulf Oil Corporation pleaded guilty in a federal district court in Washington to charges of contributing $100,000 to President Nixon's reelection campaign plus $15,000 to the campaign of Representative Wilbur Mills (D-Ark) and $10,000 to that of Senator Henry Jackson (D-Wash).[7] Claude C. Wild, Jr. pleaded guilty to charges that he consented to the $100,000 contribution to the Nixon campaign. The Federal District Court imposed the maximum fines of $5000 for the company and $1000 for Wild. Criminal charges, which also could have resulted in prison sentences, were filed by the office of the new special Watergate prosecutor, Leon Jaworski.

The two congressmen involved immediately took action in response to the disclosure. A spokesman for Senator Jackson pointed out that the money was received as a personal contribution to the campaign committee from Claude Wild with no knowledge that corporate funds were involved. It was also made public that the campaign committee's treasurer had previously told the Senate Watergate Committee about the contribution.[8]

An aide to Representative Mills noted that the congressman had stated that he hadn't at any time been associated with any fund-raising activities and had no knowledge of this particular contribution. Mills indicated he would determine if a refund was in order. If a decision was made to make the refund, the congressman further indicated that he would make the refund from his personal funds, mainly because the campaign committee's books already had been closed.[9]

Cloyd Mellot, an attorney for Gulf, told the Federal District Court that the company had established "procedures and controls" under the direction of its chief financial officer to ensure that illegal contributions would "never again" be made. He further made the point that the political system does exert pressures on corporations and officers to make contributions to campaigns, and that neither Gulf nor Wild had benefited from the campaign in return for the contributions. In pleading for a lenient sentence for Wild, Mellot observed that his crime wasn't a "crime of violence." But the court declared that "it may be a much worse crime because what you're doing is corrupting our government." [10] The court in this instance used the situation to point to the seriousness of this crime and to further point out that it takes two to commit such an offense. It observed that it was the special prosecutor's job to complete the work of bringing guilty parties to trial.

Testimony indicated that Gulf was "solicited" by Lee Nunn, an official of the reelection committee, whose authenticity was attested to by John Mitchell while he was still Attorney General. Gulf submitted the requested amount using money from its Bahamian subsidiary on the theory that it was both "discreet" and "close." After hearing the testimony, Senator Sam Ervin, chairman of the Senate committee, observed that the corporate community seemed to feel it needed a friend in government and that the way political campaigns had been financed in the past amounted to extortion. [11]

Shareholder Suits

On January 7, 1974, word was leaked that Gulf shareholders would file suit demanding that corporate executives involved in the illegal campaign contributions be punished. [12] The suit called for the board to slap heavy fines against the executives named in the criminal charges filed in 1973 by the Watergate special prosecution force. The suit also demanded that the executives pay any money spent by the company in defending themselves. The action against Gulf was filed on behalf of the Project on Corporate Responsibility, according to Joseph Gebhardt, a Washington lawyer representing the shareholder group. This was an organization initially formed by Ralph Nader to pressure the General Motors Corporation to become more sensitive to its social responsibilities.

Several events then occured subsequent to the first court settlement of shareholder suits. It was first reported that Wild, the individual in whose name the illegal contribution was made, had resigned his position as Gulf's Washington representative. Wild's resignation came to light in a proxy statement mailed to shareholders prior to the company's April 23 annual meeting. The company indicated it was considering whether to seek reimbursement from its former Washington based representative for the $5000 fine paid by the corporation in connection with the illegal political gift. Gulf also indicated in the proxy that it had established a policy that would prevent a recurrence of the incident. The policy required that responsible corporate officials advise the company in writing every year that they had not made any illegal political contributions. Shareholders had planned to introduce at the annual meeting a proposal barring all political contributions by Gulf. Company officials claimed that the new policy eliminated any need for such proposals. [13]

In June 1974 began the first court hearings on the shareholder suits. Gulf again promised in court to tighten its procedures to prevent any further illegal political donations. The rule-tightening called for, among other things, the board of directors to be notified immediately if Gulf were approached by any political unit soliciting an illegal contribution. Also at this time Wild agreed to pay the company $25,000 in connection with past donations.[14]

Part of the settlement reached in court also stipulated that Gulf directors would have the authority to rehire Wild during the following five years so long as it gave 15 days notice to the Project on Corporate Responsibility. There had been some confusion about this part of the settlement because the *Wall Street Journal* had initially reported incorrectly that the company could not rehire Wild for at least five years unless an "emergency situation developed."[15]

Another Accusation Directed at Gulf

Senator Henry Jackson, who had received an illegal gift of at least $10,000 from Gulf, in January 1975 accused a subsidiary of the Gulf Oil Corporation of blackmailing the Defense Department by threatening to cut off certain fuel supplies unless the company was exempted from some legal requirements. Jackson stated that the Gulf Trading Company had failed to renew its supply of a special kind of cold weather fuel for the Navy's Operation Deepfreeze in Antarctica; at the same time it was asking to be freed of an obligation to furnish the cost and pricing data required of all defense contractors. However, it was noted that Gulf had not stated directly that it would cut off supplies if it were required to furnish the data to justify its prices. But the Defense Department had essentially been given a "take it or leave it" proposition. Jackson wanted an investigation on the matter.[16]

Gulf immediately denied the charges and stated that it had submitted a bid on September 27, 1974 to supply the fuel for Operation Deepfreeze. Gulf further argued that it had asked to have the cost accounting regulation waived, a request that had been granted in the past. The grounds for such a waiver were that foreign operations that supply the fuel use accounting procedures set by laws of those nations and the information is not readily transferable nor is it relevant to United States accounting requirements. A company official stated that Gulf had been making these specialized products in its refinery in Venezuela where the Navy was expected to pick it up by January 9. He further said, "We don't have the contract as yet and we know that the regulation has not yet been waived. We nevertheless will have the fuel available and will do our best to abide by the requirements of the regulation."[17]

The SEC Files Suit

The Securities and Exchange Commission (SEC), in March 1975 charged the Gulf Oil Corporation with falsifying its reports to hide the existence of a $10 million secret fund that was used to make illegal political contributions between 1960 and 1974. The violation of the securities laws for which Gulf was charged involved the alleged falsification of a long list of corporate reports and filings in which the true financial condition of the company was obscured, to the extent that the $10 million in diverted funds was improperly hidden. The SEC simultaneously announced that the company had agreed to an order against it that would bar it from taking similar illegal action. As a part of this requirement the company took action to discover just how the illegal fund was set up and by whom and to correct its false reports.

The SEC complaint did not specify to whom the illegal contributions were given. However, it was known that an excess of $10 million in corporate funds had been laundered by being channeled to Bahamas Exploration, Ltd., a wholly owned Gulf subsidiary, and other subsidiaries, beginning in 1960. A total of $5.4 million apparently went to Bahamas Exploration and was converted to cash and returned to the United States for political contributions and related expenses, most of which were unlawful.[18]

According to testimony that was taken in late 1973 by the Senate Watergate Committee, Gulf had a system whereby Wild, in Washington, made the decision as to which political candidates should receive campaign contributions. He then ordered the controller of the various Bahamian subsidiaries, William Viglia, to transmit the needed amounts of laundered cash to him for transmission to the candidates. Mr. Viglia had since left the company. The SEC complaint named only Wild as a defendant and no agreement had yet been made to a settlement of the charge against him. It was curious to some that Wild was the only individual named as a defendant. However, the SEC would not discuss the matter. The SEC complaint also asked the district court to order Wild to repay Gulf all corporate funds that he had illegally donated to political campaigns or used for other unlawful purposes.[19]

At this point in the investigation other members of the oil industry became quite critical of Gulf. The company was frequently described as something of an outsider or a maverick company in the industry. The company was not only criticized for the secret fund but also because of its stand in Washington. Wild, his actions, and his ties were highlighted. Industry executives seemed to be generally angered because they felt Gulf was drawing unfavorable attention to the oil industry at a time when the industry was already under strong criticism in Congress because of high profits, the Arab embargo, and certain tax laws such as the depletion allowance.[20]

Wild Is Rehired

Shortly after the first charges were brought against Gulf by the SEC it was revealed that the company had rehired Wild. He had apparently been secretly rehired as a consultant the previous August. The rehiring was acknowledged at the same time the company admitted in its annual report to shareholders that between 1960 and 1973 it had channeled about $10.3 million in corporate cash into secret funds from which illegal contributions were made.

When the rehiring was made public a great deal of pressure was exerted on Gulf for it to explain its action. Company officials argued that Gulf had decided to retain Wild because pending legislation in Washington, including moves to abolish the depletion allowance, could have a very substantial impact on the organization. However, Wild's retainer and exact duties were not disclosed. At this time, Gulf reiterated that it had voluntarily approached the special prosecutor in July 1973 when it appeared likely that a lawsuit filed by Common Cause would force the White House to release a list showing Gulf's $100,000 donation. Gulf again maintained that Wild was solely responsible for the illegal contributions, acting without the knowledge or approval of the company's senior management and board. Wild, in fact, told the Senate Watergate Committee that he had made the contributions without telling anyone else at Gulf. [21]

Other Lawsuits Are Filed

A second charge was filed in federal court by the SEC alleging that Gulf and Wild also violated the agency's full-disclosure regulation. The regulation requires the public disclosure of important business and financial information to enable investors to make informed decisions. It was alleged that the company failed to include in its proxy statements and annual reports the fact that it had created a secret fund of corporate moneys for the making of unlawful political contributions and other purposes. The SEC also charged that Gulf's balance sheets were understated because they failed to reflect the slush fund's value. [22]

Just four days after the second SEC suit was filed the first of several shareholder suits was filed in federal court. The suit was an attempt to force eight present and past officers and directors and Price Waterhouse & Co., the company's independent auditor, to pay the corporation $20 million in damages. Charges were filed by William Shlensky, an owner of 13 shares of Gulf stock. He charged that the defendants secretly converted and wasted corporate funds for illegal purposes such as unlawful political contributions while refusing to disclose the existence or purpose of those funds on Gulf's balance sheet. The suit further contended that Price Waterhouse willfully and negligently violated its professional duties to Gulf and its stockholders and was thus guilty of malpractice. [23]

Later in April 1975, a second shareholder suit was filed against Gulf officials based on the SEC charges. The suit filed on behalf of Fred and Doris Horenstein, owners of 300 shares of Gulf stock, charged Dorsey, Gulf chairman of the board, and nine other current directors, as well as Price Waterhouse, with failing to have adequate procedures to prevent the unlawful diversion of corporate funds. All of the defendants were accused of filing false and misleading proxy statements with the SEC from 1960 to the date of the suit because they didn't disclose the slush fund's existence. The suit also noted that neither the Gulf Good Government Fund, the corporation's vehicle for legitimate political contributions, nor any of the top 50 Gulf executives was listed as contributing to the Nixon campaign. The suit asked the court to require the ten directors and three former executives to reimburse the company the money channeled into the slush fund. [24]

Slush Fund Details

As a result of these lawsuits the details of how Gulf managed its massive slush fund in almost complete secrecy for 13 years came to light. The details included the following:

> —Although Bahamas Exploration bylaws required an annual audit of its books, Gulf's independent auditor indicated none was conducted in recent years.
> —Gulf apparently transferred much of the $10.3 million to Bahamas Exploration as "capital investments" made with after-tax dollars. Such a move could help minimize its vulnerability to many of the possible tax-fraud headaches facing other companies that charged off illegal political donations as business expenses in their U. S. operations.
> —Illegal contributions from the slush fund apparently went to as many as two dozen congressional candidates during the election year of 1970 and the prior year. These congressional contributions totaled at least $60,000.[25]

The Internal Revenue Service had been intently investigating the slush fund, but Gulf maintained it wasn't aware of any "tax problems" stemming from its illegal political activity.

The key man in the day-to-day operation of the slush fund, William Viglia, refused to discuss the slush fund or who authorized him to follow Wild's orders. He referred all questioners to members of top-level management. It did not appear that Viglia could be forced to testify about his role in the slush fund, since he is outside the United States.

Is Gulf Stonewalling It?

Despite what information had been made public to this time, the *Wall Street Journal* commented that it seemed clear that the full story of the slush fund and the millions in illegal contributions made from it were emerging more slowly at Gulf than the details of secret political operations at other companies. The article further accused Gulf management of "stonewalling it" rather than actually cooperating with the investigation.[26]

The paper noted that expanded revelations about the slush fund generally came only when government investigators and others had turned up additional evidence. Gulf officials argued that their primary concern was protection of the corporation and the right of executives to play "hardball" when their jobs and reputations were at stake. The company also felt that stockholders did not have the right to know everything.[27]

Also it was not made clear who knew about the slush fund. Wild testified that he referred to the $100,000 Nixon contribution during a 1972 conversation with William Henry, a Gulf executive vice president and one of the company's half dozen top officers in Washington. Yet Henry would not comment.

Further, it was not determined whether or not Wild was the only officer to mastermind the operation of the slush fund since its initiation in 1960. Since Wild joined Gulf as a legislative representative in 1959, it appeared unlikely that a person in that position would have immediately been capable of wielding the clout necessary to start moving hundreds of thousands of dollars around the corporation for unstated purposes. Certainly some executives other than Wild in Gulf's U. S. operations would have had to approve the "capital investments" totaling $10.3 million in the near-dormant Bahamian subsidiary.[28]

Even members of the company itself were concerned about the question of why Gulf quietly retained Wild as a consultant when it publicly branded him as the sole culprit in the affair. Dorsey attempted to quiet these concerns by pointing out that Wild had made the illegal donations in what he believed to be the best interests of the corporation and the payments were made without personal gain or profit.[29]

Those questioning Gulf's sincerity were also raising questions about what happened to the results of the "thorough" investigation initiated by the Gulf board in August 1973. Gulf never indicated whether the probe was concluded or what it discovered. In any case, it was clear that, whatever the results, none of the information would be shared with the stockholders.

Another issue brought to light during the shareholder suits was the role of Price Waterhouse, the company's independent auditor. Price Waterhouse had indicated Gulf never asked it to conduct any special checks that might have helped ascertain more quickly the full extent of the slush fund's activities.[30]

It appeared at least to many outside observers that Gulf was creating unnecessary headaches and public relations damage for itself by taking such a hard line on the slush fund matter. Neither Gulf's management nor its board of directors publicly expressed any remorse or regret to shareholders about the creation of the slush fund or the illegal contributions. In its annual report mailed to stockholders Gulf continued to maintain that all of the $10.3 million was used in an effort to further a corporate purpose believed at the time to be in the best interest of the company and its stockholders. One of the lawyers involved in the case stated: "Gulf is not humble."[31]

Watergate Special Prosecution Force Reopens Investigation

In April 1975 information reached the public that the Watergate special prosecution force was reopening the investigation of illegal political contributions by Gulf. Several rumors were floating around the Washington press. Apparently several special prosecution investigators expressed doubt privately that the Gulf consultant, Wild, was actually the sole executive involved in the slush funds operation. Also most of the charges to which Gulf and Wild pleaded guilty were based on information that the lawyer representing both the corporation and the former vice president (Wild) voluntarily provided to the special prosecutor's office.[32]

The Annual Stockholders Meeting—1975

During the annual meeting held in late April, stockholders repeatedly bom-
barded Gulf chairman, Dorsey, with questions about the slush fund. The chairman would not respond in detail about the $10.3 million secret fund. He did dis-
close that the consulting arrangement with Wild had been terminated, due to the
enactment of major tax legislation, which ended the need for his services. The
arrangement was to have ended April 1, although a company official had twice
stated during April that Wild was still a consultant for the company.[33]

One stockholder tried unsuccessfully to have each director tell the meeting
whether he had ever questioned the slush fund but Dorsey refused to let the
directors answer the question. The chairman pointed out that a special stockholders'
meeting would be called for election of new directors if a review committee investigating the secret political contributions uncovered information that led the board
or the SEC to conclude that new elections of directors should be held. Dorsey
commented further that he believed there was a feeling that possibly the board and
the officers had not been properly concerned about the matter. He felt, however,
that no incident in his 30-odd years with the company had caused the company
more concern or more grief. He believed there was a great deal about the fund that
had been misunderstood, but he pointed out that it had been a grievous affair and
the officers of the company had taken it very seriously and were very concerned
about it.[34]

Finally in response to a stockholder question, Price Waterhouse volunteered
that no member of the accounting firm had any knowledge of the political contributions until the SEC published the charges.[35]

Foreign Contributions

Just prior to the company's annual meeting Gulf's top officials disclosed additional uses of the $10.3 million slush fund. They told the government that politi-
cians in a foreign country compelled the company to pay $4 million in two succes-
sive cash "contributions" in order to stay in business there. The SEC was told that
identification of the recipients of the extorted payments would jeopardize Gulf investments of $700 million in that country. The company emphasized that the
moneys were not paid as a result of requests but as a result of specific and absolute
demands made for contributions to a political party. According to Gulf, the political
party was still in existence and the leaders of that party were still in office. Gulf was
also required to pay approximately $200,000 in order to obtain permits necessary to
begin operating a foreign oil installation in which the company had just invested
$150 million. This payment was made in the same country as the others.[36]

The amounts disclosed accounted for much of the $4.9 million the SEC had
charged that Gulf distributed overseas in cash between 1960 and 1973. At this point
there was some question among members of the SEC as to whether or not to push
for further disclosure. Investors had a right to know if the company resorted to the

use of under-the-table payments to win business opportunities, yet some members expressed the belief that detailed disclosure of foreign payoffs could jeopardize a company's business dealings and assets in certain countries.[37]

Testimony did disclose that the payments again were charged to the Bahamian subsidiary as "expenses." Also an audit of the subsidiary had been stopped by Gulf executives after these payments.[38]

Shortly after the initial disclosure of the foreign payments, officials in Venezuela and Ecuador denied that Gulf was required to pay $4 million to operate in their countries.[39] Two days after this denial Venezuela ordered Gulf to say within 48 hours whether Venezuelan officials or politicians were involved in charges that the company had bribed politicians. The Venezuelan government threatened that if Gulf failed to clarify the allegations by 6:00 P.M. of the stated date, it would suspend all company activities in the country. The decision to ask for clarification was made by President Perez and his cabinet with the support of the political parties. Also at this time the Venezuelan congress opened investigations into the reported $4 million contributions.[40]

The following day Gulf denied that the political contributions involved Venezuela or Ecuador, but declined to identify the country involved.[41]

That same day Bolivia demanded that Gulf disclose whether any of the $4 million in payoffs had gone to politicians in that country. Gulf replied that it was investigating the possibility that Bolivian officials were involved. However, if Bolivia was the country to which contributions were made, Gulf's original statement had to have been highly inaccurate. Gulf did not have any assets to lose in Bolivia, since the company's operations were nationalized in 1969. Gulf did promise to make known all facts as soon as they became available and also commented that a fear of jeopardizing foreign investments wasn't the only reason the company was refusing to name the countries involved in its overseas contributions.[42]

Bolivia then elected to employ the same strategy used by the other Latin American countries. Bolivia gave Gulf 48 hours to reply to a request about involvement in that country or have payments stopped on the compensation. Bolivia was paying Gulf for oil installations nationalized in 1969.[43] Gulf then told the Bolivian government that it was not the nation involved in the $4 million contribution. However, Gulf also stated it was still investigating whether any political contributions were made in Bolivia.[44]

Unlike the other countries involved, Peru gave no hint of its intentions. On May 14, 1975, the Peruvian revolutionary government announced the cessation of all operations in Peru of Gulf Oil, and the immediate expropriation of all its assets in Peru.[45] Peru's government stated that because of Gulf's "notorious immoral conduct" it was taking over Gulf's marketing operations. The company calculated this consisted mainly of 13 service stations worth a total of $2 million.[46]

Recipients of Contributions Identified

After a great deal of pressure, Dorsey, on May 19, identified the recipients of the Gulf contributions. He itemized each of the secret payments. The ruling political party of President Park Chung Hee of South Korea received $4 million. The gift of a helicopter valued at $110,000 was sent to the late President Rene Barrientos of Bolivia and $350,000 was sent to the late president's political party. Gulf also donated $50,000 to finance Arab propaganda in the United States.[47]

As one might suspect the announcement by Dorsey provoked reactions abroad as well as annoyance on the Senate subcommittee. Leaders of the political opposition to President Park expressed outrage at Gulf's $4 million contribution to his ruling party. It was claimed that President Park narrowly won reelection in 1971 with Gulf's help. The following year Park proclaimed martial law and in May 1975 he banned all internal dissent, possibly in anticipation of Gulf's disclosure. As a result of the edict, South Korean newspapers did not report Dorsey's testimony. At the same time the Bolivian cabinet, after an emergency session, demanded total clarification of this matter in order to apply the maximum punishment established by law to those found guilty.[48]

Dorsey testified that Gulf contributed to the Korean Democratic Republican party in response to a demand by high party officials that was accompanied by pressure that left little to the imagination as to what would occur if the company chose to turn its back on the request. He was told by the fund raisers that all foreign companies were expected to contribute. Dorsey also stated he took full responsibility for the action. He indicated he regretted that the decision to pay had embarrassed Gulf's stockholders and had brought anguish to Gulf employees and those with which the company transacted business around the world.[49]

Apparently only four to six corporate officers were aware of the payoffs and even Dorsey had no knowledge of the Bolivian contributions until just before the company announcement. The funds were channeled through Bahamas Exploration, which now appeared to be virtually a dummy corporation. Dorsey agreed that the reason the funds went through the company was to conceal their origin.[50]

Meanwhile in testimony before the Senate committee, Dorsey argued strongly for the passage of a law that would prohibit payments to foreign officials of the kind made by Gulf. He believed that a law of this kind would permit multinational companies to resist such pressures.[51]

Gulf Official Jailed

The Bolivian government reacted to the disclosure by jailing Gulf's representative to that country and ordering Gulf "criminally prosecuted" for making illegal political contributions. A summons was issued for Dorsey to appear in Bolivian court to name the officials who received $460,000 in contributions. The government also asked the Organization of American States to condemn Gulf for its activities. Gulf stated that its Bolivian chief, Carlos Dorado, was not involved in the company's payments and asked that he be released without delay. Eight days later Dorado was released, after his lawyer argued he had no legal responsibility for the company's contribution.[52]

Internal Investigation

As a part of the consent agreement entered into by Gulf and the SEC following a lawsuit in March 1975, the company was required to conduct an internal investigation to be completed by June 11, 1975. Gulf's board set up a "special review committee" to carry out the investigation. The chairman of the committee was John J. McCloy, who had frequently represented Gulf on various foreign matters.[53] The company indicated that the broad scope of the committee's investigation might carry it beyond the inquiries that produced the $10.3 million slush fund.[54] For this reason the company also announced that the amount of corporate funds it channeled into political activities in the United States and abroad might be found to exceed the original $10.3 million figure. One day after the study was to be completed Gulf asked the SEC for a three-month extension in order to broaden the investigation into payoffs discovered after the original consent agreement had been established. The SEC agreed to the three-month extension.[55]

On July 28, 1975, shortly after the extension was granted, the SEC accused Wild in court of having "substantially hindered" the work of the special review committee. Wild's lawyers argued the assessment was unfair because the committee had never approached their client directly seeking information. However, it was revealed that the committee staff had indirectly sought Wild's cooperation and had been rebuffed.[56]

Wild's lawyers also attempted unsuccessfully to bar the SEC from trying to examine their client under oath. Wild invoked his Fifth Amendment rights in November 1974 in refusing to answer SEC questions about the illegal political donations on the grounds of possible self-incrimination. His lawyers told the court that Wild would again invoke the Fifth Amendment if pressed to identify the recipients of the "donations." It was also confirmed that the Watergate special prosecution force had reopened its investigation of Gulf.[57]

Further Reverberations of the Gulf Contributions

In early fall of 1975, the Internal Revenue Service (IRS) asked the federal court to order Price Waterhouse to turn over certain documents the government wanted in connection with a criminal tax fraud investigation of Gulf's political contributions between 1971 and 1973. The IRS charged that Gulf's independent auditor had refused since last April 1975 to make audit "workplans" and "workpapers" available in response to a government subpoena. The Price Waterhouse partner in charge of the Gulf account stated the firm had "a duty under the law to its clients and their stockholders, as well as to its profession and itself, to resist whatever legal counsel has advised as to be an improper and unlawful demand for all of our files.

We don't believe the IRS is automatically entitled to complete access to all of the audit files that were prepared in our role as the independent auditors of Gulf Oil." [58]

Price Waterhouse stressed that it had given the IRS all the available documents from its files for the entire 14-year period beginning in 1960 that in any way related to the special Gulf subsidiaries that were the subject of IRS investigation. [59]

FOOTNOTES

[1] "The Fortune Directory of the 500 Largest Industrial Corporations," *Fortune*, May 1975, pp. 210–211.

[2] Robert P. Hanson, ed., *Moody's Industrial Manual*, Vol. 1, A-I, 1973 (New York: Moody's Investors Service, Inc., 1972), pp. 679–680.

[3] Monroe W. Karmin, "Firms Disclosing Campaign Gifts to Nixon to Increase; Gulf, Goodyear Reveal Theirs," *The Wall Street Journal*, August 13, 1973, p. 8.

[4] *Ibid.*

[5] *Ibid.*

[6] *Ibid.*

[7] "Two More Firms, Officers Fined for Election Aid: Gulf, Ashland Oil Unit Are Penalized for Giving Funds to Nixon, Other Campaigns," *The Wall Street Journal*, November 14, 1973, p. 48.

[8] *Ibid.*

[9] *Ibid.*

[10] *Ibid.*

[11] "Gulf, Ashland Oil 'Laundered' Their Gifts to Nixon's Campaign via Overseas Units," *The Wall Street Journal*, November 15, 1973, p. 15.

[12] Mitchell C. Lynch, "Shareholders Demand Firms Punish Officers Over Illegal Gifts to Nixon Re-election Drive," *The Wall Street Journal*, January 7, 1974, p. 5.

[13] "Gulf Oil Officer Resigns in Wake of Gift to Nixon," *The Wall Street Journal*, March 20, 1974, p. 4.

[14] "Gulf Vows to Guard Against Illegal Gifts in Settling Lawsuit," *The Wall Street Journal*, June 28, 1974, p. 6.

[15] "Corrections and Amplifications," *The Wall Street Journal*, July 1, 1974, p. 6.

[16] "Oil Company Blackmail Is Alleged by Jackson," *The New York Times*, January 3, 1975, p. 53.

[17] *Ibid.*

[18] Eileen Shanahan, "Gulf Oil Accused by SEC of Hiding $10 Million Fund," *The New York Times*, March 12, 1975, pp. 1, 9.

[19] *Ibid.*

[20] William D. Smith, "Gulf Oil: Maverick Company," *The New York Times*, March 13, 1975, pp. 57, 67.

[21] *Ibid.*

[22] "Again, Political Slush Funds," *Time*, March 24, 1975, p. 54.

[23] "Gulf Oil Holder Sues Certain Officers, Auditor Over Secret Channeling of Funds," *The Wall Street Journal*, March 28, 1975, p. 6.

[24] "Gulf Oil Holders Sue Officials to Reimburse Company $10 Million," *The Wall Street Journal*, April 4, 1975, p. 21.

[25] Byron E. Calame, "Gulf Oil Unit Struck Out as a Driller But Was a 'Gusher' on Political Scene," *The Wall Street Journal*, April 3, 1975, p. 10.

[26] Byron E. Calame, "Stonewalling It at Gulf Oil," *The Wall Street Journal*, April 18, 1975, p. 12.

[27] *Ibid.*

[28] *Ibid.*

[29] *Ibid.*

[30] *Ibid.*

[31] *Ibid.*

[32] Byron E. Calame, "Investigation of Gulf Oil's Political Fund Said to be Reopened by Watergate Office," *The Wall Street Journal*, April 22, 1975, p. 2.

[33] Byron E. Calame, "Gulf Oil's 1st Period Earnings Plunge, Slush Fund Shares Spotlight at Meeting," *The Wall Street Journal*, April 23, 1975, p. 11.

[34] William D. Smith, "Gulf to Change Directors if Warranted by Inquiry," *The New York Times*, April 23, 1975, p. 59.

[35] *Ibid.*

[36] Jerry Landauer, "Costly Concession: Gulf Oil Admits It Paid $4.2 Million to Officials Abroad to Shield Assets," *The Wall Street Journal*, May 2, 1975, pp. 1, 25.

[37] *Ibid.*

[38] *Ibid.*

[39] "Ecuador, Venezuela Deny They Required Payoffs From Gulf Oil," *The Wall Street Journal*, May 5, 1975, p. 20.

[40] "Gulf Oil Is Told by Venezuela to Clarify Bribe Charges There," *The Wall Street Journal*, May 7, 1975, p. 5.

[41] "Gulf Says $4 Million Political Donations Involved Neither Venezuela nor Ecuador," *The Wall Street Journal*, May 8, 1975, p. 9.

[42] "Gulf Studies Possibility Bolivian Figures Were Recipients of Firm's 'Contributions,' " *The Wall Street Journal*, May 9, 1975, p. 10.

[43] William D. Smith, "Gulf Cites Study of Bolivian Role," *The New York Times*, May 9, 1975, p. 47.

[44] "Gulf Oil Corp. Says Bolivia Didn't Get $4 Million Payment," *The Wall Street Journal*, May 12, 1975, p. 2.

[45] "Peru Seizes Gulf Oil Assets," *The Wall Street Journal*, May 14, 1975, p. 3.

[46] Kenneth H. Bacon, "Telling All: Full-Disclosure Push by SEC on Companies Worries Some Critics," *The Wall Street Journal*, May 15, 1975, p. 1.

[47] Jerry Landauer and Kenneth H. Bacon, "Gulf's Account of Political Gifts Abroad Stirs Anger Overseas, Questions at Home," *The Wall Street Journal*, May 19, 1975, p. 2.

[48] *Ibid.*

[49] *Ibid.*

[50] *Ibid.*

[51] *Ibid.*

[52] "Bolivia Judge Orders the Release from Jail of Gulf Oil Official," *The Wall Street Journal*, May 29, 1975, p. 28.

[53] Michael C. Jensen, "More Time Asked for Gulf Inquiry," *The New York Times*, June 12, 1975, pp. 53, 60.

[54] "Gulf Oil Indicates Its Political Donations May Top the $10.3 Million Cited Earlier," *The Wall Street Journal*, June 10, 1975, p. 10.

55 "Gulf Oil Says Panel Studying Payoffs Is Given More Time," *The Wall Street Journal*, June 13, 1975, p. 12.

56 Byron E. Calame, "Ex-Gulf Aide Is Accused of Hindering Panel Investigating Illegal Political Gifts," *The Wall Street Journal*, July 28, 1975, p. 5.

57 *Ibid.*

58 "Gulf Oil Inquiry Leads IRS to Seek an Order for Auditor's Data," *The Wall Street Journal*, September 12, 1975, p. 17.

59 *Ibid.*

QUESTIONS

1. Discuss the nature of Gulf's coping strategy after discovery of the illegal contributions. What sanctions does it attempt to avoid?
2. Discuss the role of the Securities and Exchange Commission as it relates to Gulf's illegal donation to the Nixon campaign organization and as it relates to the South Korean political party.
3. What social expectations appear to be the main influence on Gulf's decisions to make the political donations? Discuss these circumstances as they may affect a firm's responsiveness to the environment.
4. Discuss the concept of role strain as it relates to Gulf in this case.
5. How would you characterize Gulf's top management in terms of the classification presented in the first section of this text?
6. What were the major ramifications on the environment of Gulf's payment to the South Korean political party?
7. Discuss the nature of the moral dilemma for multinational companies such as Gulf as opposed to national conglomerates. Explain.
8. What in your view would have been the consequences of Gulf's not contributing the $100,000 to the Nixon campaign?
9. What are the implications for private industry of the role played by the Nixon campaign organization as described in this case?
10. What would be the impact of a federal law making illegal payments to foreign officials by multinational companies?

CHAPTER 12

THE
ENERGY
QUESTION

CASE 14
THE OIL CRISIS

The energy crisis has been an emergent one for a number of years. Economists, politicians, academicians, and environmentalists have been urging the United States to develop a comprehensive energy policy that addresses both sides of the issue—our ever-increasing demand for energy and the dwindling supply of fossil fuels. The issues are global and complex. They are politically and economically the most important issues facing the future. Our life style, our standard of living, our international relations are all oriented toward the extravagant use of energy.

The crisis in the marketplace precipitated by the Arab oil boycott has brought the problem to the forefront of political debate. One thing seems certain: energy is going to increase in price. How to pay for it as a nation remains to be decided. When prices increase rapidly, the typical reaction is to look for a scapegoat, not a reason. This case in some respects describes the scapegoating of the oil industry.

Energy Use, Oil Supply, and the American Oil Industry

The Oil Crisis

In recent years there has been concern expressed by many groups in society about our use of energy. Conservationists are concerned about the impact of increased energy use on our health, our natural environment, and our future economic well-being. Economists have pointed out that the United States' economy is highly dependent upon the availability of abundant supplies of energy and, indeed, our high standard of living has resulted from the plentiful supply of cheap energy. But the era of cheap energy may have ended for the United States in the decade of the seventies and a period of national energy conservation appears to have begun.

The chief source of energy in the United States has been petroleum. More than 75 percent of our nation's energy has come from petroleum and one of our strengths as an industrial power has been domestic petroleum production. However, in recent years increases in domestic production have fallen behind increases in the demand for petroleum products in the United States and we have turned to international markets to fuel our growing needs. For the United States, at least, this growing dependence on foreign oil has resulted in a major reappraisal of foreign policy, domestic energy production, energy sources, and industry practices. Figure 12.1 demonstrates:

> U.S. self-sufficiency in oil ended by 1970. Although consumption grew less rapidly in the United States than it did in the rest of the world, the nation was already consuming so much that each year's increment was very large. The discovery of new domestic supplies of oil and natural gas barely kept up with the depletion of known reserves. Domestic production leveled off and by 1968, spare capacity fell below the level of oil imports. By 1973, imports had grown to one-third of U.S. oil consumption, and because consumption was growing more rapidly than production, the nation's dependence on foreign oil continued to increase. Prior to the crisis of October 1973, it was projected that U.S. imports of oil and gas would be 11 million barrels per day by 1980 and 14 million barrels by 1985, or approximately half of U.S. oil consumption. Total energy imports were projected to be one-fourth of total U.S. energy consumption in 1985.[1]

This crisis of October 1973 was precipitated by international political as well as economic conditions in major oil exporting nations in the Arab world. All during

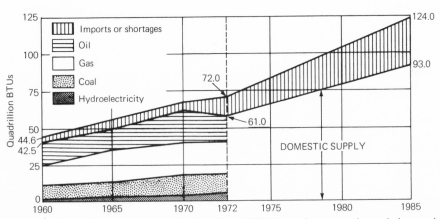

FIGURE 12.1 U.S. energy gap projected to 1985, based on supply and demand trends prior to oil boycott.

Source: *U.S. Congress. Joint Committee on Atomic Energy, "Understanding the National Energy Dilemma"* (Washington, D.C.: U.S. Government Printing Office, 1973), foldout 'L.'

the 1960s there was a buyer's market internationally. In addition, the United States had imposed quotas on oil imports, leaving the already soft market to the other industrialized nations of the world. As a result of the low prices the major oil exporting nations, led by the Arab countries, formed the Organization of Petroleum Exporting Countries (OPEC) to gain control over both international oil production and oil prices. Early in 1970 the international oil scene began to change. Production was curtailed in some of the producing nations. The Arab-Israeli conflict had kept the Suez Canal closed resulting in increased transportation costs for Middle East oil, and OPEC was able to increase oil prices and oil taxes dramatically. Table 1 is a chronology of Middle East price increases.

In addition to price increases, Arab exporting countries attempted to bring political pressure to bear on those industrialized countries of the world dependent upon Middle East oil. The Arab-Israeli conflict had long been a source of international controversy whereby Israel and the Arab nations attempted to align the United States and Western Europe with their respective causes. Israel appeared to have more support in the West than most of her Arab foes. In 1973 another round of the Middle East war broke out and the oil producing nations cut off oil shipments to the United States and other countries that aligned themselves with Israel.

The immediate effect of the Arab oil embargo was to cause gasoline and heating oil shortages to appear in many parts of the United States but this soon ended

TABLE 1 The Dramatic Jump in Middle East Crude Prices

Period	Posted price *	Arab tax	Total cost (production cost plus tax)
1960–65	$1.80	$0.82	$0.92
1966–67	1.80	0.85	0.95
1968–69	1.80	0.88	0.98
Jan. 1–Nov. 14, 1970	1.80	0.91	1.01
Nov. 15, 1970–Feb. 14, 1971	1.80	0.99	1.10
Feb. 15–May 31, 1971	2.18	1.26	1.37
June 1, 1971–Jan. 19, 1972	2.28	1.32	1.43
Jan. 20, 1972–Jan. 1, 1973	2.48	1.44	1.55
Jan. 1–Mar. 31, 1973	2.59	1.51	1.62
Apr. 1–May 31, 1973	2.75	1.61	1.71
June 1973	2.90	1.70	1.80
July 1973	2.95	1.74	1.84
Aug. 1973	3.07	1.80	1.90
Oct. 1–Oct. 15, 1973	3.01	1.77	1.87
Oct. 16–Dec. 31, 1973	5.12	3.05	3.15
Jan. 1, 1974	11.56	7.00	7.10

* Posted price is the base on which OPEC countries figure their tax; it bears little relationship to the producers' selling price.

Source: *Business Week*, February 2, 1974, p. 54.

with the lifting of the embargo in 1974. However, the long-term repercussions, both political and economic, were still being felt in the United States. The long lines at gasoline stations, the obvious hardships that occurred in some parts of the country because of short supplies of fuels, and the sharp increases in gasoline and fuel oil prices precipitated a policy debate in government and among oil companies. The consuming electorate focused its anger and frustration on government and the oil industry. The oil industry blamed federal policies for the crisis and Congress began investigations in search of causes, solutions, and scapegoats.

The View From Mobil—What Went Wrong [2]

The Arab oil embargo focused public attention on energy problems as no other issue could. Shortages and high prices at the gasoline pump dramatically demonstrated what many economists, government agencies, and the petroleum industry had been saying for a decade. The United States was increasing petroleum consumption faster than domestic production capacity and therefore was becoming dependent upon foreign sources—mainly Middle Eastern oil. As a result of this dependence on foreign oil the Arab nations were able to disrupt economic and political balances in the United States. The domestic oil industry came under intense pressure to do something about the shortages quickly and Mobil, Exxon, Sohio, and others began a media campaign to defend their actions. Mobil Oil Company was and continues to be an articulate spokesman for the gasoline industry, and this firm's views are widely adhered to by many of the other major gasoline producers. Mobil attributes the oil crisis to several sources:

First, the federal Mandatory Oil Import Program did not limit the importation of low-cost foreign oil sufficiently to provide incentives to increase domestic production.

Second, environmentalists and politicians reacted with hostility against off-shore oil exploration and legal action against the oil companies delayed large-scale exploration. "In short, the nation badly overreacted to off-shore drilling in the wake of the Santa Barbara spill [in 1969]. As a consequence, the United States has lot vital time when off-shore exploration could have been taking place."

Third, after discovery of large reserves in Alaska in 1968, pipeline construction was delayed as a result of the 1969 National Environmental Policy Act, which required that a detailed environmental impact statement be prepared. The environmental study took two years and cost $6 million.

"The total result was to delay construction work on the line until 1974, five years later. Proponents of the line protested in vain that hundreds of test borings had been made to select a route that would take the line through rocky and stable areas for most of its journey and to design the pipeline so that the permafrost would not melt. Once the issue had gone to the courts, construction was postponed until the energy crisis made it apparent that the line was vital to the national interest."

Fourth, concern over federal air pollution standards caused a switch to fuel oil away from high sulfur coal in many industries. This widened the gap between consumption and production of domestic oil as did the new standards for automobile emissions. Furthermore, the company stated:

> In 1967, Mobil Oil Corporation and the Ford Motor Company agreed on the basic arrangement for an Inter-Industry Emission Control program (IIEC). The IIEC soon included 13 oil and auto companies. By 1970 it had developed emission-control systems so effective they could be engineered to meet the needs that were then foreseen for the 1980s.
>
> The IIEC goals—established in 1967—were about the same as those proposed to Congress in 1970 by the Federal Department of Health, Education and Welfare.
>
> But Congress chose to ignore the HEW proposals, and enacted legislation that required far more severe standards to be met by 1975.
>
> At that time Congress had no ideas what sort of ambient air standards were needed, how much these emission-control levels would contribute toward achieving those air-quality standards, or even whether the technology could be developed to meet the requirements of the law. Congress simply passed a law decreeing that it be done.
>
> Congress also had no idea of the lead times involved. The amendments to the Clean Air Act were passed at the very end of 1970, which gave the auto makers just about two years to freeze a design and start preparing for mass production.
>
> The direct result was the catalytic converter. It was the only device that could be developed, even partially proven, and engineered, within the allotted time frame.
>
> Ironically, the Environmental Protection Agency has now announced that the catalytic converter may cause emissions even more harmful than those it was designed to prevent. Although cars with catalytic converters do emit fewer hydrocarbons than those without them, it appears that they add sulfuric acid mists.
>
> This sequence of events illustrates the very real risks involved when laws are passed hastily by legislators who do not understand their implications. The decisions in the early 1970s cost the public billions of dollars, increased national consumption of petroleum, and created new problems for the environment.

This reasoning is not without merit; however, there is more to explain the problem than Mobil has pointed out. Table 2 reviews gasoline supply and demand during 1972 and 1973 with forecasts made for 1974 and 1975. Forecast A was made in 1973 and assumes a slight increase in refinery efficiency in the United States. However, the point to be observed is that U.S. refineries in 1973 were operating at a high percentage of capacity and 92 percent is considered the highest sustainable utilization rate. Therefore, not only had demand in the U.S. outpaced oil production, but it also had exceeded domestic refinery capacity. In other words, regardless of crude oil supplies, the U.S. oil industry had not invested sufficient capital in new refineries to avoid dependence upon foreign oil.

TABLE 2 Gasoline Supply and Demand, 1972–75 (In thousands barrels per day)

	1972	1973	1974(A)	1974(B)	1975(A)	1975(B)
Refinery capacity	11,210	11,350	11,500	11,500	11,650	11,500
Runs	9,815	10,410	10,638	10,580	10,776	10,580
Percent	(87.9)	(91.7)	(92.5)	(92.0)	(92.5)	(29.0)
Unfinished	102	110	110	110	110	110
Refinery input (excludes natural gas liquids)	9,947	10,520	10,748	10,690	10,886	10,690
Gasoline yields	46.9	47.0	48.0	48.0	48.0	48.0
Gasoline:						
Refinery output	4,615	4,947	5,159	5,131	5,225	5,131
Natural gas liquids	719	784	780	780	780	780
Total refinery output	5,454	5,731	5,939	5,911	6,005	5,911
Imports	18	145	237	265	478	572
Net flow to and from PAD V	(−17)	(−64)	(−64)	(−64)	(−64)	(−64)
Supply	5,455	5,813	6,112	6,112	6,419	6,419
Demand	5,473	5,783	6,083	6,083	6,390	6,390
Change in stocks (million barrels)	—	(+10.8)	(+10.4)	(+10.4)	(+10.7)	—
Stocks end of year (million barrels)	190.5	201.3	211.7	211.7	222.4	222.4
Days supply *	34.81	34.81	34.81	34.81	34.81	34.81

* End of period stocks divided by average demand for year. 1972 ratio of 34.81 days supply was held constant in 1973–75 period. See table below:

	Days supply
1965	40.3
1970	38.0
1971	38.2

Source: United States Congress, Subcommittee on Consumer Economics, *The Gasoline and Fuel Oil Shortage.* Hearings Before the Subcommittee on Consumer Economics, Joint Economic Committee, 93rd Congress, May 1, 2, and June 2, 1973 (Washington: U.S. Government Printing Office, 1973), p. 8.

Future Supply and Demand

Table 3 depicts a 1972 prediction of the extent to which the United States would become dependent upon foreign energy supplies by the year 2000. The intervening of the 1973 oil boycott has caused a rethinking of the problem and there has been considerable thought given to lessening our dependence upon foreign energy supplies. Oil reserves, as Figure 12.2 illustrates, are considerably enhanced by the addition of the Alaskan discovery. But, this does not prove sufficient to supply our growing needs unless alternative sources are utilized. The greatest potential fuel source in the United States using existing technology is our great reserves of coal. However, the efficient mining of coal fields disturbs the environment and may alter it radically. Moreover, the high sulfur content of most coal reserves requires expensive technology to avoid air pollution when coal is burned. A more feasible ap-

TABLE 3 United States Energy Shortfall

Domestic Supply	10^{15} BTU				
	1971	1975	1980	1985	2000
Natural gas	21.810	22.640	22.960	22.510	22.850
Petroleum	22.569	22.130	23.770	23.600	21.220
Coal	12.560	13.825	16.140	21.470	31.360
Hydro	2.833	3.570	3.990	4.320	5.950
Nuclear	0.391	2.560	6.720	11.750	49.230
Total	60.163	64.725	73.580	83.650	130.610
Domestic Consumption	68.728	80.265	96.020	116.630	191.900
Shortfall to be satisfied by imports	8.656	15.540	22.44	32.980	61.290

Source: United States Department of Interior, "United States Energy Through the Year 2000," December 1972.

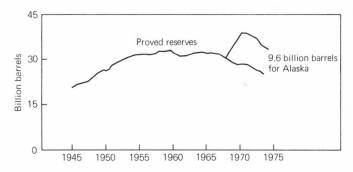

FIGURE 12.2 Oil reserves.
Source: *American Petroleum Institute.*

proach to expanding reserves would be to improve the technology for oil recovery. Stephen Gardner, an economist with the Federal Reserve Bank, argues:

> Because this country has been a major oil producer so long, there are many fields that could be reworked even further, vastly improving prospects for output.

> Probably some 434 billion barrels of crude have been discovered in the United States so far. Of that, only about 141 billion barrels can be recovered by conventional methods, leaving 293 billion barrels in known reservoirs as a target for improved recovery technology.

> Estimates of how much of this residual can be added to the nation's reserves over a reasonable length of time vary. There seems to be some consensus, however, that only about a fifth of the residual can be made available by the turn of the century. The estimates range from a practically assured 19 billion barrels to an optimistic 55 billion.

295

Only about 1 percent of all crude production in the United States comes from use of methods beyond conventional flooding and repressurization. But with continued incentives, and further technological improvements, tertiary recovery—recovery spurred by the introduction of heat or chemicals to loosen oil from the sand and speed its flow through formations—could make an important contribution to the nation's crude supply by 1985.

That places crude produced by tertiary methods as far out as some of the other sources of energy to be developed over the next ten years or so. But there will still be a need for this oil as the nation moves to primary dependence on other energy sources.

Continued incentives are important in promoting further technological improvements. Tertiary recovery takes large amounts of high-cost chemicals and equipment. And though the location of the oil is known, because the processes involved in recovering it will still be new, initial costs could be high, making financial risks heavy. For the processes to be helpful, their costs will have to be kept below the value of the oil recovered. [3]

Other proposals abound but a review of the problem by the Research and Policy Committee of the Committee for Economic Development makes the general case for changes in public policy. The Committee recommends the following:

1. All appliances should be labeled with information about how much energy they consume.
2. Individual meters should be installed in multifamily dwellings to allow each family to monitor its energy use.
3. Rate structures for electricity and gas should be reviewed to ensure price differentials that will encourage efficient use of these two energy sources.
4. The use of public transportation should be encouraged.
5. Better fuel efficiency should be built into automobiles and the current 55 miles per hour highway speed retained.
6. A federal government priority and allocation plan should be developed for all critical materials including oil and gas.
7. Oil and gas prices should be de-controlled and the marketplace should determine price and supply allocations.
8. The government should fund research into new technologies that more efficiently extract energy from fossil fuels, develop synthetic fuels, and develop alternative energy sources such as solar and nuclear power. [4]

These are the highlights of the committee's recommendations; they represent the typical view of the business community toward the energy crisis and should be considered in that light. More radical views and suggestions less favorable to the oil industry and business in general have emerged from numerous quarters.

Profits and Problems in the Industry

In the wake of the Arab boycott, higher prices for imported oil resulted in higher prices at the gasoline pump and much higher profits for most integrated oil companies. Figure 12.3 demonstrates the changing fortunes of the industry and there is no doubt that the large oil firms have increased profits as a result of the worldwide shortage of petroleum products. For example, Phillips' net income rose 55 percent in 1973 over 1972, 71 percent in 1974 over 1972, and 31 percent in 1975 over 1972. Mobil Oil Corporation's net income rose 48 percent in 1973 over 1972 and rose 82 percent in 1974 over 1972. These were typical increases for integrated oil companies and became somewhat of a *cause celebre* for many groups that contended that the oil companies were responsible, at least in part, for the energy crises. Oil industry representatives denied responsibility vehemently and argued that on balance the companies did not reap untold benefits from the oil crises. For example, Mobil stated that much of the increased profits resulted from two factors:

> The first factor accounting for part of the companies' profit increase was a rise in "currency" profits. These resulted from the dollar's weakness in international markets during 1973, which had the effect of translating foreign earnings into more dollars.

> The second factor involved so-called inventory profits. Many companies were using accounting systems which automatically showed large increases in apparent profits when the 1974 cost of oil rose sharply above what they had previously paid for the oil they held in inventory. These inventory profits, however, provided no net cash to the companies since they had to be instantaneously reinvested in re-

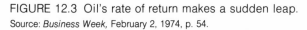

FIGURE 12.3 Oil's rate of return makes a sudden leap.
Source: *Business Week,* February 2, 1974, p. 54.

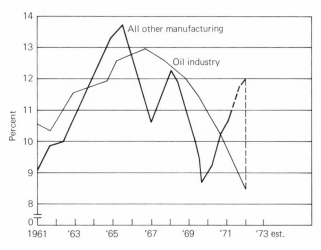

placement stocks at the new prices. Indeed, they were a cash drain because the companies had to pay taxes on them. Some companies have since changed their accounting systems so that these inventory profits would no longer distort their real profitability. The damage to oil industry credibility, however, had already been done.

On the other side of the picture, several companies during 1974 pointed out that U.S. marketing and refining profits and rates of return on investment were inadequate and falling. In Mobil's particular case, the company actually lost money in 1974 on its entire U.S. marketing and refining operations. On a world-wide basis, only the inclusion of one-time inventory profits kept Mobil's 1974 rate of return on average total assets from falling to the lowest level since 1960.

In looking at profits, it is essential to remember that investments to develop additional sources of energy can only be made if companies have the money to make them, and they will only be willing to commit the money if they have a reasonable rate of return on investments.[5]

The latter consideration is one that is argued by nearly all of the firms in the oil industry as well as regulated utilities in gas and electric. What is a sufficient return on investment? Theoretically, it is a return high enough to attract adequate capital for additional exploration, increased refining capacity, and the development of new technologies. In a comparison of the average rate of return in stockholders' equity (ROI) between the petroleum industry and all manufacturing firms for the period 1973–1976, it appears that ROI was 12.3 percent in both cases. In recent years ROI in the petroleum industry has exceeded the average for all manufacturing and as the following analysis demonstrates, the present governmental pricing regulations have spurred a lot of activity in oil exploration and production and have caused a number of other problems not favorable to the public image of the industry.

In an effort to encourage new production, the Cost of Living Council established a two-tier price system for crude oil. Not only could imports be priced at cost; so-called new and released domestic crude oil was freed from controls in order to seek the import price level. New crude oil was defined as production from a leasehold above the level of production achieved during 1972. For every barrel of new oil a producer was permitted to sell one barrel of released oil at whatever the market would bear. Subsequently, as part of the Emergency Petroleum Allocation Act of 1973, Congress also deregulated stripper-well crude. This is defined in the law as crude produced by wells yielding less than 10 barrels per day.

The two-tier system was designed to increase domestic crude oil production by raising the crude price at the margin while allowing the lower average price of crude to determine refined-product prices. The results of this scheme have been spectacular. The old crude oil ceiling price is now $5.25; the price of new, released, and stripper crude is over $10, a level more than enough to provide adequate incentives for new production. Drilling activity has been intense. The Hughes's rig count, which measures the number of rigs in operation, is perhaps the best indicator of this activity. By March 1974 it had risen by 40 percent above its level 1 year earlier, and it rose again in April. As a result of the two-tier price system, nearly 40 percent of all domestic oil in the United States has now been deregulated.

Although the crude oil program has encouraged new exploration and development, it has also created problems for the industry. For example, because each refiner does not have access to the same proportion of old and new crude oil, or domestic and imported crude oil, the two-tier pricing system has resulted in significant price differentials between the products of competing refiners. This has, in turn, contributed to the difficulties of those refiners and marketers who, by happenstance, sell refined products manufactured from higher-priced crude oil.

Initially, the ceiling price on old crude oil was to have been reviewed periodically and eventually raised to the level attained by deregulated and imported oil. Old domestic crude oil prices have, in fact, been allowed to increase significantly since the beginning of Phase 4. However, the sharp rise in crude oil prices has led to strong criticism by certain members of Congress and some segments of the public. There have been several efforts by congressional critics to enact laws requiring the rollback of all crude oil prices to $5.25 and old oil prices to $4.25. As a result, further increases in old oil prices by the administration are now more difficult, particularly as long as oil company profits are rising sharply. At the same time, producer interests have strongly opposed any administration ceiling or rollback of deregulated crude oil prices. This has resulted in a Mexican standoff. What was to have been a flexible ceiling price on old oil has become, instead, an inflexible freeze price. The two-tier price system has been cast in concrete.

The two-tier price system is the primary reason why two gasoline stations in the same area of the same city may charge prices that differ by as much as 12¢ per gallon. This, in turn, is resulting in very substantial pressures, particularly by those refiners who have historically relied heavily on imported crude oil for "price allocation," an extension of the existing allocation program to assure that low-priced crude oil is shared "equitably" by all the industry. Interests that in the 1960s and early 1970s fought to obtain special privileges from the government to import low-price oil from the Middle East, Venezuela, and Canada are now trying to obtain $5.25 domestic oil under the federal allocation program. Various ways have been suggested for sharing low-price oil. All of them involve some form of domestic ticket or entitlements systems. Those refiners consuming low-price crude oil would first have to obtain a ticket from the government or purchase a ticket from another refiner who has, in turn, obtained that ticket from the government. The entitlements program would offset one of the bad effects of the two-tier price system. As often happens, one control begets two, two begets four . . .

The two-tier price system invites manipulation. Old oil cannot be physically distinguished from new, released, or stripper crude. They are all blended in the same pipeline. A refiner has no way of knowing for sure whether the oil that is emerging at the end of that pipeline is, in fact, new or old oil and, for this reason, has no way of policing the system.[6]

Beyond the concern over excess profits earned by the major oil companies there is an even broader antitrust issue that has been the subject of several bills in Congress. High rates of inflation in the recent past were not easily controlled through monetary and fiscal policies. A rising unemployment rate, declining industry output, coupled with rapidly rising prices were not supposed to occur according to current economic theory. Prices should fall during times of rising unemployment and idle industrial capacity or, at the very least, stop rising. Since the economic policies of the Nixon administration failed to stem the "stag-flation" during the 1971–75 period the explanation for their failure is thought by many economists and politicians to be in the structure of the economy. It was argued that the lack of competition in many industries prevented monetary and fiscal policies from curing our economic ills.

Consequently, there has been renewed interest in "trust-busting" among federal agencies and Congress. The oil industry, with its obvious increases in profits and the integrated nature of many firms, has become the target for recent legislation aimed at forcing large firms to divert themselves of some phases of the business and/or limit their products to only one type of fuel. For example, one proposal would force companies operating retail outlets for the sale of gasoline and other petroleum products to choose either to engage in retailing and wholesaling only or to divest themselves of the retail business and remain in oil production, refining, and wholesale distribution. The proponents of this view argue that this would result in more price competition in the industry and lower prices for the consumer.

The issue of price competition was raised by the independent marketers of petroleum products. During the Arab boycott, private brand dealers—companies that are either wholesalers or retailers of petroleum products purchased from major producers such as Exxon, Gulf, or Mobil—were able to purchase only about one-half or less gasoline and fuel oil than they could prior to the crisis. In comparison, retail outlets owned or franchised by the major producers were receiving up to 90 percent or more of their previous allocation of gasoline, diesel fuel, and heating oil. The congressional testimony of Dean Walcutt illustrates the problem.

> I am Dean Walcutt and I am executive vice president of Certified Oil Co. We operate in Ohio, Kentucky, West Virginia, Indiana, and Pennsylvania.
>
> I am also one of the founders of the new Independent Gasoline Marketers Council and I am appearing here today on behalf of that council.
>
> Perhaps I should state at the outset that the council consists of 19 of the leading independent gasoline marketers in America, doing business from coast to coast. Collectively, they operate over 3,500 retail service stations and employ over 12,000 people. Their aggregate gross sales are about 4½ percent of all gasoline sold in the United States. The council represents 20 to 30 percent of the entire independent marketing segment of the gasoline industry.
>
> The supply problem facing the independent marketer is deadly. The loss of employment and the financial hardships endured by individuals and small companies are not realistically reflected in the broad statistical picture. Nevertheless, let me give you the best figures the council is able to produce concerning the shortage.
>
> The shortage of gasoline experienced by the members of the council at the present time is estimated at 1,480 million gallons. This is about 49 percent of last year's requirements for the same group of companies. This means that the independent sector, as a whole, is short about 6 billion gallons of gasoline. How does this come about?

The United States simply does not have enough refining capacity. Therefore, the integrated manufacturers of gasoline react by cutting back or cutting off their sales to independent marketers. The refiners prefer to reserve their limited supplies for their own integrated marketing outlets. Hence, the independent marketer is unable to buy the quantity of gasoline he requires.

In contrast, the integrated marketer is being supplied as fully as his in-house refiner can supply him. For example, it was announced a few days ago that Sun Oil Co., identified as the 10th largest oil company in America, has been obliged to ration its sales to its jobbers and dealers. The essence of the announcement was that Sun Oil Co. would have to limit deliveries to about 90 percent of normal. Indeed, it was stated by a representative of Sun that its retail dealers would probably not run out of gasoline, thus forcing the public to do business with Sun exclusively.

My purpose here is not to criticize Sun Oil Co. My purpose is to illustrate the problem. It is natural that the integrated refiner would cut off sales to outsiders. But, when this natural behavior occurs throughout the entire oil industry, the result is that the independent marketer is forced out of business.[7]

The private dealers are frequently referred to as the discounters because typically they attempt to sell gasoline and other products substantially below the price charged by major brand retailers. The gasoline price wars in the 1960s and early 1970s can be attributed to the price differentials maintained by the independents. Consequently, it would be in the financial interest of the major brand retailers if this source of downward pressure on prices were eliminated. Further congressional testimony from Professor F. C. Allvine of the Georgia Institute of Technology analyzes this problem:

The shortage of gasoline has already had an adverse impact on competition in the gasoline industry. As the gasoline shortage situation intensifies over the next 2 or 3 years, it could seriously injure and possibly destroy a very significant competitive force in the selling of gasoline to the public.

Independent private brand marketers, the major source of price competition in the gasoline industry, have severely suffered as a result of the supply shortage. This situation is extremely unfortunate for consumers since such independents are specialists in efficient techniques of selling gasoline which result in substantial savings for the public. Already several independent private brand marketers have been forced out of business because of supply shortages. Unless conditions change fairly soon many more independents face the same prospect over the next year or two. If this is allowed to happen competition in the gasoline industry will suffer a major setback.

For the past several years, and until very recently independent discount gasoline marketers have sold gasoline at much lower prices than their major brand competitors largely because of their relative efficiency.

The marketing cost including profit for many independents is about 5 to 7 cents per gallon. This would be in contrast to the cost of major brand marketing ranging from 10 to 12 cents or more per gallon. The independents are more efficient because of their discount, mass-merchandising method of marketing private-brand gasoline on a high-volume, high-turnover, low-cost and low-price basis. This is in contrast to the high priced method of selling major-brand gasoline. In the latter case, the costs of selling are much greater because of brand-name advertising, distribution of gasoline through large numbers of service stations, high priced locations, very elaborate facilities and costly sales promotion efforts including credit cards, trading stamps, games, and premiums.

The private-brand discount gasoline marketer accounted for an estimated 12–15 percent of the 70.5 billion gallons sold to the public through retail outlets during 1972. At a savings of around 4 cents per gallon, which is a major oil company estimate, the independent private branders directly saved the public around $375 million last year. Furthermore, when price reductions by the majors in response to the independents are included, the savings attributed to the independent discount gasoline marketers run well over half a billion dollars per year.

Prior to the last 6 to 9 months, the independent discount method of selling gasoline was actually forcing a revolution in the major brand methods of gasoline marketing. Through their pioneering efforts with self service, the independents over the last 4 years had actually reduced their costs while the costs of selling major brand gasoline were either constant, or had increased. The improved efficiency of the independents led to their acquiring an increasing market share at the expense of the major brand marketers. As a result of the intense competitive pressures of the independents, the costly major brand method of marketing was starting to crumble. The consumer savings from more efficient methods of marketing would have been substantial. Now, however, with the extraordinary developments in the gasoline industry, the competitive pressures of the efficient independent discount gasoline marketers are no longer being felt.

Ironically the efficient discount gasoline marketer, the primary force against inflation in the gasoline industry, is facing the realistic possibility of extinction. The critical problem confronting the independent discount gasoline marketers is obtaining economical supplies of gasoline to sell to their customers. As crude oil and refined products have grown exceptionally tight some refineries have taken advantage of the situation. They have diverted crude oil and refined products from independent refineries and discount marketers to their direct controlled operations. Many of the independents having supplies substantially reduced have been forced to increase their prices, reduce hours of operation, and to lay off employees in order to try and hold their operations together. Those that have been particularly hard hit by severe cutbacks in supply have ceased to operate.

The net effect of diverting products from the independents and reducing their supply has been to neutralize the independent price marketer as a viable competitive force in the marketplace. [8]

The oil companies responded vigorously to these charges and to the threat of antitrust action. Howard Blauvelt, chairman and chief executive officer of Continental Oil Company responded to the above statement in the following manner:

Most of the larger oil companies in this country—including all of the top 20—are vertically integrated in varying degrees. My own company, Continental, provides a good example of the reasons for integration. Back in the late 1920's, just before the stock market crash, Conoco was basically a marketing company, selling refined products throughout the West. Since we had no crude oil production or refining capacity, our supplies were insecure, and more costly, and thus we were having difficulty competing. At the same time, an Oklahoma-based company called Marland Oil had its own crude oil production and refining capacity, but it didn't have an adequate marketing structure. For both companies, a merger made sense, and was consummated. The combined company weathered the Depression—something that the old Continental and the Marland Oil Company separately might not have been able to do.

What was gained? Efficiency, balance, and stability, factors that have been the underlying rationale for integration in a large sector of American industry, ranging from food to textiles, from metals to publishing. The advantages to integrated operation accrue not only to industry, they also benefit the consumer. Vertical integration in the American petroleum industry has resulted in reduced risks, better product quality, and lower petroleum prices. Even today, the petroleum prices paid by Americans are among the lowest in the world. Many of our foreign competitors are recognizing the inherent benefits of integration and are themselves becoming fully integrated.

In view of the many benefits of integrated operations, let us examine what the architects of divestiture claim it would bring about and a more realistic scenario of what would occur.

Underlying all the arguments for vertical divestiture is the assertion that the petroleum industry isn't competitive enough. This assertion flies in the face of the facts. Petroleum is one of the most competitive industries in the country. Despite the size of the largest petroleum companies, no one company controls as much as eleven percent of any major phase of the business—crude oil production, natural gas production, refining, or marketing. Even the top four companies combined have only about thirty percent and the top eight companies combined have only about half of the total business. If concentration in the oil business should be applied across the entire U.S. manufacturing sector as a standard for breakup, it would mean breaking up quite a few industries—including automobiles, steel, aluminum, aerospace, computers, and others.

There is intense competition at every stage of petroleum operations—ranging from vigorous bidding for exploratory leases (bringing billions of dollars into the federal coffers) all the way to gasoline retailing. As they drive across the nation, motorists can pick from some 2,500 different brands of motor fuel.[9]

Exxon made the case for competition in the oil industry in even stronger terms:

Concentration ratios in 1973 for the top four participants in every phase of petroleum activity—exploration and production, refining, marketing, and transporation—are below 33%. This is well below the 39% four-firm average for all U.S. manufacturing.

More than 10,000 companies compete in oil and gas exploration and production in the U.S.; 131 companies operate 260 refineries; about 100 pipeline companies transport crude oil and products; and there are more than 15,000 wholesalers of petroleum products and more than 300,000 retailers of motor gasoline, most of whom are independent businessmen.

While many oil companies are large in absolute terms, the national market for petroleum products is also large and can support many large and small firms alike. If the term "majors" is limited to companies that are integrated in at least three functions (production, refining, and marketing) and which market their own brand in full line service stations, there are 16 such companies. This large number of large companies is hardly representative of a market structure dominated by a few.

Concentration ratios for total energy production (oil, gas, coal, uranium) are even lower. The top four companies accounted for only 22% of total energy production on a BTU basis during 1973, and the top eight had only 35%. The entry of oil companies into coal and uranium has had beneficial effects and has not increased energy concentration.

Both large and small firms in the petroleum industry are vertically integrated. Vertical integration is an efficient form of organization which allows improved coordination and planning among various segments. Vertical integration in petroleum activities cannot be used to "squeeze" out firms operating at only one level. Even the largest refiners must purchase significant amounts of crude oil to run their refineries, so substantial intermediate markets for crude exist despite vertical integration.[10]

Public response to the problems in the oil industry are probably dependent more on the price and availability of products than arcane economic arguments. But public concern and mistrust remain unabated even as the price of gasoline stabilizes and the availability seems little changed from the 1960s. The energy crisis is more than a memory of bad times—it remains at the policy level in government and industry as an unresolved dilemma.

FOOTNOTES

[1] *Achieving Energy Independence* (New York: Committee for Economic Development, 1974), p. 8.

[2] The source of the quotes and views in this section are from "Toward A National Energy Policy—What Went Wrong," Mobil Oil Co. pamphlet.

[3] Stephen L. Gardner, "Better Use of Existing Reserves May Yield More Than Exploration," *Business Review*, 8 Federal Reserve Bank of Dallas, Texas, April 1975, pp. 4–5.

[4] Committee for Economic Development, *Achieving Energy Independence*, pp. 22–25.

[5] "Toward a National Energy Policy," pp. 4–5.

[6] William A. Johnson, "The Impact of Price Controls on the Oil Industry: How to Worsen an Energy Crisis," in Gary D. Eppen (ed.) *Energy: The Policy Issues* (Chicago: The University of Chicago Press, 1975), pp. 109–110.

[7] United States Congress, Subcommittee on Consumer Economics, *The Gasoline and Fuel Oil Shortage*, Hearings Before the Subcommittee on Consumer Economics, Joint Economic Committee, 93rd Congress, May 1, 2, and June 2, 1973 (Washington: U. S. Government Printing Office 1973), pp. 41–42.

[8] *Ibid.*, pp. 98–99.

[9] Howard W. Blauvelt, "Petroleum Divestiture: An Untenable Solution to a Nonexistent Problem," Address Before the Columbia Business School Club of New York, Feb. 24, 1976.

[10] Howard W. Blauvelt, "Competition in the Petroleum Industry," pamphlet printed by Exxon Corporation, p. ii.

QUESTIONS

1. What are the policies and issues faced by the large firms in the oil industry?
2. Explain the nature of the environment the oil industry faces.
3. What role behavior is justified by the chief executive of Mobil? Of Certified Oil Company?
4. What are the major public policy issues to be resolved?
5. How would you differentiate between the environment faced by Mobil and that of Certified Oil Company?
6. Should the oil industry be regulated to the same extent as gas and electric?

CHAPTER 13

CONSUMERISM

CASE 15
CONSUMER MOVEMENT

Theoretically, under constraints of a laissez-faire market, the consumer is protected by the market's free operation. Consumers buy what best satisfies their needs and when the competitive market is in operation, there is no need for government action to make corrections. The market automatically corrects undesirable behavior by companies.

Those that feel the free market is still the best protection for the consumer argue that consumerism is a term created to describe a concerted disruptive ideology concocted by self-appointed bleeding hearts and politicians who find it pays off to attack the corporation.[1]

Others speculate, however, that several critical assumptions about the market's capabilities of protecting the consumer are no longer warranted in most market situations.[2] For example, buyers and sellers have formed groups or coalitions to influence the market. Buyers and sellers do not have complete information and full freedom of choice to react to information. Buyers and sellers may not always act rationally. Under such conditions, an alternative perception of the consumer movement argues that the consumer has needs and rights that require protection. Some areas in which protection is needed include truth in packaging, honest advertising, product safety, warranties and guarantees, and pricing.

This case presents an environment characterized by a variety of organizations that relate to one another through strategies ranging from cooperation to competition. These organizations include private corporations, government agencies, independent consumer pressure groups, and research organizations. In this case the common component relating all these organizations is a particular issue—deceptive advertising.

FOOTNOTES

[1] Ralph Nader, "The Great American Gyp," *The New York Review of Books,* November 21, 1968, p. 27.

[2] Jerome Rothenberg, "Consumer's Sovereignty Revisited and the Hospitality of Freedom of Choice," *American Economic Review,* May 1962, pp. 260–68.

Advertising Policies of the American Home Products and Sterling Drug Companies: Consumerism in the Drug Industry

"The myth of the defenseless consumer is one of the most enduring outputs of social critics of advertising. Yet, a substantial body of consumer behavior research tells us that the consumer is hardly a helpless pawn manipulated at will by the advertiser. We know, for example, that almost all consumers are very selective in what advertising they pay attention to, perceive, evaluate, and remember—let alone act upon" [1] Yet, if the consumer is the victim of false or misleading advertising, the character of this selectivity may be significantly affected. The Federal Trade Commission (FTC) has been charged with responsibility for dealing with such unfair practices.

The Federal Trade Commission

The Federal Trade Commission Act was first passed in 1914 and signed into law by President Wilson. The key section of the act, Section 5, held that "unfair methods of competition in commerce are hereby declared unlawful." [2] A recent book on the FTC states:

> The original FTC Act dealt only with unfair methods of competition, and that is where the Commission's regulatory efforts were concentrated. It soon became apparent, however, that situations occurred in which the public was victimized by false claims for a product or service that did not involve an adverse effect on competition. Under the existing law, the FTC was prevented from stopping such practices unless it could show anti-competitive effect. That changed in 1938 with passage of the Wheeler-Lea Act which gave the Commission a mandate to act whenever deception of the public was involved. After Wheeler-Lea, the Commission began to move consistently against such deceptive practices as false advertising. . . . [3]

Today, government control over advertising is vested primarily in the FTC. Section 5(b) of the FTC Act empowers the commission to issue orders requiring any "person, partnership, or corporation" to "cease and desist" from "using any unfair method of competitive or unfair or deceptive act or practice in commerce." [4] For the most part, past cease and desist orders issued by the commission in deceptive advertising cases have been framed solely to prohibit certain practices, without requiring any particular affirmative action by the respondent.

The implementation of such orders have proven difficult to achieve without incurring extreme delays. For example, in action against Carter's Little Liver Pills, it took the FTC 16 years to get the respondent to drop "Liver" from its name. A 16-year delay is rare, but three to five years is common from time of original action by the FTC until a cease and desist order is issued.[5] The procedure the FTC goes through to issue a cease and desist order is as follows:

> If the FTC finds "reason to believe" that an unlawful practice has been employed, it may proceed against the allegedly offending party with varying degrees of formality. Most cases are disposed of through the Informal Enforcement Procedure, which may take the form of an oral promise, an exchange of letters, or a more formal Assurance of Voluntary Compliance. If no agreement is reached at this stage, the Consent Order Procedure is employed. The Commission notifies the suspected party of its intention to institute proceedings, and with the notice serves a "proposed complaint." If the respondent agrees to the consent order, he is bound as if the matter has been fully adjudicated. Only if a consent order is not agreed upon does the Commission issue and serve the formal complaint. In those few cases in which no settlement can be reached, evidence is presented by both sides before a hearing examiner, whose decision may be appealed by either party to the full Commission. If an order to cease and desist is ultimately issued, the respondent can obtain review in a United States court of appeals.[6]

During the mid-1950s, a number of new combination drug products came on the market and each was accompanied by a number of advertised claims. For instance, it was claimed that several products including Bristol-Myers Company's Bufferin did not create side effects and provided more rapid relief than plain aspirin. Yet, very few of these products had been properly tested to determine how they actually compared with plain aspirin.[7]

The first significant test of combination products was carefully contrived by Dr. Robert C. Batterman, associate professor of medicine at New York Medical College. He set up double-blind tests on a large group of patients with both acute and chronic pain. Double blind means that neither the patients nor those conducting the tests know who is getting what drug until all evaluations are made. Specifically the tests were designed to discover how likely aspirin was to cause stomach distress, and whether this likelihood was affected by the small amount of antacid in Bufferin. Also, tests were carried out to determine speed, degree, and duration of relief from discomfort produced by the buffered and unbuffered aspirins. Results of the tests revealed that on every question no significant difference could be discerned between Bufferin and ordinary aspirin.[8]

In the early 1960s the FTC in an attempt to gain additional information about advertising claims, authorized a study of Bayer aspirin, St. Joseph's aspirin, Bufferin, Excedrin, and Anacin at Baltimore City Hospital. The findings reported in the *Journal of the American Medical Association*, December 29, 1962 were that there were no significant differences in ability to ease pain among the five brands during the first three hours of observations.[9]

Shortly after the report was published the manufacturer of Bayer aspirin and the distributor of St. Joseph's aspirin capitalized on the fact their products came out well in the study. Both the FTC and the American Medical Association were disturbed that advertising for Bayer aspirin boasted that a "government-supported medical team," whose findings "were reported in the highly authoritative *Journal of the American Medical Association*" had found the Bayer product equal to the higher-priced pain reliever. The advertisement also claimed "Bayer Aspirin brings relief that is as fast, as strong, and as gentle to the stomach as you can get. . . . . Bayer Aspirin had a somewhat higher pain relief score than any of the other products."[10]

The FTC believed this was a distortion of emphasis of the Baltimore study and issued a complaint against the distributor of Bayer aspirin and its advertising agency, charging that the findings had been misrepresented. The FTC sought a temporary injunction from a Federal court to stop the claims immediately. The complaint alleged

> . . . that the findings and conclusions reached by the medical team of clinical investigators were their own and had not been endorsed or approved by the United States Government, by the American Medical Association, or by the medical profession. The FTC also argued that, contrary to Bayer's claims, the clinical investigators did not state as a finding that Bayer aspirin will not upset the stomach, is as gentle to the stomach as a sugar pill, or is as gentle to the stomach as any analgesic product containing more than one ingredient.[11]

The Federal Court denied the FTC's request for a temporary injunction and ruled the advertisements did not misrepresent the findings of the study. Thus, the claims and counterclaims continued among companies producing and marketing analgesics.

In July 1967, the FTC announced it was considering the formation of a trade rule regulation covering the advertising of analgesics. The manufacturers of analgesics quickly responded to this announcement and court fights ensued. March 1969 found the FTC proposing "guidelines" to assist the manufacturers in advertising over-the-counter drugs. When neither the proposed rules of 1967 nor the guides of 1969 were adopted, the FTC announced in January 1971 that it was dropping its effort to have a rule adopted and that new investigations of analgesic advertising would be opened. The April 20, 1972 statement was the result of these new investigations.[12] In the 11 years, from 1961–1972, the FTC had come full circle and had again cited specific companies and their products with false advertising.

During the late 1960s, consumer advocate Ralph Nader put a task force to work at the FTC and came up with a report that the agency was so ineffective it should be abolished. The American Bar Association, in another report, found incompetence among FTC staff members, misallocations of funds and personnel, and poor morale throughout the agency.[13] As a result, President Nixon ordered the FTC "cleaned up" after he took office. His first appointee as chairman was Casper Weinberger, a California state official with a reputation for efficiency. On June 8, 1970, less than a year after assuming control, President Nixon moved Weinberger to the position of deputy director of the Office of Management and Budget and named Miles W. Kirkpatrick, head of the Bar Association group that criticized the FTC, to be its new chairman.[14]

When Kirkpatrick became chairman in late 1970, he announced, "The little old lady of Pennsylvania Avenue (the FTC) has taken off her tennis shoes and put on cleats." [15] Kirkpatrick, along with fellow Republican commissioners David S. Dennison, Jr. and Mary Gardiner Jones, succeeded in dominating the FTC. Democrats Paul Rand Dixon, who chaired the commission under Presidents Kennedy and Johnson, and H. Everette MacIntyre completed the five-member commission.[16] Both Dixon and MacIntyre contended that the FTC had become anti-business and these feelings were not limited to only the commissioners. Democrats and Republicans, as well as those businessmen who had recently incurred the FTC's wrath concurred. Chairman Kirkpatrick replied, "We Republicans believe in the free-enterprise system. That's why we have always been tougher enforcers of the antitrust laws than the Democrats." [17]

While a majority vote of the commission is necessary for any action to be taken, much of the impetus for any decision is given by the staff. Under the Nixon Administration, this staff became a hard-driving group of young consumer-oriented lawyers. Weinberger, Nixon's first chairman of the FTC, began the massive house-cleaning that resulted in the recruitment of a staff from the top law schools and law firms. At the time Weinberger stepped down as chairman to become deputy director of the Office of Management and Budget, Commissioner Dixon denounced the new Republican staff saying, "I don't buy the Chairman's idea of bringing in so many of these lawyers from the Northeast. I've found too many revolutionaries from up there. Anyway," Dixon concluded, "We should stop assuming that all the bright people come from one section of the country and all the dumb ones from another." [18]

During this time, the FTC had attempted to strengthen its position in the area of deceptive advertising in selected areas. In March 1969, guidelines were issued for the advertising of over-the-counter (OTC) drugs. The guides stated that advertising should not misrepresent the benefits, effectiveness, or safety of drugs and provided that advertisers must avoid untruthful claims of the superiority of one product over another. The guides were advisory and were intended to encourage voluntary compliance with the unfair methods of competition and deceptive advertising section of the FTC Act.[19] By June 1969, the FTC and the Federal Drug Administration (FDA) had jointly sought action to require manufacturers of OTC drugs to give consumers fuller, more factual information on which to base their purchases of such products as analgesics and antacids. Retail sales of OTC drugs amount to approximately $1.4 billion annually, and the economic implications affecting the advertising of such drugs are substantial.[20]

The commission's most influential staff member with respect to the advertising of OTC drugs was Robert Pitofsky, a member of the New York University law faculty on leave of absence, who was in charge of the Bureau of Consumer Protection. Pitofsky's critics in the business world, who referred to him as the FTC's "wild-man," claimed he refused to rely on voluntary self-regulation by businessmen. Pitofsky's reply: "In the past, this agency tended to rely on voluntary compliance and nobody took us very seriously. Now that we have demonstrated to the business community that we are prepared to litigate, voluntary compliance is bound to follow." [21]

However, six guidelines were set forth in November 1972 by the FTC for product endorsements. It was emphasized the guidelines were not mandatory but would be used by the FTC to determine possible false advertising violations. A summary of the guidelines follow:

1) Evaluation of organizations' endorsements of products would be more stringent than individuals' endorsements because such endorsements imply that the products have met organization standards.
2) Disclosure of connection between advertiser and endorser must be made when such a connection is "material"—paid for. However, an actor would not have to disclose that he was paid to advertise a given product.
3) Endorsers represented as experts must possess such expertise as represented.
4) Endorsements by experts must be based on experience, not just the fact that they are receiving compensation for the endorsement.
5) Testimonials about a "typical" consumer's experience with a product must indeed be typical.
6) Endorsements addressed to children would be subject to special limitations. The endorser must be qualified to determine characteristics that make the toy or product good for children. [22]

During the period of turmoil and change in the FTC, the business community developed a somewhat apprehensive attitude toward what the commission might do next. One example of fueling such apprehension was the action taken against Charles Pfizer and Company for deceptive advertising of its Un-Burn Sunburn Ointment. A Pfizer spokesman said, "The central issue in the proposed FTC complaint has to do with the amount and kind of proof necessary to document claims of effectiveness for this or any other drug. Indeed, the proposed complaint does not contend that the requisite type and amount of proofs are not now available to document these statements (about the effectiveness of Un-Burn), but contends that such proofs were not available before these statements were initially made. The challenged advertising statements for Un-Burn are true and supported by controlled clinical studies conducted by eminent experts in the field of dermatology. In this proposed complaint, the FTC is seeking to establish new legal theories that have no precedent in cases that have been decided by the courts or by the FTC." [23] The FTC examiner later recommended dismissal of the complaint because scientific tests conducted by Pfizer after the FTC action was brought did substantiate the product's probable effectiveness. [24]

During this same period in late 1970, Ralph Nader, on the basis of a report prepared by himself and an assistant, Aileen A. Cowan, specifically asked the FTC to adopt a trade regulation rule requiring national advertisers to give the agency scientific evidence supporting claims for products' safety, effectiveness, or performance before such claims were made. A year-long study by Cowan of TV and print ads showed that "much of the advertising in the media is blatantly or subtly deceptive." [25] In announcing his petition, Nader charged that "big business systematically refuses to document its wide ranging claims." He and Cowan wrote 58 companies seeking substantiating evidence for 68 advertising claims, but received data from only three. [26]

One point of contention growing out of the Pfizer suit and Nader report was the problem of corrective advertising. Pitofsky claimed, "It's really a very mild remedy because it would only require a company to use a small block of time each week— say five to fifteen minutes—to counter previous false claims for its product." [27] Democrat Dixon countered by saying, "It's one thing for a businessman to stop doing something wrong. But the idea of forcing him to spend his own money to tell the public he did wrong is too much to take." [28] In a 3–2 vote by the FTC favoring the requirement that three companies under investigation submit to corrective advertisement, the two Democratic commissioners cast the dissenting votes.

Yet, according to the *Harvard Law Review*, "The FTC in particular was created to explore and develop a field of law in which much pioneer work was needed. The corrective advertising order is a legitimate and potentially useful contribution to that field of law." [29]

In response to Nader's petition and pressures from other consumer groups, such as Consumers Union, the FTC began an advertising substantiation program in July 1971, and by March 1972 had requested documentation of claims from companies in six major industries: automobiles, televisions, electric shavers, cough and cold remedies, air conditioners, and dentifrices. FTC Chairman Kirkpatrick appearing in October 1971 at the congressional hearing on S-1461, the "Truth in Advertising Act," testified that Congress should refrain from passing any advertising legislation until after the effects of the substantiation campaign could be measured. [30] Senator Frank E. Moss of Utah, chairman of the Consumer Subcommittee of the Senate Committee on Commerce, in a letter of transmittal for the FTC staff report on the substantiation program stated:

> For the benefit of the members of the Commerce Committee let me offer the following brief conclusions which I have drawn from this exercise:
>
> 1) The FTC's ad substantiation program has been successful, indeed startling, in revealing the widespread and flagrant absence of adequate substantiation for advertising claims and the overriding need for a systematic means of holding advertisers' feet to the fire of public scrutiny. While several of the responses do indicate that substantiation exists for many claims and that in certain cases the FTC's staff judgments may have been unjustifiably harsh, the report remains unimpaired in its basic conclusion that a substantial number of ad claims are backed by nothing but hot air.
>
> 2) The FTC's substantiation program is nevertheless not a satisfactory mechanism

for supplying useful consumer information in a timely manner: the ads are chosen on a selective basis; the process is time-consuming and inevitably results in the airing of stale claims; finally, neither individual consumers nor the FTC have the technical capacity to evaluate the validity and relevance of much of the data.

In my judgment, what this report and the responses indicate is (1) the need for a system which would enable the individual consumer viewing an ad which contains performance or other claims to obtain quickly and simply a coherent, digestible summary of the data the advertiser believes substantiates his claim, and (2) where any such summary raises questions as to the adequacy and meaningfulness of the supporting data, there is a need for a mechanism by which competent, objective, private, and public technical organizations, such as Consumers Union and the National Bureau of Standards, can obtain, evaluate, and interpret the underlying technical data.[31]

Given these factors, attempts by the FTC to meet the demands of customers and revitalize its image have left the commission with some major problems. These include:

1) The FTC lacks the personnel to extend its ad substantiation program beyond the six industries previously mentioned.
2) The considerable time lag between the time ads are published or broadcast and the time of the substantiation information is made public.
3) The uselessness of gathering substantiation data if the FTC takes no indicated legal action once the data are gathered.
4) Much of the substantiation information requires a level of expertise not available within the FTC.
5) Slowness by the FTC in implementing corrective action leads the public to believe that deceptive ads are in fact correct.[32]

Finally, a *Wall Street Journal* editorial on the FTC ad substantiation program disagreed with the whole idea on the basis that the FTC had overstepped its boundaries and that except for correcting flagrant abuses, the consumer remained the most effective control over business excesses.[33]

In the midst of the controversy over the proper source of consumer protection, congressional remedies in the form of two bills came before the 92nd Congress. One required advertisers to provide documentation for their claims to any customer seeking it, and the other established a major study on the impact of advertising.[34] The more controversial of the two bills was the "Truth in Advertising Act." The bill, sponsored by George McGovern (D-SD) and Frank E. Moss (D-Utah), required any advertiser to provide documentation on the safety, performance, and efficacy of any advertised product or service to anyone who requested it. The only charge that the advertiser could make for such information would be for the actual costs of duplicating the documentary material. Such information must include descriptions of research and testing of the product offered for sale and comparisons with other products, including names of testing agencies, brand names tested, technical names of ingredients, and comparative prices. The only exemption from such disclosure would be trade secrets. The publications or broadcasting stations running the advertisements were required to give the name and address of any advertiser to anyone upon request. Enforcement would be handled by the FTC under rules it would promulgate after enactment of the law.[35]

Senator McGovern, testifying at the congressional hearings for the bill, stated what the bill would do:

1) It would make it unlawful for any person to advertise concerning the safety, performance, efficacy, characteristics, or comparative price of any product without having substantiating documentation available for public inspection in person or by mail at its principal office.
2) It would require media for the dissemination of advertising to furnish on request the name and address of advertisers and to inform the public that documentation for advertising claims is available upon request from the advertiser.
3) It would give the FTC power to insure that the two previous points are enforced.

and what the bill would not do:

1) It would place no additional burden on advertisers who today base their claims on substantiated research.
2) It would not create a new federal bureaucracy. The FTC would intervene only when an advertiser failed to supply information requested by an individual.
3) It would not require that radio and television broadcast a public service announcement concerning the name and address of advertisers every time they broadcast an advertisement.
4) It would not require advertisers to submit their documentation to any government agency prior to beginning their advertising campaign.[36]

Since no action was taken on the proposed bill (S-1461) by the 92nd Congress, it is now dead. It was not resubmitted to the 93rd Congress for consideration.

Sterling Drug Inc.

In 1971, Sterling Drug Inc., New York, had sales covering 124 countries and totaling $708,453,000, a 10 percent increase from 1970's total of $643,873,000. Overseas sales comprised 37.2 percent of Sterling's total with a record $263,543,000 volume. Pharmaceutical sales totaled $243,413,000 or 34.3 percent of the total, and proprietary medicines comprised 28.4 percent of the total with $200,926,000 in sales.[37] Sterling's performance placed it 195th among *Fortune's* top 500 in total sales.[38] Sterling ranked 11th in national advertising, spending $80,000,000 in 1971.

Outside observers of Sterling Drug describe the company as being conservative and cautious with solid financial management. Each product is judged independently. Advertising support can range from nothing to as high as 50 percent of sales.

Advertising Expenditures *

	1971	1970
Newspapers	$————— **	$ 1,169,800
Magazines	10,717,600	10,003,300
Farm Publications	314,600	162,000
Business Press	460,900	442,800
Spot Television	12,300,400	12,940,400
Network TV	46,329,000	41,324,000
Spot Radio	4,468,000	4,495,000
Network Radio	2,965,000	2,975,000
Total Measured	77,555,500	73,212,500
Unmeasured	2,444,500 ***	3,687,500
Estimated Total	80,000,000	76,900,000

* *Advertising Age*, August 28, 1972, p. 165.

** Not available, but estimated by AA at $1,000,000 ($617,000 of it in supplements), included in unmeasured.

*** Includes $350,000 in p.o.p.

Every six months, major policies and procedures are reviewed and, if necessary, revised. This flexibility in marketing policy results in some products being tested for varying lengths of time, while others may be introduced nationally without any previous testing at all. "If you think this is vague," one executive remarked on the operations of the company, "I've been here for five years and still can't figure out the key." [39] The decision whether or not to introduce new consumer products is usually made by Chairman J. Mark Hiebert after studies are conducted by the marketing department. Hiebert also is involved in advertising approvals. The chairman emphasizes that Sterling, while being conservative, does not believe in "doing things because that's the way they've always been done." [40]

Sterling's divisions operate almost autonomously and are expected to meet volume and profit goals set for them by top management. How each division meets these goals, including the introduction of new products and the use of advertising, is determined by the division itself. Advertisement of a Sterling product varies greatly from division to division. Breon Laboratories uses advertising to support only one of the seven products in its Diaparene lines. Conversely, Lehn and Fink, maker of Lysol brand products, advertises each product separately. The lack of rules has not hindered Sterling's growth. During the last 21 consecutive years, the company has increased both sales and earnings. Earnings for the last 10 years have been consistently 10 percent of sales. However, the percentage of sales in each of Sterling's divisions has changed for these same 10 years. Pharmaceuticals, household products, and cosmetics have increased their share of sales while proprietaries have decreased and the remaining industrial products have stayed constant. [41]

Glenbrook Laboratories, the company's major proprietary products division, was Sterling's leading advertiser with $41,181,000 spent in 1971. [42] Glenbrook's leading products include Bayer aspirin, Bayer Timed-Release aspirin, Bayer children's aspirin, Phillip's Milk of Magnesia, Vanquish and Cope analgesics, Haley's M-O, and Campho-Phenique. Regular Bayer aspirin, a Sterling product for 53 years, received $17,380,000 in measured support, of which $13,230,000 went for network television. Yet, Bayer aspirin continued to trail American Home Products' Anacin in food and drug dollars with 14 percent and 15.4 percent shares respectively. Vanquish, another Glenbrook pain killer, had 1.4 percent share of the market and was supported by $2,080,000 in advertising. Cope, supported by $590,000, had a share too small to register on national charts.[43] Glenbrook's advertising of Bayer aspirin has repeatedly stressed two themes—Bayer's superiority over all other aspirins on the market and aspirin's superiority over any other type of pain reliever. In 1971, Glenbrook used a "Bayer man" ad format, featuring a question-and-answer series of commercials. Expert opinion and the latest available research was cited in what the company said was a campaign to provide the consumer with in-depth factual information about nonprescription pain relievers available to them. The campaign resulted in a $1,500,000 class action suit filed in February 1972 by a Michigan attorney.[44] The American Medical Association was named as co-defendant because the Bayer advertisements cited an AMA Council on Drugs report. The AMA revealed it had complained to Glenbrook and that the company had removed a photo of the AMA report from Bayer's ads printed in newspapers and magazines. An advertising campaign initiated in 1973 equated the notion that all aspirins are alike with such previous mistaken beliefs as "the world is definitely flat" and "if man were meant to fly he'd have wings." Consumers were informed that they could write to Bayer for the booklet containing tests conducted by Bayer to show that its product is superior.

Sterling's official policy statement concerning Bayer aspirin is set forth in the booklet, *Nonprescription Pain Relievers: A Guide for Consumers*, published by the Bayer Company. Interested consumers are encouraged in the company's advertisements to send for one of the booklets which is sent free of charge.

The introduction to Bayer's booklet states that it "has been prepared to assist you in making informed and intelligent decisions about the nonprescription pain reliever you buy. It provides independent, expert scientific opinion on various types of pain relievers. It provides, as well, the results of the Bayer Company's own extensive research on various brands of pain relievers." [45] Acknowledging that there are many types of pain relievers available and that deciding on the best pain reliever to buy is not a simple matter, the introduction continues: "There is significant misinformation about them [pain relievers] and it is difficult, at times, for the consumer to determine the quantities of the individual active ingredients in combination products. Finally, there is a scarcity of authoritative information about them available to the consumer." [46] Concluding, the introduction states, "It is for this reason that the Bayer Company has prepared this booklet that summarizes, for the first time, available information to guide consumers in choosing pain relievers." [47]

The booklet proceeds to divide pain relievers into two general groups: prescription drugs, obtainable only by a doctor's prescription, and nonprescription drugs, obtainable without a doctor's prescription. "They [nonprescription pain relievers] have a long-established and recognized role in relieving such nearly universal problems as headaches, minor aches and pains, the fever and discomfort associated with colds and flu." [48] Only pain relievers of the nonprescription type are considered in Bayer's booklet.

Part I of the booklet is entitled, "Evaluation and Selection of Pain Relievers." Commonly used pain-relieving ingredients discussed include aspirin, phenacetin, acetaminophen, and salicylamide. Nonpain-relieving ingredients considered are caffeine and buffers (antacids). A discussion of each ingredient and combinations of ingredients is based on "many scientific sources, what is believed to be a consensus of scientists, expert in evaluating medicines—first, on the individual ingredients, and second, on certain combination product formulations on the American market." [49]

1. Aspirin—"It has gained authoritative medical acceptance as an effective pain reliever, fever reducer, and anti-inflammatory agent. . . . Aspirin is, by far, the most recommended and most used nonprescription pain reliever, alone ('straight aspirin') or in combination with other analgesic and non-analgesic ingredients." [50] The "Handbook of Nonprescription Drugs" and the 1971 "AMA Drug Evaluations" are both cited as sources concurring that aspirin is the best pain reliever. Additionally, the testimony of a "leading medical scientist" before a congressional hearing is quoted: "There is no good evidence that any analgesic obtainable on an over-the-counter basis, either a single entry or a drug mixture, can provide greater relief of pain than an adequate dose of plain aspirin." [51] After a listing of the possible side effects involved with the use of aspirin and a warning to consult your physician on the use of aspirin if these symptoms should occur, the discussion on aspirin concludes, "Bayer Aspirin is the most widely used aspirin product." [52]

2. Phenacetin and Acetaminophen—Discussed together because they belong to the same chemical family, these two drugs, like aspirin, effectively reduce fever and relieve pain but, unlike aspirin, are not effective in reducing inflammation. There is an indication that prolonged use of both drugs, especially phenacetin, may cause kidney damage. The Food and Drug Administration requires a warning notice regarding possible side effects be placed on products containing phenacetin and a warning to consumers be placed on packages of acetaminophen not to use the medication for more than ten days without consulting a physician. Empirin contains phenacetin, as well as aspirin and caffeine, while Tylenol is straight acetaminophen.

3. Salicylamide—Few studies have been conducted on this drug, but those undertaken do indicate this drug is less effective than aspirin. A "noted scientist" is quoted as stating that "patients taking products containing salicylamide derive little benefit from its presence." [53] Excedrin is the only major advertised analgesic containing salicylamide.

4. Caffeine—Caffeine has no pain relieving effect, and its inclusion in combination pain relievers has been questioned. The booklet reports the testimony of "a leading medical expert" before a congressional subcommittee, stating: "there is no

evidence that the rather small dose [30 mg] usually present in OTC [nonprescription] analgesic mixtures . . . either exerts a direct analgesic effect or potentiates the action of other analgesics." [54] A suggestion is made that caffeine may even contribute to stomach upset.

5. Buffering—Claims that buffered aspirins provide faster relief and reduce the chance of stomach upset are disputed. A 1971 report of the National Academy of Sciences/National Research Council Drug Efficacy Study Panel's evaluation of the nonprescription buffered aspirin, which was made public, is quoted as saying the product's claim to act "twice as fast as aspirin" was "ambiguous and misleading." With regard to its claim that it helps "prevent the stomach upset often caused by aspirin," the panel concluded that ". . . there is little difference in the incidence or intensity of subjective gastrointestinal side effects after ingesting Bufferin or plain aspirin." [55] Bufferin is mentioned as the leading buffered aspirin.

6. Combination Pain Relievers—Combination pain relievers are analyzed similarly to the preceding five compounds, and it is concluded that they, too, are less effective than aspirin (with a possible increase in side effects).

Part I is then summarized:

> In summary, medical experts in the evaluation of medicines are in broad agreement on the following points:
>
> 1) Aspirin is the only nonprescription pain ingredient that effectively provides all three major therapeutic benefits: analgesic (relief of pain), antipyretic (fever reduction), and anti-inflammatory (reduction of swelling).
> 2) Aspirin is the best nonprescription product available today for the relief of headaches, fever, and discomfort accompanying colds and flu, muscular aches and pain, the minor pain of arthritis and other kinds of mild to moderate pain.
> 3) The addition of buffers or caffeine to aspirin, or the combination of other pain relieving ingredients with aspirin or their substitution for aspirin, has not been proved to result in faster, gentler or stronger relief of pain.
> 4) Although there is no one pain reliever for everyone, aspirin comes closest to this ideal.
> 5) If you have any question about your use of pain relievers, consult your physician. [56]

Part II is entitled "Evaluation and Selection of a Straight Aspirin Brand" and begins by asking, "Is all aspirin alike?" Part II attempts to answer this question by reporting the results of a "four-year quality comparison carried out by the Bayer Company. The study covered 221 different straight aspirin products on the American market as well as the three largest selling combination products, each of which uses aspirin as a basic ingredient." [57] Samples of each product were obtained from the shelves of retail stores. The tests conducted fell into the following categories: aspirin content, free salicylic acid, disintegration, color, odor (as a measure of deterioration), tablet count, tablet breakage, label legibility, indications (label instructions, for example), sealed cartons/bottles, condition of container, package insert, quality control numbers, and general appearance and condition. In all 13 categories, Bayer aspirin met or exceeded the requirements of the U.S. Pharmacopoeia

Convention, a private organization that establishes legally recognized standards for the manufacture of medicines. Failure to meet these minimum requirements is a violation of the law.[58] Other aspirins were found defective in one or more areas. The summary states: ". . . this extensive comparison of aspirin quality shows:

1) All aspirin is not alike.
2) Studies such as this—indicating the superiority of Bayer Aspirin tablets to all 220 brands of aspirin—demonstrate that the quality of aspirin, like the quality of any generic drug, can vary depending upon the manufacturing process by which it is made and the controls for quality to which it is subjected.
3) For the consumer, the purchase of Bayer Aspirin provides—as does the purchase of no other aspirin product—the assurance of having for use, when needed, a pain relieving, fever-reducing, anti-inflammatory agent of exceptional quality. Bayer's self-imposed standards, more rigid than those imposed by the U.S.P., insure this quality." [59]

"Keys to Bayer Quality and Difference" were then given. These included the fact that only selected raw materials are used in a batch process that enhances quality control. The nonaqueous nature of the Bayer manufacturing process is stated as a reason for the production of a more stable aspirin. The manufacturing process also involves the blending of two types of aspirin crystals which, it is claimed, contributes to Bayer aspirin's "rapid and uniform disintegration within two seconds after swallowing." Bayer purchases no aspirin from outside suppliers. Finally, "more than 100 different chemical tests and quality inspections are carried out for each batch of Bayer Aspirin." [60]

Part III is entitled "Prices of Pain Relievers." General considerations, such as the fact that consumers' choice is usually made on "best value" rather than "cheapest price" and that prices fluctuate depending on retail outlet, are mentioned. A paragraph headed, "Bayer and other straight aspirin" reviews the reasons that have been presented in an attempt to dispel the myth that all aspirins are alike. It points out that the unique process used by Bayer to manufacture aspirin is substantially more costly to perform, but concludes that even so, Bayer aspirin still costs the consumer only about a penny per tablet. No direct price comparisons with other straight aspirin brands are made. Leading combination pain relievers are said to cost 40 percent to 50 percent more than Bayer aspirin. Leading acetaminophen products are said to cost about twice as much as Bayer.

The Bayer Company concludes its booklet with Part IV: "Now you decide."

> The Bayer Company believes that an objective evaluation of the medical consensus (Part I) and its own extensive research (Part II) clearly leads to the following conclusions.
>
> 1) Aspirin is superior to other analgesic entities because of its broader activity, high efficacy, relatively low toxicity and few side effects.
> 2) All leading nonprescription pain relievers advertised to the public depend wholly, or chiefly, on aspirin for analgesic activity.

3) Aspirin is preferred to any combination product by medical experts in their evaluation of medicines.

4) Aspirin is the standard against which pain relievers are measured.

5) Like all effective medicines, aspirin is not totally free of adverse side effects. However, extensive research has established that only a small fraction of the total population need avoid aspirin.

6) Aspirins are not the same pharmaceutically. Bayer produces a superior quality aspirin, proved in tests, by virtue of a unique manufacturing process and the excellence of its ingredients and quality controls. Bayer proved to be superior in quality, showing greater reliability, stability, purity and freshness than other aspirin products.

7) Bayer Aspirin is the superior value in the pain relief category.[61]

American Home Products, Inc.

American Home Products' (AHP) particular qualities and success trace back to the late Alvin G. Brush, a Quaker accountant-turned-dentifrice salesman (Dr. Lyon's toothpaste), who became the company's first president in 1935. The company had been founded nine years before by a group of Sterling Drug Company executives who consolidated a handful of small independent proprietary drug companies into a new company. Brush expanded the business with a number of acquisitions and established the basic operating patterns to which AHP still conforms.

Today, AHP is a little-known corporate giant with an austere managerial style that contrasts sharply with the flamboyant, hucksterish nature of the business it is in. Company policy focuses on achieving "anonymity" rather than "identity" or "image." Its products, which include Dristan, Anacin, Sani-Flush, Chef Boyardee, and BiSoDol, never display the company name, and its 25-story mid-town Manhattan headquarters is identified by a barely discernible name plate. Its switchboard operators respond curtly to outside callers, and persons in the traditional role of receptionist are not to be found at its Manhattan headquarters.[62]

AHP's controversial, strong-willed president, William F. LaPorte, who shuns the press, says that one reason for the maintenance of its low profile is a desire to shield its ethical drug business, which accounts for around 35 percent of sales and over 40 percent of its earnings. LaPorte says, "There's a great deal of difference between an injectable drug and an oven cleaner." [63]

AHP's profits are consistently above the average for the ethical drug and consumer packaged-goods industries. Its 25 percent return on investment has been one of the highest among the billion dollar industrial companies.[64] The company has reputed record sales and earnings for the 21st consecutive year.

The often seemingly over-simplified platitude, describing a company's purpose as maximizing profits by minimizing costs and returning their earnings to the stockholders, apparently has become a dogmatic way of life at AHP.[65] Some aspects of the strategy, employed to achieve these objectives, are presented below. Company missions are achieved:

1) by having only modestly furnished offices, even for President LaPorte.
2) through limited research and development spending. AHP spends only 7 percent of its ethical drug sales dollar on R and D as compared to 10 percent for the industry.
3) by not fighting for market share on an individual product. Rather says LaPorte, "I prefer a smaller share and a bigger profit to a bigger share and a smaller profit." In short, AHP will not spend excessively to corner the market on a particular product. The company is content with a lesser share of the market as long as profits grow.
4) by introducing new products only after other companies have established a market for them. Accordingly, AHP has rarely fallen on its face with the costly introduction of new items. In respect to the introduction of a new product, an AHP executive says, "We'll do the typical American Home trick, we're letting the other guys create the market. We'll wait and then come out with our product with a discernible improvement. We won't own the market. That's not our aim. But we'll sop up our share and be content with the profit we can get out of it."
5) by pursuing a policy of strict central monetary control. For instance, a voluminous manual spells out in detail the expenditures that need New York's (the corporate staff's) approval for everyone of the company's 55 domestic plants, laboratories, warehouses, or field offices. Virtually every non-budgeted expenditure of $250 or more must be explained in a detailed report and no contribution to a local charity of more than $10 can be made without LaPorte's approval.
6) by maintaining a financial position of unusually large amounts of assets, cash and marketable securities, and limited amounts of long-term debt. In 1969, AHP had $725.5 million in assets, $113.2 million in cash and marketable securities, and only $10.9 million in long-term debt.[66]

In 1969, AHP budgeted $87 million for advertising, which placed it eighth among the nation's largest advertisers. In 1971, the company raised its advertising budget to $88 million and became the third largest spender for TV commercials at $39+ million.[67] AHP adheres to a policy of hard-sell, shock-type advertising of the "old school" variety with monotonously repeated messages and a penchant for interior views of stomachs and heads. In the initial six months following the lifting of the TV code ban on ads for hemorrhoid preparations, AHP spent an estimated $650,000 for the promotion of its hemorrhoidal ointment, Preparation H. Many of AHP's ads tout the superiority of its products over its competitors'.[68]

Controversy with the FTC

In June 1969, the FDA and the FTC jointly sought action to require over-the-counter drug producers to give consumers fuller, more factual information on which to base their purchases of such products as analgesics. Claims for the drugs were to be edited, and it was expected that such editing would result in a single allowable claim for analgesics. For example, one claim might proclaim being useful only for "simple relief of pain" for a period of perhaps a week with the warning that a physician should be consulted if pain persists. Promotions for pain killers, such as Anacin, would no longer be allowed to claim the products' effectiveness for the treatment of tension, tension headaches, irritability, migraine headaches, sleeplessness, or lumbago. The new labeling requirements for OTC drugs were designed to give the FTC maximum legal leverage in proceeding against false and misleading promotion.[69]

At the close of 1970, the FTC dropped the industrywide proceeding it had initiated in 1967 on the proposed trade rule to regulate the advertising of nonprescription analgesic drugs. The FTC decided instead to tackle the problem on a case-by-case basis. The new investigations were to cover analgesic advertising from January 1, 1969 to the present, and the FTC staff was authorized to use subpoenas or other "compulsory" measures to gather necessary information.[70]

On April 20, 1972, the FTC, claiming that one nonprescription pain killer is about as effective as another, accused the makers of Anacin, Bufferin, Excedrin, and Bayer aspirin of deceptive advertising.[71] In the words of Robert Pitofsky, TFC's consumer protection director, the companies had failed in their "attempt to establish a 'significant difference' between their products."[72] The FDA, in conjunction with the FTC, released scientific evaluations challenging the effectiveness of many widely used over-the-counter pain relievers and antacids. These evaluations were conducted by the National Academy of Sciences, a non-government academy that has reviewed the efficacy of all drugs marketed between 1938 and 1962.[73] The three companies involved, American Home Products Corp., Bristol Meyers Co., and Sterling Drug, Inc., had spent a combined total of $80 million on advertising of nonprescription pain killers in 1970 and had captured two-thirds of the $330 million over-the-counter drug market in that year.[74] The commission's proposed complaint would prohibit the future use of the advertisements in question. As stated above, by a 3–2 vote of the commissioners, the FTC suggested that the manufacturers involved be required to run corrective advertisements that would be separate from any sales effort. Because of the large volume of advertisements in this area and the length they had run, the FTC demanded two years of corrective advertisements be run.

The FTC specifically charged Sterling Drug, Inc., makers of Bayer aspirin, Cope, and Vanquish with "making deceptively inconsistent claims for its Bayer aspirin on the one hand and its Cope and Vanquish on the other."[75] The corrective ad the commission hoped to require Sterling to use concerning Cope, Vanquish, and Midol read: "It has not been established that these products are more effective for the relief of minor pain than aspirin, that Cope relieves nervous tension, anxiety, irritability, or enables a person to cope with ordinary stresses of personal life; that Vanquish causes gastric discomfort less frequently than aspirin, or that Midol will relieve nervous tension, nervousness, stress, fatigue, or cure depression or improve the user's mood."[76] The corrective advertisement regarding Bayer aspirin read: "It has not been established that Bayer aspirin is more effective for the relief of minor pain than any aspirin which meets the standards set out by the U.S. Pharmacopoeia." [77] Commissioner Pitofsky suggested that up to 25 percent of the company's advertising budget could be spent promulgating these ads.

The FTC has the power to issue complaints when it has "reason to believe" that the law has been violated. Such action does not, however, imply any judgment of the charges by the commission. If consent agreements cannot be reached between the FTC and the parties involved, the complaints are sent down for a hearing before an FTC examiner. The commission will ultimately issue a ruling on the charges, and this ruling can be appealed to a federal court. Immediately following the FTC's announcement, Sterling issued a statement that it would fight the FTC and that it was "fully confident that the advertising claims for Bayer aspirin and Sterling's other nonprescription pain relievers are accurate and truthful and that they will be completely substantiated in any formal hearing." [78] Most of the parties involved agreed that years of litigation lay ahead.

One of AHP's major over-the-counter nonprescription drugs is Anacin. Through "hard sell" advertising, the product has become the No. 1 analgesic tablet rather than a simple pain killer. A typical critique of an ad for the product is, "If you didn't have a headache before you saw or heard an Anacin commercial, you will after." [79] Among other claims, AHP has promoted Anacin as containing one-fifth more aspirin than an ordinary aspirin pill. Consumers Union warns that an individual who buys Anacin pays an extraordinarily high premium for a small amount of extra aspirin. [80] Anacin's other ingredient is caffeine, which doesn't add anything beneficial according to Consumers Union and may sometimes actually be harmful according to a recent medical report in the *Reader's Digest*. Patients with fevers resulting from a cold or flu are often advised by their doctors to take aspirin and drink hot tea which contains caffeine. Aspirin does reduce high temperature, but caffeine appears to keep body heat up. Thus, the two substances cancel each other's effect. As a result, the report advises fever sufferers to avoid medications containing caffeine. [81]

In addition, the FTC charged AHP with making misleading and false claims about the effectiveness of Anacin. For instance, the FTC challenged the claim that a survey showed Anacin as "the pain reliever preferred by twice as many doctors." Typically, AHP withheld comment until the complaints could be studied. [82]

Not only has AHP been involved in a long, drawn-out controversy with the FTC over its advertising of Anacin, but in 1970, the company was requested by the American Medical Association (AMA) to discontinue the use of the organization's name in its advertising campaign for the analgesic. AHP voluntarily agreed to discontinue the campaign that referred to an article in the journal of the AMA. The article was a review of scientific literature on pain relievers that found aspirin favorable to other commonly used pain killers. The AMA spokesman said the organization objected to the Anacin campaign because "We don't feel that the AMA name should be used to promote a proprietary drug." [83]

The Mayo Clinic Report

On April 22, 1972, the Mayo Clinic of Rochester, Minnesota, reported the results of tests conducted concerning pain relievers.[84] Fifty-seven inoperable cancer patients were given various drugs. A generic form of aspirin was used rather than any brand name. Aspirin was shown to be a powerful pain killer, outranking eight common prescription drugs such as codeine, Darvon, and Talivin. Doctors conducting the study listed aspirin's cheap price and the absence of side effects as some of the advantages of its use and concluded, "These advantages should make aspirin the drug of preference for any pain problem requiring an oral analgesic." [85] Also included among the eight prescription drugs was Zactane made by Wyeth Laboratories Division of AHP. Zactane, it was reported, is not significantly different from a placebo used in the study and is significantly inferior to aspirin. A spokesman for Wyeth Labs said the company could not comment on the study's findings on Zactane until it had seen the report, but he added that the company had done extensive studies on the drug and had submitted the data to the FDA for its evaluation.[86]

Stern Concern

On April 29, 1972, consumer advocates began to mount a drive to compel the broadcasting of free "public service" messages concerning aspects of advertised products that were misrepresented, ignored, or obscured in paid commercials.[87] The drive was spearheaded by the Stern Concern, a non-profit group of communications experts directed by Marvin J. Segelman. Stern Concern, which later changed its name to Concern Firm, was the creation of Philip M. Stern, a philanthropist and writer, his wife, Leni, Tracy A. Western, director of the Stern Community Law Firm, and Segelman.[88] The group produced messages based on the claim that broadcasters must serve the public interest and urged the TV networks to air their work. Efforts were also made to have newspapers, magazines, and local broadcasters carry public interest messages.

One such public interest message was a 30-second television spot narrated by actor Burt Lancaster. The spot went:

> I'd like to talk to you about a drug problem called Excedrin, Emperin, Anacin, Cope, Vanquish, and Bufferin [all these on a table in front of him]. The American Medical Association has found remedies like these to be either irrational, not recommended, or unsound. As for plain aspirin, there's no persuasive scientific evidence one brand is more effective at relieving headaches than another [holds up Bayer] . . . although the major brand costs a lot more. So, next time you buy something for your head, use your head. Buy the least expensive plain aspirin you can find [holds up plain aspirin].[89]

Thus far, the TV networks have refused to air the Stern commercials, fearing such messages would drive away advertisers. Their refusal is being appealed to the Federal Communications Commission by the firm. The appeal is part of the three-step strategy Stern devised "to put a megaphone on the facts" developed by the consumer movement. The facts behind the commercial claims are researched, a celebrity is found to tape spots, and the Stern Concern sues to get the message on the air.[90]

Consumer Reports

In August, 1972, Consumers Union published an article in its magazine, *Consumer Reports*, entitled "Aspirin and Its Competitors." The *Wall Street Journal* commented the article "could prove [a] headache for branded aspirin." [91] The report included studies of Bayer aspirin, Bufferin, Excedrin, Vanquish, Cope, and commentary on FTC and FDA actions concerning these products. Conclusions were based on "extensive review of scientific literature as well as congressional hearings and statements by organizations such as the AMA and the National Academy of Sciences/National Research Council Panel on Drugs." [92] Consumers Union did no actual testing. The evaluation by *Consumer Reports* was felt to be a timely one for several reasons. More than $1 billion is spent on these types of nonprescription drugs a year; 80¢ out of every dollar spent on these drugs was used to purchase aspirin's far more costly competitors. Most significantly, recent FTC and FDA actions had focused consumer attention on these over-the-counter drugs.

"Quick relief" was stressed in Bayer's new campaign: "For quick relief—always say 'Bayer' aspirin when you buy." [93] Consumers were urged to prove for themselves Bayer's claim of quick relief by dropping a Bayer aspirin tablet and another aspirin tablet into a glass of water. They were assured the Bayer tablet would begin to disintegrate "in 2 seconds by the stopwatch." *Consumer Reports* remarks: "That proved nothing, of course, except that some tablets disintegrate faster than others in a glass of water." [94] The article continues, "[t]here's an important difference between simply disintegrating [breaking apart] and dissolving [changing into a liquid solution]." [95] Investigations conducted by Dr. Gerhard Levy observed that the disintegration times of the aspirins tested had "no relation whatsoever to biological availability," [96] (the amount of active medication that actually enters the blood stream). Regardless of these findings, company literature still stressed Bayer's tablet-disintegration time.

Price studies were conducted by Consumers Union showing that Bayer sold for two to four times the price of "ordinary" aspirin. But Consumers Union claimed there is no clinical evidence to support Bayer's claim that it relieves pain better than any other five-grain aspirin tablet. "CU knows of no reason to buy Bayer aspirin instead of a cheaper brand." [97]

Consumers Union then turned its attention to those pain relievers with a combination of ingredients (including aspirin) such as Anacin, Excedrin, Bufferin, Vanquish, and Cope. Each product's claims were summarily attacked. Regarding the last two drugs, Consumers Union stated: "The most remarkable fact about Vanquish and Cope, however, is that both are marketed by the Glenbrook Laboratories Division of Sterling Drug, Inc.—the same division of the same company that markets Bayer aspirin. So Sterling Drug is advertising that there is nothing better for pain relief than Bayer aspirin at the same time that it advertises that there are two products far better than any aspirin." [98]

Consumers Union applauded the attempts of the FDA, which has jurisdiction over over-the-counter drug labels, and the FTC, which has jurisdiction over over-the-counter drug advertising. It warned, however, that both agencies have enormous tasks confronting them. An FDA program involving the establishment of criteria upon which the efficacy of drugs can be judged and the FTC's attempt to require corrective advertising are both steps in the right direction according to Consumers Union. Enthusiasm for these moves was tempered with the realization that they may be a long time in reaching fruition. Based on the fact that present regulations are ineffective, Consumers Union set forth two recommendations:

"First, distrust all claims for over-the-counter drug products, especially analgesics. Urge your friends to distrust them, too, and encourage your children to be skeptical of all such advertising.

Second, when selecting an analgesic, limit your consideration to the cheapest available brand of plain aspirin or the cheapest brand of acetaminophen. (In Canada, "aspirin" is still a Bayer trade name, so other brands are identified by the acetylsalicylic acid or ASA)." [99]

Sterling Drug's reply to the article stated that Consumers Union "errs in perpetuating the myth that all aspirins are alike." [100] The company stated that a four year study by Bayer showed Bayer superior in "reliability, stability, purity, and freshness" to more than 200 other brands tested. Sterling agreed with Consumers Union that aspirin is still the drug of choice among nonprescription pain relievers. Finally, Sterling said it "has never claimed that . . . Vanquish and Cope are superior to Bayer or any other aspirin. The Consumers Union statement to this effect is in error." [101]

The Food and Drug Administration

For some time, the FDA had been pressing for a legislative change that would give them control of over-the-counter drug advertising. So far, the proposed change had received little attention in Congress. One FDA official, while hesitating to openly criticize the FTC, stated that, "while we have control over over-the-counter labeling claims, a great deal of benefits are either implied or stated in the advertising that could never be put on labels," and although the FDA has a liaison with the FTC on drug advertising, "there are a lot of things that fall through the crack." [102]

A published report entitled "A Study of Health Practices and Opinions," issued by the FDA during the week of October 16, 1972, appeared to boost that agency's case for taking over regulation of nonprescription drug advertising.[103] The report was initiated by the Senate committee on aging, but went well beyond the habits and views of older consumers. According to the FDA, the findings were the result of "a representative sampling of the U.S. population" [104] consisting of almost 3000 people in 106 communities. Conclusions and findings in the report included:

1) 38 percent of the consumers interviewed agreed that ad claims for over-the-counter remedies must be correct or the government would not permit the advertisers to use them.
2) Based on projections of the interviews, 33 percent of the public would take an over-the-counter remedy against a doctor's advice.
3) Many consumers believe that nonprescription treatment will cure, "rather than merely provide relief for" asthma, allergies, diabetes, and hemorrhoids.
4) "It is probable that there is an enormous waste of money, not to mention adverse health effects, from misguided consumer experimentation with health products. . . ." [105]

National Association of Broadcasters

In February 1973, the television code review board of the National Association of Broadcasters issued a set of new rules and limitations on TV drug ads.[106] Adopted by a unanimous vote of the board, the rules went into effect September 1, 1973, and included the networks and most stations.

The new rules require an "overt reference" to the need to follow directions and cautions on the labels. The rules ban:

1) "Personal testimonials or endorsements of products by authority figures or celebrities."
2 Use of children in commercials for drugs taken by adults.
3) "On-camera taking of pills or capsules." [107]

Capability claims "shall be directed to symptoms/conditions for which the product is intended and for which substantiation has been supplied." [108] The intent, as stated by the board, is to encourage drug ads that provide factual information about products consistent with package and label information and that avoid "overstatement in both audio and video." [109]

Rep. Paul Rogers (D-Fla) who helped work out the regulations, said the board's action was "a public service of the first magnitude," and continued that he was hopeful the rules "will result in the end of the Cinderella syndrome which over-the-counter drugs have created on TV." [110]

The FTC's New Chairman

On February 20, 1973, Lewis Engman became the new chairman of the FTC, succeeding Miles Kirkpatrick, who resigned. Robert Pitofsky, consumer protection chief, also resigned, stating the expiration of his leave of absence from NYU law faculty as his reason.

In testimony before the Senate commerce committee, Engman stated that he did not believe "as some apparently do" that advertising was inherently suspect, "but I believe it has to be truthful." [111] Engman also said his predecessors, Weinberger and Kirkpatrick, had followed "a very laudatory course," vowing that the FTC "will continue to explore imaginative and innovative techniques for fulfilling its responsibility." [112] Although he considered himself a "novice" to advertising, Engman did say he approved moves toward ad substantiation and tougher penalties for false advertising. "There have been abuses," he told the committee, "and we must continue to seek effective means of dealing with these abuses without imposing burdens on legitimate business practices." [113] Throughout the hearing, Engman clearly made a determined effort to dispel the speculation that the FTC would be put back into mothballs. Indications were that the commission would begin to concentrate on establishing rules and regulations, relying on state and local agencies to assist it in the enforcement of the guidelines.

The Advertising Industry

Tom Dillon, president of the advertising agency, Batten, Barton, Durstine, and Osborn, Inc., believed that getting public attention is as much the FTC's goal as it is Madison Avenue's. Prodded by consumerists and legislators anxious to show their constituencies that someone is looking out for their welfare in Washington, the commission has to react strongly.

Dillon said of that reaction,

> Their own survey showed that only 5 percent of complaints are about advertising, and I'll bet only a fraction of those have anything to do with network TV. But the FTC does not have the staff or the money to go after the little guys. They have to go after the highly visible advertiser and that means attacking network television.

Dillion further comments:

> It's difficult to say what the commission should do. They are widening the parameters of their presumed responsibility—they are trying to regulate communication—and I wish journalists were as concerned with their aims as they are about the Defense Department's. We will probably have to get into court to find out if the FTC is empowered to expand into some of the areas it wants to get into —such as the idea that for every positive claim you make, you will have to make a non-positive one. [114]

Some ad men have scoffed at the suggestion that a client spend one-fourth of his annual budget on ads that say, for example, "It has not been established that Anacin is more effective for relief of minor pains than aspirin." [115] However, a number of companies, as previously noted, have already agreed to run corrective ads, and many in the ad industry agree with the need for the FTC actions that the consumerism movement has stimulated. One of these, Ernest Brower, the twenty-seven-year-old special projects chairman of the Los Angeles Junior Advertising Club, blistered the ears of the Western Region American Advertising Federation members in November 1969 with a plea for more responsibility in advertising. Brower asked his audience to:

. . . consider for a moment our hollowed consumer. Now this poor bastard is being pummelled by over 1,500 messages a day. Some are good. Perhaps the majority. But almost as many proffer products dishonestly, insult the intelligence, are presented in bad taste, or are just no damned good at all. As an industry, we frolic precariously close to the edge of the consumer's tolerance level. . . . As we edge toward the saturation point, it becomes harder and harder to distinguish the good from the bad. And that's a shame. Admit it, we've built many of our ads to conform to his faults, to play on them—indeed to prey on them—and it won't be the consumer's fault if through the morass of kitchen giants and detergent doves, he (more likely she) opts not for the credible, but for the crap . . . In many circles we are gaining our reputation as predators, fabricators, as rapidly as we are losing it as communicators . . . The proliferation of inane, hypocritical advertising is a slap in the face of the pool from which we must draw our future ranks and insure our future success, namely the young.[116]

His speech was met by the advertising industry with mixed reactions, about half for and half against.

In an attempt to meet criticisms of the ad industry, the National Advertising Division (NAD) of the Council of Better Business Bureaus and a separate "court of appeals," the National Advertising Review Board (NARB), were set up during the latter part of 1971. But only since January 1973 have they become serious and, thus, controversial. William H. Ewen, executive director of the NARB, points out that everyone connected with NAD-NARB was aware that critics would label it an apologist for the advertising industry at first, "but now we think we have changed some minds." [117]

With an eye on potential legislation that threatened to curtail their industry, the major ad groups—American Association of Advertising Agencies, American Advertising Federation, and the Association of National Advertisers—moved to prove they could handle the problem. A decision was made to work with the Council of Better Business Bureaus, which itself had been under attack by consumerists and had been restructured and revitalized to take a more active consumerist role. The NAD is the complaint bureau, and it screens complaints lodged by citizens, consumerists, rival advertisers, and others, serving first in a grand jury capacity to determine if the facts call for a fuller investigation. If they do, the NAD calls on the advertiser or agency for comments, substantiation of claims, and other material needed to reach a decision. Of some 511 complaints submitted to the NAD thus far, more than 400 have been processed, and about 150 have been dismissed after consideration.[118]

If complainants or advertisers are not satisfied with the NAD findings, they can ask for an appeal to the review board. About 10 cases have gone to the NARB, but they have been the ones that made the headlines in the advertising trade press. The decisions have also pleased some industry supporters of the operation, riled others, and drawn consumerists' blasts. In the NARB procedure, a panel of five judges rules on the merits of each complaint. The panel is drawn from 50 high-ranking executives on call, 30 of whom are from advertisers, 10 from agencies, and 10 from what might be considered the ranks of consumers in that they are lawyers, college professors, etc. Each panel is assembled in a 3-1-1 ratio, and members are called in from across the country.

The procedure troubles Ms. Angevine of the Consumer Federation. "I used to think the FTC was slow," she says. Of 35 complaints filed by the Consumer Federation in the past year, she complains, only 17 have been acted upon and none has been upheld. "We won't be sending any more complaints," she says. "We simply don't have the time and energy for such a charade." [119]

On the other hand, the NARB director, Ewen, thinks much good has come from the operation. In addition to its role as an arbiter, it has fastened the first of several consultative panels to study such things as how women are portrayed in ads and whether some ads may cause unsafe behavior. [120]

The Continuing Controversy

On March 13, 1973, after eleven months of negotiation, the FTC announced that it would issue complaints against AHP, Bristol Meyers Company, and Sterling Drug, Inc., the same firms which received consent orders on April 19, 1972, because no agreements could be reached with the firms on claims of misleading advertising for their pain killers. Specifically, the FTC said it could find no proof of these advertising claims:

1) That the Bayer products are superior to other aspirins.
2) That Cope is more effective in killing headache pain than any other nonprescription internal analgesic.
3) That Vanquish upsets the stomach less frequently than other pain killers.
4) That Bufferin and Excedrin have double the pain killing power of aspirin.
5) That Excedrin PM is a mild sedative or a better pain reliever than aspirin.
6) That Anacin is better than any other nonprescription pain killer on the market. [121]

The complaint also stated there was no real scientific evidence that any of the products ease nervous tension or help people get through the ordinary stresses of everyday life. The FTC further accused the manufacturers of combination pain killers of representing the main ingredient of their products as something other than aspirin. [122]

FOOTNOTES

[1] Stephen A. Greyser, "Advertising: Attacks and Counters," *Harvard Business Review*, March–April 1972, p. 24.

[2] Susan Wagner, *The Federal Trade Commission* (New York: Praeger Publishers, 1971), p. 17.

[3] *Ibid.*, pp. 152–153.

[4] "Corrective Advertising Order of the Federal Trade Commission," *Harvard Law Review*, December 1971, pp. 477–506.

[5] *Ibid.*

[6] *Ibid.*

[7] " 'Buffered Aspirin' the medicine show technique again," *Consumer Reports*, May, 1958, p. 278.

[8] *Ibid.*, p. 278–279.

[9] "Advertising and the government missed the boat on the validity of aspirin advertising" *Consumer Bulletin*, May, 1963, p. 36.

[10] *Ibid.*

[11] *Ibid.*

[12] "FTC Plans to Renew Complaints Against Analgesic Makers," *Advertising Age*, April 17, 1972, p. 97.

[13] "Federal Agencies Under Fire," *U.S. News and World Report*, November 9, 1970, pp. 82–84.

[14] *Ibid.*

[15] Yale Brozen, "The FTC and Trial by Publicity," *Advertising Quarterly*, Spring 1972, p. 27.

[16] Gerald Rosen, "The FTC Cracks the Whip," *Dun's Review*, January 1973, p. 40. Reprinted with the special permission of *Dun's Review*, January 1973. Copyright, 1973, Dun & Bradstreet Publications Corporation.

[17] *Ibid.*, p. 40.

[18] *Ibid.*, p. 42.

[19] "FTC Proposed Guides for Advertising Drugs Over the Counter," *The Wall Street Journal*, March 19, 1969, p. 14.

[20] Jonathan Spivak, "FDA, FTC Devising Joint Drive to Limit Nonprescription Drug Promotional Claims," *The Wall Street Journal*, June 27, 1969, p. 8.

[21] Rosen, "The FTC Cracks the Whip," p. 42.

[22] "FTC Plans Product-Endorsement Guides with Organizations' Plugs the Main Target," *The Wall Street Journal*, November 28, 1972, p. 5.

[23] "Charles Pfizer and Company's Advertising of a Sunburn Reliever is Challenged by FTC," *The Wall Street Journal*, April 17, 1970, p. 4.

[24] "FTC Aide Bids to Drop Complaint Citing Pfizer," *The Wall Street Journal*, May 10, 1971, p. 16.

[25] "Nader's Bid to Require Proof of Ad Claims to be Studied by FTC," *The Wall Street Journal*, December 14, 1970, p. 8.

[26] *Ibid.*

[27] Rosen, "The FTC Cracks the Whip," p. 42.

[28] *Ibid.*

[29] "Corrective Advertising Order of the FTC," p. 506.

[30] "Deceptive Advertising: Pressures for Change," *Congressional Quarterly Weekly Report*, April 1, 1972, pp. 727–730.

[31] Staff Report to the FTC Commission on the Ad Substantiation Program Together With Supplementary Analysis of the Submissions and Advertisers' Comments, 92nd Congress, 2nd Session, Washington, D.C.: U.S. Government Printing Office, 1972, p. 67.

[32] "Deceptive Advertising: Pressures for Change," pp. 727–730.

[33] "Review and Outlook—This Way to the Egress," *The Wall Street Journal*, August 28, 1972, p. 6.

[34] "Deceptive Advertising: Pressures for Change," pp. 727–730.

[35] *Ibid.*

[36] U.S. Senate Committee on Commerce Advertising Hearing on S-1461, 92nd Congress, 1st Session (Serial No. 92-31), October 4, 1971.

[37] "Advertising Marketing Reports on the 100 Top National Advertisers," *Advertising Age*, August 28, 1972, p. 165.

[38] "The Fortune Directory of the 500 Largest Industrial Corporations," *Fortune*, May 1972, p. 196.

[39] Nancy Giges, "Lysol, Bayer and New Products Keep Sterling Sales Rising," *Advertising Age*, November 20, 1972, p. 90.

[40] *Ibid.*

[41] *Ibid.*

[42] "Advertising Marketing Reports on the 100 Top National Advertisers," p. 165.

[43] *Ibid.*

[44] *Ibid.*

[45] *Nonprescription Pain Relievers: A Guide for Consumers*, The Bayer Company, 1971, p. 1.

[46] *Ibid.*

[47] *Ibid.*

[48] *Ibid.*, p. 2.

[49] *Ibid.*, p. 5.

[50] *Ibid.*, p. 5.

[51] *Ibid.*, p. 6.

[52] *Ibid.*, p. 6.

[53] *Ibid.*, p. 8.

[54] *Ibid.*, p. 9.

[55] *Ibid.*, p. 9.

[56] *Ibid.*, p. 11.

[57] *Ibid.*, p. 13.

[58] *Ibid.*, p. 14.

[59] *Ibid.*, p. 19.

[60] *Ibid.*, p. 20.

[61] *Ibid.*, p. 25.

[62] "American Home, A Reticent Giant," *Business Week*, March 21, 1970, pp. 76–77.

[63] *Ibid.*, p. 76.

[64] *Ibid.*, pp. 76–77.

[65] *Ibid.*

[66] *Ibid.*

[67] Hy Gardner, "Danger Makes the Act, Senior Wallenda Says," *The Roanoke Times*, January 29, 1973, p. 16.

[68] "Company Performance Roundup," *Business and Society Review*, Autumn 1972, p. 87.

[69] "FDA, FTA Devising Joint Drive to Limit Nonprescription Drug Promotional Claims," p. 8.

[70] "FTC Canceled Move to Set Regulations on Analgesics Ads," *The Wall Street Journal*, January 6, 1971, p. 2.

[71] John D. Morris, "FTC Assails Pain Killer Ads: Says They Mislead the Public," *New York Times*, April 20, 1972, pp. 1, 28.

[72] "FTC Hits Ads of Three Aspirin-Item Makers; FDA Challenges Value of Many Analgesics," *The Wall Street Journal*, April 20, 1972, p. 4.

[73] *Ibid.*

[74] *Ibid.*

[75] *Ibid.*

[76] Stanley E. Cohen, "FTC Spells Out Corrective Ad Proposals for Analgesics," *Advertising Age*, April 24, 1972, p. 1.

[77] *Ibid.*

[78] "FTC Hits Ads of Three Aspirin-Item Makers; FDA Challenges Value of Many Analgesics," p. 4.

[79] "American Home, A Reticent Giant," pp. 768–77.

[80] Barry Kramer, "Consumers Union Rx Could Prove Headache for Branded Aspirin," *The Wall Street Journal*, August 4, 1972, p. 17.

[81] "News From the World of Medicine," *Reader's Digest*, January, 1973, pp. 181–182.

[82] "FTC Hits Ads of Three Aspirin-Item Makers; FDA Challenges Value of Many Analgesics," p. 4.

[83] "Makers of Anacin Agree to Drop AMA-Linked Ads," *The Wall Stret Journal*, December 29, 1970, p. 8.

[84] Jane E. Brody, "Pain Killer Test is Led by Aspirin," *New York Times*, April 22, 1972, p. 30.

[85] *Ibid.*

[86] "Pain-Reliever Study Promises a Headache for Aspirins' Rivals," *The Wall Street Journal*, April 13, 1972, p. 23.

[87] John D. Morris, "Free Consumer TV Ads are Demanded," *New York Times*, April 29, 1972, p. 37.

[88] "Advertising, Marketing Reports on the 100 Top National Advertisers," p. 165.

[89] U.S. Senate Committee on Commerce Advertising Hearing on S-1461 and S-1753, 92nd Congress, 2nd Session (Amendment No. 1118), p. 68.

[90] ". . . And Now a Word from Our Non-Sponsor . . . ," *The Wall Street Journal*, August 7, 1972, p. 4.

[91] "Consumers Union Rx Could Prove Headache for Branded Aspirin," p. 17.

[92] *Ibid.*

[93] "Aspirin and Its Competitors," *Consumer Reports*, August 1972, pp. 540–544.

[94] *Ibid.*, p. 541.

[95] *Ibid.*, p. 541.

[96] *Ibid.*, p. 541.

[97] *Ibid.*, p. 541.

[98] *Ibid.*, p. 542.

[99] *Ibid.*, p. 543.

[100] "Consumers Union Rx Could Prove Headache for Branded Aspirin," p. 17.

[101] *Ibid.*

[102] "Study Cites Over-Use of OTC Drugs; FDA Bids for FTC's Power Over Ads," *Advertising Age*, October 16, 1972, p. 2.

[103] *Ibid.*, p. 96.

[104] *Ibid.*, p. 2.

[105] *Ibid.*, p. 96.

[106] "Guarded Reaction by Drug Ad Critics to New O-T-C Rules From Code Board," *Advertising Age*, February 26, 1972, p. 1.

[107] *Ibid.*

[108] *Ibid.*

[109] *Ibid.*, p. 157.

[110] *Ibid.*

[111] Stanley E. Cohen, "Engman Says He'll Continue FTC Present Course on Ads," *Advertising Age*, February 12, 1972, p. 3.

[112] *Ibid.*, p. 59.

[113] *Ibid.*, p. 3.

[114] "Madison Avenue's Response to Its Critics," *Business Week*, June 10, 1972, pp. 46–50.

[115] *Ibid.*

[116] Jacqueline Eagle, "Stormy Weather in Media City," *Media Scope*, February 1970, pp. 29–32.

[117] "The Industry Gets a Controversial Watchdog," *Business Week*, May 12, 1973, p. 130.

[118] *Ibid.*

[119] *Ibid.*, p. 133.

[120] *Ibid.*

[121] "Pain Killer Ads Misleading Agency Says," *The Roanoke Times*, March 13, 1973, p. 1.

[122] *Ibid.*

QUESTIONS

1. What in your opinion are the underlying reasons for the different approaches by Sterling and AHP to their environments?
2. What roles do the government agencies perform? Are they a necessary part of the environment?
3. Do environmental pressures call for conflicting behavior by OTC drug companies? What is the nature of the conflict if it does exist?
4. What type of management role do the top managements of the two companies in the case exemplify?
5. How effectively have these companies responded to the expectations of consumers?
6. What alternative tools are required to further strengthen government agency's hand in protecting the consumer?
7. What is implied about the current concept of consumerism based on the actions of the FTC and FDA?
8. Discuss the effectiveness of the coordination between the FTC and FDA.
9. What roles were played by pressure groups such as the Stern Concern and Consumers Union?
10. What changes were made in the FTC's coping strategy during the case and what were the reasons for these changes?
11. Discuss the adequacy of the claims made in the booklet published by Sterling to differentiate Bayer aspirin. Were claims substantiated?
12. What are the variations in coping strategies and organizational roles performed by Sterling and AHP?
13. What was the nature of role strain resulting from coping strategies developed by the two drug companies?

14. What appears to have been the impact of attempts by the various governmental and independent groups to protect the consumer?
15. Are these companies required to respond effectively to the expectations of society? Explain your answer.

CHAPTER 14

OWNERSHIP
CLAIMS

CASE 16
CAMPAIGN GM

When the role expectations of at least some segment of a society are in conflict with the self-perceived social role of a large powerful corporation operating in that society, how is such a corporation pressured to be more responsive to society's expectations? Corporations normally interrelate to varying degrees with several relevant publics including employees, suppliers, owners, and customers. Many firms might be prepared to undertake a variety of socially oriented expenditures if they could reconcile them with stockholder interests.

Possibly with this in mind several individuals formed an association designated Campaign GM, purchased a few shares of General Motors Corporation (GM) stock, then attempted to introduce changes in company policy and structure via the proxy procedure. These changes, the group believed, would make GM more responsive to its several constituencies. A second purpose of this group was to force the board of directors to be more active and responsive to social problems. One of the demands of Campaign GM was that the GM board be enlarged so that it could not only effectively represent the stockholders but also the public interest.

The question of whether a board of directors should represent clientele groups other than the owners has been debated for many years but no debate has been more enlightening and more relevant today than that held between Professors Berle and Dodd during the early 1930s.

> A classic debate on the question was conducted by Professor Berle and Professor Dodd almost thirty years ago, and Professor Berle has now concluded that Professor Dodd was right in the first place. As is the case in many debates, the theses of the protagonists turn out on inspection to be quite compatible. Professor Berle starts with the proposition that all corporate powers are powers in trust, 'nec-

essarily and at all times exercisable only for the ratable benefit of all the stock-holders as their interest appears'. In the light of this premise, he makes illuminating comments on a number of controversial issues of corporate law and practice. Professor Dodd agrees that corporate powers are powers in trust, to be sure. But the use of private property, he urges, is deeply affected with a public interest, and the development of public opinion is more and more acutely conscious of that fact. Recognition of the public interest in the use of corporate property, Professor Dodd contends, requires that directors be viewed as trustees for the enterprise as a whole—for the corporation viewed as an institution—and not merely as 'attorneys for the stockholders'. To this Professor Berle replied by agreeing that the use of private property, notably in the case of large corporations, was indeed a matter of the highest public importance. But, he said, 'I submit that you cannot abandon emphasis on the view that business corporations exist for the sole purpose of making profits for their stockholders until such time as you are prepared to offer a clear and reasonably enforceable scheme of responsibilities to someone else'. We have no such directing rule. In its absence, the consequence of Professor Dodd's argument would be to submit the control of corporations, and the orientation of their poli-cies, entirely to the management. The older rule, Professor Berle contended, offers the only chance of ordering business affairs in ways which would minimize mana-gerial oversearching and self-seeking. With this position, Professor Dodd then agreed, although he felt that the rule had lost all contact with reality, and with public aspiration.[1]

FOOTNOTE

[1] Eugene V. Rostow, "To Whom and For What Ends is Corporate Management Re-sponsible?" in Edward S. Mason (ed.) *The Corporation in Modern Society*, (Cambridge: Har-vard University Press, 1964), pp. 61–62.

Minority Stockholders Challenge General Motors: Owners' Claims

In early 1970, Ralph Nader, the advocate of consumer interests and critic of the au-tomobile industry, announced the opening of a national campaign to make GM responsible. Several of Nader's colleagues, mostly young lawyers based in Washing-ton, D.C., had formed a Project on Corporate Responsibility to conduct the cam-paign. Nader indicated that he would not be directly involved in the project. The project purchased 12 of GM's 285 million shares of stock to give it a voice in the company's business affairs.

The founders indicated the basic purpose of the campaign would be to alert and inform the public about their omnipresent neighbor, GM, and how it behaves. For instance, Nader accused GM of creating 35 percent of the country's air pollu-tion, of collusion in design and marketing practices, of violating air pollution and safety laws, and of manufacturing shoddy cars that caused rocketing repair bills.[1] Nader also stated that it was time shareholders exercised some right of ownership and that consumers should be represented on the GM board of directors. Further, he contended during the announcement of the project that GM's board must take more responsibility for social problems such as pollution, highway safety, and minority-group employment.[2]

SEC Rules on First Dispute

The project first developed several proposals that it hoped to present for stockholder action at GM's annual meeting in May 1970. Among the resolutions submitted for inclusion in the company's proxy to be voted on by the stockholders were:

(1) To expand the board of directors from 24 to 27 members.

(2) To limit GM's business purposes to those consistent with the laws of public health and safety.

(3) To require management to set up a shareholders' committee to watchdog the public impact of GM's decisions and determine its proper social role.

(4) To require GM to allocate "a fair proportion" of its dealer franchises to members of minority groups and to increase its employment of minorities in managerial and other skilled jobs.

(5) To improve the design of GM cars so that occupants wearing proper seat and shoulder belts could survive without injury crashes at 60 miles an hour.

(6) To make GM cars comply as promptly as possible with the standards for emissions from vehicles recommended by the National Air Pollution Control Administration, to be in effect by 1975.

(7) To require GM to support, rather than lobby against, allocating of federal tax money to finance studies aimed at improving mass transit facilities.[3]

While the project exercised its right as a stockholder by presenting all proposals for inclusion in the company's proxy statement, the first three were given greatest emphasis. More detailed descriptions of each of these proposals are presented below.

(1) The expansion of the board of directors from 24 to 27 members was to include three new members representing the public interest. The project's choices were: (a) Betty Furness, former White House consumer affairs advisor, (b) Rene DuBois, noted biologist and ecologist, and (c) Channing Phillips, president of the Housing Development Corporation in Washington, D.C.[4]

(2) GM should limit business to that consistent with the laws of public health and safety. This was an amendment to the company's certificate of incorporation. The amendment stated that none of the purposes of the corporation could be implemented "in a manner which is detrimental to the public health, safety, or welfare, or in a manner which violates any law of the U.S. or of any state in which the corporation does business." [5]

(3) Management should set up a shareholders' committee to watchdog the public impact of GM policy and determine the company's proper social role. Top pri-

ority should be given to the company's effort to design a "non-polluting" car with substantially lower accident and repair cost potential. The watchdog committee would consist of 15 to 25 persons appointed by a majority vote of 3 people—one representing the project, one representing the United Auto Workers (UAW), and one representing the GM board.[6]

As one might expect, GM protested the attack on its integrity, and appealed the inclusion of these proposals to the Securities and Exchange Commission (SEC). The SEC directed GM to include in its proxy to be voted on by the stockholders proposals #1 and #3 above. None of the other proposals were supported. The SEC ruling included the following:

> Management may exclude a shareholder's proposal if it is 'not a proper subject for action by security holders' under the law of the company's state of incorporation; if it asks management to act on matters related to conduct of day-to-day business normally determined by management; or if the proposal seeks primarily to enforce a personal claim or redress a personal grievance.[7]

Proposals #1 and #3 were ruled not subject to these exclusions. It was not unusual for the commission to order issues placed before a company's stockholders, but this marked the first time that consumer matters were to be put before such a group. This particular action, many believed, could lead to efforts to put consumer or environmental issues before the stockholders of other industries, such as railroads, power companies, oil companies, and pesticide manufacturers.

However, GM stated its lawyers believed that all the resolutions were illegal and the stockholders should not vote on such issues, but the company would not fight the commission's order. The company further stated that while it was deeply concerned about the problems of environment and urban society, this did not make them proper subjects for a corporate proxy statement.[8] On the other hand, one of the directors of the project pointed out that its continued purpose was to make corporations accountable, to expand business law and make new use of traditional business procedures, and to raise issues such as desegregation, pollution, and product safety.

The 1970 Campaign

GM shareholders, in addition to private individuals, also include such institutions as banks, churches, universities, private foundations, pension funds, and mutual funds. The company began its own campaign to woo its 1.3 million stockholders by sending them a 21-page book defending its actions. The book outlined GM's safety efforts and its emission control devices which were said to eliminate most of the major pollutants from new car engines. It also spelled out plant pollution control efforts and developments in the mass transit field. Finally, it set forth GM's record in hiring and promoting blacks and investing in black projects.

Also, GM took issue with the two proposals presented by the project in its own proxy statement. With regard to the first proposal, the proxy stated that the three additional directors would not be selected "on the basis of their interest in the process of the corporation, but rather on the basis of their sympathy with the special interests of the proponents of the resolution." With regard to the second proposal, GM argued that such an arrangement would give campaign GM and the UAW "majority vote" with the power to elect the entire committee. The company also pointed out the objective of the resolution was "to interpose a body purportedly investigatory in nature but structured for harassment and publicity." [9]

In addition to these actions, the company ran full-page advertisements in about 150 daily and college newspapers around the country asking, "Does GM care about clean air?" and answering "You bet we do." A GM spokesman said the company planned the campaign long before the project emerged, but many of the ads ran about the same time that the proxy material was mailed. [10]

However, GM's most intense efforts were devoted to personal contacts at institutions holding large blocks of its stock. Word leaking from these organizations indicated that GM had told them it wanted a record vote on the proposals. [11] One example of this tactic occurred on April 4, when GM sent Roger B. Smith, its treasurer, and Frederick W. Bowclitch, director of Emission Control Systems, to persuade the Massachusetts Institute of Technology (MIT) to vote its 291,000 GM shares against the proposals at the annual meeting. Before an 18-member panel of students, professors, and corporate members that advise the 68-member committee responsible for voting MIT's stock, Smith maintained that the company was working in the public interest. "GM's interest and the public's are the same. We cannot work for GM and against the public." University officials felt, however, that the 1968 cars topped the 1969's in pollution control devices. In a news conference held later the same day, Bowclitch admitted that MIT's contention was correct. [12]

In general, GM's stated position was that the proposals were meant to harass the corporation and its management, and to promote the particular economic and social views of the sponsor. In a letter to shareholders accompanying the company's proxy statement, James M. Roche, chairman, and Edward N. Cole, president, recommended a vote against the proposals and argued "they would restrict management's ability to meet its responsibilities to the stockholders and public." [13] The chairman and president also stated that the 12 shares were bought by the project to promote "its own particular economic and social view." [14]

On the other side, the project initiated its campaign by mailing 2000 of its 15-page proxy statements to mutual funds, brokers, universities, and other institutions that held large blocks of stock. In some cases, a spokesman stated, it wasn't known whether the institution owned GM stock. The project also planned to set up regional distribution centers where individual stockholders could pick up proxy material. The group's proxy statement contained the two proposals included in the GM proxy plus a third proposal that would amend the company's certificate of incorporation listed as #2 above.

The project also planned to hold several press conferences and sponsor conventions on corporate responsibility. These would be included with strategy meetings for GM stockholders.

Mainly because of their growing interest in environmental problems, many students at universities holding GM stock supported the project. Yet, their support did not seem to have great impact on the way most universities decided to vote their stock. For instance, student environmental leaders at the University of Michigan demanded that an open hearing be held in the "university community" to determine the way the 27,538 shares of GM stock should be voted. However, regents at both the University of Michigan and University of California rejected proposals that they order their institution's shares of GM stock voted in favor of the project. The Michigan Regents stated they had a consistent policy of voting university shares for the recommendations of the management or of withholding its proxy votes and disposing of its shares. The treasurer of Harvard University also sided with the GM position and stated that in Nader's proposal to organize the GM board of directors was "an opening wedge in a movement to socialize the traditional American way of doing business." [15]

Other kinds of institutions and individuals also made their voting intentions quite clear during the campaign. U. S. Senator Philip Hart (D-Mich) stated that he would vote his 315 shares in favor of the two proposals submitted to the annual meeting by the project. He argued that the government alone wouldn't protect the environment, so citizens must also make their influence felt through non-government channels such as the two proposals. [16] Also on May 13, the Rockefeller Foundation said that it found much to recommend in the two proposals, but that it would vote against them this time. A spokesman for the foundation stated, "We do not share the view which was expressed by management that the campaign GM proposals represent an attack on the corporation." [17]

New York City held 160,000 shares of GM stock in its pension fund and it decided to vote this block of stock against the corporate management. A spokesman for the fund noted that GM had spent $250 million on advertising the previous year and only $15 million on developing automobile pollution devices, indicating that some of GM priorities were out of order. He further stated that the city employees who ultimately benefited from the income produced by the pension funds had a right to live in a decent environment and to know that the cars they drove were as safe and pollution-free as modern technology could make them. [18]

During the final weeks before the annual meeting, shareholders were wooed by management as though a major proxy fight were on. One bank trust officer who has had intimate exposure to the GM effort stated, "We're being treated to a classic example of corporate overkill." [19]

Albert Besney, vice-president for finance and planning at Antioch College said jokingly, "Aside from feeling occasionally like our 1000 shares is a majority holding in GM, there hasn't been any pressure at all." Antioch decided to vote its shares for the project's proposals. Shortly after that decision was made, Richard Mansfield, an Antioch trustee and a vice president of a GM subsidiary, made several telephone calls and a personal visit to the college urging a reversal of the Antioch position. [20]

During this period, the project also charged that GM had spent more than $500,000 to defeat the proposals. The company refused to say what "normal" expenditures connected with stockholders' meetings had been in the past. It was also pointed out by New York attorney Stanley Kaufman, a specialist in stockholder actions, that the proposals had no chance to pass. "Even 10–15% of the vote against management would be unheard of for a shareholder proposal." [21] However, a spokesman for the project stated the campaign had already achieved a degree of success by putting GM on display. "Ironically, their asserted vigorous opposition may have helped the campaign to achieve its aim of publicizing the issue, particularly among a wider body of stockholders than the project itself might have reached." [22]

The 1970 GM Annual Meeting

Some 2000 stockholders, three times that of the previous year's meeting, crowded into Cobo Hall Civic Center, Detroit, to attend GM's annual meeting on May 22. The confrontation appeared to be less a duel between stockholder and management than between stockholder and stockholder. One frequent meeting goer, often described as a gadfly, Mrs. Soss, called Nader "the merchant of venum." She said, "I couldn't think of a worse time for Mr. Nader to pick than during a bear market to make all his extravagant demands. It all leaves me cold." She continued that in the past, she had attended GM annual meetings "to save capitalism from the capitalists by protecting shareholders' interests. Now it looks like we may have to save it from the socialists." [23]

Any concern over inroads the project might possibly have achieved during the meeting were shortlived, for GM easily turned back both proposals. The resolutions received only 2.44 percent and 2.73 percent of the stock voted. The project's plans also were frustrated in several ways during the course of the extremely long annual meeting. A handful of regular meeting goers successfully acquired one of the six microphones at least as often as the reformers. The regulars expressed views either supporting management, stressing the traditional goals of small holders for higher profits and dividends, or openly attacking the goals of the reformers as the beginning of the "end of the capitalist system." When microphones were acquired by members of the project, they were occasionally either turned off by the chairman or speakers were halted before their point could be completed. However, a number of the reformers did praise Roche, the chairman, for the manner in which he handled the meeting. [24]

During the meeting, students and other supporters of the two proposals attacked GM's role as a defense supplier, called it "racist" for doing business in South Africa, and alleged GM was and is slow to respond to the problems of auto safety and air pollution. Roche deplored the war in Southeast Asia, but said GM would continue to support the U. S. government. He denied GM was racist. Other questions and statements by project members hammered at the point that GM's directors were mainly businessmen, rather than representatives of large groups, such as consumers, who are affected by the consequences of GM's actions. [25]

Despite its lopsided victory, GM's top management wasn't feeling particularly elated over the outcome of the voting. "I don't think we won a victory," said Roche, chairman and chief executive, at a press conference after the marathon 6½-hour meeting. "We won a vote of confidence. We could lose that vote of confidence very quickly unless we respond in the way our shareholders expect us to." [26]

Philip Sorenson, one of the project leaders, said the assault on GM was "a substantial victory" because "everything they did was a direct response" to the charges of the reformers. [27]

After GM's 1970 annual meeting the project announced it would continue its campaign GM and also aim at making more responsible Ford, Chrysler, AT&T and six pharmaceutical companies. With this in mind, Nader announced that ten graduate students would spend the summer studying GM to determine whether its policies were serving consumers. The students would interview a cross-section of the 750,000 employees of the company, including retired engineers and executives.

The 1971 Campaign

During and after the 1970 campaign for proxies, both foundations and individual stockholders, although having made a decision to vote with management, wrote to the GM chairman, James Roche, expressing their lack of satisfaction with progress on safety, pollution controls, and minority hiring. This kind of pressure apparently contributed to several actions taken by GM during the next year.

For instance, in September 1970 GM announced the establishment of a public policy committee to advise the company on matters that affect the general public. The committee was made up of five members of the 23-member board of directors of GM, four of whom were outside members. The fifth was a former vice chairman of the board. The committee was an apparent direct answer to demands of the project. However, the project was not satisfied. Ralph Nader described the committee during an interview as "genuinely preposterous." He felt the fact that they could not go outside of the company for the members was an indication of GM's insecurity. He also believed it would backfire on the company. [28]

Early in January 1971, Dr. Leon Howard Sullivan, a black minister from Philadelphia who had been a pioneer in helping blacks find better jobs in industry, was elected to the board of directors of GM. The company believed the election of Sullivan, GM's first black director, would strengthen its hand in its tough new stance toward Ralph Nader and the Project on Corporate Responsibility. During an interview with Sullivan after the election, he stated that the blacks must be given a share in the American economy, but that blacks should join the free enterprise system and not strive for separation. Leaders of the project interpreted the election as another victory in their attempt to make the corporation more responsible to social problems. [29]

Again in early February 1971, GM took the initiative and created a new department to supervise company activities related to the environment. This was soon changed to a committee of six scientists with responsibility for advising the company on the environmental effects of its products and operations. The committee was headed by Dr. Charles H. Townes, professor of physics at the University of California at Berkeley, and winner of a Nobel Prize in 1964.[30]

The project called the committee an interesting and promising gesture, but added that so far there had been no real change in GM policies toward the environment and safety. Philip Moore, the executive director of the project, declared that all the members were directly responsible to the corporation and did not hold public meetings, and that there was, therefore, no way of knowing whether they were raising important issues or whether they were having a real effect.[31]

In addition to these actions, the corporation carried out several additional projects. It loaned $1 million dollars to black groups for low-income housing in two cities where the company had plants. The company deposited $5 million in black-controlled banks around the country, and it spent $188 million—according to company figures—to fight pollution from its cars and plants.[32]

While GM was taking these actions, the project began to seek support for three new resolutions to be introduced at GM's annual meeting in May 1971. According to Philip C. Sorenson, chairman of the project's board of directors, the adoption of the new resolutions would have a fundamental impact on GM's decision-making process, "opening it up to new people and new ideas." [33] The three proposals were:

(1) The "Proposal on Shareholder Democracy" would require GM to list on the proxy ballot it sends to its stockholders not only management's nominees for directors, but also candidates nominated by petition by non-management shareholders. Under the present system, GM's proxy statement lists only management's slate. According to the project, this proposal would "transform the selection of directors into a real election in which all shareholders would have the chance to make meaningful nominations and to choose among opposing candidates."

(2) The "Proposal on Constituent Democracy" would permit 3 important constituencies of GM—GM employees, GM consumers, and GM dealers—to participate in the election of 3 of the company's directors. This proposal reflects the project's belief that groups substantially affected by GM's decisions must be given a more direct and meaningful voice in the corporation's decision-making process.

(3) The "Proposal on Disclosure" would require GM to publish in its annual report hard statistics revealing GM's progress on auto-pollution control, auto-safety, and minority hiring. The project thinks such disclosures would provide GM shareholders, constituents, and the public with the minimum information needed to effectively evaluate GM's responsiveness to public needs.[34]

On April 9, GM placed in its proxy statement eight shareholder proposals, including the three proposed by the Project on Corporate Responsibility. The company said, "Despite serious reservations regarding the suitability for inclusion in the proxy statement of a number of these proposals, the board of directors decided that

GM stockholders should be afforded the opportunity to express their views on them." [35]

In a statement opposing the three proposals, GM warned that its critics were seeking to establish precedents that they would campaign for at other companies. The company argued the disclosure proposal would tie its hands on what should go in the annual report and "could lead to protracted argument and even to expensive litigation" if information was omitted. The company also stated the constituency plan would lead to a kind of popularity contest among loosely-defined groups. If elected, it would also confront the nominee with divided allegiance to the group which nominated him—the dealers, employees, or consumers—and the entire body of stockholders to whom each director has a legal responsibility. Finally, the company contended that the proposal for more candidates—up to thirty—is cumbersome and discards procedures which have contributed to the economic success of GM. [36]

In a series of statements by the chairman of the board of directors, GM further attempted to discredit the Project on Corporate Responsibility and its aim. Several critics were described as the "adversary culture" and charged with misleading the young, the courts, and the government.

"They thrive on the sensational accusations and the publicity it gains." [37]

"They jump from cause to cause going wherever popularity or expediency lead, using whatever means are at hand, inflaming any issue that promises attention." [38]

"They crusade for radical changes in our system of corporate ownership, changes so drastic that they would all but destroy free enterprise as we know it." [39]

"Make no mistake, the results of irresponsible harassment have added significantly to the cost of doing business. The higher taxes are costly. Adapting products to new regulations are costly. Meeting daily harassments, answering criticisms, defending against public attacks, all these carry costs—in time and energy as well as dollars, and the fashion is still to call for these new controls on business." [40]

Meanwhile, the project initiated its drive by writing to the 350 largest mutual funds asking them to poll or take a sample of their stockholders on the proposals that were submitted for consideration at GM's annual meeting. After completing the polls or taking samples, the funds were asked to vote their GM stock the way the fund's stockholders requested. This would presumably be a certain percentage for the project and a certain percentage for GM management. This action marked the first time an attempt had been made to persuade institutional investors such as banks, insurance companies, pension funds, and mutual funds to consider the wishes of their own stockholders on the issues that come up at stockholder meetings.

The project also announced it had written to major brokerage firms which hold stock for customers and warned them that in the project's opinion, the brokers may not legally vote this stock without special instructions from the beneficial owners.

After these actions, the project sent out its own proxies, too, and met personally with representatives of the largest institutional investors, including banks, pension funds, universities, and a few insurance companies.

GM, after taking several steps to improve its social credibility, went to work on the institutional investors, who control most of its common shares and who were most likely to support the social critics this year. The company gave the investors a special tour of GM's technical center and proving grounds near its headquarters to show what it was doing to make cars safer and their engines cleaner. Top company officials also had lengthy lunches with representatives of some of the most influential institutions holding GM stock.

Finally, the company sent a 49-page book describing GM's work in air pollution, safety, abandoned car clean-up, and minority hiring to all its 1.3 million stockholders.[41]

As during the preceding year's campaign, several institutions announced the manner in which they intended to vote their GM stock. On April 14, the First Pennsylvania Banking and Trust Company became the first bank to state it would vote its block of GM stock, 500,000 shares, for the project's proposals that year. The previous August, however, the bank had openly advocated even more drastic changes in corporate boards than those proposed by the project. In fact, to make the bank more responsive to the public, it considered turning over one-third of First Pennsylvania's 24 board seats to consumer representatives, young adults, employees, blacks, the poor, and perhaps militant feminists. A spokesman for GM said the company was surprised by the bank's action.[42]

By a narrow 8 to 7 vote, trustees of the College Retirement Equities Fund, which holds 715,000 GM shares, decided to vote its shares in favor of the project's proposals.[43]

However, on May 19, just prior to the annual meeting, GM picked up the backing of two big institutions. The Carnegie Foundation and the Rockefeller Foundation stated they would vote their 157,801 shares and 195,982 shares respectively for GM management.[44]

In accordance with the project's request, the Dreyfus Leverage Fund, Inc. polled its 127,000 holders on the proposals. Based on the poll, the fund announced its 25,000 shares would support the disclosure proposal submitted by the project. Management would be supported in the other proposals.[45]

The 1971 GM Annual Meeting

Most top executives at GM were satisfied prior to this annual meeting that they could muster enough evidence to demonstrate the company was reordering its recent actions and stepping up public relations efforts. However, these actions, with the exception of the election of Sullivan, had not impressed Nader and his associates. At an interview a day before the annual meeting, they commented that such actions were all purely cosmetic. More specifically, Nader argued that the scientific committee, including Dr. DuBridge, former science advisor to President Nixon, was "part of the scientific establishment" without "one potential troublemaker. Their first recommendation," Nader said, "will be we need more research." He felt this was simply stalling.[46]

The group further commented that while GM stated that more than half the salaried workers it had hired in recent years were from minority groups, that still represented just 3 percent of the company's salaried workers and that blacks probably had been shuffled into low-level jobs.[47]

Moore, of the project, also stated that "we don't feel that the American public should depend on the personal integrity" of corporate management, such as Roche. He further commented they were still making decisions as in the past, meaning considering profits and without inviting the public into the debate, thus any changes were transient and not permanent.[48]

During this same time, one of the proposals submitted by the project came under attack. William E. Chatlos, an expert in stockholder solicitation, after scanning the GM proxy statement, concluded that the project proposal on constituent democracy, which required the election of one director each by GM dealers, employees, and consumers was irresponsible. He argued the "massive costs" of putting such a proposal into effect were not even hinted at. He estimated that the election by consumers would cost conservatively around $100 million and additional massive efforts would be required to elect the dealers' and employees' directors.[49]

The annual meeting itself, which ran a record six hours and 56 minutes, gave stockholders little important financial information but did serve as a forum for a full-scale debate on the social obligations of the large corporation. However, unlike the previous year, the GM chairman didn't treat speakers from the audience with equal fairness. He allowed a boosters group from Flint, Michigan to speak at length on the glories of GM, often when what it was saying had nothing to do with the subject under discussion. But, he frequently cut off speakers representing the project before they had a chance to develop their point.

While both sides knew beforehand that the project's proposals did not have a chance, both were surprised by how badly they were beaten. The project had predicted around 3 percent of the vote since the previous year two proposals received 2.44 percent and 2.73 percent, yet the three proposals received only from 1.11 percent to 2.36 percent of the shares voted.[50]

Roche acknowledged after the meeting that GM's victory could be very short-lived if it didn't continue to address itself to social issues. The chairman and other top officials commented they realized after the previous year's meeting that the corporation's structure and its emphasis on profit and dividends could be jeopardized in the future unless it proved it was able to respond immediately to specific social problems. At a news conference, Roche told reporters that they could expect to see GM make "the type of changes that are necessary to cope with the problems that we are going to encounter in the days ahead, and we certainly wouldn't hesitate to change whatever structures seem to need changing to deal effectively with the problems that we have." [51]

FOOTNOTES

[1] Richard Halloran, "Nader to Press for G.M. Reform," *New York Times*, February 8, 1970, p. 44.

[2] "Nader's Pitch to G.M. Stockholders," *Business Week*, February 14, 1970, p. 30.

[3] Eileen Shanahan, "G.M. Urged to Respond to Public Need," *New York Times*, February 22, 1970, p. 49.

[4] *Ibid.*

[5] "G.M. Managers Oppose Two Proposals Urged by Nader Associates," *The Wall Street Journal*, April 10, 1970, p. 11.

[6] *Ibid.*

[7] "Nader's Pitch to G.M. Stockholders," p. 30.

[8] Jerry M. Flint, "G.M. Told to Put Consumer Moves to Stockholders," *New York Times*, March 20, 1970, p. 1.

[9] "G.M. Managers Oppose Two Proposals Urged by Nader Associates," p. 11.

[10] Norman Pearlstine, "Activist Shareholders Provoke G.M. Offensive for Its Annual Meeting," *The Wall Street Journal*, May 12, 1970, p. 1.

[11] *Ibid.*

[12] "G.M. Seeking to Kill Nader—Group Motions, Solicits M.I.T. Votes," *The Wall Street Journal*, April 14, 1970, p. 13.

[13] "G.M. Managers Oppose Two Proposals Urged by Nader Associates," p. 11.

[14] Flint, "G.M. Told to Put Consumer Moves to Stockholders," p. 67.

[15] "Harvard Supports G.M. Against Nader," *New York Times*, May 6, 1970, p. 87.

[16] "Hart to Back G.M. Insurgents," *The Wall Street Journal*, April 23, 1970, p. 29.

[17] "Rockefeller Foundation Likes Responsible G.M. Idea, But Won't Vote for It," *The Wall Street Journal*, May 13, 1970, p. 17.

[18] David Bird, "City Will Use Its G.M. Stock to Vote for Nader's Campaign," *New York Times*, May 20, 1970, p. 1.

[19] Pearlstine, "Activist Shareholders Provoke G.M. Offensive for Its Annual Meeting," p. 1.

[20] *Ibid.*

[21] "Nader's Pitch to G.M. Stockholders," p. 30.

[22] M. A. Farber, "Foundations Shy at Plan for G.M.," *New York Times*, May 3, 1970, p. 31.

[23] Art Glickman, "G.M.'s Meeting Today Will Draw Assortment of Corporate Critics," *The Wall Street Journal*, May 22, 1970, p. 17.

[24] "G.M. Easily Turns Back the First Assault From Within by the Liberal Reform Activists," *The Wall Street Journal*, May 25, 1970, p. 4.

[25] *Ibid.*

[26] *Ibid.*

[27] *Ibid.*

[28] Agis Salpukas, "G.M. Names 5 Directors As Public-Issue Advisers," *New York Times*, September 1, 1970, p. 1.

[29] Agis Salpukas, "G.M. Elects First Negro as Member of Its Board," *New York Times*, January 5, 1971, p. 49.

[30] Agis Salpukas, "G.M. Names Panel on Environment," *New York Times*, February 25, 1971, p. 28.

[31] *Ibid.*

[32] Jerry M. Flint, "G.M. Will Face Its Critics at Its Annual Meeting Today," *New York Times*, May 21, 1971, p. 53.

[33] "G.M. Managers Oppose Two Proposals Urged by Nader Associates," p. 11.

[34] *Ibid.*

[35] "G.M. Plans to Oppose 8 Holder Proposals Put in Annual Meeting's Proxy Statement," *The Wall Street Journal*, April 9, 1971, p. 20.

[36] *Ibid.*

[37] Jerry Flint, "G.M.'s Chief Scores Critics of Business," *New York Times*, March 26, 1971, p. 53.

[38] *Ibid.*

[39] *Ibid.*

[40] *Ibid.*

[41] Eileen Shanahan, "G.M. Critics Woo Fund's Investors," *New York Times*, April 14, 1971, p. 59.

[42] "First Pennsylvania Backs 1 of 3 Proposals by G.M. Citizens Group," *The Wall Street Journal*, April 14, 1971, p. 11.

[43] "Institution to Vote 715,000 G.M. Shares Against Management," *The Wall Street Journal*, May 3, 1971, p. 7.

[44] "G.M. Picks Up Backing of 2 Big Institutions Against Nader Group," *The Wall Street Journal*, May 19, 1971, p. 8.

[45] "Dreyfus Leverage's Holders Support G.M. on 4 Proxy Proposals," *The Wall Street Journal*, May 21, 1971, p. 4.

[46] Flint, "G.M. Will Face Its Critics at Its Annual Meeting Today," p. 53.

[47] *Ibid.*

[48] *Ibid.*

[49] Robert Metz, "Market Place: Weighing Cost of Nader Plan," *New York Times*, May 12, 1971, p. 56.

[50] Norman Pearlstine, "G.M. Management Wins Smashing Victory Over Social Critics at Annual Meeting," *The Wall Street Journal*, May 24, 1971, p. 10.

[51] *Ibid.*

QUESTIONS

1. How important was the coverage by the media of Campaign GM activities?
2. What are the distinctions between the public interest and GM's social role as viewed by Campaign GM?
3. What strategy was employed by Campaign GM to achieve their goal?
4. Explain the reasons for GM's response and the demands of Campaign GM.
5. What has been the traditional role of the large corporation with regard to its stockholders?
6. In what manner has the corporate system changed the concept of ownership of private property?
7. How accurately did the results of the 1970 stockholder meeting reflect the successfulness of Campaign GM?
8. If one were to use the composition of membership in Campaign GM as a basis for judging their ability to represent the social good, how effective would they be?
9. During the 1970 campaign at MIT a representative of GM argued, "GM's interest and

the public's are the same. We cannot work for GM and against the public interest." Comment on this statement.

10. What was the strategy employed by GM to counter the environmental threat imposed by Campaign GM?

11. Which of the organizational models of social responsibility set forth in the text section of this book coincides with the expectations of: (a) Campaign GM, (b) GM?

CHAPTER 15

THE
INDIVIDUAL
AND THE
ORGANIZATION

CASE 17
MAJOR LEAGUE BASEBALL

Today, professional sport is big business as testified to by the size and cost of the physical plant, TV contracts, and the salaries of the athletes, coaches, and managers. Major league baseball has often been described as comparable to a trust. The owners of the teams making up the league select a commissioner of baseball who then regulates the league members. He controls competition between members, limits entry, and regulates movements of clubs and the telecasts of home games. It is generally acknowledged that major league baseball is a legal monopoly whose most valuable asset is its players.

The Oakland A's, a professional baseball team, is a member of the American League West. The team is owned by Charles O. Finley, a maverick in many respects, who has taken the once Kansas City A's from virtual oblivion to what some have called a baseball dynasty. From at least an economic standpoint, few can argue with Finley's accomplishment. Yet, team members have little good to say about this man.

This case deals with the rights of private property. In this instance, the property includes not only physical assets, but also the field manager and team members. The issues involved are not only economic but also legal, social, and moral. Each of these issues relates either directly or indirectly to the central problem of determining an equitable balance between property rights and individual personal rights.

The Oakland Athletics and the 1973 World Series:
The Individual and the Organization

The Second Game of the 1973 World Series

The second game of the World Series turned out to be the longest and quite likely the sloppiest game in World Series history. The New York Mets defeated the Oakland Athletics 10–7 after twelve innings and four hours and thirteen minutes. The Athletics made five errors, two of them by substitute second baseman Mike Andrews in the fatal twelfth inning. Andrews had been acquired from Boston midway through the season as a pinch hitter. The game was won or lost perhaps half a dozen times by both teams on errors and misjudged fly balls.[1]

"The game assumed comedic proportions shortly after Bob Hope—who else?—tossed out the first ball. In the very first inning, after Campaneris had grounded out, Joe Rudi lofted a high fly ball into the no-man's land of left field. Cleon Jones backed up against the fence as if to make a dramatic leap and rob Rudi of an extra-base hit, perhaps a homer. He was thus braced when the ball landed about two feet to his left on the warning track. It very nearly skulled him, and it set the tone for the entire contest."[2]

Oakland was leading 3–2 at the beginning of the sixth inning when Vida Blue walked one man and singled another. Manager Dick Williams then replaced Blue with Horacio Pina. On his first pitch he struck Jerry Grote on the hand, loading the bases. His next pitch was chipped along the third base line for a single that scored one run. The next batter lined a single to right field, putting the Mets in front, 4–3.[3]

Williams now replaced Pina with Darold Knowles. The first batter hit the ball back to the mound, Knowles fielded it and threw a hurried pitch home past the waiting catcher allowing two more runs to score.[4]

The Mets were leading by two runs in the ninth inning with Oakland at bat when Mays lost track of a fly ball in the sun, then fell down chasing it, allowing a man on base. Bando drew a walk. Jackson singled both men home, putting the game in extra innings.[5]

In the tenth inning with one out Bud Harrelson of the Mets hit a fly to left field. The runner on third tagged up and ran home. He was called out in a photo finish at the plate. Berra insisted the catcher had missed the tag. All it meant was an inning ending in a double play.[6]

"Numerous television replays, from several camera angles, indicated that A's catcher Ray Fosse missed the tag on Harrelson."[7]

In the twelfth inning Harrelson doubled, then Tug McGraw bunted for a single moving Harrelson to third. The next two batters were out. Mays, up next, hit one through the middle scoring the tie-breaking run.[8]

Cleon Jones poked his third hit of the game to load the bases. "Then John Millner hit a soft roller to second. But Andrews, the A's third second baseman of the game, let the ball get past him for an error, reminiscent of the error Millan of the Mets made which gave the A's their first game victory, 2–1." [9]

"McGraw and Mays scored on the play, and as they went to the dugout Mc-Graw embraced the aging superstar. A moment later, Jerry Grote hit another grounder to Andrews, and the second baseman's throw was wide for his second straight error—Oakland's fifth of the game—and another Met run." [10]

The "error orgy" which embraced most of the second game was over with the Mets winning 10–7. "The game featured six official errors and four other balls that got lost in the outfield glare but were scored as hits." [11] The game featured eleven pitchers in the longest World Series game on record.

Shortly after the game, as the Oakland Athletics were leaving for New York, Charles O. Finley, sole owner of the club, "discharged" Andrews. But first he had Andrews sign a doctor's statement that he had a chronically injured shoulder. Finley then asked the commissioner of baseball for permission to activate Manny Trillo, a young reserve infielder who had already been ruled ineligible.

Charles O. Finley

Charles O. Finley, insurance broker and gentleman farmer, is the sole owner and general manager of the Oakland Athletics. He has proven to be quite a curious individual. He follows no set plan and has no heroes with the possible exception of himself.[12] "I am a self-made man," he says, with the accent on the "self." He seems to operate entirely by whim and yet he possesses an innate shrewdness that permitted him to drive an incredible bargain with the Oakland-Alameda County Coliseum Commission. He is a man of long memory and short temper. He does not like to be corrected, defied, or challenged.[13]

After achieving success in the insurance business, Finley looked again at one of his first loves, baseball. He made many attempts to purchase baseball clubs in the late fifties, "only to be told, privately, of course, that the other owners wouldn't approve of him." [14] Finally, in 1960 he was allowed to purchase the Kansas City Athletics (for $4 million) a team which had demonstrated no potential.

He began his tenure with the team by battling everyone in Kansas City who got in his way. He removed the Athletics' front office staff and threatened to play in a cow pasture. He punctuated his feelings by purchasing a team mascot, "Charlie O., the Missouri mule and took him on road trips, housing him in the Presidential suite at every hotel that would have him." [15] Toward the end of the team's stay in Kansas City, Finley did make temporary peace with the town.

When Finley came into baseball he was told he would need a general manager. So he went out and hired Frank Lane, who was considered the best. After a short time he decided that any average guy off the street could handle the job, so Lane was fired and Finley assumed the position. Finley officially became his own general manager, and unofficially, his own everything else, including field manager as long as telephones worked. However, after going through several field managers, he did find one he felt made a difference in the team. His name was Dick Williams.

After approximately nine years in Kansas City, Finley decided it was time to move elsewhere. He commissioned a research firm to find the perfect site for his franchise. "Allegedly—and Charlie has never denied it—he looked over the candidate cities himself, called the research firm and said: 'Tell me to move to Oakland.' " [16] A five-year television contract calling for $55 million, 25 percent of the concessions, 27½ percent of the parking and only $125,000 for the rent appeared to be major factors. When hearing the news Kansas City sports editor Joe McGruff commented that Oakland was the luckiest city since Hiroshima.

Even after the success of two world championships the other owners still regard him as an interloper. Finley argued: "They haven't accepted me and I don't expect they will. I didn't inherit a team. I didn't work my way up through the minor leagues as an executive. I'm a former Birmingham Barons' batboy who came out of the Gary, Indiana steel mills and made money accidentally in the insurance business. Now I'm ruining the sanctity of their game. If they don't get wise to themselves, they won't have any game left to be sanctimonious about." [17]

Finley has at least two traits that have served him well as a businessman. He is an extremely hard worker and a stickler for detail. No detail of his club's operation is too small to pass his attention. Bob Bestor, former publicity director for Finley's California Seals hockey team, said, "When I was with the Seals he was in our office finding out what kind of paper we used, how many pencils it took to get through the day and what each of us did with our time. I got the idea he'd like to be everywhere at once. He thinks he's God, he wants to be omnipresent." [18]

"Give Charles his due," said Phil Seghi who left Finley to become general manager of the Cleveland Indians. "He's a worker. He's a fanatic for details. People claim he's tough to work for. It's true, everything has to be checked with him. But he wants workers around him. He'll go until 4:00 A.M. and be up and going again at 8:30 A.M. If you work for him you can't worry about your own sleeping habits." [19]

Since coming to Oakland Finley has never made less than $600,000 a season despite the fact he has never drawn a million customers to the Coliseum. In 1972, when teams were unable to turn a profit, Finley bragged of a $1.3 million profit with his championship team. He frequently comments on his method of achieving financial success in organized baseball. "I can turn a profit because I don't have many unessential employees to pay big money to. I put my money into player development and I don't worry about paying $20,000 to a public relations man who can't put any extra people in the seats anyway. . . . Baseball owners tell me they can't make any money. But there's a feeling that every ex-player has to be put on the payroll as a $25,000-a-year scout. I don't see that I'm a charitable organization. A player ought to plan for his future while he's playing and while he has a big name. I've made $100,000 business loans to some of my players. I've given them tips on the market, and I've tried to give them sound business advice. I don't need some ex-player hanging around turning in scribbled, useless scouting reports. I pay the money and the profit should go to me, not him." [20]

"I got where I am by working harder than anybody else. I'm no Harvard man. I'm no brain. I take care of every detail because that's my formula for success." [21]

His formula for success was quite evident during the 1973 World Series. Games in Oakland were played in curiously drab surroundings. The Coliseum is certainly not an architectural masterpiece and for the Series Finley neglected to decorate it with the flags and bunting that are traditional to such events. This seemed especially unusual, since the Athletics owner is a great believer in lily-gilding. The only diversions he provided his spectators on these days—besides anthem singers Jim Nabors and Tennessee Ernie Ford—were Charlie O., the mule, and Cricket, the world's smallest registered horse. [22]

"His treatment of his players is a constant source of curiosity. When Reggie Jackson hit 47 home runs one season, Finley pampered him outrageously. He helped him with his business problems and his personal troubles. When Jackson came around to collect what he assumed would be an enormous contract, he found the club owner standing there with gritted teeth." [23]

"I told Dave Duncan that Finley treated his black players like niggers," Jackson said. "Dave told me not to worry or feel hurt, he said that Charlie treats his white players like niggers, too." [24] When Vida Blue won 26 games in the 1971 season, the "grand duke" bought Vida a new Cadillac, a year's supply of gasoline and gave him $2000 to get himself some decent clothes. Then when Blue and his attorney asked for a $115,000 per year contract, Finley suggested he and his attorney hold hands and jump from the 27th floor office window. Blue settled for $63,150. "That man soured me on baseball," Blue said. "No matter what he does for me in the future, I'll never forget that he treated me like a damn colored boy. That's unforgivable." [25]

In the 1972 World Series when Gene Tenace, the catcher, hit four home runs, Finley gave him a $5000 raise right there. It cost Finley a $2500 fine when the commissioner heard about it, because incentive bonuses are against baseball mores. [26] There appear to be as many Finley kindnesses to his players as there are atrocities.

Andrews' Account of Actions After the Second Game

Shortly after the second game of the World Series Mike Andrews signed a statement that he was injured. He did not make the trip to New York for the third game of the Series but later argued he was badgered into signing an untrue medical statement by Finley. Andrews also made it clear that Finley had made no overt threats, and that no rewards were offered, demanded, or given for the signature.

At a news conference on Wednesday, Mike Andrews recounted the events of Sunday evening. He first commented, "When I came back to the clubhouse I was told that the doctor wanted to see me. I couldn't believe it, so I went to my locker. [27]

"Someone came over and told me again that the doctor was waiting for me in the training room. The doctor, Harry Walker, said that Mr. Finley wanted me examined. I didn't want to do it. [28]

"I thought it was a joke. I was really shocked. Then I let him examine me—it lasted five minutes or so and seemed a very easy exam. [29] Dr. Walker told me I had a condition in my shoulder. I told him that if I had it, it didn't bother me at all. It hadn't bothered me all year. He said he'd tell Finley.[30]

"Then I was asked to go into the manager's office. Dick Williams was there, but he didn't say anything. Finley said he had the doctor's report and wanted to put me on the disabled list.[31]

"I asked Mr. Finley if he wanted me to lie," Andrews said. "He replied, no." [32]

Andrews then inquired of Finley, "Then how do I explain it? It makes me feel that I am a coward." [33]

Andrews said, "He told me it would be beneficial to the ball club. Do I want to help the club? Then he would get very upset. 'Forget everything. Don't sign. We'll get it through without you,' Finley said." [34]

Andrews continued: "I should have walked out on the doctor and Finley in the first place. But I was tired and ashamed [of the errors] and I just hung my head." [35]

Andrews noted that Williams had not said a word to this point during his conversation with Finley.

Finley then suggested that Andrews go up to his office and read the medical report. At this point Williams told Andrews to look at the report and not to sign if he didn't wish to.[36]

Andrews said, "All I could think of was, what do I do now? I was dead anyhow. Maybe Trillo could help the team. I said give me the damn thing. I'll sign it. I just wanted to hide my head. I was embarrassed. I was beaten. For the first time in my life I just quit. I said I'd rather go home." [37]

Finley apparently felt that was a good idea. It would help corroborate the fact he was disabled.

"I'm sorry I signed but if I was in the same state of mind again I'd do the same thing," Andrews continued.[38]

Andrews' attorney said his client, "had not been in complete control of his emotions. He had reached the lowest level of humiliation. At that point he might have signed over [to Finley] the deed to his home." [39]

According to speculation in the papers the events on Sunday night after the second game would seem to be an attempt by Finley to circumvent the disabled-list rules in order to activate a player—Manny Trillo—he considered more useful than Andrews.[40]

Player Reaction

Reggie Jackson, the leading hitter and player representative, said Monday night the bizarre whims of Finley could lead to a wholesale revolt by the players. "There could be a possibility of refusing to play. There are a bunch of guys who are close to that point." [41]

Jackson added, "I just felt bad for the man [Andrews]. We all do. Believe me, there are going to be a lot of holdouts in spring training next year. Some players are going to hold out just for spite." [42]

During the afternoon work out many players taped No. 17 to their shoulders.

Dick Green, the regular second baseman, said team captain Sal Bando and pitcher Vida Blue were behind the plan. [43]

Green commented, "This was a bad time to dump Mike. We got him as a pinch hitter, not as a fielder, and his arm doesn't bother him to swing the bat. Maybe I won't make the trip back to Oakland if I make a couple of errors Tuesday." [44]

Outfielder Billy Conigliaro said, "This is ridiculous. I know Andrews is not hurt, that's for sure. He was embarrassed enough because of the errors without making him look like a fool." [45]

Ted Kubiak, the person Andrews batted for on Sunday, said, "This is the worst run organization there is. The players are really mad. That man Finley has a chance to help himself and baseball and he lets it slip away." [46]

Sal Bando said, "They [management] wanted a change because they weren't happy with Andrews' performance on the field. I assume something extra was involved if he signed that letter." [47]

Darold Knowles, a pitcher, said, "This is the day and age of outspoken players and we've got them on this club. We've had problems in the clubhouse but it's obvious that they haven't hurt us on the field." [48]

Knowles did offer some kind words for Finley. He was grateful to Finley for relocating the players' wives to the lower deck of Shea Stadium to offer them greater protection from the overzealous Mets fans.

During the three games at Shea Stadium, whenever an Oakland fielder made an error, signs would be raised saying, "You're fired!" Vida Blue commented, "If I don't pitch good, they may just leave me here. Are the Jets still looking for a quarterback?" [49]

An Oakland player told the Associated Press that Dick Williams, prior to the third game, "told the team he would resign, win or lose." [50] The player said, "he told us he was in full sympathy with us over the Mike Andrews affair." [51]

When Williams was questioned about leaving Oakland and possibly going to the New York Yankees manager's job, he denied that rumor "1000 percent." [52] Williams was under contract at $75,000 a year for two more years to Oakland.

Finley was questioned about the report and said he would not stand in Williams' way if he wanted to move to the Yankees. [53] Oakland had had 10 managers in the previous 13 years.

In addition to the above comments, many players voiced their dissatisfaction with the way Finley had run the team in general. Several expressed a desire to be traded, commented on the depressing thought of having to play out a career under Finley, and criticized the inept front office. [54] It is true that Finley runs his own show. Yet with smart trades, bonus money, followed by hefty salaries, Finley molded a dynamic team which in 1971, 1972, and 1973 brought an extra paycheck of up to $20,000 per man.

Because of the tight organization it was also very likely understaffed. Of course this may have been one reason he has been able to pay his players their inflated salaries in a city that turned out less than a million fans in a championship season.

Finley is certainly not a diplomat and often puts his worst foot forward, but when pressed, the players could not come up with anything substantial against him, except for the Andrews affair.[55]

In order to balance the ledger a little, there are many people knowledgeable about professional sports that feel that it is a fiction, well maintained, that today's athletes are exploited by management. On the contrary, they argue that most athletes (and their agents) are unashamedly selfish and greedy, and that the owners of the pro teams do more for their employee-players than do employers in any other business in the country.[56]

Commissioner Rules

On October 16, 1973 Commissioner Bowie Kuhn ruled against Finley in the Mike Andrews' case. Kuhn said, "There is no basis to grant the request and it is accordingly denied.[57]

"I might add that the handling of this matter had the unfortunate effect of unfairly embarrassing a player who has given many years of able service to professional baseball. It is my determination that Andrews remains a full-fledged member of the Oakland World Series squad.[58]

"There is no suggestion that this condition [Andrews shoulder] has changed or worsened since the Series began, or has been injured in this Series. The fact that Andrews was used in Game No. 2 by the Oakland club appears to indicate to the contrary." [59]

Finley took Kuhn's ruling calmly, saying, "The commissioner saw fit to disallow the disqualification despite the doctor's letter and the player's signature. We will have to govern ourselves accordingly and play the Mets with 23 players. I am not disappointed or disturbed, but I do think we should have been granted our request." [60]

Although not stated explicitly, the thrust of the ruling implied Finley was trying to circumvent the eligibility rules for the Series. To be eligible a player must be on the roster on August 31 or before. He wanted to activate Manny Trillo, who joined the club late in the season, in Andrews' place.

Finley later commented, "It is my ballclub, and I don't appreciate anyone telling me how to spend my money to run my business. As long as I own this ballclub, I will operate it my way." [61] Finley owns thirty percent of the stock; his wife and children own the rest.

Finley contended it was not Andrews who was embarrassed but himself when his request was turned down by Commissioner Kuhn. He said, "I don't think the baseball commissioner treated us fairly in turning down this request. He's talking about embarrassing Andrews. We're not out to embarrass Andrews. But I sure as hell was embarrassed by what he did. He released his letter [a formal letter denying the A's request to put Andrews on the disabled list] before I ever received it." [62]

Mike Andrews returned to play during game four. Finley indicated no bitterness for him and was not disturbed when he came to bat as a pinch hitter in the eighth inning. As soon as Andrews walked out of the dugout to the on-deck circle the capacity crowd started cheering. When he went to the plate the crowd rose again.[63]

Andrews said, "It brought tears to my eyes."[64] They "made me feel good. I don't think I ever had one [the ovation] before in my life. It gave me chills. I didn't think of anything, it just made me happy. Maybe it's the little guy rebelling against the boss."[65]

Finley said, "I was hoping Andrews would put the ball out of the park and had he put it out of the park, I would have had to eat crow—and I would have enjoyed eating that crow."[66]

After the World Series

The World Series ended with Oakland winning the final game on Sunday 5-2 over the New York Mets. This gave Oakland two consecutive world championships, the first team to do so since the New York Yankees in 1961–62.

Minutes after the game Williams announced his resignation from Oakland; Finley said he "would not stand in his way."[67]

Three days later at an American League meeting, Finley stunned the New York Yankees by refusing to release Williams. Finley said he had not finished his sentence on Sunday. He said he would not stand in Williams' way "if the Yankees compensate me . . . handsomely."[68] Finley said without compensation "there will be court action."[69]

Finley relied on history to cite cases of such compensation and the legality of pro sports contracts. He mentioned the time Clark Griffith of Washington sent his son-in-law, Joe Cronin to the Red Sox for $250,000 and Lyn Lary, but in that deal Boston was buying a star shortstop, not a nonplaying manager. In 1960 the Indians and Tigers swapped managers, Joe Gordon for Jimmy Dykes, even up. In 1967 the Mets gave cash and a pitcher, Jack Denehy, to Washington for Gil Hodges, whom New York had released as a player in 1963 so he could manage the Senators.[70]

Williams said of Finley's reaction to his resignation, "He's the one that brought it up on national TV. He said he knew a couple of days before that I was leaving and he wished me well and said he wouldn't stand in my way. He's been a man of his word. We've hit it off real well and I'm surprised at the turn of events."[71]

Williams said the cases Finley cited were not similar to his situation. The only similar case was Ralph Houk's resignation from the Yankees to join the Detroit Tigers as their manager.[72]

"Houk also resigned, didn't he?" Williams said. "And the Yankees accepted it? Finley accepted mine. He accepted it on national TV. It seems to me that if I re-sign and have no contract with any other club, then if somebody were interested in my services they should be able to talk to me without even asking permission. The man has been very nice to me and has never gone back on his word, but evidently he is now."[73]

"We just have to wait and see if he's available," said Gabe Paul of the Yankees. "If he isn't there are other candidates." [74]

Also Mike Andrews, the center of controversy during the Series, was given his unconditional release by the Oakland Athletics. The team announced that Andrews, placed on waivers, was unclaimed. Any other major league team could have acquired him for $1.

Even at that bargain price, there were no takers and there was no action even when he became a free agent available for nothing.

"After what happened, I think people will sort of shy away," Andrews said by phone from his home in Peabody, Massachusetts. "I really don't expect to hear from too many people. All of this has discredited my ability." [75]

"I was unsure of myself at second base," Andrews said. "I had troubles with throwing the year before and it got to be some sort of a mental block. I never fielded more than six ground balls in any game, including spring training. I think I had a total of 20 ground balls all year at second base." [76]

Finley Fined and Placed on Probation

Charles O. Finley was fined $7000 by the commissioner of baseball, Bowie Kuhn, for three cases of misconduct during the 1973 World Series: a $5000 fine for his conduct concerning Mike Andrews after the second game; a $1000 fine for the announcement at the opening game that the Mets would not allow his team to add Manny Trillo to its roster; a second $1000 fine for ordering the lights turned on during the ninth inning of the second game, a prerogative of the Series umpires. [77]

Finley was also placed on probation by the commissioner at the same time. Kuhn stated, "I also determine that you personally shall be placed on probation until further notice and warn you that further conduct not in the best interest of baseball may lead to disciplinary action against you as provided in Article I of the major league agreement." [78]

Article I gives the commissioner the power to remove an owner from a club if he feels it is in baseball's best interests. [79]

Finley said, "I don't have that much comment to make, other than to say that regardless of hell or high water, fines or no fines, once more in '74. And by that I mean the World Series." [80]

However, after taking some time to think things over Finley decided he would take Commissioner Bowie Kuhn to court to fight the fines and probation. Finley said, "I continue to feel that the commissioner has acted beyond his authority in this matter, that his fines were unjustified, and I will seek relief from the courts." [81]

Negotiations for Williams

Progress was made in the managerial problems of Oakland and New York during the winter baseball meetings, when the Yankees agreed, in principle, to give the Athletics compensation for the right to hire Dick Williams. Before the winter meetings, Finley had said he wanted either Thurman Munson, Bobby Murcer, or Mel Stottlemyre as compensation. No one took that seriously. By the time the Athletics' owner arrived in Houston for the meetings, he'd scaled his requests down to two Yankee farm hands, pitcher Scott McGregor and outfielder Otto Velez. "No way," Gabe Paul, General Manager of the Yankees replied. "Those are our crown jewels." When the parties to the dispute met for 110 minutes behind closed doors, Finley made another offer. He asked for either McGregor or Velez, plus cash. Paul refused again. [82]

American League President Joe Cronin, being pressed to make a decision in the dispute, didn't seem in any hurry despite the fact that his term of office was due to end December 31. Commissioner Bowie Kuhn said publicly that he wasn't going to intrude, but he was believed working behind the scenes to have Cronin come up with an answer.

The Yankees didn't seem anxious to come up with a solution right away pending the outcome of a meeting scheduled between them and the Tigers on December 18 in Boston. The Yankees disputed the right of the Detroit Tigers to sign Ralph Houk, who quit his New York job after the regular season. He also had two years to go on his contract. [83]

Finley commented on the Boston meeting, "What happens between Detroit and the Yankees is none of my business. I've got enough problems of my own without worrying about that. [84]

"The business of managers not honoring their contracts is horsemeat. It's about time Ralph Houk and Dick Williams honored their contracts. They [managers] expect to be paid off if they're fired." [85]

In later negotiations the Yankees offered Horace Clarke but Finley insisted he would only accept one of the Yankees' premier young farm club players. Paul again apparently believed Williams was not worth the nucleus of future Yankee ballclubs.

The Yankees had appealed to American League President Joe Cronin for a ruling in a letter sent on November 8. When no answer was forthcoming, the Yankees decided to act. On December 28 the New York club named Dick Williams their 19th field manager. In making their decision they defied Charles Finley, challenged him—even dared him to sue. The contract was believed to be for three years and $100,000 per year. The team apparently based their right on the public announcements of resignation by Williams and public, as well as private, acknowledgement of that resignation. [86]

"I'm happy and proud to be a member of the New York Yankees," Williams said. "I was an extra man with the Brooklyn Dodgers and we continuously were getting beat by the Yankees. I always have felt that New York City is the place to be and since I live on the east coast of Florida, I'm happy to be closer to home than I was." [87]

Then eleven days before he was to leave office and approximately a week after the Yankees signed Williams, Joe Cronin made his decision. He disallowed the acquisition of Williams by the Yankees but freed Ralph Houk to become manager of the Detroit Tigers without requiring compensation. Williams was not free to manage the Yankees for the next three years without the approval of Finley.

Williams had earlier stated he would not go back to Oakland no matter what, intimating he would do anything rather than submit to Finley. After the judgment he stated he still expected to be the manager of the Yankees.[88]

In two consecutive days of testimony the Yankees had tried to convince Cronin that the Houk-to-Detroit and Williams-to-New York cases were similar. The Tigers argued they were not. The Yankees had not made claims for Houk until October 24—after Finley had refused to grant them permission to talk with Williams. Cronin observed that in the last day of the 1973 season, the Yankees showed Houk a press release concerning his resignation and Houk approved it. The Yankees then started the process of ending Houk's profit sharing plan with the team, indicating termination of his contract. Also Houk had signed his three-year contract with one set of owners (CBS) and resigned after another set of owners took control.[89]

Epilogue

After Cronin's decision Williams decided to take Finley to court. "I'm taking Finley to court," he said. "I'm not done yet. . . . I'm out of baseball but not for good until my attorneys are heard from. As far as I'm concerned no one owns me." [90]

Finley already had filed suit against Williams in federal court in San Francisco, seeking to have the manager prevented from working for any other baseball team for the next two seasons. Williams's countersuit charged Finley with blocking the manager's right to work in the game.

At the same time Williams decided to take Finley to court the Yankees apparently gave up their chase for the ex-Oakland manager. The Yankees formally announced the signing of Bill Virdon, former manager of the Pittsburgh Pirates. Virdon managed Pittsburgh to the National League East title in 1972 but was fired by the Pirates in September 1973 with the club two games out of first place. He signed the Yankee contract only one month after committing himself to the minors as manager of Houston's Denver farm club in the American Association. The Yankee contract was only for the 1974 season at a salary estimated at $40,000.

When asked about the future, George Steinbrenner, general partner of the Yankees replied, "I wouldn't want to say we have abandoned Dick Williams. Virdon is our manager. We couldn't get Williams. If we could now, we'd cross that bridge when we came to it." [91]

FOOTNOTES

[1] Ron Fimrite, "Buffoonery Rampant," *Sports Illustrated*, October 22, 1973, pp. 24–27.

[2] *Ibid.*

[3] Joseph Durso, "Mets Top A's, 10–7; Even Series at 1–1," *New York Times*, October 15, 1973, pp. 1, 43.

[4] *Ibid.*

[5] Fimrite, "Buffoonery Rampant," pp. 24–27.

[6] Durso, "Mets Top A's, 10–7; Even Series at 1–1," pp. 1, 43.

[7] "Mets Win an Amazing One With 4 Runs in 12th," *Washington Post*, October 15, 1973, p. D-1.

[8] *Ibid.*

[9] *Ibid.*

[10] *Ibid.*

[11] "Sand-Lot Scramble," *Time*, October 29, 1973, p. 105.

[12] Wells Twombly, "Charlie O., The Missouri Mule," *New York Times Magazine*, July 15, 1973, p. 32.

[13] *Ibid.*, p. 12.

[14] *Ibid.*, p. 32.

[15] *Ibid.*

[16] *Ibid.*

[17] *Ibid.*

[18] *Ibid.*

[19] *Ibid.*, p. 13.

[20] *Ibid.*, p. 32.

[21] *Ibid.*

[22] Fimrite, "Buffoonery Rampant," pp. 24–27.

[23] Twombly, "Charlie O., The Missouri Mule," p. 36.

[24] *Ibid.*

[25] *Ibid.*

[26] *Ibid.*, p. 37.

[27] "Andrews: Pressured by Finley," *New York Times*, October 18, 1973, p. 57.

[28] "Finley Lied About Injury, Andrews Says," *Roanoke Times*, October 18, 1973, p. 34.

[29] "Andrews: Pressured by Finley," p. 57.

[30] *Ibid.*

[31] *Ibid.*

[32] *Ibid.*

[33] *Ibid.*

[34] George Minot Jr., "Andrews Tells of Pressure to Sign False Report," *Washington Post*, October 18, 1973, p. D-3.

[35] *Ibid.*

[36] "Andrews: Pressured by Finley," p. 57.

[37] *Ibid.*

[38] Minot Jr., "Andrews Tells of Pressure to Sign False Report," p. D-3.

[39] *Ibid.*

[40] *Ibid.*

[41] Joseph Durso, "Mets Prepare Maximum Security for Tonight," *New York Times*, October 16, 1973, p. C-55.

[42] "A's Players Up in Arms Over 'Firing' of Andrews," *Roanoke Times*, October 16, 1973, p. 12.

[43] George Minot Jr., " 'Firing' of Andrews Has A's Up in Arms," *Washington Post*, October 16, 1973, p. D-1.

[44] *Ibid.*

[45] *Ibid.*

⁴⁶ *Ibid.*

⁴⁷ *Ibid.*

⁴⁸ *Ibid.*

⁴⁹ "The World Series—Sort of," *Newsweek,* October 29, 1973, p. 61.

⁵⁰ "Williams Quitting A's, Oakland Player Claims," *Washington Post,* October 18, 1973, p. E-1.

⁵¹ *Ibid.*

⁵² *Ibid.*

⁵³ Shirley Povick, "Actually, Series Matchup is World Against Finley," *Washington Post,* October 19, 1973, p. D-1.

⁵⁴ "A's Unjust in Putting the Rap on Finley," *Washington Post,* October 21, 1973, p. D-2.

⁵⁵ *Ibid.*

⁵⁶ Robert Brinter, "Making Sport of Us All," *Sports Illustrated,* December 10, 1973, p. 36.

⁵⁷ "Kuhn Sides With Andrews," *Roanoke Times,* October 17, 1973, p. 12.

⁵⁸ *Ibid.*

⁵⁹ *Ibid.*

⁶⁰ Leonard Koppett, "Kuhn Rebuffs Finley in Andrews Case," *New York Times,* October 17, 1973, p. 48M.

⁶¹ "Finley Defends Action in l'Affaire Andrews," *New York Times,* October 21, 1973, p. 3.

⁶² "Finley Says He Was Right About Andrews," *Roanoke Times,* October 21, 1973, pp. C-4, C-10.

⁶³ William Leggett, "Mutiny and A. Bounty," *Sports Illustrated,* October 29, 1973, pp. 22–27.

⁶⁴ "Andrews Cries Over Ovation," *Roanoke Times,* October 18, 1973, p. 34.

⁶⁵ Leggett, "Mutiny and A. Bounty," pp. 22–27.

⁶⁶ "Finley Says He Was Right About Andrews," pp. C-7, C-10.

⁶⁷ "A's Manager Williams Quits," *Washington Post,* October 22, 1973, p. D-2.

⁶⁸ Shirley Povick, "Finley Eyes Dollar DP, Tigers to Yankees to A's," *Washington Post,* October 25, 1973, pp. D-1, D-6.

⁶⁹ "Finley Foils Yanks On Williams Deal," *New York Times,* October 25, 1973, p. 61.

⁷⁰ Red Smith, "Dick Was Scrubbing the Porch," *New York Times,* October 26, 1973, p. 33.

⁷¹ *Ibid.*

⁷² *Ibid.*

⁷³ *Ibid.*

⁷⁴ *Ibid.*

⁷⁵ Ron Bergman, "Andrews Sitting by Phone, But Doubts It Will Ring," *The Sporting News,* November 24, 1973, p. 33.

⁷⁶ *Ibid.*

⁷⁷ "Finley Fined $7,000, Vows to Battle Kuhn," *Washington Post,* October 30, 1973, p. C-6.

⁷⁸ "Finley Placed on Probation," *Roanoke Times,* November 1, 1973, p. 30.

⁷⁹ *Ibid.*

⁸⁰ "Finley Uncertain on Appeal," *New York Times,* October 30, 1973, p. 51.

[81] "Kuhn Upholds Fines; Finley to Sue Him," *New York Times*, December 1, 1973, p. 43.

[82] Ron Bergman, " 'I'll Go to the Courts If I'm Not Satisfied,' Says Finley," *The Sporting News*, December 22, 1973, p. 38.

[83] *Ibid.*

[84] *Ibid.*

[85] *Ibid.*

[86] Phil Pepe, "Yankees Sign Dick, Give Charlie O. the Gate," *The Sporting News*, December 29, 1973, p. 27.

[87] *Ibid.*

[88] Phil Pepe, "Cronin Leaves the Driving to Charlie O.," *The Sporting News*, January 5, 1974, p. 36.

[89] *Ibid.*

[90] "Finley-Williams Suits Loom," *Washington Post*, January 5, 1974, p. C-1.

[91] *Ibid.*

QUESTIONS

1. What managerial role or combination of roles does Finley exemplify in his behavior as owner of the A's?
2. Does the role performed by Finley appear to be in accord with social expectations?
3. Discuss the response of the social environment to Finley's self-perceived role.
4. What characteristics of the entrepreneurial role does Finley exemplify?
5. Explain Finley's concept of private property.
6. Does Finley act in accordance with his concept of the right of private property?
7. Was Andrews being asked to perform a function for which he was not hired?
8. Did Williams have the right to start negotiations with the New York Yankees?
9. Williams comments that no one owns him. Was he unduly restricted by Finley in his attempt to become manager of the Yankees?
10. Compare the Andrews and Williams incidents in terms of individual rights.
11. Did Finley change his role during the Andrews and Williams incidents?
12. Discuss the legitimacy of the role of the commissioner of baseball and the bases for that legitimacy or lack thereof.
13. Discuss similarities and differences in the Williams and Houk situations. Do you believe individual rights were violated in either case?

Abram, Morris 124
Ackerman, Robert 49
A. C. Nielsen Co. 85
Adkins, Maxine 121
Advertising 307–331
African Methodist Episcopal Church 162
Air Force (United States) 110–111
Air Force, Office of Special Investigations 223
Air Force, Systems Command 222–223
Airline Pilots Association 134, 141
Air piracy 129–146
Air Transport Association 132, 137–138
Alaska Pipeline 292
Allied and Technical Workers Union 106
Allison, Roger 105
Allvine, F. C. 17
American Academy of Allergy 91
American Airline Pilots Association 136–138
American Bar Association 310
American Furniture Company 113
American Home Products, Inc. 321–324
American Life Convention 156
American Medical Association 317, 324
American Motors Corporation 199
American Telephone and Telegraph 194
Anderson, Jack 94, 246–248
Andrews, Kenneth R. 53
Andrews, Mike 354–355, 357–362
Appalachian Power Company 107

Aptitude tests 170
Arab-Israeli conflict 291
Argyris, Chris 15
Army Corps of Engineers 79, 125–126
Artistic model 21, 47
Atkinson, Brooks (Judge) 67
Atomic Energy Commission 68–69, 71, 73, 79
Atomic power 65, 70
Audubon Society 67
Austere model 19–20, 117
Austin, Richard B. 240
Autrey, F. E. 76

Bahamas Exploration, Ltd. 278
Balboa, Enrique 265
Bando, Sal 359
Bankers Life Company 159
Bannon, Ken 204
Barrientos, Rene 284
Batterman, Robert C. 309
Bauer, Raymond A. 55
Bayh, Birch 248
Beal, Orville 157
Beard, Dita: see Dita Beard memo
Bechtal Corporation 72
Bendix Reinhard 8, 12–13
Bennaton, Abraham 256, 265–267
Bennett Mechanical Aptitude Test 171